THE SENSE OF DECADENCE
IN
NINETEENTH-CENTURY FRANCE

ARCHIVES INTERNATIONALES D'HISTOIRE DES IDEES

INTERNATIONAL ARCHIVES OF THE HISTORY OF IDEAS

7

KOENRAAD W. SWART

THE SENSE OF DECADENCE
IN
NINETEENTH-CENTURY FRANCE

KOENRAAD W. SWART

THE SENSE OF DECADENCE
IN
NINETEENTH-CENTURY FRANCE

MARTINUS NIJHOFF / THE HAGUE / 1964

TO INEKE

CONTENTS

INTRODUCTION

"It was the best of times. It was the worst of times." The famous opening sentence of Charles Dickens' *Tale of Two Cities* can serve as a motto to characterize the mixture of optimism and pessimism with which a large number of nineteenth-century intellectuals viewed the condition of their age. It is nowadays hardly necessary to accentuate the optimistic elements in the nineteenth-century view of history; many recent historians have sharply contrasted the complacency and the great expectations of the past century with the fears and anxieties rampant in our own age. It is often too readily assumed that a hundred years ago all leading thinkers as well as the educated public were addicted to the cult of progress and ignored or minimized those trends of their times that paved the way for the catastrophes of the twentieth century.

In the nineteenth century the intoxicating triumphs of modern science undeniably induced the general public to believe that progress was not an accident but a necessity and that evil and immorality would gradually disappear. Yet fears, misgivings, and anxieties were not as exceptional in the nineteenth century as is often imagined. Such feelings were not restricted to a few dissenting philosophers and poets like Schopenhauer, Kierkegaard, Dostoevsky, Baudelaire, and Nietzsche. Complaints about the passing of the good old times were so common in the nineteenth century, even in its closing decades when the idea of progress had supposedly become a general article of faith, that some writers felt called upon to protest against the prevalent dissatisfaction with the present by pointing out that in all ages man has been inclined to idealize the past. Such criticism of the present is even found in the works of authors who on the whole subscribed to a progressive philosophy of history. Thus Chateaubriand, Auguste Comte, Saint-Simon, Fourier and Proudhon, though firmly believing in progress, were of the opinion that their own age was a period of crisis, transition, anarchy, or decadence.

It might seem surprising that the same persons often viewed the trend of their times with pessimism as well as with optimism. But it should be kept in mind that most reflections on progress and decadence are hasty generalizations made without any thorough study of either the present or the past (not to mention the future, which is necessarily a matter of pure speculation) and are greatly influenced by temporary good fortune or disillusionment. Even otherwise systematic minds have therefore often wavered between optimistic and pessimistic evaluations of the present in its relation to the past and the future.

The coexistence of pessimistic and optimistic elements in the philosophy of history of the same person is, however, not necessarily a form of inconsistency of thought. It is easily forgotten that the concepts of progress and decadence can be satisfactorily combined in a variety of ways. It is, for example, not at all illogical to be convinced that in certain fields like religion or morality serious decline has taken place and yet to believe at the same time that in other areas like science and art great progress has been achieved. Similarly a person can be of the opinion that civilization in his own country is retrogressing but that mankind in other parts of the world continues to make progress. Furthermore progress and decadence can each be restricted to different periods of history. Thus one might assume that there has been progress in the past, but feel that mankind has recently started to degenerate and that further decadence is to be expected in the future. Or one might, on the contrary, condemn most of history as a long process of gradual degeneration, but believe that a regeneration is under way and that the future will be dominated by progress. It is obvious that the doctrines of absolute, indefinite, rectilinear decadence or progress, excluding any deviation from a basic pattern, are too simplistic to be accepted by a thinker who is willing to give any attention at all to the complexity of historical processes.

This study will concentrate on France, but will occasionally compare the fears and anxieties of Frenchmen with similar feelings elsewhere. In the nineteenth century the sense of decadence was not a uniquely French phenomenon but a general European one, of which the French variety was a fairly representative specimen. In each country, of course, historical pessimism had its own distinctive features. In France despondency about the course of history was probably stronger and more widespread than in England and the United States, but less so than in Central and Eastern Europe. The French sense of decadence was especially different from that of other leading countries by being closely related to the feeling that the nation's power and prestige in the world was declining. For this reason the theme of the decadence *of* France (as distinguished from from the sense of decadence of civilization in general) will be one of the leading ideas investigated in the present study.

The following pages will deal primarily with the nineteenth century, or more precisely with the hundred years period between the fall of Napoleon and the outbreak of the First World War. But for a proper understanding of the subject it has been deemed advisable to include a short survey of the major varieties of historical pessimism in earlier centuries. This will provide a historical perspective against which the characteristics of the nineteenth-century sense of decadence will appear in sharper relief. An understanding of the older forms of historical pessimism will also be helpful because many of the old dreads such as the belief in the imminent end of the world have persisted in considerable strength until well into the twentieth century. Finally, the modern forms which the sense of decadence assumed in the nineteenth century were often little more than new variations on some basic views that can already be found in the literature of antiquity and the Middle Ages.

It has not be considered necessary to add, by way of a postscript, a brief survey of the intensified sense of decadence which began to prevail in the years following the First World War. The unprecedented catastrophes that have befallen the world during the past half century explain that outside the Communist camp only a few intellectuals nowadays still indulge in dreams of a future golden age. Many contemporary authors in France as well as elsewhere express a more truly tragic conception of life and a more utterly hopeless view of the present than is to be found in most nineteenth-century literature. If a satanic delight in decadence is no longer as fashionable as it was at the *fin de siècle* this is partly because modern writers feel that they can no longer afford the luxury of cultivating decay at a time when the very existence of civilization has become problematic.

CHAPTER I

THE OLD FEARS

The world now has grown old and does not abide in that strength in which it formerly stood . . . Even if we alleged no proofs from the Sacred Scriptures, the world itself is now announcing and bearing witness to its decline by the testimony of its failing state. In winter there is no longer enough rain to feed the crops; in summer the sun is no longer hot enough to ripen the fruit . . . The land remains without farmers; the sea without sailors; the armies without soldiers. There is no more any innocence in politics, any justice in the courts, any mastership in the arts, any discipline in moral behavior.

CYPRIANUS, *c*. 250 A.D.[1]

I

The idea of living in a period of political and cultural decline did not originate in the nineteenth century, but is as old as recorded history. In early civilizations the concept of decadence was not primarily a view of history formed after careful comparison between conditions in past and present; it would be more appropriate to call it a delusion or a myth that found ready acceptance among men who were afraid or resentful of the evil and the stupidity that so often seemed to preside over wordly affairs. This mythical character, which the idea of decadence still partly retains in scholarly studies of modern times, was especially pronounced in many religious cosmologies in which the notion made its first appearance. In nearly all ancient civilizations it was believed that after an initial period of paradisiacal felicity and innocence, man had lost his primeval virtues either as the result of a sudden fall or in the process of a gradual degradation. Such presuppositions were generally part of a cyclical philosophy of history assuming that the world was doomed to endless repetition of the same pattern of degeneration. Sometimes the apogee of the cycle was placed not in the beginning, but in the middle; but even in this instance a gloomy view was taken of human destiny since the present was believed to be located in the downward swing of the curve. All these ancient cos-

---

[1] Cyprianus, *Liber ad Demetrianum*, par. 3, Migne's *Patrologia latina*, vol. IV (Paris, 1844), 546.

mologies, then, took it for granted that mankind was living in a period that compared unfavorably with the past.

The historical pessimism inherent in these cyclical conceptions of history perhaps found its most dogmatic expression in the cosmological speculations of ancient India.[1] Brahmanism, Buddhism, and Jainism all taught that the present era was a period of darkness, the so-called age of Kali, in which man was biologically, intellectually, ethically, and socially far inferior to his ancestors. According to the dogmas of these various religions, the world was heading for a total annihilation to be followed by the creation of a new world fated to pass through the same process of gradual deterioration as the one that had preceded it.

The early mythological legends of Mesopotamian civilization, some of which date back to at least 2000 B. C., also portrayed primeval man as happier, healthier, and less wicked than his descendants. [2] Similarly most philosophers and historians of old China were convinced that they were living in a period of cultural decline; since the days of Confucius and Mencius (sixth and fifth centuries B.C.), if not earlier, the Chinese literati either looked upon the legendary reigns of the Sage Kings as the Golden Age, or viewed the history of their country as passing with each dynasty through a separate cycle of which the period of vigor already belonged to the past.[3] Related beliefs in the downward movement of history and impending doom were current among many primitive societies, like those of the Teutonic nations of northern Europe, or of the Mayas, Aztecs, and other Indian tribes of the Western hemisphere.[4]

Pessimism was also the dominant note in the historical outlook of

---

[1] See P.-E. Dumont, "Primitivism in Indian Literature," in Arthur O. Lovejoy and George Boas (eds.), *A Documentary History of Primitivism and Related Ideas in Antiquity* (Baltimore, 1935), 433–446; Mircea Eliade, *Cosmos and History. The Myth of Eternal Return* (ed. Harper Torchbooks, New York, 1959), 112–118; Grace E. Cairns, *Philosophies of History. Meeting of East and West in Cycle-Pattern Theories of History* (New York, 1962), 69–73.

[2] W. F. Albright, "Primitivism in Ancient Western Asia (Mesopotamia and Israel)," in Lovejoy and Boas, *op. cit.*, 421–432; Gerhard von Rad, *Old Testament Theology*, vol. I (Edinburgh, 1962), 164–165.

[3] Derk Bodde, "Harmony and Conflict in Chinese Philosophy," *Studies in Chinese Thought*, ed. Arthur F. Wright (Chicago, 1953), 27–36, 68, 73; William T. De Bary, "Chinese Despotism and the Confucian Ideal. A Seventeenth Century View," *Chinese Thought and Institutions*, ed. John. K. Fairbank (Chicago, 1957), 162–203; William T. De Bary and others (eds.), *Sources of Chinese Tradition* (New York, 1960), 101, 220–221, 450 ff.; Fung Yu Lan, *A Short History of Chinese Philosophy* (New York, 1958), 168–170, 278.

[4] Axel Olrik, *Ragnarök. Die Sagen vom Weltuntergang untersucht* (Berlin, 1922); H. Petriconi, *Reich des Untergangs. Bemerkungen über ein mythologisches Thema* (Hamburg, 1958), 8–9; Robert M. Lowrie, "Primitive Messianism as an Ethnological Problem," *Diogenes*, XIX (1957), 70–71.

classical antiquity.[1] Under Oriental influence the cyclical concept of eternal return was accepted by many eminent thinkers, notably the Pythagoreans and the Stoics. In classical antiquity, it is true, such cyclical doctrines never held such sway as in the Orient. But this does not mean that the Greeks and the Romans looked with greater confidence to the future. Greek thought, as an eminent scholar, B. A. van Groningen, has clearly pointed out, was "in the grip of the past."[2] In its mythology, the Golden Age of primordial times, when man had been leading a simple and virtuous life, was contrasted with the Iron Age of the present when civil strife, greed and other evils of civilization were rampant.[3] It was not only the common people, but also the intellectual elite, who held such pessimistic views of history. Almost all Greek philosophers preached some kind of primitivism, even if few of them were as radical in their opposition to the refinements of civilization as the Cynics. "The men of earlier times," wrote Plato, "were better off than we and nearer to the Gods."[4] Even such a clear and sober mind as Aristotle, who was more appreciative of the blessings of civilization than most other ancient philosophers, was in agreement with the theory that time had a destructive rather than a constructive character.[5]

Roman authors were equally outspoken in proclaiming the corrupting effect of historical change, Cicero's rhetorical exclamation, "O tempora, O mores!" is characteristic of the attitude of many prominent Roman citizens.[6] "What does not ruinous time degrade?," wrote Horace in one of his bitter moods, "The age of our parents, inferior to that of our grandparents, brought forth ourselves, who are more worthless still and are destined to have children still more corrupt."[7] Even authors like Lucretius and Seneca who, in some passages of their works, anticipated the modern idea of progress still subscribed to the gloomy doctrine of the gradual deterioration of the world.[8] In the classical world, then, decadence was regarded

---

[1] Cf. Lovejoy and Boas, *op. cit.*, *passim*; Samuel H. Butcher, "The Melancholy of the Greeks," *Some Aspects of the Greek Genius* (4th ed. London, 1916), 133–176.

[2] B. A. van Groningen, *In the Grip of the Past: Essay on an Aspect of Greek Thought* (Leiden, 1953).

[3] Cf. H. C. Baldry, "Who Invented the Golden Age," *The Classical Quarterly*, XLVI (1952) 83–92.

[4] Lovejoy and Boas, *op. cit.*, 168; cf. Werner Jaeger, *Paideia* (New York, 1944), III, 231–238.

[5] Thorleif Boman, *Hebrew Thought Compared With Greek* (London, 1960), 128.

[6] *In Catilinam*, I, i, I; cf. Joseph Vogt, *Ciceros Glaube an Rom* (Stuttgart, 1935), 33ff.

[7] *Odes*, III, vi.

[8] Lovejoy and Boas, *op. cit.*

almost as a law of nature, and as it seemed impossible to reverse an inevitable trend, degeneration was not decried with as much moralistic fervor and indignation as in modern times. A resigned, almost fatalistic acceptance of decline on the whole distinguishes the ancient attitude toward decadence from that of the moderns.

Optimistic elements were, of course, not completely nonexistent in ancient views of history. The world conflagration thas was predicted by the Stoics and other ancient philosophers did not mean the final end of human history, but was to be followed by a new world, initially far superior to existing society. For this reason many actually anticipated the destruction of the present order with hope instead of fear.[1] Moreover, some writers took exception to the widespread tendency to idealize the past. A number of Greek and Roman authors expressly ridiculed the naive belief in the virtues of the Golden Age and commented with more or less enthusiasm upon the advances made in arts, sciences, and technology.[2] Although the Greeks never hit upon a formal law of historical progress, they were fully aware of the progress that they had made in reference to the East as well as in reference to their own past. In spite of their eulogies of primitive life and their criticism of civilized society, most Greek authors praised reason and wisdom as the supreme qualities of mankind and looked with contempt on the "barbarian" world because it lacked in these virtues.[3]

Yet the ancients, although often proud of progress achieved, did not expect that progress would continue to be made in the future. One of the distinctive features of classical civilization was its low opinion of the sentiment of hope.[4] Among the down-trodden masses, it is true, many subscribed to salvationist creeds that offered the prospect of a better future for themselves, if not for the world at large. But until the triumph of Christianity such doctrines did not enjoy any prestige among the educated. According to most Greek and Roman authors, persons who were hoping for a radical improvement in man's

---

[1] This point is stressed – and perhaps somewhat overstressed – in Mircea Eliade, *Cosmos and History. The Myth of Eternal Return*; cf. Gerardus van der Leeuw, "Urzeit und Endzeit," *Eranos-Jahrbuch*, XVII (1949), 11–51.

[2] Cf. Lovejoy and Boas, *op. cit.*; Siegfried Lauffer, "Der antike Fortschrittsgedanke," *Proceedings of the XIth International Congress of Philosophy, Brussels, August 20–26, 1953* (Amsterdam, 1953), XII, 37–41; C. B. Wells, "The Hellenistic Orient," *The Idea of History in the Ancient Near East*, ed. Robert C. Dentan (New Haven, 1955), 135ff.; P. V. Naquet, "Temps des dieux et temps des hommes. Essai sur quelques aspects de l'expérience temporelle chez les Grecs," *Revue de l'histoire des religions*, CLVII (1960), 55–80.

[3] Cf. Hans Kohn, *The Idea of Nationalism* (New York, 1961), ch. II, *passim*.

[4] Cf. Butcher, *loc. cit.*

condition were guilty of forgetting the limits of the possible. In classical literature hope was portrayed as a mocking goddess, one of the deadly gifts contained in Pandora's box, that lured the weak to folly.

Complaints about existing decay and fear of impending doom also pervaded much of ancient political thought. Many Greeks and Romans, it is true, took pride in the political institutions or the power of their states. Pericles' famous oration in commemoration of the soldiers fallen in the war against Sparta testified to a highly developed self-respect that was felt by many citizens of the ancient world. Thus the idea of the greatness and the eternity of Rome became a standard theme in Roman oratory in the beginning of our era and perhaps enjoyed its greatest popularity in the second century A.D., a period which contemporaries themselves characterized as a "Golden Age."[1] To many citizens of the Empire it seemed that Rome, like the miraculous bird Phoenix, had the special gift to rise again out of its ashes.[2]

But not all Romans shared this confidence in the everlasting greatness of their Empire. Many of the preserved panegyrics on "eternal Rome" were flatteries imposed by an increasingly despotic government rather than sincere expressions of popular sentiment. In sharp contrast to the belief in the eternity of Rome stood the widely accepted view that states, like anything else in this world, were subject to the law of change and decay. Empires and kingdoms, it was commonly held, were also affected by the rotation of Fortune's wheel determining that "what goes up also come down." The Hellenized Jew Philo (first century AD..) perhaps best expressed the ancient conviction as to the inconstancy of all earthly power: "Greece was once flourishing, but the Macedonians took away her power. Macedonia was then in flower, but when she was divided, she weakened, until she entirely withered away. Before the Macedonians, Persia enjoyed good furtune, but one day laid low her great and mighty kingdom, and now Parthians, who were once the subject of the Persians, rule over them, their former masters. Egypt shone in splendor and did so for the longest time, but like a cloud her great prosperity has vanished . . . What of Europe and Asia and, in a word, of the whole inhabited world? Is it not tossed up and down and shaken like a ship at sea, now blown by favor-

---

[1] See Edward K. Rand, *Building of Eternal Rome* (Cambridge, Mass., 1953); Vogt, *op. cit.*, 72ff.; Eva M. Sanford, "Contrasting Views of the Roman Empire," *American Journal of Philology*, LVIII (1937), 436–456; Chester G. Starr, *Civilization and the Caesars. The Intellectual Revolution in the Roman Empire* (Ithaca, 1954), 34.

[2] Adolf Rusch, "Phoinix," *Pauly-Wissowa Real-Encyclopädie*, 39. Halbband (Stuttgart, 1941), col. 422–423; cf. Ronald Syme, *Tacitus* (Oxford, 1958), II, 771–774.

able, now by opposing winds? For in a circle turns the divine plan, which many name fortune."[1]

A similar view that all states pass through a cycle of growth and decline was propounded by Polybius in the second century B.C. This Greek historian masterfully described the political abuses that had led to the downfall of his native country, but he suggested that victorious Rome would also have its "fatal day."[2] The idea of the decline of Rome, thus appearing as early as the second century B.C., became almost an obsession with many later Roman writers such as Cicero, Sallust, Livy, and Tacitus.[3] Some of them accepted the conquest of Carthage as the beginning of Roman degeneration, feeling that after the defeat of this last dangerous opponent, the Romans had neglected to cultivate their military virtues. Other Romans saw in the suppression of liberty after the establishment of the principate the major cause of Rome's decadence. Despondency and despair became increasingly common during the serious crises facing Rome in the third and fourth centuries A.D. when new reasons, such as excessive taxation and the rise of Christianity, were given for the disasters befalling the Empire.[4]

The decline and fall of the Roman Empire has continued to obsess many later Europeans. Chateaubriand tracing the vogue of Romantic despair back to the decline of ancient civilization asserted that from the decay of the pagan world and the barbarian invasions the human spirit had received "une impression de tristesse et peut-être même une teinte de mélancholie qui ne s'est jamais bien effacée."[5] Most cyclical theorists of history (Giambattista Vico, Oswald Spengler, Arnold Toynbee) took it for granted that the course of ancient history

---

[1] *Quod deus*, XXXVI (173–176), as tr. in George Boas, *Essays on Primitivism and Related Ideas in the Middle Ages* (Baltimore, 1948), 7.

[2] *The Histories*, with Engl., tr. by W. R. Paton (6 vols., London, 1920–27), VI, 437, 439; on Polybius' historical pessimism as well as on the idea of decadence of Rome in general, see Santo Mazzarino, *Het einde van de antieke wereld*, tr. from Italian (Utrecht, 1963).

[3] Jean Hubeaux, *Les grands mythes de Rome* (Paris, 1945); Vogt, *op. cit.*, *idem*, "Das römische Geschichtsdenken und die Anschauung des Tacitus," *Grosse Geschichtsdenker*, ed. R. Stadelmann (Tübingen, 1949); Helm Werner, *Der Untergangs Roms. Studien zum Dekadenzproblem in der antiken Geistesgeschichte* (Stuttgart, 1939); Walter Rehm, *Der Untergang Roms im abendländischen Denken; ein Beitrag zur Geschichtsschreibung und zum Dekadenzproblem* (Leipzig, 1930).

[4] J. Geffcken, "Stimmungen im untergehenden Weströmerreich," *Neue Jahrbücher für das klassische Altertum*, XXIII (1920), 256–269; Jacob Burckhardt, *Die Zeit Constantins des Grossen* (Leipzig, 1927), 269ff.; Mazzarino, *op. cit.*, ch. II, III, IV.

[5] Chateaubriand, *Génie du Christianisme* (1802), Deuxième partie, livre III, ch. IX; a similar view was taken by Hippolyte Taine who asserted that man had lost his spiritual balance with the downfall of paganism and had not recovered it since; *Derniers Essais de critique et d'histoire* (Paris, 1903), 88.

was the pattern that any other civilization had to follow. Many other historians, convinced that there existed a remarkable similarity between the development of modern civilization and that of ancient Rome have undertaken a study of the decline of the Roman Empire in the hope of finding an answer to the question of how their own society could escape a similar fate. Thus a fierce critic of the Third Republic, Jacques Bainville, felt that the best summary of the history of Republican France was contained in Livy's gloomy appraisal of Roman history: "With the gradual relaxation of discipline, morals gave way, then sank lower and lower, and finally began the downward plunge which has brought us to the present time, when we can endure neither our vices nor their cure."[1]

Rome's downfall served the moderns as a test case that had not been available to the Romans themselves. Rome's fate, more than that of Greece, has reminded even the most dogmatic believers in progress that the forward march of history is not always rectilinear. Many later conceptions of decadence have been influenced by what was known of the corruptions of Roman society. The nineteenth-century "Decadents," for example, were greatly indebted to the Romans for their views as to what constituted depravity. Believing that their own society suffered from evils similar to that of the Roman Empire, they identified themselves with Rome in its period of decline. Their attitude was best summed up in Paul Verlaine's verse: "Je suis l'Empire à la fin de la décadence."[2]

II

The Jews developed a concept of history that was radically different from that of the Greeks and the Romans.[3] Perhaps influenced by Iranian cosmological ideas,[4] Judaism adopted the view of a definitive end of the world to be followed by an eternal life of bliss for the elect.

[1] Livy, *Ab urbe condita*, preface to book I (Loeb ed., 14 vols., London, 1919–1959), I, 7; Jacques Bainville, *La Troisième République* (Paris, 1935), *in fine*; cf. P. G. Walsh, "Livy's Preface and the Distortion of History," *American Journal of Philology*, 1955, 369–383.

[2] See *infra*, 77, 112, 161, 164.

[3] On the differences between the Jewish and Classical views of history, see: Boman, *op. cit.*; Millar Burrows, "Ancient Israel," *The Idea of History in the Ancient Near East*, 127–128; Abba Hillel Silver, *Where Judaism Differed* (New York, 1957); Joseph Klausner, *The Messianic Idea in Israel From its Beginning to the Completion of Mishnah* (New York, 1955); Eliade, *op. cit.*, 102.

[4] On Persian influences in Jewish post-exilic eschatology, see Nathan Söderblom, "Ages of the World," *Encyclopedia of Religion and Ethics* (13 vols., New York, 1908–27), I, 205–210; Alfons Maria Kurfess, "Dies Irae," *Historisches Jahrbuch*, LXXVII (1957), 328; Norman H. Snaith, *The Jews From Cyrus to Herod* (New York, 1955), 94ff.

It, moreover, taught that wordly affairs were subject to divine providence, which had a supreme purpose in mind even if its workings
might often seem mysterious. History was thus interpreted as having
an ending (*eschaton*) as well as a purpose (*telos*). This eschatological[1]
and teleological orientation gave a meaning to the course of events
that had been lacking in most earlier cosmologies based on the more
hopeless view of eternally recurring world cycles. The Jewish philosophy of history thus contained various ideas that can be considered
optimistic. Although the great religious leaders of the Jews had a
very low opinion of the present and often predicted disaster in the
near future, they never doubted that the forces of good would ultimately prevail.

Like classical civilization, Judaism has been highly influential in
shaping Western historical thinking. Many later views of past, present,
and future have been strongly colored by the Jewish tradition of
messianism, moralistic prophecy, and apocalypticism. Numerous
medieval and modern European writers interpreting the trends of
their times have borrowed their ideas, and even their terminology,
from the Old Testament. They designated the centers of contemporary
corruption as Babylon, Sodom, and Gomorrah, identified the attacking
enemies with the hordes of Gog and Magog, and indulged in visions
of a Heavenly Zion in the near future. Many Christians have also
followed the Jews in their predilection of exactly calculating the date
of the end of the world and of the coming of a savior.[2]

The Jewish view of history has been so influential because it was
adopted as the basis of the Christian philosophy of history. Like the
Jewish prophets, early Christians combined an utterly gloomy estimate
of the present with great expectations regarding the future. During the
first three centuries of our era many of them firmly believed in the
imminent coming of the millenium.[3] Millenialism (or chiliasm) was
a curious mixture of despair and hope, of belief in catastrophe and
redemption. The existing society of the Roman Empire was regarded
as irremediably doomed, but unlike the pagans the Christians antici-

---

[1] It is only in post-exilic Judaism that the eschatological (and apocalyptic) point of view
was fully developed; cf. Paul Volz, *Die Eschatologie der jüdischen Gemeinde im neutestamentlichen
Zeitalter* (Tübingen, 1934); R. Bultmann, *History and Eschatology* (ed. Harper Torchbooks,
New York, 1962), 27, 30.

[2] Cf. Volz, *op. cit.*; Abba Hillel Silver, *A History of Messianic Speculations in Israel From the
First Through the Seventeenth Centuries* (new ed., Boston, 1959).

[3] Cf. Walter Nigg, *Das ewige Reich. Geschichte einer Hoffnung* (Zürich, 1954); Norman Cohn,
The Pursuit of the Millenium (2d ed., New York, 1961); W. E. Peuckert, "Chiliasmus,"
Handwörterbuch des deutschen Aberglaubens (10 vols., Berlin, 1927–1942), II, 26–35.

pated the fall of Rome with hope rather than fear. Influenced by earlier prophecies circulating in Asia, they indulged in predictions of the approaching end of the hated Empire.[1] As envisioned in the well-known passages of the Revelation of St. John the Divine, Rome, "the ten-horned beast," was soon to be cast in a pool of fire. Then after its destruction, a new world was to be created and the faithful were to enjoy all the pleasures of Paradise. But even this future order would not be an unmixed blessing, for the millenium would last for only one thousand years and its disappearance like its establishment would be accompanied by horrible disasters.

Throughout the centuries most millenialists[2] as well as numerous other Christians held not only that the momentary state of affairs was beyond salvation but also that things have to get even worse before they will get better. The horrors of the last days, when Antichrist will rule the world, have been a constant theme in Christian literature. "It will be a time," wrote Lactantius in the second century, "when justice will be rejected and innocence odious, when the wicked will prey as enemies upon the good, when neither order nor military discipline will be observed, when none will respect grey hairs, or do the offices of piety, nor take pity upon women and children; all things will be confounded and mixed, against divine and natural law . . ."[3]

Millenialism, after having been widely accepted during the first three centuries of our era, was rejected by the Church in its hour of triumph. Criticized by the great Church Father St. Augustine and condemned by Church Councils, it remained outside the main stream of Christian thought during the subsequent Middle Ages.[4] Yet millenialism and other forms of apocalypticism survived as an important undercurrent, which re-emerged with the Protestant Reformation, and, in a secularized form, has manifested itself in Marxism and other modern philosophies of history.[5] Presenting at the same time pessimistic

[1] F. Cumont, "La fin du monde selon les mages occidentaux," *Revue de l'histoire des religions*, CIII (1931); J. W. Swain, "The Theory of the Four Monarchies: Opposition History Under the Roman Empire," *Classical Philology*, XXXV (1940), 1–21.

[2] Some later millenialists holding that the Second Coming of Christ is not needed to usher in the millenium viewed the course of history with more optimism. But these so-called post-millenialists did not become numerous until the nineteenth century.

[3] *Divinae institutiones*, VII, 17, 9, as tr. in Eliade, *op. cit.*, 127.

[4] Cf. E. Lewalter, "Eschatologie und Weltgeschichte in der Gedankenwelt Augustins," *Zeitschrift für Kirchengeschichte*, LV (1934), 1–51.

[5] Cf. Norman Cohn, *op. cit.*; Ernest Lee Tuveson, *Millenium and Utopia. A Study in the Background of the Idea of Progress* (Berkeley, 1949); "Millenial Dreams in Action. Essays in Comparative Study," Suppl. no. 2 to *Comparative Studies in Society and History* (The Hague, 1962).

and optimistic views of man's historical destiny, millenialism has played an important role in the history of the idea of decadence as well as in the development of the belief in progress.

A more genuinely "progressive" philosophy of history was presented by a number of Christian writers during the last two centuries of the Roman Empire (Arnobius, Eusebius, Orosius). Impressed by the increasing influence of Christianity, they held that the world was gradually moving toward greater perfection and that the Golden Age was not in the past, but in the present or the future. "I have discovered," wrote Orosius at the time of the collapse of the Western Roman Empire, "that the days of the past were not only as oppressive as those of the present but that they were the more terribly wretched the further they were removed from the consolation of true religion."[1] But this variety of Christian optimism also met with strong opposition. It was again St. Augustine who more than any one else was responsible for the elimination of these views from Church doctrine.[2] And it was "the fall of Rome" itself, that is the plundering of the eternal city by the Visigoths in 410, which prompted the bishop of Hippo to use the weight of his authority against a conception which, he felt, might be embarrassing to the Christians accused of being responsible for the ruin of the Empire. In earlier centuries Christians facing such charges had often argued that catastrophes had become less numerous since the birth of Christ. But in view of the magnitude of the disasters that had recently befallen Rome, St. Augustine felt that such an optimistic position was no longer tenable. Many other leading Christians like St. Jerome and St. Ambrose witnessing the collapse of Rome expressed their historical pessimism by reasserting the early Christian view that the end of the world was imminent.[3]

At this time many Christians, instead of looking upon Rome as Antichrist, assigned to the Empire the providential mission of spreading their religion throughout the world. Like earlier pagan authors they now wrote panegyrics on the greatness or even the "eternity" of

---

[1] Orosius, *The Seven Books of History against the Pagans*, tr. Irving W. Raymond (New York, 1936), 30 f.; cf. Gerhart B. Ladner, *The Idea of Reform. Its Impact on Christian Thought and Action in the Age of the Fathers* (Cambridge, Mass., 1959).

[2] Theodore E. Mommsen, "St. Augustine and the Christian Idea of Progress," *Medieval and Renaissance Studies* (Ithaca, 1959), 279–285; idem, "Orosius and Augustine," *ibidem*, 325–348.

[3] Johannes Straub, "Die Wirkung der Niederlage bei Adrianopel auf die Diskussion über das Germanenproblem in der spätrömischen Literatur," *Philologus*, 1943; idem, "Christliche Geschichtsapologetik in der Krisis des römischen Reiches," *Historia*, I (1950), 52–81; Bernard Kötting, "Endzeitprognosen zwischen Lactantius und Augustinus," *Historisches Jahrbuch*, LXXVII (1957), 125–139.

Rome or deplored its declining strength.[1] All during the Middle Ages clergymen were foremost in celebrating the glories of ancient Rome.[2] Many of them subscribed to the view that Rome, as the last of four great world empires, continued to exist in a corrupt form in their own age, and that its fall would coincide with the end of the world. Or to quote a Christian poet of the eighth century: "When Rome falls, the world will also find its end (Quando Roma cadet, cadet et mundus)."[3]

III

Pessimism as to the hopelessness of this world's redemption dominated much of the thinking in Western Europe from the fall of the Roman Empire until the Renaissance. Perhaps in no other period was mankind so much obsessed with the decay of life and the approaching end of the world. Medieval literature is filled with lamentations over the misery of man's mundane condition and with denunciations of corruptions in Church and State. In the Middle Ages Christianity did not serve as a doctrine presaging reformation of a world, which was regarded beyond salvation; rather, it was interpreted as a belief giving the individual the hope of compensating for his sufferings in this vale of tears by eternal bliss in a world hereafter.

The best that might be in store for this world was that it would last for a non-determinable length of time without undergoing any radical changes either for better or for worse. Such was the view to which the Catholic Church generally gave its official sanction and which was propounded by authoritative Catholic spokesmen like St. Augustine and Thomas Aquinas. But many Christians were inclined to take gloomier views. They held that under the cumulative effects of the Fall of Man mankind was doomed to degenerate regardless of the coming of Christ. Adopting the ancient conception of the gradual

[1] Rehm, op. cit., 29.
[2] Cf. Fedor Schneider, Rom und Romgedanke im Mittelalter (München, 1926); Percy E. Schramm, Kaiser, Rom und Renovation (Leipzig, 1929); Michael Seidlmayer, "Rom und Romgedanken im Mittelalter," Saeculum, VII (1956), 395–412.
[3] Mommsen, op. cit., 271; cf. H. von Löwe, "Regino von Prüm . . .," Geschichtsdenken und Geschichtsbild im Mittelalter, ed. Walther Lammers (Darmstadt, 1961), 120–121. Many Byzantine Christians also expected the end of the world to coincide with the fall of the Empire; cf. Charles Diehl, "De quelques croyances byzantines sur la fin de Constantinople,,' Byzantinische Zeitschrift, XXX (1930), 192–196; A. Vasiliev, "Medieval Ideas of the End of the World: West and East," Byzantion, XVI (1942–43), 462–502; Paul J. Alexander," "The Strength of Empire and Capital Seen Through Byzantine Eyes," Speculum, XXXVII (1962), 339–357.

degradation of humanity and the decay of nature, they believed that this process would go on until the very Day of Reckoning.[1] The utter state of decadence which many believed to be characteristic of their times was therefore widely regarded as convincing evidence that the Last Judgment could no longer be far away. It was especially during the early Middle Ages that this view of history was commonly accepted. Even popes such as Leo the Great and Gregory the Great endorsed the popular opinion that the frequency of political calamities as well as of natural disasters like earthquakes and famines were a sure indication that the world was drawing to a close.[2] In the tenth century the idea became almost a cliché as is evident from the standard formula that was included in many official documents: "While the world is approaching its end . . ."[3]

Unlike the ancients, medieval men looked upon decadence not as a law of nature, but as part of a divine scheme preceding the ultimate salvation of the elect. It might be true, as has been argued, that Christianity has paved the way for the ultimate acceptance of the belief in progress, but the immediate effect of the Christian triumph consisted in the strengthening rather than in the weakening of the conviction that this world was displaying all symptoms of senescence.

This pessimistic view of history did not lose much of its strength during the centuries in which medieval civilization exhibited its greatest vigor. At this time, even more than before, the Church itself was seen as being ridden with greed and ambition and undermined by division and strife. In the eleventh century, many clergymen bewildered by the crisis of the Investure Struggle came to the conclusion that the last days could not be very far away.[4] This pessimism deepened in the subsequent two centuries, when the Christians lost their possessions in the Holy Land, and the abuses in the ecclesiastical hierarchy became the subject of heated controversies.[5] The unsatis-

---

[1] Tuveson, op. cit., 20.

[2] E. Mangenot, "Fin du monde," Dictionnaire de théologie catholique, V[2] (Paris, 1913), col. 2531; Paul Vulliaud, La fin du monde (Paris, 1952), 80; G. G. Coulton, Medieval Panorama (Meridian ed., Cleveland, 1961), 9–11.

[3] Henri Focillon, L'an mil (Paris, 1952). 49ff.

[4] Erich Meuthen, "Geschichtssymbolismus Gerhohs von Reichersberg," Geschichtsdenken. . . im Mittelalter, 22, 228; Johannes Spörl, "Wandel des Welt- und Geschichtsbild im 12. Jahrhundert," ibidem, 294–295.

[5] Cf. P. Kurtz, "Gifer the Worm; an Essay toward the History of an Idea," University of California Publications in English, II (1928–29), no. 2, pp. 235–261; George J. Engelhardt, "The De Contemptu Mundi of Bernardus Morvalensis, Part One: a Study in Commonplace," Medieval Studies, XXII (1960), 108–135; P. Sabatier, Vie de S. François d'Assise (Paris, 1931), 67–68; Bertha Widmer, Heilsordnung und Zeitgeschehen in der Mystik Hildegards von Bingen (Basel, 1955), 186ff.; Achille Luchaire, La société au temps de Philippe Auguste (Paris, 1909), 1.

factory development of Christendom was frequently characterized as a form of "decay" and "decline," terms which made their first appearance in the various European languages at this time. It was the papacy especially that became the target of virulent criticism in the later Middle Ages. As early as the beginning of the thirteenth century the equivalent of our term "decadence" was used by the poet Guilhelm Figueira, accusing the papacy of being the source of all "dechesenssa."[1] Around this time many Christians came to regard the Donation of Constantine, by which the Roman Emperor had allegedly laid the foundation of the pope's temporal power, as the origin of the downfall of Christianity.[2]

The sense of living in a period of historical decline as expressed by these denunciators of ecclesiastical corruption is significant because it was based on a more realistic interpretation of history than most other forms of medieval pessimism. It had its orgin in a serious crisis in the Church, the only institution since the fall of the Roman Empire to dominate much of the social, cultural, and political life of western Europe. Even in modern times many intellectuals, non-Catholics as well as Catholics, have looked upon the collapse of the medieval synthesis as the passing of the last glorious age in European history.[3] It was especially in nineteenth-century Germany and England that the Middle Ages became the object of a cult on the part of many men of letters disgusted with the alleged materialism and individualism of modern civilization. But such "medievalism" was also a common attitude among men of letters in other countries. In America the brothers Henry and Brooks Adams regarded the dissolution of the Gothic Age as the beginning of a downward movement in Western civilization. In France writers like Gobineau and Renan asserted that the decadence of their country had started with the rise of a strong national state at the beginning of the fourteenth century; similarly the positivist philosopher Auguste Comte looked upon the centuries during which the Roman Catholic Church had imposed its control over a large part of Europe as the last constructive period of Western civili-

---

[1] J. Anglade, *Anthologie des troubadours* (Paris, 1953), 149ff. In other Romance languages similar equivalents were used: "Decadencia" (Catalonian); "scadenzia" (Italian). These terms rather than the medieval Latin "decadentia" might have been the immediate source of the French and English "decadence." The equivalent in the *langue d'oil* was originally "déchéance" from which the English "decay" was derived. Cf. M. Raynouard, *Lexique roman ou dictionnaire de la langue des troubadours* (Paris, 1836–45), II, 346, no. 14ff.; Carolus du Cange, *Glossarium mediae et infinae latinitatis* (ed. nova, 10 vols., Niort, 1883–87), III, 17.

[2] Erich Seeberg, *Gottfried Arnold. Die Wissenschaft und die Mystik seiner Zeit* (Meerane i. Sa., 1923).

[3] See *infra*, 227, 230–231, 242, 246.

zation and believed that only the establishment of a social order
similar to that of medieval society could bring an end to the continuous
state of intellectual anarchy from which Europe had suffered since
the decline of papal authority.[1]

During the many centuries of medieval civilization not all persons
were unqualified pessimists. Bitterness about the degeneration of the
present was occasionally tempered by the expectation of a renewal,
a regeneration, or a reform in the near future. In many periods of
medieval history, for example, clerics dreamed about a renovation of
the Roman Empire.[2] An even more significant expression of medieval
hope for a better world manifested itself in the agitation for a reform
of the Church in Head and Members that gained impetus in the
centuries of the Babylonian Captivity and the Great Schism.[3] The
Christian's prospect of salvation which thus far had been mainly
offered to the individual alone, was now extended to Christianity as a
social institution. The strength of later medieval reform movements is
an indication that many prominent Christians began to reject the
ancient view of the inevitability of continuous degeneration. Their new,
"regenerationist" sense of decadence left its impact on many later
secular forms of historical pessimism.

The spiritual crisis of the later Middle Ages also led to a new vogue
of apocalyptic doctrines that expressed in an intensified form the same
mixture of alarm and hope which characterizes many other speculations of this period. Most of the new prophecies were inspired by the
views of Joachim of Floris. This twelfth-century Cistercian abbot
predicted the coming of the era of the Holy Spirit, a period that would
be vastly superior to the two earlier phases of human history, those
of the Old Testament (or the Father) and the New Testament (or
the Son). This new conception of history, looking forward to a world
of love and harmony, has been regarded as a first manifestation of a
truly optimistic philosophy of history. Yet, as in the case of the
millenialism of earlier centuries and of secular utopianism of later
times, medieval apocalyptic doctrines largely served the function of
compensating for the miseries of existing society, which was considered

---

[1] See Karl Löwith, *Meaning in History* (Chicago, 1957), 74–82; the High Middle Ages
have also been glorified by many convervative French historians; cf. Frantz Funck-Brentano,
L'ancien régime (Paris, 1926), 17: "Les XIe, XIIe et XIIIe siècles français sont la plus grande
époque de l'histoire du monde."

[2] Cf. Schramm, *op. cit.*; H. von Löwe, *loc.cit.*, 132; Robert S. Lopez, *The Tenth Century.
How Dark the Dark Ages?* (New York, 1959), 2.

[3] Cf. Alexander Flick, *The Decline of the Medieval Church* (2 vols., London, 1930), I,
334ff.; Ray C. Petry, *Christian Eschatology and Social Thought* (New York, 1956).

to be in a state of total decadence. It was taken for granted that a renovation could not be expected until after Antichrist had completed his destruction of the existing order. The popularity of the Joachimist prophecies should therefore not be interpreted as indication of pride in progress hitherto achieved. [1]

A more radical departure from the gloomy appraisal of the state of the world is to be found in the views of a number of twelfth-century writers questioning the superiority of ancient civilization. Bernard of Chartres' noted statement that the moderns were dwarfs compared to the ancients, but could see farther because they were standing on their shoulders was one of the first indications of a regained self-respect in medieval times. Later on in the twelfth century, a few French authors went even a step further. No longer acknowledging a great debt to the ancients they claimed that the pre-eminence in "chivalry and learning," formerly belonging to the Greeks and the Romans, had definitively passed to their own nation. [2]

Yet the strength of this incipient secularism, though evident in some of the greatest works of medieval art, literature, and philosophy, can easily be exaggerated. The Church, even if increasingly involved in the organization of this world, did not renounce its otherwordly orientation. Innocent III, who more than any other pope acted as the supreme ruler of Christianity, yielded to few other medieval writers in bewailing the corruptions of human nature. Roger Bacon might have anticipated modern scientific progress, but he considered the thirteenth century as the worst of all times and lived in the expectation of Antichrist. Even Dante, in whom a secular, modern spirit was more strongly developed than in many of his contemporaries, believed that he lived in the last of the ages.[3]

Complacency sporadic and feeble as it might have been in the twelfth and thirteenth centuries, all but disappeared during the subsequent two centuries. In northwestern Europe at least, the "waning

[1] Karl A. Fink, "Joachim von Fiori," *Grosse Geschichtsdenker*, ed. R. Stadelmann, 96–110; Marjorie Reeves, "Joachimist influences on the Idea of a Last World Emperor," *Traditio*, XVII (1961), 233–370; Löwith, *op. cit.*, 145–159.
[2] A. Buck, "Das französische Kulturbewusztsein im 12. Jahrhundert," *Wissenschaftliche Zeitschrift der Friedrich-Schiller Universität Jena*, Gesellschafts- und Sprachwissenschaftliche Reihe, Heft 2–3, pp. 249–251; *idem*, "Aus der Vorgeschichte der *Querelle des anciens et des modernes* im Mittelalter und Renaissance," *Bibliothèque d'Humanisme et Renaissance*, Sept., 1958; William A. Nitze, "The so-called Twelfth-Century Renaissance," *Speculum*, XXIII (1948), 464–471; Ernst Robert Curtius, *Gesammelte Aufsätze zur romanischen Philologie* (Bern, 1960), 32–33; Friedrich Heer, *Medieval World in Europe, 1100–1350* (Cleveland, 1962), 230ff.
[3] George G. Coulton, ed., *Life in the Middle Ages* (4 vols., New York, 1930), II, 55ff.; H. Grandgent, *Dante* (London, 1920). 224.

of the Middle Ages" was a period of almost universal despondency expressing itself in numerous predictions of the coming of Antichrist and the end of the world.[1] Nor did these gloomy sentiments vanish in modern times. The Renaissance lacked the strong popular roots necessary for bringing about a definitive rejection of Christian super-naturalism and asceticism. Insofar as the rediscovery of antiquity introduced a heightened sense of earthly destiny, its effects were confined to a small elite. As such, moreover, its impact was weakened by the Protestant Reformation, which, far from inaugurating an era of historical optimism, actually led to an intensification of worldly despair.

The Reformation by disrupting the religious unity which western Europe had known for many centuries perpetuated the sense of crisis that had prevailed during the later Middle Ages. To numerous Catholics, needless to say, the Protestant apostasy was a source of profound alarm. Up to our own time many uncompromising, so-called "integralist" Catholics have maintained that the Reformation ushered in the downfall of European civilization.[2] Thus nineteenth-century Catholic foes of the French Revolution like Joseph de Maistre, Metternich, and Adam Müller detected the origin of the subversive spirit of their times in the Protestant Reformation.[3] "Protestantism," wrote Metternich's secretary, Friedrich Gentz in 1819," is the first, the only source of all the vast evils under which we groan today . . . Once the governments . . . granted it a place in the State beside, or even on the ruins of, the only true church, the religious, moral and political order of the world was immediately dissolved . . . The entire French Revolution, and the even worse revolution which is about to break over Germany, have sprung from this same source."[4]

Protestants have, of course rejected this interpretation of the revolt against Rome, and yet many of them have also been nostalgic for the strong religious faith that had bound Europe together during the Middle Ages.[5] And among early Protestants historical pessimism

[1] Johan Huizinga, *Herfsttij der Middeleeuwen* (8th ed., Haarlem, 1952), *passim*, esp. ch. II; Rudolf Stadelmann, *Vom Geist des ausgehenden Mittelalters* (Halle, 1929), esp. ch. V.

[2] Friedrich Heer, *Die Dritte Kraft. Der europäische Humanismus zwischen den Fronten des konfessionellen Zeitalters* (Frankfurt, 1959), 591ff.; Judith N. Shklar, *After Utopia. The Decline of Political Faith* (Princeton, 1957), 185; cf. *infra*, 50, 87–88, 150.

[3] H. J. Schoeps, *Vorläufer Spenglers. Studien zum Geschichtspessimismus des 19. Jahrhunderts* (Leiden, 1955), 20.

[4] Gentz to Adam Müller, transl. in E. J. Hobsbawm, *The Age of Revolutions. Europe 1789–1848* (London, 1962), 231.

[5] Cf. G. P. Gooch, *History and Historians in the Nineteenth Century* (Boston, 1962), 66; *infra*, 227, 230–231.

was all but universal.[1] During the sixteenth century and even a great part of the seventeenth the old views of the decay of nature and the degeneration of the world found some of their staunchest defenders in Protestant countries. Later generations might have looked back upon the Elizabethan era as a period of unsurpassed vitality and brilliancy in English history, but most English writers of the time were firmly convinced of the corruption of the world and its approaching end.[2] In Germany Protestant theologians were equally pessimistic about the state of Christendom. At this time astrological predictions of doom created serious panics among the populations of various European states.[3] As late as 1665 Louis XIV ordered the publication of treatises reassuring the French people that the appearance of comets did not signify the coming of any great disasters.[4] Even among the learned the old views were slow in dying. "Not only the vulgar, but even philosophers themselves from Antiquity down to our times," maintained the English naturalist John Ray in 1692, have believed in the doctrine that all things "successively diminish and decay in all natural . . . as well as moral qualities."[5]

John Ray himself, however, rejected this ancient theory, and many of his contemporaries shared his view. At the end of the seventeenth century the great change in European outlook on the world, which had been anticipated by some men of the Renaissance, rapidly gained ground. In the years between 1680 and 1715, the period so aptly characterized by a great French scholar, Paul Hazard, as "la crise de la conscience européenne," a new cosmology and a more accurate understanding of man's past began to replace the views that had been current until this time. As part of this intellectual revolution an important change occurred in man's view of historical decline. The old fears were definitively losing their hold on the mind of the educated.

---

[1] Cf. Paul Vulliaud, *op. cit.*, 120 ff.; Silver. *A Study of Messianic Speculations in Israel*, 162ff.; Tuveson, *op. cit.*, 32, 41–42, 225.

[2] Victor Harris, *All Coherence Gone* (Chicago, 1949); Tuveson, *op. cit.*, 93, 129; Herschel Baker, *The Wars of Truth. Studies in the Decay of Christian Humanism in the Earlier Seventeenth Century* (Cambridge, Mass., 1952), esp. ch. II.

[3] Rudolf Stadelmann, *Vom Geist des ausgehenden Mittelalters*; Erich Seeberg, *op. cit.*; W. E. Peuckert, articles "Antichrist" and "Chiliasmus," *Handwörterbuch des deutschen Aberglaubens*, I, 490–493; II, 30–34.

[4] A. Prat in his introduction to Pierre Bayle, *Pensées diverses sur la comète* (2d ed., Paris, 1939), p. vii.

[5] John Ray, *Miscellaneous Discourses Concerning the Dissolution and Changes of the World* (London, 1692), 40–41.

CHAPTER II

THE NEW SENSE OF CRISIS

Nous approchons de l'état de crise et du siècle des révolutions.
ROUSSEAU, *Emile*, Book III

I

With the coming of the Renaissance a new, more secular, and in some respects more optimistic conception of history began to emerge. First in Italy and then in northwestern Europe, the world lost some of its terror, and mythology released its grip on the understanding of the past. Petrarch was perhaps the first author clearly recognizing the decline of the Roman Empire as a purely historical phenomenon. Although still looking upon his own age as the nadir of all times, he occasionally expressed some confidence that arts and sciences would revive and his country regain its former strength.[1] And among Petrarch's admirers in the Quattrocento, somber feelings about the corruption of Italy made place for a sense of pride in the recent achievements of Italian artists and scholars. Perhaps nothing else divides so sharply the Renaissance from the Middle Ages as this new awareness of living in an era superior to the preceding period.[2]

At this time the ancient doctrine of the eternity of the world – already adopted by some medieval admirers of Aristotle – gained increased prestige among European intellectuals. Niccolò Machiavelli, Francesco Guicciardini, and Lucilio Vanini ignored, if they did not openly criticize, the Christian expectation of the end of the world and reintroduced the ancient concept of endless flux or cyclical movement.

[1] W. Mommsen, "Petrarch's Conception of the Dark Ages," *Medieval and Renaissance Studies*, 107–209; J. H. Robinson and H. W. Rolfe, *Petrarch, the First Modern Scholar and Man of Letters* (New York, 1909), 208–213. The humanists of the Quattrocento designated historical decline as "inclinatio," a term which they derived from the classical "inclinare" (a term used by Cicero and Sallust in reference to the alleged corruption of the Roman Republic); see Mazzarino, *op. cit.*, 26, 72–75. Vernacular derivatives of this Latin term (Italian: "inclinazione;" French: "inclinaison") were current in the sixteenth century but fell into disuse in the subsequent century.

[2] Walter K. Ferguson, "Humanist Views of the Renaissance," *American Historical Review*, XLV (1939), 1–28; Denys Hay, *The Italian Renaissance in its Historical Background* (Cambridge, 1961), 11.

Among the later humanists the common belief in the Golden Age in the past found its first modern critics. Some of them even dreamed about a Golden Age in the near future or proclaimed the superiority of the "moderns" over the "ancients."[1]

But the gradual replacement of Christian supernaturalism by a naturalist and secular outlook did not necessarily lead to a more cheerful view of history. On the contrary, once again, as in antiquity, the course of events often appeared as deprived of any ultimate meaning. Thus one of the most naturalist minds of the Renaissance, Leonardo da Vinci, was obsessed with visions of a catastrophic end of the world, an event that he no longer envisaged as a divine judgment consoling to the faithful, but as a disaster in which all men, regardless of their merits, would suffer the same torments.[2]

Most humanists, moreover, remained painfully aware of the superiority of classical civilization and, like the venerated ancients, placed the Golden Age in the past instead of the future. To them the idea of a "Renaissance" represented a longing for renewal rather than a proud awareness of actual accomplishments. And in many instances their high hopes for a better future were followed by bitter disillusionment. Thus Marsilio Ficino and Erasmus ended their lives without any of the youthful optimism with which they had once viewed the trend of their times.[3] The wide response to Savonarola's virulent denunciations of Renaissance society also indicates that many Italians of the end of the fifteenth century still looked upon their age as a period of crisis and corruption.[4] In other words the exuberant optimism of the Renaissance is little more than a myth.

II

One of the new secular ideals that increased in strength during the Renaissance was that of nationalism. Many Italian, German, French,

[1] Cf. Herbert Grundmann, "Die Grundzüge der mittelalterlichen Geschichtsanschauungen," *Geschichtsdenken und Geschichtsbild im Mittelalter,* 418–429; Hans Baron, "The Querelle of the Ancients and the Moderns as a Problem of Renaissance Scholarship," *Journal of the History of Ideas,* XX (1959), 3–22; Giacinto Margiotta, *Le origini italiane de la "Querelle des anciens et des modernes"* (Roma, 1953).

[2] Joseph Gantner, *Leonardos Visionen von der Sintflut und vom Untergang der Welt.* (Bern, 1958), esp. p. 197).

[3] Ferguson, *loc. cit.,* 25; Raymond Marcel, *Marsile Ficin (1433–1499)* (Paris, 1958), 449; on Erasmus' hopes and disillusions, see J. Huizinga, *Erasmus* (3d ed., Haarlem, 1936), 105–106 and *infra,* 23.

[4] Rudolf von Albertini, *Das florentinische Staatsbewusstsein im Übergang von der Republik zum Prinzipat* (Bern, 1955), 22–23, 107; Rehm, *op. cit.,* 48–50.

Spanish, and English humanists indulged in making exaggerated claims as to the superiority of their nations and their mission in the world.[1] Some of them also dreamed of reintroducing the republican institutions that were held to have been the secret of Roman greatness. When such dreams of national grandeur or political regeneration failed to materialize, a new, partly secular concept of decadence, consisting of a blend of ancient and Christian ideas, made its appearance.

The first significant manifestations of this new form of pessimism are to be found in Italy and Spain. The rather sudden and unexpected setback in power and prestige which Italy suffered in the sixteenth century and Spain about a hundred years later created a sense of crisis and decadence foreshadowing the feelings of anxiety with which many nineteenth-century Frenchmen viewed the state of their country. It is true that there were many other European countries which declined in power and prosperity in the early modern period: the Holy Roman Empire,[2] Poland, and Sweden. None of these countries, however, had progressed as far as Italy in the secularization of its culture or as far as Spain in creating a modern centralized national state. Moreover, none of these states had ever played a role of supremacy in European culture or economy and their fairly gradual, purely political or economic decline was not accompanied by a widespread sense of national and cultural crisis. The anxiety resulting from the disasters befalling these countries was still expressed in forms not yet radically different from the medieval speculations about the approaching end of the world or the transient nature of all worldly power.

The calamities befalling Italy and Spain, on the other hand, fostered a more modern kind of historical and cultural pessimism. The similarity between the situation facing France in the nineteenth century and that confronting Italy and Spain as early as the sixteenth and seventeenth centuries did not escape the attention of nineteenth-century writers speculating about the "decadence of the Latin nations."[3] At this time it was widely believed that because of a common religious, political, and racial background these countries experienced the same difficulties in adjusting themselves to the modern world. In all three countries there developed nationalistic movements that

---

[1] Denys Hay, "Italy and Barbarian Europe," *Italian Renaissance Studies*, ed. E. F. Jacob (New York, 1960), 48–68; Hubert Gillot, *La Querelle des anciens et modernes en France* (Nancy, 1914); S. Kliger, *The Goths in England* (Cambridge, Mass., 1952); Hans Kohn, *The Idea of Nationalism*, ch. IV.

[2] On the disappointment that many German humanists experienced in their nationalistic aspirations, see Kohn, *op. cit.*, 138–146.

[3] See *infra*, 124, 140, 156–157, 243–244.

aimed at reviving the national greatness of the past. This type of backward looking nationalism, which took for granted the decadence of the present, stood in sharp contrast to the future-oriented nationalism of countries like Germany and Russia, whose past, it was admitted, might be insignificant, and whose present might be mediocre, but whose future, it was confidently hoped, would be glorious.

III

Italians, "the first born among the sons of modern Europe," were also first in developing a modern concept of decadence. A sense of crisis, which had already plagued some of the earlier humanists, acquired greater urgency after the French invasions of 1494. Francesco Guicciardini, one of the most intelligent observers of the events of his time, called 1494 "the great year of misfortunes for Italy," which "had opened the door to innumerable and horrible calamities."[1] Like many other Florentines he was deeply disturbed by the collapse of republican institutions and by Italian failure to ward off foreign domination. He felt that the old strength of Italy was irretrievably lost and that the best one could do in such dark times was to withdraw from public life and to pursue his private interests.

In some of his views Guicciardini struck a remarkably modern note. His complaints that the Florentine zeal for equality would lead either to tyranny or to mob rule might easily have been made by a nineteenth-century conservative like Tocqueville. Another distinguishing feature of Guicciardini's view of history is his resigned, almost fatalistic acceptance of political decline. "All cities, states, and kingdoms," he wrote, "are mortal, since either by nature or by accident everything in this world must some time have an end. Accordingly the citizen who happens to live when his country is in its decline should not so much lament over its unhappy fortunes as over his own. For his country only suffers what it was fated to suffer. His is the infelicity of being born at the moment when his country has to fulfill its doom."[2] At first glance it might seem that Guicciardini here renewed ancient Stoicism with its belief in endless world cycles and its cult of imperturbability in the face of inevitable disaster. But it should be noted that an element of individualism crept into the attitude taken by Guicciardini,

---

[1] Albertini, *op. cit.*, 237–240; cf. *ibid.*, 95ff., 225.
[2] Francesco Guicciardini, *Ricordi*, ed. R. Spongano (Firenze, 1951), 201; Engl. tr. (New York, 1949), 262–263.

who, like some of his contemporaries, went further than the Stoics by denying any meaning to history and developing an attitude of political indifferentism or even of cynicism. Francesco Vettori, another Florentine aristocrat, went so far as to call history a concatenation of senseless wars, crimes and failures, leaving man no other choice than caring for his personal welfare.[1]

Very different in spirit from Guicciardini's attitude of detached observation and resigned acceptance of the calamities of his age was Machiavelli's reaction towards his time. More virulent in his denunciations and yet less despairing of the future than most humanists, Machiavelli was the last great exponent of republican idealism in Renaissance Italy. In his indictment of the depravity of his society he equalled preachers of penitence like Savonarola. In the present situation of Italy, he wrote, "there is nothing that redeems it from every extremity of wretchedness, infamy, and shame. There is no observance of religion or law, there is no military consciousness. Instead it is defeated by every species of abomination . . ."[2] Machiavelli also remained well within the prophetic tradition by his refusal to give up hope for a better future. However pessimistic on the existing state of his country, he was still confident that a regeneration (*ricorso*) was possible.

In the remedies he proposed Machiavelli often displayed a remarkable lack of political realism. In his obsession with a restoration of the old militia and his appeal to a strong prince to liberate his country from foreign domination he suffered from illusions similar to those of religious prophets of the past. Yet, in other respects, Machiavelli's sense of decadence was highly modern. His primary concern was not with the decline of piety and Christian morality, but with the loss of civic virtue and republican idealism. He no longer accepted the Christian views on Divine Providence but believed in the eternal flux of rising and falling states. He was convinced that the world remained basically the same as far as good and evil were concerned and that when virtue disappeared as it had done in the Italy of his time, it reappeared elsewhere. Machiavelli was also modern in his attempt to base his conviction that contemporary Italy was rotten to the core on objective historical evidence. He rejected the commonly held belief in a Golden Age and realized that the past was easily idealized

---

[1] Albertini, *op. cit.*, 251.
[2] N. Machiavelli, *Discorsi*, book II, preface, as tr. in Federico Chabod, *Machiavelli and the Renaissance* (London, 1958), 80; cf. ibid., 137, 145.

by old men whose judgment had sharpened but whose capacity for enjoyment had dulled.[1] Machiavelli's views of past, present, and future represented the first important secularized version of the Christian philosophy of history. His seemingly incongruous mixture of despair and hope anticipated the attitude with which many later European intellectuals faced the crises of their times.

The conviction that sixteenth-century Italy was in a state of decadence was not held by Florentines alone: the Venetian humanist Paolo Giovio called his period "a century of iron" in which man could not help but bewail "the heartlessness of the times;" the papal librarian Agostino Steuco likewise lamented that man had fallen on evil days. Among other reasons, the threat posed by the Protestant Reformation led many Italians to view the future with anxiety. In 1562, at the Council of Trent, a Franciscan theologian, Vicedominus, complained: "The world is falling into ruins; the Christian Republic is perishing, the stones of the spiritual temple are tumbling down. And which stones? Entire cities, provinces, kingdoms, the strength of the Empire."[2] It was especially the sack of Rome in 1527 by German Protestant soldiers that created a mood of anxiety and bewilderment. Many contemporaries comparing this disaster with the plundering of the Eternal City by the Visigoths in 410 feared that a new age of barbarism was at hand. Even outside Italy this event was regarded as a catastrophe of the first magnitude. Thus Erasmus, repeating almost exactly the words written by his venerated master St. Jerome in the fifth century, confided to a friend: "Truly, this is not the end of a city, this is the end of the world".[3]

In the following centuries of foreign domination and national disunity, when Italy lost its position of leadership in European economy as well as in arts and literature, a sense of national and cultural decline was never completely absent from the Italian mind.[4] Yet in this period the sense of crisis lost much of its urgency. In Italy the loss in power and prestige was not spectacular enough to cause lasting

---

[1] *The Discourses*, ed. Leslie J. Walker (2 vols., New Haven, 1950), book II, preface; book III, discourse I (I, 353–356; 459ff.); cf. Rehm, *op. cit.*, 55 ff.

[2] F. Chabod, *op. cit.*, 197; Albertini, *op. cit.*, 136–137, 171, 330–337; Rehm, *op. cit.*, 69–71, 73, 153; J. D. Mansi, *Sacrorum conciliorum nova amplissima collectio*, vol. XXXIII (Graz, 1961), 723.

[3] Percy S. Allen, *Opus epistolarum Desiderii Erasmi Roterodami*, vol. VII (Oxford, 1928), 509–511 (Erasmus to Jacopo Sadoleto, Oct. 1, 1528); cf. Walther Rehm. *Europäische Romdichtung* (2d ed., München, 1960), 87ff.; D. Regis de Campus, "Trois aspects du 'Jugement dernier' de Michel-Ange," *Table ronde*, Febr., 1957, 85–95.

[4] Cf. Benedetto Croce, *Storia della età barocca in Italia* (2d ed., Bari, 1946) introd., pp. 41–51, 467–490; Rehm, *Der Untergang Roms*, 73–74.

gloom about the national development. In many fields such as the arts and literature the decadence was only relative, whereas in music and science the Italians held more than their own. The establishment of legitimate dynasties, moreover, appeared to many Italians as an improvement upon the tyranny or the anarchy prevailing in the Trecento and the Quattrocento. Finally, national confidence was not greatly perturbed by the minor role that Italy played in European politics, since even in the so-called glorious centuries of the Renaissance, Italy had never been a national state acting as a major power.

It is therefore not surprising that many Italians continued to consider their country far superior to the "barbarian" nations of northwestern Europe. In the seventeenth century some Italians actually paved the way for the acceptance of the modern idea of progress by refuting the notion of the inferiority of modern civilization to that of antiquity.[1] Nor did the great philosopher of history Giambattista Vico (1668–1740) express himself pessimistically about the civilization of his time. In his famous *Principi d'una scienza nuova* he made surprisingly few strictures on his own age. Although he presented a dismal picture of the age of corruption and selfishness that he considered to be in store for every society that had run its due course, he never specifically asserted that modern civilization was approaching this fatal state.[2] Insofar as Italians continued to be haunted by the idea of decadence, it was not the decline of Renaissance Italy, but that of the Roman Empire that remained uppermost in their minds.

IV

In the seventeenth century Spaniards faced an even more serious crisis in their national existence than Italians had confronted a hundred years earlier. Probably no other leading European country renowned for its wealth, its military power, and the vitality of its arts and literature lost its prominence within such a brief period. The bewilderment of the Spaniards was the greater as they had been accustomed to think of themselves as the chosen people, vastly superior to any other nation by the excellence of their government and their devotion to the Catholic religion.

---

[1] Alessandro Tassoni, *Dieci libri di pensieri diversi* (Carpi, 1620); Secondo Lancellotti, *L'hoggidì overo Il mondo non peggiore, ne più calamitoso del passato* (Venetia, 1623); cf. Giacento Margiotta, *op. cit.*; Hans Baron, *loc. cit.*; Albertini, *op. cit.*, 310; Chabod, *op. cit.*, 198.
[2] Giambattista Vico, *La scienza nuova*, ed. F. Nicolini (2vols., Bari, 1928), II, 162; cf. R. Stadelmann, "Giambattista Vico," *Grosse Geschichtsdenker*, 142–146; Richard Peters, *Der Aufbau der Weltgeschichte bei Giambattista Vico* (Stuttgart, 1929), 164ff.

The downward trend of the country began to be a common topic of discussion during the reign of Philip III (1598–1621).[1] As early as 1600, an astute political analyst, Martin González de Cellorigo, asserted that all Spaniards agreed in considering the present vastly inferior to the past. "It seems," he wrote, "as if one wished to reduce these kingdoms to a republic of bewitched beings, living outside the natural order of things." Being one of the first to apply the term "decline" (*declinación*) to the recent development of his country, he did not indulge in nostalgic lamentations over the passing of the good old times, but presented a cool statement supported by precise evidence. González de Cellorigo was mainly concerned with the unsatisfactory state of Spanish economy, which he attributed to the backwardness of Spanish technology. "Our republic," he complained, "has come to an extreme contrast of rich and poor. We lack people of the middle sort whom neither wealth not poverty prevents from pursuing the rightful kind of business . . ." "Those who can, will not," was his bitter comment, "and those who will, cannot."[2]

An even more impressive manifestation of growing concern about the state of the country is the somber warning given by the Council of Castile in 1619. After having pointed to the many serious abuses from which the country was suffering, it concluded: "The nation's sickness is grave indeed; it cannot be cured by ordinary means. Bitter remedies are most likely to be efficacious for those who are ill: in order to save the body, one must often remove the arm; to cure the cancerous, one must employ fire." It further pointed out that "cities, kingdoms, and monarchies perish, as do men and all things created," and illustrated this view by the fate which had befallen the empires of the Medes, Persians, Greeks, and Romans. It felt that the virtues which had made for Spanish greatness in the past no longer existed and recommended radical reforms in order to restore the country to its former strength.[3]

[1] This is not so say that before this time various Spanish writers did not lament the downfall of their nation. The fall of Visigothic Spain was an important theme in Spanish medieval literature; cf. Pedro Sáinz y Rodríguez, *La evolución de las ideas sobre la decadencia española* (Madrid, 1925), 8, 21 and Luis Díez y Corral, *De ontvoering van Europa*, tr. from Spanish (Utrecht, 1961), 66. On sixteenth-century pessimism in Spain, see Victor Harris, *op.cit.*, 88, 212; John L. Phelan, *The Millenial Kingdom of the Franciscans in the New World, a Study of the Writings of Gerónimo de Mendieta (1525–1604)* (Berkeley, 1956), 102–105, 142–143.

[2] Martin González de Cellorigo, *Memorial de la política necessaria y util restauración a la República de España* (Valladolid, 1600) as quoted by Vicente Palacio Atard, *Derrota, agotamiento, decadencia, en la España del siglo XVII* (Madrid, 1949), 113; and John Elliott, "The Decline of Spain," *Past and Present*, no. 20 (nov., 1961), 53, 73.

[3] *La Junta de reformación. Documentos procedentes del Archivo nacional y del General de Simancas*, ed. Angel González Palencia, *Colección de documentos inéditos para la historia de España y de sus*

Public opinion as expressed in the publications of that time went even further than this official report in castigating the corruption of the Spanish nation. Many poets and novelists complained about the increasing effeminacy of the younger generation, their indolence and excessive love of luxuries, their delight in gambling, women, and the theater, and also about the new pretensions of Spanish womanhood and the ever worse plague of prostitution. In a barely disguised parody the poet Matías de los Reyes ridiculed the confusion of government circles and their failure to take energetic action to stem the national decline. The Latin poet Juvenal serving as his mouthpiece admitted Spanish superiority over the Romans in the field of satire, because in this genre, he felt, eminence largely stems from the viciousness of the age in which a satirist was born. It was therefore natural, according to him, that in a society as decadent as that of seventeenth-century Spain the satirical vein was more fecund than it had ever been in the Roman Empire.[1]

Other early seventeenth-century publicists concentrated their criticisms on the numerous evils in the Spanish government and economy. Distinguished authors like Saavedra Fajardo and Fernández Navarrete as well as a host of obscure pamphleteers diagnosed the maladies from which their country was suffering and suggested remedies for its recovery. In the numerous political treatises dealing with the Spanish crisis the depopulation of the countryside was singled out as one of the most serious sources of national weakness. Other frequently discussed abuses were the neglect of agriculture and industry, the rapid rise in prices, the heavy, unequally distributed tax load, the sale of public offices, and the corruption and inefficiency of the administration of justice and finances.[2]

Many authors took the position that the misfortunes of Spain were not due to any undesirable national characteristics but should be blamed on pernicious foreign influences. Instead of conceding any basic inferiority of the Spanish people, they felt called upon to make extravagant claims for its superior qualities and to defend their country

---

Indias, vol. V (Valladolid, 1932); cf. Ruth Lee Kennedy, "The Madrid of 1617–25. Certain Aspects of Social, Moral, and Educational Reform," *Estudios hispanicos. Homenaje a Archer M. Huntington* (Wellesley, Mass., 1952), 275–309.

[1] Ruth Lee Kennedy, *loc. cit.*; cf. Pierre Vilar, "Le temps du Quichotte," *Europe* (Paris), CXXIV (1956), 3–16.

[2] Sáinz y Rodriguez, *op. cit.*, 23–25; John C. Dowling, *El pensamiento político- filosófico de Saavedra Fajardo. Posturas del siglo XVII ante la decadencia y conservación de monarquías* (Murcia, 1957).

against foreign detractors.[1] The gifted satirist Francisco de Quevedo, though admitting that his contemporaries had lost the military ardor of their forbears, held that the Spaniards had been corrupted through their communication with other nations: they would not have known any excesses in drinking and eating if the Germans had not introduced them; they had learned unnatural vice from the Italians and had had to use the Inquisition because of Luther's and Calvin's heresies. To bring back the old virtues he advocated a complete cultural isolation from the rest of Europe and a renewal of war.[2] A similar point of view was presented in the 1620's by a Spanish diplomat, who preached war against England because this country was supposed to have infected Spain with heresy and to be responsible for the loss of Spanish commercial and political influence in the world.[3]

During the first decades of the seventeenth century many Spaniards were still confident that a reform of the government or the pursuit of a different foreign policy would restore the former power of the country. But as the century progressed, the hope for a national revival grew fainter. It was especially after the numerous insurrections and military defeats of the early 1640's that many Spaniards began to despair of the future. At this time Quevedo lost his confidence in the regeneration of his country. "I do not know," he wrote in 1645, "whether the end is coming, or whether it has already come."[4] In 1640 a historian, Juan de Palafox y Mendoza, wrote a secret memorandum on the downfall of Spain in which he contrasted the short duration of Spanish greatness (thirty years) with the much longer periods of supremacy enjoyed by the Assyrians, Greeks, Romans, and other leading peoples in world history. Like many of his contemporaries he came to the conclusion that Spain had failed because her resources had not been equal to the great tasks which she had set herself. Instead of a policy of peace, an overaggressive foreign policy was now blamed for the decline of the country. A melancholy mood also pervaded much of the imaginative literature of this period. The early reformist zeal was largely replaced by stoic resignation, an

[1] Fidelino de Figueiredo, *Las dos Españas* (Santiago, Chile, 1936), 71–72; Manuel de Montolíu, *El alma de España y sus reflejos en la literatura del Siglo de Oro* (Barcelona, 1942), 9–133; Sverker Arnoldsson, *La Leyenda Negra* (Göteborg, 1960); Ramón Menéndez Pidal, *The Spaniards in Their History* (New York, 1950), 226.

[2] Figueiredo, *op. cit.*, 112–113; Menéndez Pidal, *op. cit.*, 224–226; Sáinz y Rodriguez, *op. cit.*, 20–21, 32.

[3] "Memoria sobre las causas de la decadencia de España desde Cárlos V hasta 1629, "*Colección de documentos inéditos para la historia de España*, vol. LV (1870), 5–25.

[4] Menéndez Pidal, *op. cit.*, 227.

attitude which many later writers came to consider as typical of the Spanish national temper.[1]

A new note in Spanish speculations on the decline of their country made its appearance in the eighteenth century when a number of Spaniards influenced by French thought began to blame Spanish "decadencia" (a neologism derived from the French "décadence") on the unenlightened policies of religious intolerance and administrative corruption.[2] As a result, the Spanish people became sharply divided in their attitudes toward the decline of their country. Whereas many Spaniards continued to ascribe national weakness to the perverting influence of foreign ideas, an increasingly strong minority attributed it to a policy of cultural isolation. Down until our own time the problem of Spanish decadence has continued to obsess the Spanish mind and to provoke passionate and inconclusive debates in which liberals and conservatives have taken opposite positions.[3]

The sense of political decline thus contributed to the division of the Spanish people into two camps with conflicting explanations of the national reversal. In France, as will be pointed out, the feeling of decadence had a similar effect. In Spain, as later on in France, the misfortunes befalling the nation also fostered an exclusive concern with national interests and a withdrawal of the nation within itself. There are still other similarities between the feeling of national decline in Spain and that in France. In the nineteenth century the same reasons were often advanced for the so-called decadence of France as had been presented for the decline of Spain in an earlier period: depopulation, pernicious foreign influences, backwardness of science and industry, an overambitious foreign policy, and excessive centralization. It is therefore not surprising that next to the fall of Rome, the decline of Spain was often cited as a warning example by Frenchmen alarmed at the state of their nation.

On the other hand, there also existed significant differences between the speculations about national decline in the two countries. In the Spanish Old Regime a strict censorship of the press made it impossible

[1] Juan de Palafox y Mendoza, "Juicio interior y secreto de la monarquía para mí solo," ed. José María Jover Zamora, Cuadernos de historia de España, XIII (1950); Jover, Historia de una polémica ... 1635 (Madrid, 1949); Dowling, op. cit.,, 232ff.; Luis Sánchez-Agesta, "España y Europa en la crisis del siglo XVII (Raíz histórica de una actitud polémica)" Revista de estudios políticos, no. 91 (1957); Azorin, "La decadencia de España," Clásicos y modernos (Madrid, 1919), 29-30.

[2] Sáinz y Rodriguez, op. cit., 58ff.; J. Corominas, Diccionario crítico etimológico de la lengua castellana (Berna, 1954), I, 574; Martín Alonso, Enciclopedia del idioma. Diccionario histórico y moderno de la lengua española (Madrid, 1958–   ), II, 1396.

[3] See infra, 240-243.

to discuss many aspects of the problem of decadence. Opinions that were critical of royal absolutism were not likely to be published or even written. Publicists also suffered from lack of reliable information on such important aspects of national decline as the population trends and the economic productivity in various periods of Spanish history. Like earlier authors many Spanish writers still indulged in idealizations of a primitive, very imperfectly known past.[1] Some of these myths have been exploded by recent Spanish writers, who have sometimes gone so far as to reject the thesis of Spanish decadence altogether. Considering Spain's relatively limited resources, it has been argued, the real problem is not that its period of greatness came to an abrupt end, but that for a short while it was able to play such an important role.[2]

Finally it should be noted that most Spanish writers speculating on the decadence of their country still subscribed to a traditional, largely Christian philosophy of history. Accordingly, the disasters befalling their country were widely explained as a divine chastisement for the nation's immorality. The wide acceptance of the view that worldly splendor is transitory and that earthly kingdoms are bound to decline after having reached a certain peak of power predisposed many Spaniards to face the national misfortunes with a sense of resignation.[3] Their Christian beliefs, it is true, did not preclude all hope for a regeneration. But the almost universal sway that orthodox Christianity held over the Spanish mind of this period did not leave much room for either utopianism or despair. Just as the pessimism of this age was tempered by a belief in Divine Providence, so optimism found its limitation in the Christian view that human nature was corrupt and that this world would come to its end in a not too distant future. For these reasons the sense of decadence prevalent in Spain of this period was not yet radically different from that current in the Middle Ages. It was not until after the traditional Christian explanation of the world had been rejected that a new sense of decadence could emerge.

---

[1] Cf. Dowling, op. cit., 94, 212–213; Sáinz y Rodriguez, op. cit., 13–15.

[2] See infra, 242; see also José Martin Blázquez, "Anotaciónes sobre un ensayo acerco de la decadencia española," Cuadernos de historia de España, XVII (1952).

[3] Dowling, op. cit., 106 ff., 156, 282.

V

During the centuries in which Italy and Spain lost their position of prominence in European culture and politics, the star of France was in the ascendency. It is understandable that in an era of French political and cultural supremacy, many Frenchmen were inclined to look with confidence upon the course of history. At this time "douce France" was not only noted for its lighthearted gaiety, but also distinguished itself from almost all other nations by its cheerful way of looking forward to the future. In no other country did the new belief in progress find so many prominent adepts.

But although this growing confidence in man's historical destiny was one of the distinguishing trends in French intellectual history from the Renaissance to the Revolution of 1789, this new optimism was not yet representative of the historical outlook of the majority of the French people. Even in the eighteenth century, when historical optimism began to appeal to an influential segment of the population, contrary views remained strong and widespread.

Bleak visions of the future were especially common at the end of the sixteenth century, when France passed through one of the most serious crises in its history and many leading Frenchmen expressed themselves gloomily about the prospect of their country and that of European civilization. This wave of pessimism followed closely upon an era in which French national self-confidence, originating in the twelfth century, had reached a new high pitch; in the first half of the sixteenth century, numerous French poets, historians, and humanists, resenting Italian condescension toward Northern "barbarians," had claimed that France had fallen heir to ancient civilization and, in government and cultural achievements, compared even favorably with Greece and Rome. [1] Such Frenchmen, firmly believing in the superiority of their nation, were rudely shocked by the disasters befalling France in the period of the religious wars during the last four decades of the century. The internal divisions and the diminished position of the country in European politics led the Huguenot historian Jacques-Auguste de Thou to contrast "la décadence des François" with "la grandeur et la puissance des Espagnols."[2] Similarly the distinguished lawyer

---

[1] Hubert Gillot, *La querelle des anciens et modernes*, esp. first chapters discussing the ideas of Claude de Seyssel, Ch. Longueil, Étienne Dolet, Étienne Pasquier, Joachim du Bellay, and others; William J. Bouwsma, *Concordia Mundi: the Career and Thought of Guillaume Postel (1510–1581)* (Cambridge, Mass., 1957), 216ff.; J. B. Bury, *The Idea of Progress.* (London, 1920), 35ff.

[2] J. A. de Thou, *Histoire universelle* (Basle, 1742). I, 28–29, 30.

and antiquarian Etienne Pasquier, who had been one of the emphatic defenders of France against Italian denigrators, lost all confidence in his country during the last years of his life. A person who had slept for forty years, he lamented in the 1590's, would discover a corpse instead of the prosperous country he had once known. He felt that his country was mortally sick and could be compared with Rome in the period of its decline: "Notre France est parvenue à une extrême vieillesse, laquelle l'a faite tellement malade, alangourie et abattue en elle-même, qu'elle sent le mal présent et pressant qui la rend flottante, chancelante et tirant aux derniers traits de la mort."[1]

Many other leading French men of letters bewailed the disasters of the period, in which France seemed to have entered a phase of decline ("déclination," "déclinaison," "inclinaison," or, increasingly currently, "décadence"). A gloomy appraisal of the state of affairs, for example, pervaded the *Essais* of Michel de Montaigne. "Tournons les yeux par tout," he wrote, "tout crolle autour de nous, en tous les grands estats, soit de Chrestienté soit d'ailleurs." Confronted with this "evident menasse de changement et de ruyne" and with what seemed to be "la mort publique" of France, he attempted to make the best out of a bad situation by adopting an individualistic philosophy of withdrawal from public affairs, which allowed him to take an almost perverse delight in the universal decay that he observed around him. Like other authors of his time, he had a foreboding that the European world was approaching its end and that it might pass the torch of civilization to the new world that was rising in the West.[2]

Another indication of the widespread concern about the state of France is the fact that French humanists began to follow their Italian colleagues in their interest in speculations about the rise and decline of empires and republics. Jean Bodin and Louis Le Roy are among the best known French publicists of the late sixteenth century who developed cyclical theories of history.[3] Under the influence of these writers, Claude Duret composed his elaborate treatise *Discours de la vérité des causes et effects des décadences . . . et ruines des monarchies, empires . . .*

[2] Gabriel Hanotaux, *L'Énergie française* (Paris, 1902), 339; Étienne Pasquier, *Œuvres* (Amsterdam, 1723), II, 265, 328, 448; cf. Robert Bütler, *Nationales und universelles Denken im Werke Étienne Pasquiers* (Basel, 1938).

[2] *Essais*, livre III, ch. VI, IX, XII (ed. Bibl. de la Pléiade, Paris, 1934), pp. 880–881, 886, 931–932, 1016–1017); cf. Justus Lipsius, *Two Books of Constancie* (New Brunswick, 1939) François de La Noue, *Discours politiques et militaires* (n.p., 1599), 355.

[3] Jean Bodin, *Les six livres de la Republique* (Lyon, 1593), I, preface; p. 503; Louis Le Roy, *De la vicissitude ou variété des choses en l'univers* (1577); Bodo L. O. Richter, "The Thought of Louis Le Roy According to His Early Pamphlets," *Studies in the Renaissance*, VIII (1961)' 173–196; René de Lucinge, *De la naissance, durée et cheute des Estats* (Paris, 1588).

et républiques (1595), discussing the validity of a variety of reasons that had been held responsible for the decline of formerly powerful states.

Yet even in the middle of the religious and political crisis a distinguishing feature of the French view of history was its relative optimism. The predictions of impending doom in which many French Huguenots indulged seemed to have received a warmer reception across the Channel than in France itself.[1] French cyclical theorists of the period, unlike most similar thinkers in other societies, were convinced that their times were part of an ascending curve of civilization. Although Bodin, Le Roy, and Duret did not yet go so far as to reject the belief in the end of the world altogether and were still anticipating a catastrophic decline of civilization in the future, they no longer accepted the traditional views regarding the Golden Age in the past and the inferiority of modern civilization to that of the Greeks and the Romans. Taking pride in the cultural achievements of their native country, they came close to a formulation of a theory of historical progress.[2]

After the end of the religious wars national self-confidence rapidly regained its former strength. The eulogies on France, widely known as "le plus beau royaume après celui du ciel,"[3] reached their highest pitch in the reign of Louis XIV, when even many foreigners grew rhapsodic in singing the praise of the country. "Nothing has ever been undertaken in Christendom and nothing ever will be in the future without the participation of this generous nation," reported a Venetian ambassador, Marco Antonio Giustinian, in 1668, "It is certain that the virtues have chosen France as their habitat. It is only there that the art of war can be learned and that religion receives its sincerest tribute. It is only this country that contains the purest elements of humanity."[4]

At the end of the seventeenth century the view that the moderns were superior to the ancients found wider support in France than ever before. The former veneration for classical civilization was gradually undermined by the brilliancy of French civilization as well as by the impressive triumphs of modern science and the anti-authoritarian

---

[1] Cf. Victor Harris, *All Coherence Gone*, 95–96, 97–98, 108, 117, 213, 215.

[2] Jean Bodin, *Method for the Easy Comprehension of History*, ch. VII, VIII, ed. B. Reynolds (New York, 1945), 291–302, 324, 326, 333; Duret, *op. cit.*, (2d. ed, Paris, 1598), 487, 489–490, 492, 493, 509ff.

[3] An expression perhaps first used by Hugo Grotius; cf. Othon Guerlac, *Citations françaises* (Paris, 1931), 245. See also R. von Albertini, *Das politische Denken in Frankreich zur Zeit Richelieus* (Marburg, 1951).

[4] *Le relazioni degli stati europei lette al Senato dagli ambasciatori veneti nel secolo decimosettimo*, Serie II (Francia), vol. III (Venezia, 1863), 170.

philosophy of Cartesian philosophy. One of the most intelligent defenders of the cause of the moderns, Fontenelle, formulated the first theory of indefinite progress of knowledge. Another enthusiastic champion of the moderns, Charles Perrault, proclaimed: "Je me réjouis de voir notre siècle parvenu en quelque sorte au sommet de la perfection."[1]

A certain note of optimism can even be detected in the views which the Catholic bishop Bossuet presented on the course of history. Firmly convinced that Divine Providence was the final agent directing all historical change, he seemed to have believed that the world had made considerable progress under the influence of Christianity. He considered France "le royaume le plus illustre qui fut jamais sous le soleil" and did not indulge in any gloomy predictions concerning the approaching end of the world.[2]

Yet in the seventeenth century this optimistic mood was still challenged by strong pessimistic countercurrents. As in Spain, the traditional Christian philosophy of history, opposed to any doctrine of indefinite progress and inclined to look upon man as a sinful being, survived in considerable vigor among men of letters as well as among the populace. Thus Bossuet's ultimate view of history was hardly more cheerful than that of Saint Augustine. He referred to the rise and fall of empire as "ce fracas effroyable qui vous fait sentir qu'il n'y a rien de solide parmi les hommes, et que l'inconstance et l'agitation est le propre partage des hommes."[3] French Calvinists and Jansenists subscribed to even more pessimistic interpretations of Christianity and continued to denounce the sins of their age and to prophesy the coming of Antichrist and the the Day of Reckoning.[4]

A more modern form of historical pessimism manifested itself in a number of political pamphlets criticizing the abuses and the political absolutism of the Old Regime. In France's so-called "Grand Siècle" many Frenchmen were alarmed by the state of their country, which, they felt, was suffering from serious evils behind a glittering façade of social life. In 1687, a French refugee published a pamphlet entitled *Histoire de la décadence de la France* in which he contended that France had lost more power since the Revocation of the Edict of Nantes

---

[1] Charles Perrault, *Parallèle des anciens et des modernes, en ce qui regarde les arts et les sciences* (2 vols., Amsterdam, 1693), I, 67.
[2] "Oraison funèbre de Marie Thérèse d'Autriche," *Oraisons funèbres, panégyriques* (ed. Bibl. de la Pléiade, Paris, 1950), 128.
[3] *Discours sur l'histoire universelle* (Paris, 1886), 453,
[4] Vulliaud, *op. cit.*, 145ff.

(1685) than it had gained during the forty years preceding it and that the country was doomed to suffer the same fate as the Holy Roman Empire and Spain.[1] As in many other contemporary and later publications the concept of decadence was here handled as an ideological weapon against a detested regime. But this does not mean that such a somber statement should be dismissed as a perfunctory expression of political resentment. In many official reports as well as in numerous pamphlets written during the later years of Louis XIV's reign the very foundations of the Old Regime were subjected to a devastating criticism.[2] Even a court poet like Boileau intimated his serious misgivings about the state of French society in his translation of Longinus' *Treatise on the Sublime,* in which he used the expression "décadence des esprits" in obvious reference to the depravity of his own age.[3] If it had not been for governmental control of public opinion, the often deplorable condition of the French people would have been the subject of even more bitter and numerous lamentations.

During the reign of Louis XIV the idea that France was on its road of decline found its most prominent and articulate spokesmen in a number of aristocrats disgruntled about the loss of privileges and political influence. The nostalgia with which they viewed the past was best expressed by Comte Henri de Boulainvilliers (1658–1722), whose *Histoire de l'ancienne gouvernement de la France,* published in the beginning of the reign of Louis XV, idealized the freedom and equality enjoyed by the French in the time of Charlemagne and traced the beginning of decay back to the strengthening of royal authority by Philip the Fair.[4] Boulainvilliers's attack on the principles of the centralized monarchy made a profound impact on public opinion and anticipated the "medievalism" that characterized the ideas of many nineteenth-century traditionalists, like Josoph de Maistre, Frédéric Le Play, and Gobineau.

---

[1] Anon., *Histoire de la décadence française* (Cologne [Hollande], 1687), 4.

[2] F. Kleyser, *Der Flugschriftenkampf gegen Ludwig XIV. zur Zeit des pfälzischen Krieges* (Berlin, 1935); Martin Göhring, *Die Ämterkäuflichkeit im Ancien régime* (Berlin, 1938), 171ff., 214ff., 299ff.; Alexis de Tocqueville, *L'ancien régime* (Oxford, 1933), 175.

[3] Nicolas Boileau-Despréaux, *Œuvres complètes* (7 vols., Paris, 1941–43), IV, 120–124, 155–156, 228. Around this time the literal meaning of "décadence" – the falling into ruins – became obsolete; cf. Père Bouhours, *Remarques nouvelles sur la langue françoise* (Paris, 1675), 268–269. Henceforth "décadence" and "déclin" became the two standard terms designating historical retrogression, triumphing over their various competitors like "déclinaison" and "inclinaison." "Décadence" is often preferred to designate conditions in which an element of moral corruption is involved and in which regeneration is not excluded. "Déclin," on the other hand, does not necessarily imply a sense of guilt and often refers to a more definitive kind of historical retrogression.

[4] Peter Stadler, *Geschichtschreibung und historisches Denken in Frankreich, 1789–1871* (Zürich, 1958), 26–28.

VI

At first glance it might seem unlikely that decadence was a serious topic of discussion in the eighteenth century, for this period was characterized by an increasing note of self-esteem and confidence in the future. A high appraisal of contemporary achievements, which had made its first, still diffident appearance among French men of letters in the twelfth century and which had grown in strength at the time of the Renaissance and during the age of Louis XIV, was more widely and emphatically voiced in the eighteenth century than ever before. It was the very essency of the Enlightenment that it considered itself superior to an ignorant, fanatic, and superstitious past. A habitué of the Parisian salons, Melchior Grimm, remarked in the 1750's: "Il me semble que le XVIIIe siècle a surpassé tous les autres dans les éloges qu'il s'est prodigués à lui-même."[1] Around the same time Voltaire struck a note of jubilance in numerous letters to his friends: "Ce siècle," he wrote to Helvetius in 1760, "commence à être le triomphe de la raison." Another devotee of the new philosophical ideas, François Jean de Chastellux, told his contemporaries: "Vous qui vivez, et surtout ceux qui commencez à vivre au dix-huitième siècle, félicitez-vous."[2]

It was widely felt that just as the present was superior to the past, the future would greatly excel the present. Especially at the end of the eighteenth century many Frenchmen looked forward to a great "revolution" that would destroy all vestiges of prejudice, ignorance, and oppression, and inaugurate a new, even more glorious era in the history of mankind. This confidence in the perfectibility of mankind found its most dogmatic expression in Condorcet's philosophy of history predicting unlimited progress of man's mental, moral, and physiological qualities.

Yet the eighteenth century was not an age of unqualified optimism or excessive complacency with existing conditions. It is now easily forgotten that many of Voltaire's and Condorcet's contemporaries did not share their enthusiasm about the increasing enlightenment and their belief in future progress. The *philosophes* themselves recognized the strength of a pessimistic countercurrent. "On crie toujours que ce monde dégénère . . ." complained Voltaire in 1744, and fifty years

---

[1] Friedrich Melchior Grimm, *Correspondance littéraire, philosophique et critique* (Paris, 1877–82), III, 327.

[2] Paul Hazard, *La pensée européenne au XVIIIème siècle de Montesquieu à Lessing* (3 vols., Paris, 1946), I, 373–375; III, 109–110.

later Condorcet noted that numerous persons were still bewailing the decadence of knowledge, and the imminent advent of a state of barbarism, ignorance, and slavery.[1] In France as well as in other European countries Christians continued to prophesy the approaching end of an increasingly sinful world.[2] A more significant expression of historical pessimism is found in the numerous writings of the French *"anti-philosophes"* (Caraccioli, Rigoley de Juvigny, Sénac de Meilhan and Simon Linguet) who anticipated many of the somber interpretations of modern civilization which were expressed in nineteenth-century political publications: the pernicious influence of foreign literatures, the dangers of utopianism and intellectualism, and the definitive decadence of literary taste.[3] With the same nostalgia as reactionaries of the next century, Jean Clément evoked the virtues of the past when:

> Le François étoit gai, brave et peu raisonneur,
> Aimant son roi, sa dame, et plus que tout, l'honneur.[4]

Moreover, pessimism was not the monopoly of those who detested the new ideas. The enlightened writers themselves shared many of the misgivings of their opponents. To most of the *philosophes* belief in progress was not a firmly held conviction but a cautiously expressed hope. Although encouraged by the progress in rationality and tolerance, they recognized that the forward march of humanity had been frequently interrupted in the past and that the progress made in their time might come to an abrupt end in the near future. Progress and decline, it was widely felt, both had their place in the development of history; and the increasing interest in the former automatically led to new speculations on the latter. Many of the prominent writers of the period (Montesquieu, Diderot, and to a less extent Voltaire and Rousseau) occasionally subscribed to cyclical theories of history. Like the Italian humanists of the sixteenth century, they interpreted history neither as a gradual development toward greater perfection nor as a course of events guided by Providence, but as an arbitrary process of rise and fall. Again, like Guicciardini and his congeneries, some of

---

[1] Voltaire, *Nouvelles considérations sur l'histoire* in *Œuvres historiques* (ed. Bibl. de la Pléiade, Paris, 1957), 48; M. J. A. N. Caritat de Condorcet, *Esquisse d'un tableau historique des progrès de l'esprit humain* in *Œuvres complètes* (12 vols., Paris, 1947–49), VI, 195–196.

[2] Vulliaud, *op. cit.*, 163ff.

[3] Henry Vyverberg, *Historical Pessimism in the French Enlightenment* (Cambridge, Mass., 1958), 79, 80, 88–94, 116–117, 217–221; cf. Kurt Wais, *Das antiphilosophische Weltbild des französischen Sturm und Drang, 1760–1789* (Berlin, 1934), 86–93, 213ff.

[4] Jean-Marie-Bernard Clément, *Satires* as quoted in Vyverberg, *op. cit.*, 127.

the *philosophes* advocated an attitude of resignation to the inevitable miseries of human life and of withdrawal from the public scene. The best advice which Voltaire's spokesman Candide could give after his many ordeals was: "Il faut cultiver notre jardin."[1]

The confidence of the *philosophes* was in the first place tempered by a serious concern about the unsatisfactory state of France. The numerous social and political abuses as well as the diminished position of France in European affairs created an atmosphere propitious to despondency. It is true that the *philosophes* often criticized the Old Regime in the hope of bringing about a reform. But not all denunciations were prompted by such a political motivation. On many important questions of the time their despondency was sincere and profound.

It was especially during the reign of Louis XV that the future of the country was widely viewed with alarm. Government circles themselves were occasionally obsessed by a sense of imminent doom. Every one is familiar with the ominous words reportedly spoken by the royal mistress, Madame de Pompadour, after the defeat of the French army at Rossbach (1757): "Après nous le déluge." An equally pessimistic view was expressed by the Marquis d'Argenson (1694–1757), calling France "a white sepulchre whose external splendor conceals the rottenness within."[2]

Numerous Frenchmen of this time made comparisons between the degeneracy of French society and the state of Rome in its period of decline. In an essay describing the corrupt mentality of the Roman Empire, which his contemporaries easily recognized as a piquant parallel to the situation of their own time, Diderot described the feverish excitement and somber prophecies circulating in a critical period of history.[3] Similarly Montesquieu's interest in the decadence of Rome and that of modern Spain largely stemmed from his concern about the weakening vitality of the French nation. Believing that the population of France was decreasing in size, he regarded this phenomenon as a symptom of decadence that his country had in common with declining societies of the past.[4] Montesquieu as well as many

---

[1] For a fuller treatment of the pessimistic views held by eighteenth-century *philosophes*, see Vyverberg, *op. cit.*, esp. ch. XV–XIX.

[2] Guerlac, *Citations françaises*; Ernst Cassirer. *The Philosophy of the Enlightenment* (2d ed. Boston, 1955), 265.

[3] Vyverberg, *op. cit.*, 193ff., Reinhart Koselleck, *Kritik und Krise. Ein Beitrag zur Parthogenese der bürgerlichen Welt* (München, 1959), 211.

[4] G. Chinard, "Montesquieu's Historical Pessimism," *Studies in the History of Culture*, ed. American Council of Learned Societies (Menasha, Wisc., 1942), 161–172; Rehm, *op. cit.*, 99–100; Robert Shackleton, *Montesquieu, a Critical Biography* (New York, 1961),

of his contemporaries also denounced the enervating effects of luxury. They held the increase in material comfort responsible for a decline in literary and artistic standards as well as for the corruption of morality and the effeminacy of the younger generation. Such moralistic indignation about the depravity of the age was not a novel attitude, but it acquired a new sense of urgency in the artificial atmosphere of eighteenth-century society. Many of the prominent authors like Diderot and Rousseau advocated a return to a simpler, agrarian way of life because they feared that excessive prosperity would lead to the neglect of virtue and the true graces of life.[1]

Other eighteenth-century writers like Voltaire were not concerned about the corrupting influence of luxury or about the threat of depopulation. They ridiculed the idealization of primitive life and fully appreciated the blessings of civilization. They no longer believed either in the existence of the Golden Age in the past or in any basic superiority of the ancients over the moderns. But even these writers did not look upon their own age as in every respect superior to the past. The "moderns" they admired above all were the writers and the artists of the *"grand siècle"* of Louis XIV. At least as far as literature was concerned, Voltaire and many of his contemporaries felt that their own age was one of irremediable decline. "N'espérez pas rétablir le bon goût"; wrote Voltaire to La Harpe in 1770, "nous sommes dans le temps de la plus horrible décadence."[2] Since literature was widely regarded as the finest product of civilization, this veneration for French classicism indicated a feeling of cultural inferiority with regard to the seventeenth century and implied the view, which was taken up by many nineteenth-century conservatives, that the reign of Louis XIV was the last great period in French history.

It is likely that many other aspects of the French old regime would have been denounced as indications of political or social decline if a strict censorship had not restricted a free discussion of many of the glaring abuses. It is symptomatic of the caution which had to be used that some of the gloomiest views of the state of France were expressed in the disguise of a fictional satire or were not published until after the author's death. Speculations on political and economic decadence also suffered from a lack of reliable data. Although much progress

---

146–150, 157–158; see also Montesquieu, *Œuvres complètes* (ed. Bibl. de la Pléiade, Paris, 1949), I, 1509.

[1] Vyverberg, *op. cit.*, 126–130, 162, 203.

[2] Voltaire to La Harpe, April 23, 1770, *Voltaire's Correspondence*, ed. Theodore Besterman, vol. LXXV (Genève, 1962), 38–39; cf. Rehm, *op. cit.*, 159; Vyverberg, *op. cit.*, 184–186.

was made in the realistic study of the past and the present during the eighteenth century, many writers of the age still indulged in generalizations based on insufficient or inaccurate evidence. Montesquieu, for example, held that the population of France was declining whereas actually the opposite was true. There exists an even more important reason why the decadence of France did not become a major theme in eighteenth-century literature. Although the country had lost the political supremacy that it had enjoyed during the reign of Louis XIV and showed many disturbing signs of social degeneration and financial weakness, its leading position in European culture was less contested than ever before or after. Even opponents of the *philosophes* as well as many foreign writers admitted the radiation of French civilization.[1] In an age when Voltaire, Montesquieu and Rousseau dominated European cultural life, it was unlikely that France would be singled out as a nation whose vitality was declining.

It was less the unsatisfactory state of France than the evils of modern civilization in general which were at the source of much of eighteenth-century despondency. In all highly developed European countries of the period numerous men of letters bewailed the lost harmony of primitive society. [2] At the end of the century this cult of primitivism was often accompanied by a sense of cultural crisis that found its most eloquent expression in the works of Jean-Jacques Rousseau.

Rousseau's originality consisted not so much in the novelty of his ideas as in the intensity and sincerity of the feelings with which these views were presented. Frustrated and unbalanced, Rousseau was perhaps the first prominent European man of letters suffering from a strong sense of alienation. In his disgust with the artificiality and the immorality of the society of his time, he interpreted most of history as a process of degeneration and exalted the virtues of primitive societies.[3]

Rousseau's works, it is true, are full of apparent contradictions which have baffled many of his later interpreters. His disciples as well as his opponents have seldom done full justice to the complexity

[1] Cf. L. Réau, *L'Europe française au siècle des lumières* (Paris, 1938); Hazard, *op. cit.*, II, 229ff.

[2] Cf. Lois Whitney, *Primitivism and the Idea of Progress in English Popular Literature of the Eighteenth Century* (Baltimore, 1934); Edith Amalie Runge, *Primitivism and Related Ideas in Sturm und Drang* (Baltimore, 1946), esp. ch. VI; Rehm, *op. cit.*, 164–165.

[3] Cf. Bertrand de Jouvenel, "Rousseau, the Pessimistic Evolutionist," *Yale French Review*, XXVIII (1962), 83–96; Georges May, "Rousseau and France," *ibidem*, 122–135; H. Steinhauer, "Rousseau and Modern Pessimism," *The University of Toronto Quarterly*, XX (1950), 1–20.

of his thought. Rousseau was not an unqualified opponent of civilization and cannot be held mainly responsible for the Romantic revolt against reason and social restraints. Nor did he share the confidence of many of his later admirers that the corrupt political order of his time could easily be replaced by a republic of virtue. In his hopeful aspirations as well as his disparagement of civilization Rousseau maintained much of the caution with which most eighteenth century French writers approached the problems of their age. [1]

Nevertheless, Rousseau played a major role in introducing a personal note of bitter discontent and hopeful longing into Western civilization. Whereas many other *philosophes* assumed an individualistic attitude of resignation similar to the one adopted by Guicciardini, Rousseau's moralistic reaction towards the problems of his time had much in common with that of Machiavelli Like the Italian humanist, he was a secular prophet preaching repentence and regeneration. But Rousseau has been much more influential in spreading this new gospel than Machiavelli for he raised problems of a more universal importance and expressed his views in a more personal and emotional form.

Another eighteenth-century French author who left a profound impact upon the development of the idea of decadence was the Marquis de Sade. His sinister influence, although less readily avowed than that of Rousseau, has also been substantial among nineteenth-century authors. His attitude towards the evils of his times was diametrically opposed to that taken by Rousseau. The corruption of his time, which Rousseau decried, was welcomed by Sade as the prerequisite for the pursuit of happiness. Sade's view that "l'état le plus heureux sera toujours celui où la dépravation des mœurs sera la plus universelle,"[2] sharply contrasted with Rousseau's longing for a primitive, virtuous society. Sade's delight in perversion anticipated the cult of decadence that became a characteristic tenet of the ideology of many men of letters of the late nineteenth century.

Sade's radical break with regenerationist aspirations remained, however, an unique phenomenon in the eighteenth century, at the end of which idealistic fervor and utopian dreams became even stronger and more widespread than before. With the appearance of

---

[1] Cf. Vyverberg, *op. cit.*, 60–61; Arthur O. Lovejoy, "The Supposed Primitivism of Rousseau's Discourse on Inequality," *Essays in the History of Ideas* (Baltimore, 1948), 14–37; F. C. Green, *Rousseau and the Idea of Progress* (Oxford, 1950).

[2] A. E. Carter, *The Idea of Decadence in French Literature, 1830–1900* (Toronto, 1958), 31; cf. Vyverberg, *op. cit.*, 223–228.

revolutionary and patriotic ardor the cautious and realistic views of the course of history which had prevailed among the leading *philosophes* gave way to a growing impatience with the existing abuses and to a widespread conviction that a "revolution" was imminent and desirable. Whereas Rousseau had still expressed some apprehension about "the state of crisis and the era of revolutions" which he saw approaching,[1] the younger generation, inspired by the struggle for freedom in the New World, became desirous to destroy the oppressive and arbitrary regime in their own country. Many expected that a great crisis was at hand, and they had no longer any serious misgivings about its outcome. "In a little while," wrote a French admirer of the American Revolution, "there will be nothing to which man cannot attain."[2] At least, a growing part of the French people felt that a miraculous renewal of the old, decadent world was imminent.

VII

The mood of utopianism that began to gain ground at the end of the eighteenth century explains that the Revolution of 1789 was widely acclaimed as the beginning of a regeneration of the world. In France as well as in other European countries the overthrow of the Old Regime was often interpreted as the inauguration of a new and glorious era in the history of mankind.[3] The introduction of a new Republican calendar gave an official sanction to this conviction that France had broken with the errors of the past. A heightened sense of self-esteem became current among the French, now that their country was placed once again in the vanguard of humanity. This national self-confidence found perhaps its most exalted expression in a speech by Robespierre asserting that "le peuple français semble avoir devancé de deux mille

---

[1] *Emile, Œuvres complètes* (13 vols., Paris, 1905), II, 166; Bernard Groethuysen, *J. J. Rousseau* (Paris, 1949), 206ff.

[2] "Dans peu l'homme ne verra plus rien où il ne puisse atteindre;" J. B. Mailhe, *Discours . . . sur la grandeur et l'importance de la révolution qui vient de s'opérer dans l'Amérique septentrionale* (Toulouse, 1784), 29; cf. Robert R. Palmer, *The Age of Democratic Revolution. A Political History of Europe and America, 1760–1800* (Princeton, 1959), 258; Daniel Mornet, *Les origines intellectuelles de la Révolution française (1715–1788)* (4th ed., Paris, 1794), 144; Koselleck, *op. cit.*, 209.

[3] Cf. Hanno Kesting, *Geschichtsphilosophie und Weltbürgerkrieg. Deutungen der Geschichte von der Französischen Revolution bis zum Ost-West Konflikt* (Heidelberg, 1959), 16–18; K. F. Helleiner, "An Essay on the Rise of Historical Pessimism in the Nineteenth Century," *Canadian Journal of Economics and Political Science*, VII (1942), 514–536; George P. Gooch, *Germany and the French Revolution* (London, 1920), *passim*.

ans le reste de l'espèce; on serait tenté même de le regarder, au milieu d'elle, comme une espèce différente."[1]

The spectacular victories of the Revolutionary armies seemed the most convincing evidence of the historical significance of the Revolution. "At this place and at this time a new era in world history has started," Goethe told the German soldiers after their defeat in the battle of Valmy, "and you can say that you were there."[2] Even such determined opponents of the revolutionary principles as Edmund Burke and Joseph de Maistre could not fail being impressed by the newly gained strength of the country that at this time became widely known as "la grande nation."[3]

The dramatic events of the period of the Revolution and Napoleon, then, did not create any misgiving about the vitality of the French nation. But they did engender a new, more urgent sense of crisis and a widespread feeling that civilization might have started its downward course. From the very beginning, the Revolution was detested by most members of the privileged classes who, like Talleyrand, were convinced that those who had not lived before 1789 had never known the joy of living.[4] Most orthodox Christians also took a dim view of a regime that confiscated the properties of their Churches and subscribed to a secular philosophy. "La génération présente," wrote Joseph de Maistre in 1796," est témoin de l'un des plus grands spectacles qui ait jamais occupé l'œil humain. C'est le combat à outrance du christianisme et du philosophisme. La lice est ouverte, les deux ennemis sont aux prises, et l'univers regarde."[5] Needless to say, in many European countries religious zealots imagined that the Revolution signified the reign of Antichrist and that the end of the world could no longer be far away.[6]

Unqualified opponents of the revolutionary principles were not the only persons who viewed the course of events in France with alarm. Many who had initially hailed the Revolution as the greatest stride

---

[1] *Moniteur*, (new ed., Paris, 1854), XX, 404.

[2] Goethe, *Französische Feldzug* in *Sämtliche Werke* (Jub. Ausg. 40 vols., Stuttgart, 1902–12), XXVIII, 60.

[3] Guerlac, *op. cit.*, 273; Karl Epting, *Das französische Sendungsbewusstsein im 19. und 20. Jahrhundert* (Heidelberg, 1952), 21–24.

[4] Jacques Godechot, *La Contre-révolution, Doctrine et action (1789–1804)* Paris, 1961).

[5] Maistre, *Considérations sur la France* (1796), ch. V, in *Œuvres* (7 vols., Bruxelles, 1838), VII, 75; cf. M. Leroy, *Histoire des idées sociales en France* (3 vols., Paris, 1946–54), III, 139.

[6] Vulliaud, *op. cit.*, 169ff.; LeRoy Edwin Froom, *The Prophetic Faith of Our Fathers* (Washington, 1946–54), II, cf. 32ff.: Shirley J. Case, *The Millenial Hope. A Phase of War-Time Thinking* (Chicago, 1918), 197; Francis Ley, *Madame de Krüdener et son temps, 1764–1824* (Paris, 1961), 273, 296–300.

forward which mankind had ever made in its march toward perfection, lost their enthusiasm when mob rule and terror became the order of the day. The ultimate failure of the first experiment in democracy, and the establishment of a new tyranny leading to bloody wars and oppression of national aspirations further undermined the great expectations with which the outbreak of the Revolution had been greeted. The general disillusionment was deepened by the vogue of Romantic melancholy which became a current affliction of the younger literary generation after the turn of the century.[1]

This was not the first time that radical historical change produced a sense of crisis and anxiety. But in no earlier period was this sentiment as consciously experienced as in the time of the French Revolution. Even in an abstract metaphysical treatise like Hegel's *Phenomenology of the Mind* (1806) the contemporary period was characterized as a critical period of transition.[2] The French Revolution was, moreover, unprecedented in the almost world-wide repercussion that it immediately produced. The stirring episodes of the Revolution affected public opinion and government policies in almost all civilized countries. "The French Revolution," declared one of the most astute German political commentators, Friedrich Gentz," ... is an event of such dimensions that it is hardly permissible to occupy oneself in its presence with any subordinate interests."[3] The greatest of all adversaries of the French Revolution, Edmund Burke, expressed himself even more emphatically as to the unique significance of this historical event: "It appears to me as if I were in a great crisis, not of the affairs of France, but of all Europe, perhaps of more than Europe. All circumstances taken together, the French Revolution is the most astonishing thing that has hitherto happened in the world."[4] Similar views continued to be expressed long after the revolutionary events had taken place. Thus Thomas Carlyle, in 1870, still regarded the "Great Revolution" as "a celestial-infernal phenomenon – the most memorable in our world for a thousand years."[5]

---

[1] See *infra*, 72ff., 244ff.
[2] G. F. Hegel, *Phänomenologie des Geistes* in: *Sämtliche Werke*, ed. G. Lasson (Leipzig, 1920 –31), II, 15.
[3] Gooch, *op. cit.*, 101–102.
[4] Edmund Burke, *Works* (2 vols., London, 1848), II, 284.
[5] Thomas Carlyle, "Latter Stage of the French-German War, 1870–1871," *Works* (Centenary ed., 30 vols., London, 1930), XXX, 56; cf. also Lenin's statement quoted in B. Réizov, *L'historiographie romantique française* (Moscou, n.d.), p. 5: "Le XIXe siècle qui a donné la civilisation et la culture à l'humanité, a passé sous le signe de la Révolution française."

It is no mere coincidence that at a time that the conscious feeling of living in a critical period reached a new intensity, the term "crisis" in its meaning of a decisive turning point in history gained general currency. It was especially the social theorist Henri de Saint-Simon who was influential in popularizing the new word as well as its corresponding adjective "critical."[1] In his philosophy of history these terms still expressed an intensity of feeling which they have lost today after a century and a half of indiscriminate usage. "L'espèce humaine se trouve engagée," he wrote in 1813, "dans une des plus fortes crises qu'elle ait essuyées depuis l'origine de son existence."[2] Saint-Simon interpreted the French Revolution as the product of the "critical" or "negative" philosophy of the eighteenth century. This "most remarkable event that has ever taken place" had ushered in a "critical" period of history, which he hopefully anticipated, would be followed by an "organic" or "positive" period. Even if Saint-Simon, during most of his life, looked with confidence to the future, he spoke about the "frightful crisis" of his own age with anxiety rather than with jubilance.[3]

In France the full strength of the new pessimism was not revealed until after the final defeat of Napoleon, when the Napoleonic adventure stood condemned in its futility and criminality, and a free expression of discontent became a possibility. Henceforward the view that the French Revolution constituted the greatest catastrophe in western civilization has never lacked support. Much of nineteenth-century political philosophy consisted in reflections on the dramatic events of the Revolutionary era. Not all commentators drew pessimistic conclusions from their study, but few looked upon the revolutionary change with the same optimism and illusions as had been current in France during the last decades of the eighteenth century.

Since the French Revolution mankind has been living in an almost permanent state of political, economic, or cultural crisis. At least the *feeling* of living in a transitional age of revolutionary and radical change has never been fully absent from Western consciousness during the last century and a half. Some have faced this challenge with buoyant optimism. "Out of every crisis," said Franklin Roosevelt,

---

[1] Nicolaus Sombart, *Die geistesgeschichtliche Bedeutung des Grafen Henri de Saint-Simon. Ein Beitrag zu einer Monographie des Krisenbegriffs* (Heidelberg, 1950), esp. pp. 44–45.

[2] *Mémoire sur la science de l'homme*, as quoted in M. Leroy, *op. cit.*, II, 204.

[3] Kesting, *op. cit.*, 33–36; on the hypothesis developed by Saint-Simon in 1815 concerning the catastrophe awaiting humanity in a distant future as a result of a gradual desiccation of the globe, see Frank Manuel, *The New World of Henri Saint-Simon* (Cambridge, Mass., 1956), 161.

"mankind rises with some share of greater knowledge, higher decency, purer purpose."[1] But not all witnessing the convulsions of their age have been able to share the cheerful conviction of the American President. It is with their views of history that the major part of this study will be concerned.

[1] Quoted by Koselleck, *op. cit.*, 218.

CHAPTER III

PROPHECIES OF HOPE AND DESPAIR
1814–1848

Vielleicht naht Frankreich einer schrecklichen Katastrophe . .
Das französische Volk, welches die grosse Revolution Europas
begonnen, geht vielleicht zu Grunde, während nachfolgende
Völker die Früchte seines Beginnens ernten.

HEINRICH HEINE in 1837[1]

Que la France soit une, un instant, elle est forte comme le
monde.

MICHELET[2]

Je suis venu trop tard da ns un monde trop vieux.

ALFRED DE MUSSET[3]

I

"La France," wrote the Comte de Henri de Saint-Simon in 1814,
"est placée sur un volcan dont l'explosion sera d'autant terrible qu'on
tardera plus à l'éteindre." Twenty years later Félicité de Lamennais
predicted that a religious renovation would be preceded by great evils,
violent crises, and catastrophes such as the world had yet seldom seen.
In the 1840's Chateaubriand concluded his memoirs with the lamen-
tation: "Nous, l'Etat le plus mûr et le plus avancé, nous montrons de
nombreux symptômes de décadence."[4] These views represent a fair
sample of the strong pessimistic strain in French thought of the early
nineteenth century. There were, of course, many Frenchmen who
disagreed with these somber statements, but words like crisis, old age,
decadence, corruption, degeneration, and catastrophe were on the
lips of many commentators on the state of the nation and modern
civilization.

[1] Heinrich Heine, "Über die französische Bühne. Vertraute Briefe an August Lewald,"
Sämtliche Werke (10 vols., Leipzig, 1910–14), VIII, 66.
[2] Michelet, *Le peuple* in *Œuvres complètes* (40 vols., Paris, 1893–99), XXXI, 25–26.
[3] Alfred de Musset, *Rolla* (1833) in *Poésies complètes* (ed. Bibl. de la Pléiade, Paris, 1951),
282.
[4] Henri de Saint-Simon and Augustin Thierry, *De la réorganisation de la société européenne*
(2d ed., Paris, 1814), 92; *Confidence de La Mennais, lettres inédites de 1821 à 1848*, ed. Arthur du
Blois de La Villerabel (Nantes, 1886), 96; Chateaubriand, *Mémoires d'outre-tombe* (ed. du
Centenaire, Paris, 1949), II, 579. For similar statements see M. Leroy, *Histoire des idées
sociales*, II, 22–26; and Dominique Bagge, *Les idées politiques en France sous la Restauration*
(Paris, 1952), 1ff.

The anxiety of the age was in the first place fostered by the weakened international position of France. The fall of Napoleon and the peace treaties which followed deprived France of the dominant position that it had enjoyed in the preceding twenty years. All the victories won by the Revolutionary and Imperial armies had ultimately led to a situation in which France was the only European power that had not acquired any additional territory. Russia more than any other state had strengthened its position on the Continent and now became the bugbear of almost all Frenchmen concerned with the place of their nation in the world.[1] It was widely feared that the Russian colossus would not be satisfied with the recent annexations in Eastern Europe, but would continue its westward expansion and upset the balance of power. France's hereditary enemy, "perfidious Albion,"[2] also emerged from the Napoleonic wars stronger than ever before. Great Britain had increased her lead in industrialization over France, extended her trade relations, and acquired additional overseas territories. Compared to these two giants, Austria and Prussia appeared as less serious rivals to defeated France, but these states had also every reason to be satisfied with the final settlement. During the next forty odd years many Frenchmen felt hurt in their national honor by what they called the shameful treaties of 1814 and 1815. Taking full advantage of the relative freedom of the press which the French were enjoying for the first time in their history, they blamed the Bourbon and July Monarchies for perpetuating the downfall of the nation.

Frustration of nationalistic dreams was, however, not the only source of the pessimistic mood of the period. Unlike the French defeats in 1870 and 1940, the downfall of Napoleon was not widely experienced as a national disaster of the first magnitude. It was actually received with a sense of relief by many Frenchmen who were tired of despotism and continuous warfare and who yearned for an era of peace and stability. The restoration of the legitimate dynasty was, of course, welcomed by all unqualified opponents of the Revolution. But many other Frenchmen were pleased by the defeat of Napoleon

---

[1] Cf. Michel Fridieff, "L'empire russe vu par les hommes de la Restauration," *Revue internationale d'histoire politique et constitutionelle*, Nouv. ser., XXII (1956), 108–124; Peter Stadler, "Politik und Geschichtschreibung in der französischen Restauration," *Historische Zeitschrift*, CLXXX (1955), 278; Oscar J. Hammen, "Free Europe Versus Russia," *American Slavic and East European Review*, XI (1952), 27–41; Heine, *loc. cit.*, VIII, 66ff.

[2] H. D. Schmidt, "The Idea and Slogan of Perfidious 'Albion'," *Journal of the History of Ideas*, XIV (1953), 604–616; Georg Büchmann, ed., *Geflügelte Worte* (30th ed., Berlin, 1961), 621–622; Pierre Reboul, *Le mythe anglais dans la littérature française sous la Restauration* (Lille, 1962), *passim*.

as is attested by the rise in the quotations of government securities at the news of Waterloo.[1] Even many liberals were gratified by the end of the Napoleonic tyranny. "Les flammes de Moscou," wrote their leading spokesman, Benjamin Constant, "ont été l'aurore de la liberté du monde."[2]

A more important reason perhaps for the widespread despondency was the realization that the period of crisis that had been opened by the Revolution of 1789 had not yet come to a close. The compromise of the Constitutional Monarchy between the principles of innovation and conservatism satisfied neither the traditionalists on the one hand nor the liberals and the radicals on the other. Each of these political groups watched the contemporary scene with a sense of crisis and anxiety, agreeing only on deploring the division of the French people in diametrically opposed camps.

While the breach created by the French Revolution was yet unhealed, the coming of the Industrial Revolution added to the tensions and dissatisfactions in French society. The opposition to the new industrial order came from various quarters: artisans unable to compete with the more efficient methods of mechanized industry; farmers alarmed at seeing the government falling into the hands of an oligarchy of industrialists and financiers; the old landed aristocracy resentful of being ousted from its leading position in society. From a more idealistic point of view, the Industrial Revolution was condemned by humanitarians shocked by the horrible living conditions of the new industrial proletariat; by moralists concerned about the increasing quest for material success; and by esthetes disgusted by the drabness of industrialized cities and the mechanical nature of work on the assembly line.

A final factor that should be considered in understanding the widespread mood of pessimism and anxiety was the vogue of Romantic despair or *mal du siècle* that began to affect the younger French generation after the battle of Waterloo. Romantic despondency, although partly a pessimistic response to the political and economic upheavals of the period should be distinguished from the usual discontent about the degeneracy of the age. The pessimism of the Romantics had its source not only in a deep concern about contemporary corruption, but also in a personal sense of frustration and insecurity. Their sense

---

[1] D. W. Brogan, *The French Nation From Napoleon to Pétain* (New York, 1963), 69.
[2] Benjamin Constant, *De l'esprit de conquête et de l'usurpation* (1814) in *Œuvres* (ed. Bibl. de la Pléiade, Paris, 1957). 985; cf. B. Réizov, *L'historiographie romantique française*, 83, 195.

of decadence stemmed from a troubled heart as much as from a critical mind. The men of letters suffering from the *maladie du siècle* were not self-assured moralists whose equanimity was hardly disturbed by the evils they denounced, but highly sensitive minds, who were bewildered by the religious, political, and social crises of their times and who were tormented by metaphysical anxieties and doubts. They were too sceptical to believe either in the ideals of the past or in the new secular creeds that were embraced by many of their contemporaries. Like Nietzsche, they had made the discovery that God was dead. Yet they strongly felt the need for some faith in transcendental values that would give meaning and purpose to life. Religious minds without a religion, they loathed themselves as much as the society in which they had been born.

It was not only the loss of religious assurances, but also the break-up of the old social order that depressed many of these romantic authors. Like contemporary socialists and conservatives, but with greater emotional involvement, they lamented the atomization of modern society. Feeling that all sense of community was disappearing, they sought refuge in a cult of individuality, yet blamed their age for the alienation and loneliness from which they suffered.

The intensity of this Romantic despair, of course, varied greatly. In many instances the *maladie du siècle* was little more than a vague feeling or a literary pose assumed by intellectuals who were actually more satisfied with their lot than they felt it proper to admit. More often than not the Romantics lacked the intellectual discipline required to analyze the causes of their bewilderment or to diagnose the evils of their times. Egotistic in their preoccupation with their own predicament, they gave little serious consideration to the problems of their age. But in other cases the despondency went much deeper than was apparent to the outside world. And some of them combined a perplexed heart with a keen insight into themselves and the world around them and formulated some of the most original views of history that were produced in the nineteenth century.

II

The most pessimistic interpretation of the political and cultural development of modern France is encountered in the writings of the traditionalists, who looked nostalgically back to the old French monarchy as the best of all forms of government. To them the outbreak of the Revolution of 1789 was a horrible crime against humanity as well as the divine order. During the Revolutionary period they had hoped that the aberration of the French people would be only temporary and in 1814 they entertained the illusion that the Bourbon monarchy would restore a clerical and aristocratic regime. But they soon recognized that the detested principles of eighteenth-century philosophy had not yet lost their strength. To their great disappointment the new king maintained most of the revolutionary innovations; liberalism once again raised its head, and the enormous sales of the works of Voltaire and Rousseau were a clear indication that atheism, individualism, and democracy still had as much popular appeal as ever. The enemy was obviously far from beaten.

The two leading spokesmen for the reactionary camp, Joseph de Maistre and the Vicomte de Bonald, expounded an almost identical philosophy of history: Joseph de Maistre with greater literary talent and Bonald with more profundity and common sense. Because of their veneration for the wisdom of the past they were called "the prophets of the past;" the Greeks were right, stated de Maistre, in placing the Golden Age in the beginning of history.[1] "O Français!" exclaimed Bonald, "peuple jadis si aimant et si sensible! revenez à vos institutions et vous reviendrez à votre caractère aimable, à vos vertus douces, à votre bonheur."[2] These writers were also known as the "théocrates," because they believed that no political order could last without the recognition of an ultimate spiritual authority as embodied in medieval papacy. To them as to most later French traditionalists, the French Revolution was the product of a destructive, egotistic mentality that had made its first appearance with the Protestant Reformation and had been more fully accepted by the *philosophes* of the Enlightenment. They, of course, rejected the eighteenth-century doctrine of the rights of man: Bonald asserted that "l'homme n'existe que pour la société; la société ne le forme que pour elle-même,"[3] and Joseph de Maistre characterized the principles of the Revolution as "le protestantisme politique poussé jusqu'à l'individualisme absolu."[4] Modern religious and philosophical doctrines were thus held responsible for having dissolved the organic community of the past and for having created a state of anarchy.

---

[1] *Soirées de Saint-Pétersbourg*, 2me entretien (9th ed., Lyon, 1867), I, 77, 78, 98, 99.

[2] Louis de Bonald, *Théorie du pouvoir politique et religieux dans la société* in *Œuvres complètes* ed. Migne (3 vols., Paris, 1859), I, 450.

[3] *Ibid.*

[4] *Œuvres complètes* (14 vols., Lyon, 1884–86), XIV, 286.

The despondency of this school reached its greatest intensity in the early publications of a sincere disciple of the theocrats, Félicité de Lamennais. Renewing the apocalyptic tradition of Christianity, he felt that the future had little else in store than calamities, revolutions, and interminable wars. "Il me semble," he confided to Maistre in 1821, "que tout se prépare pour la grande et dernière catastrophe."[2] A later French traditionalist called Lamennais' indictment of democracy "le suprême avertissement, l'ultime anathème d'une race avec qui va s'éteindre la grandeur de la France."[1] Accusing democracy of promoting, among other things, atheism, venality, despotism, corruption, political instability, and materialism, Lamennais visualized a future in which mankind would devote all its talent and energy to a mad pursuit of material possessions and would continue to boast of the progress of civilization "jusqu'au moment où cet édifice d'illusions et de folies disparaîtra dans le gouffre d'une ruine universelle."[2]

Such utter despair of the future, implying the imminent coming of the Last Judgment, was not an uncommon attitude among the lower clergy and their rural fold, but most theocrats had still some illusions concerning the future. Thus Joseph de Maistre, in one of his more cheerful moods, looked forward to a world in which goodness, clemency, and justice would once again be respected.[3] It was only at the very end of his life that despair began to overmaster him. "Je meurs avec l'Europe," he wrote to Bonald in 1819. Yet, when chided by his correspondent for his lack of faith, Maistre admitted that he had been carried away by a momentary feeling of discouragement.[4]

The theocrats' refusal to despair of the future was intimately connected with their nationalistic messianism. The belief in a mission for France, which was so widely accepted by French men of letters in the nineteenth century, also formed a part of Maistre's and Bonald's interpretations of history. The leading role that France had played in European civilization was seen as a clear indication of that nation's superiority: it was the French who had given the bishops of Rome their uncontested authority over the Catholic Church; who had led Christendom in the conquest of the Holy Land; and who, in modern

---

[1] Dominique Bagge, Les idées politiques en France sous la Restauration, 276.

[2] Lamennais, De la religion considérée dans ses rapports avec l'ordre politique et civil (Paris, 1825), I, 46; cf. Henry Tronchon, "1830. Une crise d'âmes," Romantisme et préromantisme (Paris, 1930), 12; Maistre, Œuvres complètes, XIV, 369-372.

[3] Stadler, Geschichtschreibung, 52-53.

[4] Œuvres complètes, XIV, 183, 190-192, 345, 350; cf. F. de Champagny, "Lettres et opuscules inédits du comte Josoph de Maistre," Correspondant, XXVIII (1851), 513-526; Georges Cogordan, Joseph de Maistre (Paris, 1894), 127-128.

times, had held a position of intellectual hegemony over the entire civilized world.[1] Bonald asserted that since the time of Charlemagne no great action had ever been undertaken without France, and he predicted that no great action would ever be performed without her. Maistre admired France even under the vicious revolutionary regime: "Vive la France, même républicaine."[2]

In their confidence in France's destiny the traditionalists of the nineteenth century renewed the old Jewish belief in the providential mission of their people, and the almost equally old Jewish predilection for apocalyptic prophecies. Although Maistre looked upon the French Revolution as the work of Satan, he still felt that the Jacobins were used by God to chastise mankind for its errors and to pave the way for a salvation of France and the world.[3] The leaders of the theocrats never gave up their hope that a regeneration was coming, even it had to be postponed into the distant future. When Maistre realized that Louis XVI had made a pact with the revolutionary spirit, he predicted another revolution and another exile for the royal family.[4]

Joseph de Maistre tried to justify his frequent prophecies by declaring: "il n'y a eu dans le monde de grands événements qui n'aient été prédits de quelque manière."[5] This view was at variance with the antagonistic attitude that the Catholic Church had traditionally taken toward speculations about future events. It was partly as a result of Maistre's influence that wild prophecies assuring the faithful that their present tribulations would not remain unrevenged became a characteristic feature in popular Catholic literature of the nineteenth century. As in other times of adversity, the Christians turned to predictions of miraculous interventions to give meaning to their suffering. But the new apocalyptic literature was often more animated by the secular desire to restore the Old Regime than by any spiritual longings for a heavenly Jerusalem.

In the course of the nineteenth century French reactionaries were repeatedly disillusioned in their confidence in Providence. The revival of liberalism in the late 1820's created a mood of panic among con-

---

[1] Maistre, *Considérations sur la France* (1796), ch. II; *idem, Du pape* (1819). ch. "La France et l'Eglise;" *idem, Les soirées de Saint-Pétersbourg* (1821), ch. "Le génie de la langue de la France."

[2] Bonald, *Réflexions sur l'intérêt général de l'Europe* (1815) as transl. in Hans Kohn, *The Making of the Modern French Mind*, 24–25; Francis Bayle, *Les idées politiques de Joseph de Maistre* (Paris, 1945), 20.

[3] *Considérations sur la France* (Paris, 1880), 34–35.

[4] Maistre, *Œuvres complètes*, XIV, 345.

[5] Vulliaud, *La fin du monde*, 9.

servatives, fearing a repetition of 1789.[1] After the July Revolution their denunciations of contemporary society reached new heights. One of their spokesmen, Alexis Dumesnil, tracing the progressive decadence of France since 1789, surpassed even Lamennais in the vehemence of his assault on the hypocrisy, greediness, materialism, and immorality of his period.[2] An equally reactionary point of view was taken by Maurice Rubichon, who discerned the beginning of the national downfall in Louis XI's decrees against primogeniture and advocated a complete return to the Old Regime. Holding Paris, "this modern Babylon," mainly responsible for the degeneration of the French people, he proposed to transfer the capital of France to the provincial town of Bourges, "l'endroit le plus triste, le plus mono-tone et le plus ennuyeux du royaume," where frivolous people would no longer exert their influence on the royal government.[3] A more gifted disciple of the theocrats, Honoré de Balzac, interspersed his novels with numerous passages blaming the individualistic and materialistic spirit of contemporary society on the Protestant Refor-mation and the French Revolution.[4]

Although under the July Monarchy the chances of a restoration of the Old Regime became increasingly illusionary, many reactionaries stubbornly refused to give up their hopes for a miraculous turn for the better. In a sketch of the degeneration of France, an eccentric admirer of Maistre, Antoine Madrolle, reiterated his master's views on the superiority of the French nation. The present situation, he admitted, was worse than ever before, but he considered this a hopeful sign as, according to him, nothing was more propitious to greatness than decadence.[5] Such wishful thinking also appealed to many Catholic clergymen who reacted to the rising secularism of their times by predictions by catastrophe and redemption. The persisting strength of the apocalyptic view of history is witnessed in the following prophecy, current in 1837 and accepted by the Bishop of Strasbourg: "C'est en 1838 que sera renversé dans le sang le trône de Juillet élevé dans la boue. Il sera renversé par les républicains: ils seront la verge

---

[1] Stanley Mellon, *The Political Uses of History. A Study of Historians in the French Restoration* (Stanford, 1958), 83, 86, 87.

[2] Alexis Dumesnil, *Histoire de l'esprit public en France depuis 1789, des causes de son altération et de sa décadence* (Paris, 1840), idem, *Le siècle maudit* (Paris, 1843).

[3] Maurice Rubichon, *Du mécanisme de la société en France et en Angleterre* (Paris, 1833), 420; cf. Sainte Beuve, "La réforme sociale en France . . . par M. Le Play," *Nouveaux lundis*, vol. IX (Paris, 1867), 184–189.

[4] Cf. Bernard Guyon, *La pensée politique et sociale de Balzac* (Paris, 1947).

[5] Antoine M. Madrolle, *Tableau de la dégénération de la France. Des moyens de grandeur* (Paris, 1834), pp. i-iv, xx.

de fer dont le ciel dans sa justice se servira pour châtier la France.
Ils domineront pendant une partie de 1838 et de 1839. Mais le grand
monarque les écrasera comme des vers de terre. Sa gloire sera courte . .
Et notre Henri régnera paisiblement en 1840."[1]

III

Whereas the attitude of French conservatives was fundamentally
pessimistic, the liberals looked upon the events of their age with
great confidence. The first half of the nineteenth century was the
Golden Age of French liberalism when it enjoyed more intellectual
prestige than ever before or after and when society seemed to move in
the direction of the ideals outlined by Benjamin Constant: "la liberté en
tout, en religion, en philosophie, en littérature, en industrie, en politique."[2] It is not surprising, then, that unqualified pessimism was a rare
phenomenon among those who subscribed to the seemingly triumphant
liberal credo. In contrast to the traditionalists, they felt that their own
country had made an important step forward with the overthrow of
the old regime. Prominent liberals like Guizot, Mme de Staël, and
Cousin never seemed to have doubted that progress was the law of
history.[3]

After the July Revolution of 1830, which brought many liberals
into a position of political power, many of them carried this confidence
to the point of complacency. There existed among them the tendency
to consider the existing society as the best of all possible worlds. Such
a self-satisfied mentality was especially characteristic of Guizot, who
served as prime minister from 1840 to 1848. He failed to see that the
liberal compromise between conservative and revolutionary principles was all but universally detested by the French people. It was not
until after the Revolution of 1848 that Guizot realized that in
seventeen years his party had used up "tout le capital de bon sens et de
courage politique que le pays avait amassé depuis 1789."[4]

Yet even prior to the Revolution of 1848 the optimism of many
liberals was tempered by fears and misgivings. Some of their leaders
like Benjamin Constant were plagued by the idea that with the progress
of material civilization mankind was in danger of losing the vigor and

---

[1] René Rémond, *La droite en France de 1815 à nos jours* (Paris, 1954), 278.
[2] Benjamin Constant, *Mélanges de littérature et de politique* (1829), preface, in *Œuvres*, 835.
[3] Cf. Henry Tronchon, "Histoire et philosophie de l'histoire aux alentours de 1830,"
Romantisme et préromantisme, 23–77; J. B. Bury, *The Idea of Progress*, ch. XIV.
[4] François Guizot, *Lettres de M. Guizot à sa famille et à ses amis* (2d ed. Paris, 1884), 255.

simple virtues of their ancestors.[1] As students of French history they, moreover, realized that the ideal of freedom had not such strong roots in their country as in England and that any hasty attempts to correct existing abuses might easily lead, as in the time of the French Revolution, to mob rule and tyranny.

French liberals, in sharp contrast to Frenchmen of other political persuasions, tended to be great admirers of English political institutions. This is not to say that they were in every respect fervent Anglophiles: like many other Frenchmen they often complained about English materialism and hypocrisy and were occasionally shocked by the influence which a "feudal" aristocracy still wielded in English society and politics. Yet in spite of such feelings most liberals were greatly impressed by the spirit of freedom and economic enterprise that prevailed in early nineteenth-century England. Although they were generally convinced that in cultural matters France was the leading European nation, they readily admitted that England was superior in the fields of politics and economy and that this country therefore represented the wave of the future. "Aucun peuple de l'Europe," wrote Madame de Staël in 1817," ne peut être mis en parallèle avec les Anglais depuis 1688; il y a cent vingt ans de perfectionnement social entre eux et le continent."[2]

This profound respect for England easily led French liberals to the conviction that their own country was backward, if not decadent. It is true that they were greatly encouraged by the July Revolution which, they hoped, would do for France the same that the Glorious Revolution had accomplished in England: the termination of a period alternating between royal absolutism and mob rule and the beginning of a stable political system in which the enlightened segment of the population held the reins of government. But the prevalence of electoral corruption and ministerial instability during the July Monarchy convinced even some liberals that parliamentary institutions did not work as satisfactorily in France as across the Channel.[3]

It was especially in the economic field that comparisons between England and France made many French liberals painfully aware of

---

[1] R. A. Lochore, *History of the Idea of Civilization* (1830–1870) (Bonn, 1935), 13.

[2] Mme de Staël, *Considérations sur les principaux évévemens de la Révolution française* (3 vols., Paris, 1818), III, 168; cf. Bagge, *op. cit.*, 62–64, 77–78. The subject of French opinion on England in the period of the Restoration recently found its perceptive historian in Pierre Reboul, *Le mythe anglais dans la littérature française sous la Restauration* (Lille, 1962).

[3] Prosper Duvergier de Hauranne, "Du gouvernement représentatif en France et en Angleterre," *Revue des Deux Mondes*, May 15, 1847; Henri Martin, *De la France, de son génie et de ses destinées* (Paris, 1847).

the relative inferiority of their country. After a visit to England in 1824, the liberal economist Adolphe Blanqui wrote an enthusiastic report on the industrial progress and the high standard of living of the English nation. Similarly, in 1827, Charles Dupin presented a survey of the magnificent results obtained by mechanized industry in Great Britain and urged the French to introduce all the features of the manufactual system that had brought England to such a high degree of power and wealth. He pointed out how favorably parts of Northern France where the English economic methods had been applied compared with Southern France with its almost purely agricultural economy.[1] In the same vein Michel Chevalier, a former disciple of Saint-Simon, told the French how much they could learn from the English in *sang-froid*, perseverance, precision, and strict morality, – the qualities which were the secret of England's spectacular success in industrial enterprise.[2]

One feature of the English economic system that, above all, French liberal economists hoped to introduce into their country was the policy of free trade. From the late 1820's onward they attempted to focus public attention on the nefarious effects of the prohibitive or protective tariff. Unless the French imitated the English, warned an enthusiastic advocate of laissez faire, Frédéric Bastiat, they would soon be driven from all foreign markets.[3]

Liberal economists tended to blame all the misfortunes of their country on what they considered a mistaken economic policy. In their leading organ, the *Journal des économistes*, they held the relative absence of economic freedom responsible for the instability of French political institutions. They criticized specifically the rapid increase in the number of government officials and recommended a drastic reduction of government expenses and the abolition of the standing army. One of the leading champions for economic freedom, Adolphe Blanqui, considered the protectionist tariff that had been established in the reign of Louis XVI the main cause of all the political and economic unrest from which France had suffered since that time. He blamed this system for having made French industry less competitive and more sensitive to recurrent economic depressions with their concomitants of unemployment, strikes, and revolts. Blanqui called

---

[1] Alban de Villeneuve-Bargemont, *Histoire de l'économie politique* (2 vols., Paris, 1841), II, 342–344, 354; Reboul, *op. cit.*, 171–175, 241–243, 398.

[2] Michel Chevalier, *Lettres sur l'Amérique du Nord* (Paris, 1836), first letter.

[3] Arthur L. Dunham, *The Industrial Revolution in France, 1815–1848* (New York, 1955), 388–392; *idem, The Anglo-French Treaty of Commerce of 1860* (Ann Arbor, 1930), 14–17.

free trade "le seul ancre de salut qui reste à notre agriculture et à notre commerce maritime" and made a statement that has been reiterated by many later French economists in almost identical terms: "Le mal fatal de l'industrie française est de vivre d'une vie artificielle et précaire."[1] The future, he feared, would belong to such nations as the English and the Americans, "qui s'attachent à triompher de la matière par le travail, et qui perfectionnent leurs institutions avec maturité au lieu d'en improviser sans cesse de nouvelles et d'user leurs forces vives à la poursuite des chimères sociales."[2]

Apart from a number of professional economists, few Frenchmen of this period took these warnings seriously. Actually many men of letters looked upon England as a decadent country and regarded the imitation of the English political and economic system as a great threat to the health of their country.[3] Even a number of liberal writers were concerned about the horrible living conditions of the new industrial proletariat and warned against a rapid industrialization of French economy. As early as 1819 Simonde de Sismondi presented a dismal picture of the living conditions of the English working classes: "Aucun spectacle n'est plus effrayant que celui que présente l'Angleterre, au milieu de cette opulence qui éblouit d'abord les yeux ... La nation anglaise cède la place à la machine à vapeur." Under the Bourgeois Monarchy many other liberals lamented the abuses of the new industrial system. "De cet égout immonde," remarked Tocqueville after a visit to Manchester in 1835, "l'or pur s'écoule. C'est là que l'esprit humain se perfectionne et s'abrutit, que la civilisation produit ses merveilles et que l'homme civilisé redevient presque sauvage."[4] In his investigation of the condition of the laboring classes in 1848 Adolphe Blanqui expressed himself much more sceptically about the blessings of modern industry than he had done a twenty years earlier.[5] He discovered that the standard of living in Southern France, where the modern factory system had not yet penetrated, compared favorably with conditions in the horrible basement apartments in Northern industrial cities like Rouen and Lille. For this reason

---

[1] Adolphe Blanqui, *Histoire de l'économie politique* (2 vols., Paris, 1837–38); *idem, Des classes ouvrières en France pendant l'année 1848* (Paris, 1949), 177–178.

[2] Blanqui, *Des classes ouvrières*, 158.

[3] See *infra*, 67.

[4] Reboul, *op. cit.*, 121; A. de Tocqueville, *Voyages en Angleterre, Irlande Suisse et Algérie*, in *Œuvres complètes*, ed. J. Mayer, vol. V (Paris, 1958), 82.

[5] Blanqui, *op. cit., passim*; cf. Georges Duveau, *Histoire du peuple français de 1848 à nos jours* (Paris, 1955), 167–168.

he was opposed to continued industrialization and recommended a policy of return to the countryside.

Liberal misgivings about the abuses of the industrial revolution stemmed not so much from humanitarian sentiments as from fear of a social revolution. The increasing strength of republicanism and socialism made many liberals afraid that a new era of terror and violence was imminent. As early as 1832 a liberal minister complained that the persistence of the revolutionary spirit was the greatest plague of France.[1] In the subsequent fifteen years the ruling classes were increasingly haunted by the specter of communism. The numerous revolts of the populace demanding a fairer share in national production were currently compared with the barbarian penetrations into the Roman Empire. It was feared that the irruption of these new "barbarians" would entail the end of all higher forms of civilization which Europe had enjoyed for many centuries.[2]

It was not only as the cradle of the modern factory system that many Frenchmen detested England. England was still above all the hereditary enemy of France who had defeated her at Waterloo, and for this reason the supposed Anglophile foreign policy of the July Monarchy came in for severe strictures by most French nationalists, including some liberals. On occasion of the war scare of 1840 Guizot was criticized by some of his fellow liberals for his policy of appeasement toward Great Britain. Guizot's statement that it was no longer the mission of France to conquer territories, but to conquer the mind and the soul was interpreted as an abdication of the national honor. One of Guizot's former admirers. Prosper Duvergier de Hauranne, decried the timidity of the government policy, which, according to him, had resulted in the downfall of the nation.[3]

French liberals did not constitute a group with a clearly defined political program. They all subscribed to an abstract ideal of freedom, but did not present a united front on many specific questions. There were political and economic liberals, conservative and progressive liberals, Catholic and anticlerical liberals. Alexis de Tocqueville, the most distinguished of all French political analysts of this period, does not fit neatly in any of these categories. The liberalism of this perceptive

---

[1] Narcisse-Achille de Salvandy, *Vingt mois, ou la Révolution et le parti révolutionnaire* (1832) (new ed. Paris, 1849), 1.

[2] Oscar J. Hammen, "The Spectre of Communism in the 1840's," *Journal of the History of Ideas*, XIV (1953), 408–409; Eugène Buret, *De la misère des classes laborieuses en Angleterre et en France* (2 vols., Paris, 1840), I, 9.

[3] Paul Thureau-Dangin, *Histoire de la Monarchie de Juillet* (5th ed., Paris, 1912), IV, 385–386.

critic of his times was not of the doctrinaire kind. He called himself "un libéral d'une espèce nouvelle," who was balanced between the past and the future with no instinctive attraction to either. The division of his country into two camps "d'un côté les hommes qui prisaient la moralité, la religion, l'ordre, et de l'autre côté ceux qui aimaient la liberté, l'égalité des hommes devant la loi," struck him as "le spectacle le plus extraordinaire et le plus déplorable qui ait jamais pu s'offrir aux regards d'un homme."[1] He mercilessly castigated the Bourgeois Monarchy for its shameless materialism and predicted its downfall with an uncanny instinct. Speaking to the Chamber of Deputies, where he was greeted with ironical cheers, he said on January 29, 1848, one month before the outbreak of the February Revolution: "Je crois que nous nous endormons à l'heure qu'il est sur un volcan."[2]

Tocqueville's deep concern about the state of France prompted him to study his nation's past as well as the operation of the American democracy. More clearly than most of his contemporaries he perceived the irresistible modern trend toward equality, but this insight was to him a source of pessimism rather than of optimism. He feared that the triumph of democracy, especially in France, where it was likely to meet strong opposition, would lead to despotism and mediocrity. In France he held the situation to be worse than in other countries since a highly centralized form of government originating under the Old Regime had weakened public spirit and love of freedom and had instilled in the French people the mentality of expecting all improvement from government action. Tocqueville also apprehended that the rise of democracy would greatly strengthen the spirit of individualism, which like so many of his conservative and socialist contemporaries he considered one of the most depressing features of modern society.[3] He feared that France, like all old nations, was approaching a period of intermittent anarchy and his aristocratic love of refinement, freedom, and honor made him as opposed to the vulgar age of the masses as to the autocratic rule of a tyrant. His own fate, he was convinced, would be to lead a miserable life "au milieu de réactions alternatives de license et d'oppression."[4]

Tocqueville's attitude toward the problems of society was inspired

---

[1] Letter to Eugène Stoffels of July 24, 1836, Œuvres complètes (9 vols, Paris, 1861–66), V, 432–433.

[2] Œuvres complètes, IX, 520ff.; cf. Tocqueville, Souvenirs, ed. Luc Monnier (Paris, 1942), 32–35.

[3] A. de Tocqueville, Democracy in America (Vintage Books ed., 2 vols., New York, 1954), II, 104–113, 129–132, 388.

[4] Tocqueville, Souvenirs, 75.

by a vague but sincere religious belief. As such his point of view had much in common with that of a small, but influential group of Catholic liberals, who perceived in the decay of moral and religious values a major threat to civilization and felt that only a return to Christian principles could save France and the world. Unlike most Catholics of their times, they did not preach a restoration of the old political and social order, but accepted most of the revolutionary principles and believed in the perfectibility of mankind.

The most original thinker among these Catholic liberals was Pierre-Simon Ballanche, who attempted to reconcile such seemingly contradictory concepts as the Fall of Man and the progress of civilization. In his progressive philosophy of history, the efforts of man to atone for his original sin resulted not only in his own moral rehabilitation, but also in an improvement of society and was as such the major factor responsible for the progress made in the course of history. The central idea of this philosophy was the old Christian concept of religious rebirth or regeneration (*palingenesis*) but with more emphasis on social change than it had ever had before in Christian thought.[1] This new social orientation of Ballanche's Christianity explains the considerable popularity it enjoyed among French intellectuals in the late 1820's and early 1830's. It was partly under Ballanche's influence that Chateaubriand revised his early pessimistic views on the course of history and came to his conviction that "l'homme tend à une perfection indéfinie." [2] Ballanche's ideas on the urgency of a religious revival also greatly impressed many Saint-Simonians, who were alarmed by the increasing materialism and individualism of their time.

Ballanche subscribed to a typical philosophy of crisis: "Nous sommes arrivés à un âge critique de l'esprit humain, à une époque de fin et de renouvellement . . . Nous sommes semblables aux Israélites dans le désert." [3] His great confidence in the ultimate historical destiny of mankind did not exclude a deep sence of anxiety about contemporary immorality and atheism. This same combination of alarm and hope was characteristic of the attitude of most liberal Catholics. In the same year that Chateaubriand confessed his belief in the perfectibility or mankind, he wrote: "Il est possible que nous-

---

[1] Albert Dollinger, *Les études historiques de Chateaubriand* (Paris, 1932), 300ff.
[2] Chateaubriand, *Etudes historiques* in *Œuvres complètes* (12 vols., Paris, 1859–61), IX, 106ff.; cf. Sainte-Beuve, *Chateaubriand et son groupe littéraire* (Paris, 1861), I, 150.
[3] Ballanche, *Essai sur les institutions sociales dans leur rapport avec les idées nouvelles* (Paris, 1818), 66.

mêmes, comme nation, nous entrions dans les jours de décrépitude. Tout paraît usé: art, littérature, mœurs, passions; tout se détériore." [1]

This belief in the degeneration of the present combined with a hopeful expectation of a regeneration in the near future is, as we have seen, of ancient origin. It was held by many Christian idealists in the course of the centuries and was also a distinguishing feature of Machiavelli's and Rousseau's attitude toward the problems of their times. The originality of nineteenth-century writers holding these views was to put greater emphasis on the inevitability of the ultimate triumph of the forces of progress. They were willing to admit that progress is often interrupted by periods of decadence and that they themselves were living in such an era. But this decadence of the old order was necessary for the birth of a new superior phase of civilization. "La société," wrote Chateaubriand, "tout en ayant l'air de rétrograder, ne cesse de marcher en avant; elle gagne chaque jour quelque chose dans son véritable chemin."[2] Like many of their contemporaries, the Catholic liberals were convinced that they were living in a critical period in which old religious and social concepts were losing their strength and new ideas were slowly finding their form. Far from being resigned to the corruption of their period, they were determined to make their contribution to a moral and religious regeneration which they believed would lead to a higher type of civilization than had ever existed in the past.

IV

A more purely secular and nationalistic variety of this belief in regeneration was held by many republicans. In spite of, or perhaps because of, their disgust with the political and economic system of the Bourgeois Monarchy, they firmly believed in progress. They vehemently denounced the selfish and materialistic spirit of the ruling classes, but had a naive, Rousseau-like confidence in the virtues of the common people and did not lose their faith in a renewal of their country.

Unlike the liberals, from whom they began to distinguish themselves as a separate political group after the July Revolution, the republicans placed as much emphasis on the revolutionary principle of equality

---

[1] Chateaubriand, *De la nouvelle proposition relative au bannissement de Charles X et de sa famille* (Paris, 1831), 42.
[2] Chateaubriand, *Études historiques, loc. cit.*

as on that of liberty. They tended to accept the Revolution en bloc, even those aspects such as the Reign of Terror that were held in abhorrence by the liberals. Their glorification of the Revolution made them disposed to look with disdain on the less heroic present. "De ces nobles élans d'enthousiasme," complained a leftist critic in 1841, "de ces sublimes inspirations de l'Humanité, il ne reste plus aujourd'hui qu'un nationalisme exclusif, méfiant, un patriotisme de boutique et de coin de feu . . ."[1] And Lamartine asked in 1843: "Si l'Assemblée nationale sortait aujourd'hui du tombeau et se retrouverait en présence de son œuvre ainsi défigurée, quel est celui des hommes d'Etat qui reconnaîtrait la Révolution dans nos mains?"[2] Whereas the liberals criticized contemporary France by using the yardstick of England's political and economic developments, the republicans came to a similar low appraisal of the present on the basis of their conception of French greatness in the period of the Revolution.

Almost all republicans were not only fervent democrats but also ardent nationalists convinced that France had a special mission in the world. Although conservatives and socialists also dreamed of restoring France to its former position of hegemony in Europe, the republicans surpassed all other Frenchmen in their dreams of national grandeur. They attributed almost superhuman qualities to the French and for this reason were bound to be disappointed in their nation, or even despair of it, when their dreams did not materialize.

Dissatisfaction with the position of France in Europe began to be an important political issue during the Restoration Monarchy. The failure of this regime to revenge the humiliating defeats of 1814 and 1815, and thus to placate the French thirst for national greatness was among the various factors contributing to its downfall.[3] After the July Revolution many young republicans hoped that the new government would undertake another French crusade against the "despots" of Europe. Armand Carrel, one of the leading champions of such an adventurous foreign policy, admitted that the acceptance of such views might lead, as in 1793, to a general war between France and the rest of Europe, but he asserted "qu'il faut mieux faire la guerre un peu plus tôt sur le Rhin qu'un peu plus tard aux portes de Paris." "Faites

---

[1] "Les deux époques," La Phalange, Jan. 31, 1841; cf. Étienne Cabet, Révolution de 1830 et situation présente (septembre 1832) expliquées et éclairées par les révolutions de 1789, 1792, 1799, et 1804 et par la Restauration (Paris, 1832).

[2] Henri Guillemin, Lamartine et la question sociale (Genève, 1946), 70.

[3] Michel Mohrt, Les intellectuels devant la défaite de 1870 (Paris, 1942), 117; H. F. Stewart and Paul Desjardins, French Patriotism in the Nineteenth Century, 1814–1833 (Cambridge, 1923), 155, 159.

cette guerre, faites-la au plus vite," he exclaimed, "Que vienne cette lutte que nous appellons de tous nos vœux et qui peut seul vider la querelle entre la vieille et la nouvelle Europe."[1]

The extreme Left was bitterly disappointed when the government of Louis-Philippe refused to come to the aid of the revolutionary movements outside France. Having raised many expectations that were not fulfilled, the July Revolution, like the Revolution of 1789, disillusioned many of its initial supporters.[2] "Le rôle providentiel de ce grand peuple," commented Louis Blanc, one of the many republicans who fully favored the use of force against the conservatives powers of Europe, "semblait epuisé." When the Polish revolution collapsed, many radical Parisians looked upon this event as another battle of Waterloo. "La population," wrote Louis Blanc, "s'en allait par les rues consternée, silencieuse, et comme affaissée sous le poids d'une irréparable humiliation."[3]

This effacement of France in European politics, so sharply contrasting with the role that the country had played in the years following the Great Revolution of 1789, partly explains the appearance of the theme of French decadence in leftist publications after 1830. "Notre calme est celui d'épuisement," wrote Louis Blanc in 1841, " ... Dix ans de paix nous ont plus brisés que n'eût fait un demi-siècle de guerres; et nous ne nous en apercevons pas! Dieu nous garde pourtant de désespérer de notre pays!"[4]

The outcry over the weak foreign policy of the July Monarchy reached its peak during the Near Eastern Crisis of 1840. The refusal of the government to risk a European war in defense of what were considered to be legitimate French interests greatly contributed to the feeling that France was a declining power.[5] The proposals to fortify the city of Paris were strongly opposed as implying a purely defensive policy unworthy of a great nation like France. Legitimists, liberals, and socialists as well as republicans expressed their concern about what

---

[1] Armand Carrel, *Œuvres politiques et littéraires* (Paris, 1957), I, 393; cf. Thureau-Dangin, *op. cit.*, I, 214ff.; A. Loubère, "Les idées de Louis Blanc sur le nationalisme, le colonialisme et la guerre," *Revue d'histoire moderne et contemporaine*, IV (1957), 35.

[2] See Sainte-Beuve's analysis of this disillusionment, *Portraits littéraires* (Paris, 1862), I, 298.

[3] Louis Blanc, *Histoire de dix ans, 1830–1840* (5 vols., Bruxelles, 1843), III, 74, 159–160.

[4] Blanc, *Histoire de dix ans, 1830–1840* (5 vols., Paris, 1844), V, 505.

[5] Cf. Prosper Duvergier de Hauranne, *De la politique extérieure et intérieure de la France* (Paris, 1841), pp. i, xvi; Pierre Leroux, "La France sous Louis-Philippe," (1842), *Œuvres* (Paris, 1850), I, 391–393; Douglas Johnson, *Guizot, Aspects of French History, 1787–1874* (London, 1963), ch. VI; Pierre-Antoine Berryer, *Œuvres* (5 vols., Paris, 1885–91)III, 40ff.

they considered an abdication of France under pressure of foreign powers. The French people, as a perspicacious German resident of Paris, Heinrich Heine, remarked, suffered from the uneasy feeling that the era of French greatness was rapidly coming to an end. "France," he wrote in 1841, "lives no longer in the wild intoxication of invincible power; it is sobered by the Ash Wednesday, conscious of its vulnerability. The fortifications of Paris are perhaps the giant-coffin which the giant, moved by gloomy forebodings, prepared for himself."[1]

Of all French critics of the July Monarchy, Edgar Quinet, a historian and a fervent democrat, made the most alarming diagnosis of the state of the nation. In a number of widely read pamphlets he introduced the theme of the decadence of the Latin nations: "Si les hommes qui observent attentivement ce pays s'accordent sur quelque chose, c'est pour reconnaître parmi nous plusieurs signes qui marquent le dépérissement d'une société. Malgré cela la France ne croit pas à la mort. Elle se rit de ses prophètes. Est-ce légèreté, imprévoyance ou instinct profond de l'avenir? . . . Il est une réflexion qui devrait nous réveiller de notre stupeur. La famille à laquelle nous appartenons étroitement par le sang et l'origine comprend l'Espagne, l'Italie, la France. De ces trois sœurs les deux premières sont dans le tombeau. La France seule survit, qui, à son tour, commence à palir, pendant que la race slave et la race germanique aspirent, de son vivant, à essayer sur leurs têtes la couronne de la civilisation."[2] Quinet had not yet given up all hope. He exhorted his compatriots to risk war and their lives to save France, to save the future, and to save all that was dying. "O France . . . ." he exclaimed, "qu'arriverait-il si ton nom n'était plus une protection et ta force un refuge pour tous les faibles? Ce jour-là, il faudrait croire les prophéties de mort qui annoncent la chute des sociétés modernes et la ruine de toute espérance."[3]

Quinet's fears were shared by his close friend and fellow historian Jules Michelet. As is well known, Michelet was one of the most fervent nationalists of his time, who held the French nation far superior to any other national group.[4] Like most democrats of this period he entertained exaggerated ideas on the mission of the French people. At the same time, however, he had serious misgivings about their future.

---

[1] Heinrich Heine, *Lutezia*, Feb. 13, 1841, *Sämtliche Werke*, IX, 153; see also the quotation heading this chapter.

[2] Edgar Quinet, "1815 et 1840," *Œuvres complètes* (Paris, 1858), X, 21; cf. *idem*, "Avertissement au pays," *ibid.*, 31, 36.

[3] *Ibid.*, X, 27.

[4] Cf. Michelet, *Introduction à l'histoire universelle* (Paris, 1831), 73, 92ff., 94–99, 102.

"Je vois la France baisser d'heure en heure." he wrote in 1846, "s'abîmer comme une Atlantide . . . Notre ruine est absurde, ridicule, elle ne vient que de nous. Nous avons vieilli dans nos vices, et nous n'en voulons pas guérir." "N'expliquez pas sa décadence par des causes extérieures; qu'il n'accuse ni le ciel, ni la terre; le mal est en lui."[1]

As is implied in Michelet's remarks, the weak foreign policy of the July Monarchy was not the sole reason for the Left's despair. The republicans were also depressed by the domestic policies of the ruling classes, who had betrayed the revolutionary principles of equality by limiting the suffrage to a small group of propertied citizens and by opposing any form of social legislation. They were disconcerted by seeing how the French middle classes, so soon after their rise to power, had lost their strength. "Il n'y a pas d'example," said Michelet, "d'un déclin si rapide. Ce n'est pas nous qui disons cela. Les plus tristes aveux lui échappent sur son déclin et celui de la France qu'elle entraîne."[2] Similarly, Quinet remarked: "Si la bourgeoisie avait une mission dans le monde, c'était assurément de devenir le guide, l'instituteur, ou plutôt la tête du peuple; c'était là une mission sacrée pour laquelle elle avait reçu l'intelligence, la science, l'expérience des temps passés . . . Loin de là, à peine parvenue à posséder l'autorité, la bourgeoisie en est infatuée comme tous les pouvoirs qui l'ont précédée; . . .elle se répète à son tour par mille bouches: l'Etat, c'est moi."[3]

The corruption of the bourgeoisie was actually one of the few questions on which almost all writers of the period, regardless of their political views, agreed. Catholics like Frédéric Ozanam and Alban de Villeneuve-Bargemont denounced the selfishness of the ruling class with as much vehemence as the socialists and the republicans.[4] The middle class according to Tocqueville, was only concerned with promoting its own interest and was more completely in control of the government than any aristocracy had ever been.[5] Bohemian men of letters were even more vociferous in decrying the complacency and the hypocrisy of the bourgeoisie.[6] The solid qualities that recent scholars[7]

---

[1] Michelet, Le peuple in Œuvres complètes (40 vols., Paris, 1893–99), XXXI, 25; cf. ibid.' 5, 7, 256; idem, Histoire de la Révolution française, preface 1847 (ed. Bibl. de la Pléiade, Paris, 1939), I, 3.
[2] Le peuple, loc. cit., 111–112.
[3] Quinet, Œuvres complètes, X, 35.
[4] Henri Guillemin, Histoire des catholiques français au XIXe siècle (Genève, 1947), 112–113.
[5] Alexis de Tocqueville, Souvenirs, 16–17.
[6] Cf. Edith Melcher, The Life and Times of Henry Monnier, 1799–1877 (Cambridge, Mass., 1950), 127.
[7] Cf Charles Morazé, La France bourgeoise (Paris, 1952), 94–96, 134–136.

have attributed to the early nineteenth-century bourgeoisie, which, according to them, did not start to degenerate until after 1848 or 1870, were not manifest to most contemporary authors.

The situation was all the more serious, it was felt, because bourgeois materialism threatened to infect the other classes of the population. Greediness, and exclusive preoccupation with making as much money as possible were supposedlly replacing honor, love, and faith as the motives of behavior. The new mercenary spirit was alleged to have penetrated the sacred domain of literature to the great alarm of an author like Sainte-Beuve, who started a campaign against what he called "the industrialization of literature."[1] Balzac, himself one of the authors driven by pecuniary motives, nevertheless characterized this mentality as the major evil of modern civilization. In his *Comédie humaine* the great novelist has given us an unforgettable picture of a society in which money seemed to have become the sole concern of its members. He fully shared the view of doctor Bianchon, one of the principal persons in his novel series, according to whom contemporary society suffered "du manque de religion et de l'envahissement de la finance. L'argent autrefois n'était pas tout . . . Il y avait la noblesse, le talent, les services rendus à l'état; mais aujourd'hui . . . les héritages perpétuellement divisés obligent chacun à penser à soi dès l'âge de vingt ans."[2]

This materialistic spirit of modern French society was seen fully manifested in the ruthless methods of modern capitalism. Industrialization, for this reason, was widely regarded as a curse to be avoided at all costs. Catholic economists like Villeneuve-Bargemont and Bigot de Morogues preached the return to the countryside as the only way to restore a sound social order and to prevent pauperization and revolutionary agitation; but also many of the early French socialists like Fourier and Cabet saw the salvation of mankind in the establishment of small agrarian communities; even a liberal economist like Adolphe Blanqui had, as we have seen, serious misgivings about the introduction of the factory system into France.

In spite of their misgivings about the political and economic system of the Bourgeois Monarchy, the republicans firmly believed in the

---

[1] C. A. Sainte-Beuve, "De la littérature industrielle," (1839) *Portraits contemporains* (new ed., 5 vols., Paris, 1870–72), II, 444–471; cf. Ch. M. Des Granges, *La comédie et les mœurs sous la Restauration et la Monarchie de juillet (1815–1848)* (Paris, 1904), 108–109; A. Cassagne, *La théorie de l'art pour l'art en France chez les derniers romantiques et les premiers réalistes* (Paris, 1906), 21ff.; Jules Bertaut, *L'époque romantique* (Paris, 1947), 24.

[2] *La cousine Bette* (1846) in *Œuvres complètes* (ed. M. Bouteron and H. Longnon, 40 vols., Paris, 1912–40), XVII, 472.

inevitability of progress and the superior qualities of the masses of the French nation. They had not yet given up hope that in the near future France would again lead humanity in the forward march of civilization. They praised France as more fortunate than England where the exploitation of the laboring classes had supposedly taken much more brutal forms.[1] The strong Anglophobe sentiment of the period was fed by descriptions of the appalling condition in the English industrial centers. On this matter an aristocrat like Baron d'Haussez who questioned whether the slaves of Jamaica were worse off than white workers in the slums of Birmingham and Manchester was in full agreement with a social reformer like Flora Tristan who spoke of London as a monster-city.[2] Numerous French authors called England a decadent country.[3] Many other Frenchman indulged in somber predictions of its future. Thus Villeneuve-Bargemont held that a country like England in which the majority of the population was reduced to the status of paupers was doomed to perish; before his visit to England in 1835, Tocqueville was convinced "que ce pays était sur le point d'être précipité dans les malheurs d'une profonde révolution;" and Eugène Buret, whose work on the condition of the laboring classes in France and Great Britain was awarded a prize by the Académie des sciences morales et politiques, asserted that England was engaged on a hopeless struggle which would lead either to ruin or to the most radical and probably the most terrible revolution ever to take place.[4]

V

The socialists differentiated themselves from the republicans by considering social and economic reorganization more essential than political reform. Not all of the many sects into which they were divided belittled the importance of political equality: Louis Blanc, for example, combined socialist aspirations with an ardent belief in democracy and should therefore be regarded both as a socialist and a republican. Most socialists, however, deemed the conquests of the polls utterly

[1] See, in addition to Reboul's study: Frédéric Bastiat, "Anglomanie et anglophobie," (1847) Œuvres complètes (Paris, 1864), VII; Hans Kohn, "France Between Britain and Germany," Journal of the History of Ideas, XVII (1956), 283–299; Schmidt, loc. cit.
[2] Charles Lemercher de Longpré, baron d'Haussez, La Grande-Bretagne en 1833 (Paris, 1833); Flora Tristan, Promenades dans Londres (Paris, 1840), pp. vii, 386.
[3] Elias Regnault, Histoire criminelle du gouvernement anglais depuis les premiers massacres de l'Irlande jusqu'à l'empoisonnement des Chinois (Paris, 1841); Alexandre A. Ledru-Rollin, De la décadence de l'Angleterre (2 vols., Paris, 1850); see also Reboul, op. cit., 71–78.
[4] Alban de Villeneuve-Bargemont, Économie politique chrétienne (Paris, 1834); Reboul op. cit., 246; Eugène Buret, op. cit., II, 475.

unimportant as compared with the introduction of a radically new system of economic production and distribution.

The early French socialists believed even more firmly than the democratic Left in the inevitability of progress. Saint-Simon's statement, "l'âge d'or qu'une aveugle tradition a placé jusqu'ici dans le passé, est devant nous," became one of the favorite slogans of all French socialists.[1] But the socialist concept of progress was not one of a continuous, gradual march toward perfection, but a spiral movement in which temporary retrogression is necessary to pave the way for the next, higher jump forward. They believed that their own times constituted such a period in which disintegration and decadence prevailed, and many of them felt that further degeneration and corruption could be expected before any improvement would take place.

It is therefore not surprising that most socialists portrayed their society in gloomy terms. Constantin Pecqueur, for one, wrote in 1842: "Nous ne pouvons nous le dissimuler: les choses les plus augustes sont profanées; les prestiges les plus édifiants n'ont plus de puissance ... A voir la fragilité des consciences; la débilité des convictions, l'impudence des apostasies; le matérialisme et le cynisme des caractères; la bassesse et la mauvaise foi des partis, et tant d'aveuglement et de corruption, on peut craindre que le foyer de la civilisation ne soit deplacé et que déjà nous ne ressentions les symptômes du déclin. Nos sociétés agonisantes ... ont été palpées et scrutées dans toutes leurs plaies par les meilleurs médecins: elles n'en écoutent aucun, comme si elles s'étaient bien promis de pourrir et de s'éteindre dans le marasme des vieilles civilisations."[2] Around the same time, another socialist, Pierre Leroux, decried the ugliness of the contemporary world and the disappearance of the old virtues of honor and justice. France, he asserted, had become another Carthage in which merchants dominated the government.[3]

The Saint-Simonians, the most important sect among the early French socialists, were convinced that they were living in a period of crisis vastly inferior to earlier, more constructive periods in which commercial speculations and moral corruption had not pervaded the entire social fabric. Their master believed to have found the key to

[1] Hill Shine, *Carlyle and the Saint-Simonians; the Concept of Historical Periodicity* (Baltimore, 1941), 46; Walter M. Simon, "History for Utopia: Saint-Simon and the Idea of Progress," *Journal of the History of Ideas*, XVII (1956), 311–331.
[2] Constantin Pecqueur, *Théorie nouvelle d'économie sociale et politique* (Paris 1842), p. xxi.
[3] Henry Mougin, *Pierre Leroux* (Paris, 1938), 156–157; Pierre Leroux, *Œuvres* (Paris, 1851), I, 391–427.

the understanding of history in a law prescribing the alternation of organic and critical periods. Calling himself a philosopher of crisis he held that all of Europe was passing through an era of disintegration that had started with the Protestant Reformation and reached its culmination in the destructive philosophy of the eighteenth century.[1] The social dissolution was obvious in all facets of civilization: the individualistic economy, the liberal ideology with its emphasis on individual rights, the breakdown of moral and religious certainties. Saint-Simon's onetime assistant, the philosopher of positivism, Auguste Comte, held similar ideas on the negative and destructive character of his period. "La grande crise politique et morale des sociétés actuelles," he wrote, "tient, en dernière analyse, à l'anarchie intellectuelle."[2]

Saint-Simon and Auguste Comte were in their philosophy of history greatly influenced by the ideas of the theocratic school, particularly in their appreciation of the Middle Ages as an organic period superior to later times, when society was rent asunder by the spirit of individualism. Like Maistre and Bonald they condemned the French Revolution and held that authority and organization were the prerequisites of any improvement. The term "individualisme" was actually brought into current usage as a term of opprobrium by the Saint-Simonians immediately after the death of their master in 1825. The unfavorable interpretation of the development of modern civilization as the result of the rise of individualism found its most dogmatic form in the works of Louis Blanc who, in his introduction to his *Histoire de la Révolution française* (1847), indicated how European history since the Reformation had been dominated by the various manifestations of this egotistic mentality in the fields of religion, philosophy, economics, and politics.[3]

For their analysis of society the Saint-Simonians did not depend solely on the theocratic school. They also owed a great debt to Charles Fourier, one of the most orginal and virulent critics of the political and economic order of his time. Undoubtedly influenced by Rousseau, he proclaimed the decadence of "civilization," a term which he arbitrarily used to designate the commercial and industrial order of modern times. Fourier's philosophy of history is a highly complicated

[1] Cf. Nicolaus Sombart, *Die geistesgeschichtliche Bedeutung des Grafen Henri de Saint-Simon*, 35, 43–45; Kesting *op. cit.*, 33, 35–36; Pierre Leroux, *Discours sur la situation actuelle de la société et de l'esprit humain* (new ed., Paris, 1847), II, 138; Frank Manuel, *op. cit.*, 214.

[2] Bagge, *op. cit.*, 411, 415.

[3] Louis Blanc, *Histoire de la Révolution française* (2d ed., 12 vols., Paris, 1860–70), I, *passim*, esp. 9–11; cf. my article " 'Individualism' in the Mid-Nineteenth Century (1826–1860)," *Journal of the History of Ideas*, XXIII (1962), 77–90.

variety of the cyclical theory. He did not believe in indefinite progress, but limited the history of mankind to a period of 81,000 years, the first half of which was an era of progress in which humanity developed from complete anarchy and barbarism to the highest form of harmony; the latter half was an era of decline, ending with the final extinction of all animal and vegetable life. Each of these two major eras was again subdivided into an intricate system of shorter cycles, so that even within the first half of mankind's history progress and decline were alternating. Yet until 41,000 years after the beginning of history, when the peak of social harmony and prosperity would be reached, each period of decline would be followed by a new cycle operating on a higher level than the preceding one.[1]

Now Fourier held that mankind was still young (not more than 5000 years old). For this reason, he did not consider the decadence of his times as definitive, but was convinced that mankind would soon re-enter into the ascending curve of history.

The most important part of Fourier's speculations consists in an analysis of the civilization of his time. His picture of contemporary society was extremely gloomy. He listed not less than twenty-four characteristics of degeneration caused by what he called "industrial, commercial, and financial feudalism." He used a strange terminology to designate some of the abuses of his time, such as "naumachies littéraires" and "tendance au tartarisme." Fourier's mind was somewhat unbalanced as is obvious, for instance, from his denunciations of the Jews as the leading agents of social disintegration. On the other hand, many of the evils that Fourier decried (political centralization, civil wars, industrial scandals, progress of fiscality) corresponded to real maladies from which modern civilization has been suffering. It is as an astute critic of the inhumanity of modern capitalism that Fourier has made an important and not always fully recognized contribution to the development of cultural pessimism in the nineteenth century.[2]

In their utopianism the French socialists believed that the period of crisis and degeneration in which they lived would bring forth a social order superior to any one existing previously. In this regeneration of European society, they held, France would play a leading role. Just as the democratic Left, the socialists assigned a special

---

[1] See esp. Fourier's *Le nouveau monde industriel et sociétaire* (1829), in *Œuvres complètes*, vol. VI (Paris, 1848); cf. Hubert Bourgin, *Charles Fourier*, (Paris, 1905); Robert F. Byrnes, *Antisemitism in Modern France* (New Brunswick, 1951), 118–119.

[2] Cf. Henry Michel, *L'idée de l'Etat. Essai critique sur l'histoire des théories sociales et politiques en France depuis la Révolution* (3d ed. Paris, 1898), 377.

mission to France in the world. It was the duty of France, according to the Saint-Simonian Transon, to regenerate Spain, liberate Italy, free Germany, re-establish Poland, and turn Russia's interests away from the Western world.[1] The forces of disintegration and decadence were perhaps most pronounced in France, but this meant that rebirth would also start in this country. It was entirely in the tradition of the Saint-Simonian school that Auguste Comte proposed to make Paris the capital of his future Western Republic (including France, Italy, England, and Germany).[2] Pierre Leroux also predicted that France would continue to play a role of supremacy as otherwise progress would cease, not only in France but in all of Europe.[3] In his early years Proudhon was an equally great admirer of France, "la plus spirituelle et la plus généreuse des nations."[4] Even Fourier, who was more critical of the French than most other socialist theorists, held that this nation would lead the world in the inauguration of social harmony.[5]

Like the republicans, the socialists looked upon England as an unprogressive country which would thwart the regeneration of the world. The only country other than France that was sometimes assigned an important role in the realization of the desired social order was the United States.[6] Thus Saint-Simon, after he had abandoned his earlier liberal views, lost his high regard for English political institutions and predicted that the free workers of the American Republic would become the pioneers in the reorganization of society.[7] Prior to the Revolution of 1830 the American dream also appealed to many republicans and liberals, some of whom like Charles Dunoyer and Chateaubriand looked to the United States as the country that would take over the leadership of Western civilization from an old and decaying Europe.[8]

---

[1] Leroy, op. cit., III, 326.

[2] Auguste Comte, Discours sur l'ensemble du positivisme (1848) (Paris, 1907), 33, 88.

[3] Pierre Leroux, Discours sur la situation actuelle, II, 121ff.

[4] Proudhon to Ackermann, Oct. 4, 1844, Correspondance (14 vols., Paris, 1875), II, 155.

[5] Fourier, Théorie de l'unité universelle (1822) in Œuvres complètes, vol. V. (Paris, 1846), 368ff.; Victor Considérant, De la politique générale et du rôle de la France en Europe (Paris, 1840), 24.

[6] Only a few Frenchmen shared the Slavophile dream that Russia would play a leading role in bringing about a higher social order; cf. Rohr, Un missionnaire républicain en Russie (Paris, 1852).

[7] Manuel, op. cit., 236; 282. 290; cf. Doctrine de Saint-Simon, in Saint-Simon and Enfantin, Œuvres complètes, XLI (Paris, 1877), 167ff.; Reboul, op. cit., 320–322.

[8] Hubert Gillot, Chateaubriand, ses idées, son action, son œuvre (Paris, 1934), 370; cf. Bagge, op. cit., 148. Under the July Monarchy many radicals and liberals lost their infatuation with the American dream; see the perceptive study by René Rémond, Les Etats-Unis devant l'opinion française, 1815–1852 (Paris, 1962).

VI

Much of the pessimism current in France during the first half of the nineteenth century had its source in a Romantic feeling of discontent with modern civilization, the so-called *mal du siècle*. Many writers puzzled by the prevalence of Romantic despondency in a nation traditionally known for its cheerful temperament attributed the appearance of this gloomy mood to the various political disasters that had befallen France in the period of the Revolution and Napoleon. France's "public misfortunes," Victor Hugo asserted in 1824, had left his generation with no other choice than that between resignation and despair.[1] According to Alfred de Musset, young Frenchmen were plagued by boredom and anxiety because they had hoped to emulate the great deeds of their fathers but were doomed to live in the uninspiring atmosphere of a prosaic, bourgeois society: "Toute la maladie du siècle présent vient de deux causes: le peuple qui a passé par 93 et par 1814 porte au cœur deux blessures. Tout ce qui était n'est plus; tout ce qui sera n'est pas encore. Ne cherchez pas ailleurs le secret de nos maux."[2] A similar explanation of the prevailing feeling of spiritual emptiness was offered by Chateaubriand: "Retomber de Bonaparte et de l'Empire à ce qui les a suivis, c'est tomber de la réalité dans le néant, du sommet d'une montagne dans un gouffre. Tout n'est-il pas terminé avec Napoleon?"[3]

This explanation is, however, not fully convincing. Romantic despondency was also a common phenomenon in many countries that had not experienced such upsetting events as the Reign of Terror or the Napoleonic downfall. Romantic anxiety afflicted the younger generation wherever orthodox Christianity was losing its sway and where the justification of the old social order was called into question. Romantic anxiety was therefore caused not so much by the political events of the period as by the awareness that the traditional explanations of the existence of evil and suffering were no longer valid. This explains that the Romantic disease made its first appearance before the outbreak of the Revolution. This was especially true of

---

[1] "Sur lord Byron, à propos de sa mort," *Littérature et philosophie mêlées* (2 vols., Paris, 1834), II, 71–72; cf. Marcel A Ruff, *L'esprit de mal et l'esthétique baudelairienne* (Paris, 1955), 65; Armand Hoog, "Who Invented the *Mal du Siècle?* A study in Responsibilities," *Yale French Studies*, no. 13 (1954), 42–51.

[2] Alfred de Musset, *La confession d'un enfant du siècle* (1836) in *Œuvres complètes en prose* (ed. Bibli. de la Pléiade, Paris, 1951), 94.

[3] *Mémoires d'outre-tombet*, ed, Centenaire, III, 9–10.

Germany where men of letters, unable to account for the imperfections of man's mundane existence, began to suffer from *Weltschmerz* as early as the 1770's.

In France, on the other hand, the *mal du siècle* remained relatively exceptional as long as political utopianism or intoxication with military glory filled the vacuum left by the decline of the old certainties. But when, after 1814, dreams of political regeneration and national grandeur were discredited, many young Frenchmen suddenly experienced a sense of spiritual emptiness.

In France, Romantic despondency never took the form of a national epidemic. There are many indications that the French never suffered as much from the *mal du siècle* as the Germans did from *Weltschmerz* or the English from "spleen".[1] The lamentations of a writer like Lamartine, the most popular Romantic poet in the 1820's, easily resolved themselves in an attitude of resignation to the inevitability of evil and were mild compared with the bitter diatribes of a writer like Byron. In the beginning of the nineteenth century many writers, French as well as foreign, continued to contrast the cheerfulness of the French with the somber temperament of other nations. Thus Alfred de Musset asserted that the lighthearted French, unlike the serious-minded Germans and English, were incapable of true despair; they suffered merely from boredom and scepticism.[2] The general image of France was still that depicted by Goldsmith:

> Gay, sprightly land of mirth and social ease,
> Pleased with thyself, whom all the world can please.[3]

Neither did French poets and historians go so far as many German authors in their glorification of the past. Victor Hugo, Michelet, and Barante portrayed the Middle Ages as a period repulsive in its barbarism and superstition, although fascinating, highly colorful, and

---

[1] The appearance of pessimism in nineteenth-century France was frequently attributed to German influence; see *infra*, 160, 188. As early as the beginning of the eighteenth century the English were generally considered to be extraordinarily subject to melancholia; all over the Continent, gloom was known as "the English malady;" see C. A. Moore, *Backgrounds of English literature, 1700–1760* (Minneapolis, 1953), ch. V. The English kept this reputation during the first half of the nineteenth century; cf. Pierre Jourda, *L'exotisme dans la littérature française depuis Chateaubriand. Le Romantisme* (Paris, 1938), 50ff.; Reboul, *op. cit. passim.*

[2] Alfred de Musset, *La confession d'un enfant du siècle, loc. cit.*, 91–92.

[3] Oliver Goldsmith, *The Traveller or a Prospect for Society* (1765), line 241. An exception was Heinrich Heine, who, in 1837, remarked: "The French are by no means a gay and cheerful people. I begin to believe that Laurence Sterne was right when he asserted that they are much too serious." (*Sämtliche Werke*, VIII, 46).

bursting with energy. Many French authors, it is true, reiterated the old clichés about the aging of the world, but the main purpose of these complaints, it seems, was to justify the Romantic break with literary tradition. Thus Charles Nodier declared that the corruption and mediocrity of a declining society left the artistic soul with no other choice but to escape into a world of fantasy and Victor Hugo proclaimed that mankind had reached a period of old age, of which Romanticism was the true literary expression.[1] "Je suis venu trop tard dans un monde trop vieux," sighed Alfred de Musset's hero Rolla.[2] But such lamentations of a "lost generation" did not lead to the elaboration of any systematic philosophies of history as were formulated on the other side of the Rhine.

Many French Romantics actually looked with confidence to the future. Until the late 1820's, it is true, most of them subscribed to conservative and Catholic doctrines, but in the years immediately preceding the July Revolution, they began to endorse the new secular creeds of liberalism, socialism, and humanitarianism and to place the golden age in the future instead of in the past.[3] Victor Hugo and Edgar Quinet wrote Romantic poems inspired by the new doctrine of the perfectibility of mankind,[4] Lamennais stated hopefully that a new era was beginning, and Lamartine felt that he was living in a period of innovation comparable with the beginnings of Christianity.[5] The expected regeneration, many writers felt, would take place along the principles outlined by socialist theorists like Saint-Simon and Fourier. As so-called Social Romantics, they now condemned the cult of Romantic individualism and the excessive preoccupation with purely literary questions. "Les écrivains affectaient alors dans leurs préfaces," declared Alfred de Musset, "de parler de l'avenir, du progrès social, de l'humanité et de la civilisation."[6] Sympathizing with the underprivileged classes, they became interested in the realistic portrayal of the social conditions of their own time, instead of seeking

---

[1] Charles Nodier, "Du fantastique en littérature," *Revue de Paris*, Nov., 1830; cf. Pierre-Georges Castex, *Le conte fantastique en France de Nodier à Maupassant* (Paris, 1951), 64–65, 143–144; Victor Hugo, *Cromwell* (1827), preface (ed. Paris, 1941), 4.

[2] Alfred de Musset, *Rolla* (1833) in *Poésies complètes* (ed. Bibl. de la Pléiade, Paris, 1951), 282.

[3] Cf. David O Evans, *Social Romanticism in France, 1830–1848* (Oxford, 1952); Roger Picard, *Le Romantisme social* (New York, 1944); H. J. Hunt, *Le socialisme et le Romantisme en France; étude de la presse socialiste de 1830 à 1848* (Oxford, 1935); Guyon, *op. cit.*, 760–768.

[4] Cf. Leon Cellier, *L'épopée romantique* (Paris, 1954).

[5] Henri Guillemin, *Le "Jocelyn" de Lamartine* (Paris, 1936), 96–97; idem, *Lamartine et la question sociale*, 83.

[6] "Lettres de Dupuis et Cotonet," *Œuvres complètes*, IX (Paris, 1881), 212.

consolation in idealized societies of the past or escaping in a world of dreams.

Most French Romantics, then, did not distinguish themselves by the intensity of their pessimism or by the articulateness of their views of history. After 1830, however, a new, exacerbated and more original form of Romantic discontent made its appearance in France. A number of men of letters known as "la jeune France," disillusioned by the outcome of the July Revolution, came to be affected by a serious variety of the *mal du siècle*. These "angry young men," regarding themselves as the elite of the nation and shocked by the mediocrity and the vulgarity of the ruling classes, developed into bitter or cynical bohemians, rejecting the utopian illusions that were still entertained by most other French intellectuals.[1] As great admirers of Byron, they often favored an attitude of absolute revolt against all social conventions. One of the disenchanted writers, Antoine Rey-Dusseuil, went so far as to see the only hope for the future in the utter destruction of the world by a comet, which had been predicted for the year of 1832.[2] Others advocated suicide as the only logical step in a world essentially vile and miserable.[3]

It was in this mood of profound disillusionment with all political and social idealism that some men of letters like Théophile Gautier and Pétrus Borel began to preach the doctrine of art for art's sake.[4] Breaking with the generous aspirations of Social Romanticism, they openly professed themselves individualists, totally uninterested in the reform of a society that they regarded as irremediably corrupt. All his life Théophile Gautier declaimed against "cette sotte chose que cette prétendue perfectibilité du genre humain dont on nous rebat les oreilles."[5] "Qu'a-t-on fait," he wrote," qu'on ne fit aussi bien et mieux avant le déluge." In her early years George Sand shared many of the feelings of this group: "Société, institutions, haine à vous! haine à mort!" she wrote in 1832, "Et toi Dieu, qui livre les faibles à tant de despotisme et d'abjection, je te maudis."[1] If some of these

---

[1] Bertaut, *L'Époque romantique*, 54–55; Ruff, *op. cit.*, ch. x; Edmond Estève, *Byron et le romantisme français* (2 vols., Paris, 1927).

[2] Antoine F. M. Rey-Dusseuil, *La fin du monde, histoire du temps présent et des choses à venir* (Paris, 1830); cf. Vulliaud, *op. cit.*, 211–212.

[3] Cf. P. F. J. Servan de Sugny, *Le suicide* (Paris, 1832); Louis Maigron, *Le Romantisme et les mœurs* (Paris, 1910), 312–350.

[4] Cf. A. E. Carter, *The Idea of Decadence in French Literature, 1830–1900* (Toronto, 1958), 36ff.; Cassagne, *op. cit.*

[5] Théophile Gautier, *La Préface de Mademoiselle de Maupin*, ed. Georges Matoré (Paris, 1946), 33ff., 38; cf. Castex, *op. cit.*, 143–144.

ferocious foes of society still supported socialist and republican movements, they did so out of purely egoistic considerations. Pétrus Borel's
explanation of why he was a republican is revealing of the new mentality: "Oui! je suis républicain, mais ce n'est pas le soleil de juillet
qu'a fait éclore en moi cette haute pensée, je le suis d'enfance ... j'ai
besoin d'une somme énorme de liberté: la République me la donnera-
t-elle? Je n'ai pas l'expérience pour moi. Mais quand cet espoir sera
deçu, comme tant d'autres illusions, il me restera le Missouri"![2]

A contemporary critic accused these young people of wanting
"la liberté, mais la liberté absolue, la liberté sans entraves, la liberté
de faire du tapage la nuit, ... la liberté d'enfeindre les lois ..."[3]
Thus perverting the Romantic doctrine of individuality into a cult of
selfishness and licence, they felt that a person of superior ability should
not waste his talents in attempts to reform a society which was beyond
redemption, but should strive for an idea of artificiality and defiance,
in contradistinction to bourgeois conventionality and hypocrisy.
"Dandyism," as this artistic reaction against the vulgarity of the age
was called, constituted, according to one of its most prominent
devotees, Barbey d'Aurevilly, the product of a society "horri-
blement blasée, savante, en proie à toutes les fatigues des vieilles
civilisations."[4]

The contempt for social conventions led these writers to a glorification of evil and a discrediting of virtue. In many of their literary
works, criminals, prostitutes, and adulteresses figured as heroes. Anticipating the literary schools of realism and naturalism, they indulged
in lurid descriptions of the corruption and baseness of their times.
Whereas the Social Romantics, believing in the regeneration of society,
can be considered as heirs of Rousseau, the disenchanted members of
the younger generation accepted the Marquis de Sade as their master.[5]
Basically nihilistic, they rejected the validity of all moral judgments.
In fact, they felt attracted to the diabolical and took delight in perversion. This attitude, known as Satanism or the cult of evil, amounted

---

[1] *Valentine* (1832) as quoted in Leroy, *op. cit.*, II, 419.

[2] Ruff, *op. cit.*, 115–116; cf. Enid Starkie, *Pétrus Borel, His Life and Times* (Norfolk, Conn., 1954); Mario Praz, *The Romantic Agony* (Meridian Books, New York, 1956), 131–137; G. Matoré, in Théophile Gautier, *Préface de Mademoiselle Maupin*, p. xxxvii.

[3] Bertaut, *op. cit.*, 54–55.

[4] Barbey d'Aurevilly, *Du dandysme et de G. Brummel* (1844) as quoted in Carter, *op. cit.*, 46; cf. John C. Prevost, *Le dandysme en France (1817–1839)* (Genève, 1957).

[5] In 1843 Sainte-Beuve wrote: "J'oserai affirmer, sans crainte d'être démenti, que Byron et de Sade (je demande pardon du rapprochement) ont peut-être été les deux plus grands inspirateurs de nos modernes, l'un affiché et visible, l'autre clandestin, – pas trop clandestin;" "Quelques vérités sur la situation en littérature," *Portraits contemporains*, III, 430.

to a complete break with the humanitarian aspirations of most earlier Romantics.

It was at this time that some French authors first began to dwell on the charming features of declining civilizations. Thus Théophile Gautier, one of the leading authors who indulged in fantasies of perversion and artificiality, portrayed one of his heroes as seeking relief in the debauchery of ancient Rome.[1] Like French writers of the *fin de siècle*, these last representatives of French Romanticism no longer dreamed of distant lands more virtuous and more vigorous than their own, but of societies more vicious and more decadent. Their unconventional and partly perverse mentality, repudiating traditional morality rejecting all social restraints, defying society, and taking a morbid delight in corruption, obviously constituted a radical reversal of almost all earlier attitudes towards historical decline. It was this consciously adopted ideology of Satanism, individualism, and estheticism that formed the most important legacy of French Romanticism to the so-called Decadent movement in literature at the end of the nineteenth century.

VII

The Romantics themselves, with few exceptions, did not regard their own mentality or literary style as "decadent." But this term of abuse was applied to them by many of their literary opponents. Romanticism was attacked from the very beginning of its appearance in France. For a number of years it was ridiculed mainly for its predilection for the horrible and the macabre, its mysticism and eccentricities, its taste for tombstones and moonlight. It was criticized as foreign to French taste and as an insult to all accepted literary standards. The epithets "barbare" and "frénétique" were frequently applied to the new style.

Initially the controversy between Romanticism and Classicism was still fought in the traditional form of literary quarrels in which the

---

[1] The Chevalier d'Albert in *Mademoiselle de Maupin* (1834); cf. Werner Ross, *Das Bild der römischen Kaiserzeit in der französischen Literatur des 19. Jahrhunderts* (Bochum-Langendreer, 1938), referring to a similar theme in the works of Flaubert, Louis Bouilhet and other authors of the period. As early as 1835 this identification with Roman decadence led Théophile de Ferrière to exclaim "Nous sommes tous empéreurs du Bas-Empire. Ne sommes-nous pas en décadence?"; cf. Jacques Lethève, "Le thème de la décadence dans les lettres françaises à la fin du XIXe siècle," *Revue d'histoire littéraire de la France*. LXIII (1963), 47; Thomas Couture's famous painting "Les Romains de la décadence" (1847) is another example of this new interest in Roman "decadence."

parties derided each other in satirical verses, but without complete contempt for the opponent's point of view. But when Romanticism began to display its revolutionary and individualistic tendencies, the defenders of tradition resorted to more serious forms of attack. The tone of later denunciations of Romanticism was set by the secretary of the Académie française, P. S. Auger, who, in 1824, referred to Romanticism as "cette littérature de cannibales," and declared that "cette poésie misanthropique . . . semble avoir reçu sa mission de Satan même, pour pousser au crime . . ." [1]

In the 1830's many other champions of Classicism took up arms against the new type of literature. Their foremost spokesman, Désiré Nisard, a former Romanticist himself, published a study of the literature of the late Roman Empire, attempting to show how the Latin poets of that period had indulged in the same decadent and vulgar taste as his Romantic contemporaries.[2] A classical revival undertaken by François Ponsard and others in the year 1843 was welcomed by the ruling classes, and Ponsard himself was received by the King and soon given a seat in the Académie. Various attorney generals felt it their duty to point to the pernicious effects of Romantic literature on public morality. "Je crois que notre société souffre d'un mal profond," a Parisian magistrate wrote in 1845, "et je n'hésite pas pour ma part à mettre la littérature au premier rang des causes qui ont amené ce mal. Nos écrivains ne se sont adressés aux passions que pour les flatter. Sous le beau prétexte d'individualisme, ils ont donné carrière aux pires instincts . . . Plus rien d'élevé, de noble, de généreux. Partout la satisfaction immédiate des appétits, la recherche de la jouissance, un égoïsme qui devient monstrueux . . . Je n'ose pas dire qu'on aime le mal, mais du moins on n'en a plus d'horreur; il ne déplaît pas; on dirait même qu'il intéresse, qu'il attire. On signale des cas singuliers d'aberration; il y a des perversités qui montrent le bout d'oreille. Pour peu qu'on fasse de ce côté encore quelques progrès, nous assisterons bientôt à une belle décomposition morale: les jours de la décadence romaine reviendront." [3]

---

[1] Jules Marsan, La bataille romantique (Paris, 1912), 17, 21; Pierre Martino, L'époque romantique en France, 1815-30 (Paris, 1944); Estève, op. cit., 130. Auger's attack would have fallen into oblivion if it had not been for Stendhal's retort in his new (1825) edition of Racine et Shakspeare.

[2] Désiré Nisard, Études de mœurs et de critique sur les poètes de la Décadence (1834) and "Manifeste contre la littérature facile," (1833) in Essais sur l'école romantique (Paris, 1891), 173-198.

[3] Quoted in Maigron, op. cit., 173-174; cf. ibid., 193, 332-333, 430ff.

Many socialist writers passed similar censures on the Satanistic and individualistic tendencies of French Romanticism. With the exception of the Fourierists, they bitterly denounced the cynic attitude of the younger literary generation. Even many of the older authors who, around 1830, had become more socially conscious were criticized for not having broken more radically with Romantic individualism and still seeking solace in an idealized past or a world of fantasy instead of making their contributions to the solution of contemporary problems. Philippe Buchez held novels like those written by Eugène Sue responsible for the moral turpitude of his time, accused Vigny of individualism, Victor Hugo of selfishness, and Balzac of even more serious crimes.[1] Louis Blanc and his school, the most severe of all critics, blamed Romanticism for falsifying French taste, killing all psychological insight, sacrificing classical unity to the barbarian mania for contrast, and dealing a serious blow to morality by glorifying vice and egotism.[2]

One of the numerous sins of which French Romantics were accused by their contemporaries and even more so by later critics was that they undermined French cultural traditions by their excessive admiration for foreign countries, especially England and Germany.[3] It is true that most French Romantics, in contrast to earlier French authors, were pronounced cosmopolitans. Their curiosity about foreign civilizations, like their interest in the past, often served as an escape from the supposedly prosaic world in which they were living. They felt, moreover, that French literary tradition lacked vitality and originality and was no longer suited to express the sentiments of the modern age. French literature, according to them, was doomed to sterility unless it received fresh inspiration from the poetic genius of England and Germany.[4]

Among English authors, it was notably Shakespeare, Byron, and Walter Scott who were held in high esteem. Some Romantic writers admired England not only for its literature but for its social customs and political institutions as well. Together with most liberals and a social elite they formed a small group of the French population of the period that, for a variety of reasons, were Anglophiles. Both Lamar-

---

[1] Hunt, *op. cit.*, 83–93.
[2] *Ibid.*, 167.
[3] Cf. Georges Weill, *L'éveil des nationalités et le mouvement libéral* (Paris, 1930), 222.
[4] Germaine de Staël, *De l'Allemagne*, ed. comtesse Jean de Pange (Paris, 1958), I, 24; Stendhal, *Racine et Shakspeare* (1823–25), ed. Henri Martineau (Paris, 1928).

tine and Vigny married Englishwomen and Stendhal remarked that he loved England too much to speak about it objectively.[1]

These various forms of Anglomania were, however, never popular. Anglophobia, as has been noted, was widespread in France during the first half of the nineteenth century. When English actors came to Paris in 1822 to give a performance of Shakespeare's plays, they were hooted by the populace. Even some Romantic authors had strong prejudices against the English. Victor Hugo and Michelet, for example, shared the common notion that the English people were pre-eminently selfish, undemocratic, and materialistic.[2]

German civilization had a much stronger hold on the French mind of the period. Many leading authors of the early nineteenth century were prone to admit the superiority of German culture in most fields of artistic and intellectual endeavor. It was Madame de Staël who, by the publication of her idyllic description of Germany in 1813, set the tone for the Germanomania of the next generation.[3] French intellectuals became spellbound by the picturesque charm of the German countryside, the genius of German poets and musicians, and the profundity of German philosophers and scholars. Victor Hugo proclaimed that if he had not been a Frenchman, he would like to have been a German, and Charles Nodier spoke of "l'Allemagne merveilleuse, la dernière patrie des poésies et des croyances de l'Occident, le berceau future d'une forte société à venir, s'il reste une société à faire en Europe."[4] Gérard de Nerval talked of "la vieille Allemagne, notre mère à tous! ... Teutonia ...;" Michelet characterized Germany as all "naïveté, poésie et métaphysique;" and young Ernest Renan heaved the sign: "Ah! si j'étais né protestant en Allemagne!"[5]

The country which was the object of this tremendous veneration was actually very imperfectly known to most French Romantics.[6] With very

---

[1] Stendhal, *De l'amour*, ed. Henri Martineau (Paris, 1959), 156.

[2] Cf. Jeanlouis Cornuz, *Jules Michelet. Un aspect de la pensée religieuse au XIXe siècle* (Genève, 1955), 148ff.; Hans Kohn, "France Between Britain and Germany, *loc. cit.*, Reboul, *op. cit., passim*.

[3] Cf. M. Souriau, *Histoire du Romantisme* en France (3 vols., Paris, 1927), I, 28off.; André Monchoux, *L'Allemagne devant les lettres françaises de 1814 à 1835* (Toulouse, 1953).

[4] Charles Nodier, *Le peintre de Saltzbourg*, preface of the edition of 1840, in *Romans* (Paris, 1884), 18; Victor Hugo, *Le Rhin* (1842), preface.

[5] Gérard de Nerval, "Lorely," *Œuvres* (ed. Bibl. de la Pléiade, Paris, 1956), II, 743; Guillaume Bertier de Sauvigny, *La Restauration* (Paris, 1955), 450; Ernest Renan, *Souvenirs d'enfance et de jeunesse* in *Œuvres complètes* (10 vols., Paris, 1947–61), II, 914.

[6] Cf. Jean M. Carré, *Les écrivains français et le mirage allemand, 1800–1940* (Paris, 1947); Monchoux, *op. cit.*; Albert Counson, "De la légende de Kant chez les romantiques," *Mélanges Godefroid Kurth* (Liége, 1908).

few exceptions, the French writers of this period were unfamiliar with the German language, and the characteristic works of German Romantic literature were generally unavailable in translations. At this time most Frenchmen were still completely unaware of the growing strength of German political and cultural nationalism. Germany remained to almost all Frenchmen a country of poets and thinkers, not a nation with any talent for political or military organization that might become a serious threat to France. The function that Germany served in Romantic imagination was similar to that of Spain, a country that also fascinated many writers without impressing them by its military or political strength. Edgar Quinet was the only important French author who, at this time, clearly foresaw the dangerous tendencies in German society. He was one of the few French Romantics who had acquired a thorough knowledge of Germany for he had resided many years in the country and had married a German woman. As early as the 1830's he pointed to Germany as a danger to Western civilization and predicted that within the near future France might lose her leadership to the Germanic or Slavic races.[1]

The prevalent admiration of German culture should not be interpreted as later French nationalists have done, as a lack of confidence in the strength of France. Actually, most Romantic authors were firmly convinced of the superiority of French "civilization." In proposing a close Franco-German cooperation, they never questioned that France would play the leading political role in this partnership. In fact, the cosmopolitanism, if not the exoticism, of French Romantics might be interpreted as a sign of regained confidence in the strength of their nation. It did not appear immediately after 1815, not in fact until the 1820's when France had largely recovered from the humiliation of defeat.[2] The national self-confidence of many French intellectuals of this period can be summed in a statement made by Stendhal, an author who as a voluntary exile during many years of his life cannot be suspected of undue partiality to France: "Cette grande nation, la première de l'univers."[3]

---

[1] See *supra*, 64, note, 2; cf. André Monchoux, "L'aventure allemande d'Edgar Quinet," *Revue de littérature comparée*, XXXIV (1960), 81–107, pointing out that Quinet underestimated Germany's intellectual achievement.

[2] Bertier de Sauvigny, *op. cit.*, 480.

[3] Stendhal, *De l'amour*, 148.

VIII

As has been shown, the critical state of France was attributed to a great variety of factors: the revolutionary and democratic spirit; the destructive philosophy of the eighteenth century; the excessive centralization of the government with the resulting top-heavy bureaucracy; the lack of social responsibility among the bourgeoisie; the increasing materialism and individualism; the demoralizing influence of Romanticism, to mention only the more important. A number of weaknesses that loom large in later literature on French decadence were not, or hardly at all, mentioned during the first half of the nineteenth century: the slow pace of industrialization; the irresponsible behavior of intellectuals; the lack of patriotism among the lower classes; the unprogressive character of the French educational system. Notably lacking is any unfavorable comment on the declining birth rate. The fact itself was not unknown, but at this time it was almost universally held in France as well as in other European countries that this was a desirable rather than an alarming development. In other words, Malthusianism influenced most opinions on this subject and even the few Catholics and socialists who rejected any form of birth control were not in favor of any legislation tending to promote an increase of the birth rate. The only pessimistic comment on the French demographic trend that was expressed at this time consisted of complaints made by conservatives about the depopulation of the countryside as a result of industrialization.[1]

Resentment of the diminished international position of France was an important source of the sense of decadence in the period of the Constitutional Monarchy. Public opinion was in a state of almost continuous indignation about the weakness of French foreign policy, which seemed to perpetuate the inferior rank to which France had been reduced after the battle of Waterloo. But such feelings were accompanied by the conviction that France was still "la grande nation" and would again play a great and unique role in the future. The increasing popularity of the Napoleonic legend is an indication that many Frenchmen had not yet given up the hope that their country would again play the leading role in European affairs. The belief in the greatness of France and its civilizing mission was actually

---

[1] Cf. R. Gonnard, *Histoire des doctrines de la population* (Paris, 1923), 300ff.; Joseph J. Spengler, "French Population Theory Since 1800," *Journal of Political Economy*, XLIV (1936), 743–766; *idem, France Faces Depopulation* (Durham, N.C., 1938), 36, 107–111.

a prominent tenet in many political ideologies of the period. Authors with such diverse political views as Maistre, Guizot, Michelet, August Comte, and Fourier subscribed to some variety of national messianism. In spite of all their criticisms of modern France, they still felt that the French were superior to any other nation in the world.

It is not surprising that so many Frenchmen continued to have great confidence in the basic strength of France. Between 1815 and 1848 no spectacular calamities befell the country. Although politically divided, there were no protracted periods of internal strife leading to bloody massacres or civil war. Neither was the nation involved in any foreign wars accompanied by large scale destruction of property. France, it is true, was diplomatically humiliated on a number of occasions, but it did not suffer any loss of territory. Only a few farsighted Frenchmen such as Tocqueville and Quinet perceived the shift in the balance of power that was in the making. The growing strength of an aggressive, nationalistic Germany remained almost entirely unnoticed and the potentialities of the American Republic were still grossly underestimated. The power of England and Russia was viewed more realistically, but even these countries were often not given their due. Thus Michelet called them "deux géants faibles et bouffis qui font illusion à l'Europe. Grands empires et faibles peuples! ... Que la France soit une, un instant, elle est forte comme le monde."[1]

A similar tendency to exaggerate the power of France existed also in other countries still living in the fear of a possible repetition of French aggression. The notion that France was a great and dangerous nation did not die with the battle of Waterloo. During the next half century many European statesmen anxiously watched the reactions of the French people because as an Austrian statesman, Schwarzenberg, said, "when Paris catches cold, Europe sneezes."[2] Rabid anti-French nationalists like Father Jahn who proposed to isolate the pure German fatherland from the corrupt French by a thick forest populated with elks and beavers, indirectly testified to the tremendous radiating power that the home of the Revolution still possessed.[3] Foreigners, even if they detested the individual Frenchman, had a healthy respect for the nation as a bloc. "They are like gunpowder," said Coleridge in 1831,

---

[1] Michelet, *Le Peuple* in *Œuvres complètes*, XXXI, 25-26.

[2] R. L. Williams, *Gaslight and Shadow. The World of Napoleon III* (New York, 1957), 24; cf. Metternich's statement: "Quand il pleut à Paris, nous ouvrons nos parapluies à Vienne;" Paul Henry, *France devant le monde de 1789 à 1939* (Paris, 1945), 111.

[3] Z. R. Dittrich, *De opkomst van het moderne Duitsland* (2 vols., Groningen, 1956), I, 58.

"smutty and contemptible each taken by itself, but terrible indeed when massed together."[1]

The strong Francophobia in many European countries strengthened many Frenchmen in their conviction that France was still basically strong. A nation which was widely feared and hated but never treated with indifference was obviously not in a state of utter decadence. The most serious problem weakening the country seemed to be the division of the French nation into two or more political camps irreconcilably opposed to each other. But other nations, it was felt, also had problems of their own. Thus French writers lamenting the increase of individualism in their country did not fail to point out that this mentality was essentially un-French, having originated with the Protestant Reformation and finding its fullest manifestation in contemporary Anglo-Saxon countries. Similarly, critics of chronic unemployment and other abuses of the Industrial Revolution were convinced that these evils constituted a much greater danger to the future of England than to that of their own country.

However serious any of these problems might be, they were seldom considered irremediable. They were looked upon as symptoms of change rather than of decline. One of the most distinctive features of the intellectual development of the 1830's and 1840's was the increasing popularity of belief in the ultimate triumph of the forces of progress.[2] Although the opposite of complacent, and continuously complaining about the "decadence" of their country and modern civilization, most French intellectuals interpreted this "decadence" as a concomitant of a time of crisis, in which the old order had to collapse before a new superior form of civilization could make its appearance. At the same time that the conviction that modern civilization suffered from serious maladies increased in strength, the belief in a spiral form of progress became stronger and more widely held than ever before. Many authors like Chateaubriand and Lamennais, who had been critical of the idea of progress at the beginning of their literary career, changed their views around 1830. A contemporary publicist, Joseph Ferrari, went so far as to assert in 1843: "L'idée de progrès . . . pénètre partout et se fait accepter par toutes les philosophies et par tous les partis

---

[1] Coleridge, *Table Talk and the Rime of the Ancient Mariner* (London, 1884), 127-128.

[2] Cf. Tronchon, *Romantisme et préromantisme*, 23–77.

[3] Joseph Ferrari, *Essai sur le principe et les limites de la philosophie de l'histoire* (Paris, 1843), 130–131. Cf. George Sand's characterization of the state of mind in 1818 in contrast to that of ten years later. "On aimait tant les anciens qu'on n'admettait guère l'idée du progrès. On était persuadé que l'esprit de l'homme repasse toujours par les mêmes phases, et . . .

politiques. Aujourd'hui, la nier c'est crime de lèse-civilisation: le mot de progrès est un mot d'ordre, le seul qui soit commun à toutes les opinions."[3]

This statement is too sweeping, but it can be said that in the last years of the July Monarchy only the devotees of Dandyism and Satanism together with some orthodox Christians and a few isolated reactionaries glorifying the Old Regime consistently rejected any hope for an improvement in man's mundane condition. French intellectuals, then, were in a confident, if not complacent, mood on the eve of the outbreak of the Revolution of 1848.

on croyait plus à la roue qui tourne sur elle-même qu'à la roue qui avance en tournant: cette vérité qui se répand aujourd'hui était encore très discutée il y dix ans." (*La confession d'une jeune fille* [Paris, 1865], I, 179–180).

CHAPTER IV

THE GREAT DISILLUSION
1848–1870

Notre siècle ne va ni vers le bien, ni vers le mal; il va vers le médiocre.

RENAN[1]

Si l'on n'y prend garde, la race saxonne, fortifiée par le régime de la liberté, remplacera les autres races du globe, en vertu du loi de Darwin sur la concurrence vitale.

HENRI DE FERRON[2]

The overthrow of the July Monarchy ushered in a brief period of feverish expectations. The eagerly awaited regeneration of the country seemed to be at hand. Of course, not all Frenchmen shared the illusions of the moment. But the dissenting voices of liberals and conservatives were silenced by a wave of popular enthusiasm which followed in the wake of the February Revolution. Even the clergy wholeheartedly participated in the demonstrations of loyalty to the new regime.

This mood of optimism was short-lived. In its unexpected sequel the Revolution of 1848 destroyed much of the confidence with which during the July Monarchy many French intellectuals had been looking toward the future. It shook the naive idealism which had been characteristic of French socialists and republicans; it completely shattered what had been left of the confidence which the traditionalists had had in the political capacities of the French people; it above all dealt a decisive blow to the complacency with which most liberals had previously looked upon the development of their country. 1848 was a decisive turning point in French intellectual history because after that date the doctrinaire belief in progress began to lose its intellectual respectability, if not its popular appeal. Frédéric Ozanam, a distinguished Catholic historian of democratic convictions, declared in 1852 that the best minds of his time believed in decadence and that the idea of progress had become a discredited notion.[3] "Le pessimisme,"

[1] Ernest Renan, "La poésie de l'exposition," *Œuvres complètes*, II, 250.
[2] Henri de Ferron, *Théorie du progrès* (2 vols., Paris, 1867), II, 448–449.
[3] Frédéric Ozanam, "Du progrès dans les siècles de décadence," *Correspondant*, XXX (1852), 257.

wrote the liberal Charles de Rémusat in 1860, "a fait de grands progrès, et notre temps, qui a passé pour enorgueilli de ses œuvres,
compte aujourd'hui plus de censeurs que d'enthousiastes." Many
Frenchmen, he added, who thirty or forty years ago had been full
of hope and enthusiasm for the principles of the French Revolution
had now come to the conclusion that modern democracy was not more
than "une turbulente décadence."[1]

I

The reasons for this despondency varied greatly. To the bourgeoisie
the most alarming innovation of the new regime was its experiment
in state socialism. During the short-lived Second Republic fear of
losing life and property was rampant among the propertied classes,
who began to see the salvation of their country in an intervention of
Russian troops. "Plutôt les Russes que les Rouges," was a favorite
expression used by conservatives deputies in 1849 and 1850. This fear
of socialism was the major theme of a widely read pamphlet, *Le
spectre rouge de 1852*, in which the author, Auguste Romieu, as a spokesman for Louis Bonaparte, proclaimed that the role of the bourgeoisie
was played out and that only a dictator would be able to maintain
the social order. Romieu ridiculed the idea of progress, stating that
the present time was the most ominous since the end of the Roman
Empire and that the feudal regime was the best political system Europe
had ever known. "La nation française," he declared, "n'existe plus.
Il y a, sur le vieux sol de Gaule, des riches inquiets et des pauvres
avides; il n'y a que cela."[2]

In this atmosphere of fear of popular aspirations the reactionary
philosophy of Maistre and Bonald found more disciples than ever
before.[3] A number of clergymen, such as the abbé Gorini, Mgr.
Gaume, and Auguste Nicolas, produced learned tracts tracing the
detested spirit of rationalism and secularism back to the Renaissance
and the Reformation.[4] A more distinguished exponent of traditional-

[1] Charles de Rémusat, "Du pessimisme politique," *Revue des Deux Mondes*, August 1,
1860, 729, 731.
[2] Auguste Romieu, *Le spectre rouge de 1852* (3d ed., Paris, 1851), 25–26, 43, 47, 63; see also
Henri Guillemin, *Le coup du deux décembre* (Paris, 1951), *passim* and Jean-Baptiste Duroselle,
Les débuts du catholicisme social en France (1822–1870) Paris, 1951), 483–487.
[3] Various works by Maistre and Bonald were re-edited or published for the first time
in the 1850's; see also the articles by Sainte-Beuve on the two authors in the *Causeries du
Lundi* (15 vols., Paris, 1852–62), IV, 192–216, 427–449.
[4] Jean-Marie-Sauveur Gorini, *Défense de l'Eglise contre les erreurs historiques de MM. Guizot,
Augustin et Amédée Thierry, Michelet, Ampère, Quinet, Fauriel et H. Martin* (3 vols., Paris, 1853);

ism, the country gentleman Antoine Blanc de Saint-Bonnet, believed that Europe was rushing to its irrevocable ruin. Like other conservatives, he blamed the collapse of civilization on the rise of individualism as manifested in the French Revolution and opposed liberalism as "the most terrible illusion that [had] ever taken possession of man's mind."[1]

The ultraconservative point of view found its most effective propagandist in the journalist Louis Veuillot, who was the first to use the power of the popular press in the battle against democracy and free thought. In his newspaper *l'Univers*, terms like "liberté," "science," and "progrès" were characterized as "des mèches incendiaires qu'on trouve dans toutes les débris des sociétés qui font explosion."[2] An unqualified opponent of modern civilization, Veuillot vented his disgust with the modernized French capital, its rectangular streets, horrible smells, corrupt theater, absurd science, filthy entertainment, and decadent art and literature.[3] On intimate terms with Pope Pius IX, this ultramontanist might be held partially responsible for the uncompromising stand that the Roman pontiff took against the forces of "progress, liberalism, and modern civilization" in his *Syllabus of Errors* (1864).[4]

Another prominent exponent of Catholic conservatism was the brilliant theorist of Dandyism, Barbey d'Aurevilly. Although capable of recognizing talent among his opponents and admitting the mediocrity of many of his fellow Catholics, he was as doctrinaire as Veuillot in indicting contemporary taste and morals. The great polemicist started his campaign against the modern spirit with his *Prophetès du passé* (1851), in which he presented the leaders of the theocratic schools as the "Lay Church Fathers" and pointed to the accuracy of their pessimistic predictions. As a gallant admirer of Old France, he fought a life-long battle against the forces of the modern world: against the principles of the French Revolution as well as against the modernistic views of German writers like Hegel and Goethe.[5]

Jean-Joseph Gaume, *La Révolution. Recherches sur l'origine et la propagation du mal en Europe depuis la Renaissance* (Paris, 1856–59); Auguste Nicolas, *Du Protestantisme et des autres hérésies dans leur rapport avec le socialisme* (Paris, 1852).

[1] Charlotte T. Muret, *French Royalist Doctrines Since the Revolution* (New York, 1933), 155–156.

[2] E. A. Segretain in *L'Univers*, Dec. 25, 1857.

[3] *Les odeurs de Paris* (Paris, 1866).

[4] E. E. Y. Hales, *Pio Nono. A Study in European Politics and Religion in the Nineteenth Century* (New York, 1954), 257.

[5] Besides the *Prophètes du passé* (Paris, 1851), Barbey d'Aurevilly's articles in his *Philosophes et écrivains religieux* (1861) serve as a good introduction into his traditionalist philos-

Contemporary Frenchmen who served as the favorite targets of the conservative censors were a number of prominent agnostics impressed by the scholarship and the philosophy of modern Germany. Ernest Renan became the *bête noire* of the Catholic press after the publication of his *Vie de Jésus* (1863).[1] One of his most bitter critics, the mystic Ernest Hello, carried Catholic anxiety to the point of prophesying the imminent end of the world. In his impatient expectation of a universal conflagration, he exclaimed: "Je me demande ce qu'elle attend."[2]

Even moderate Catholics were alarmed by the rising anticlerical and positivist spirit of the period. The liberal-minded Mgr Dupanloup vehemently attacked the distinguished philologist and philosopher Emile Littré when the latter ventured to apply for membership in the Académie française; in 1867 he published a pamphlet explaining the many disasters that had recently struck the world (such as wars, cholera, inundations) as a form of divine chastisement for the progress of atheism and the infringements on the temporal power of the papacy.[3]

The alarm felt by many "liberal" Catholics found its best expression in Claude Marie Raudot's *La décadence de la France* (1850), which had the merit of presenting the first systematic analysis of various symptoms of social and political disorganization from which, it was held, French society was suffering. The author emphasized a number of factors greatly undermining the strength of France: the revolutionary sentiment, the slow growth of the population, the decline of the merchant marine, the backwardness of agriculture, the weakening of the armed forces, the deterioration of the physique, and the increase in criminality. He granted that France had made some progress in various fields but asserted that, as other nations had advanced more rapidly, the French position in the world had suffered. He saw the highly centralized form of government as one of the main reasons for the unsatisfactory state of the nation and expected a recovery not from further industrialization or more political freedom, but solely from a return to the old principles of society. In spite of its obvious political bias Raudot's treatise was one of the best documented and most balanced discussions published on the problem during this period. It was widely read and commented upon at the

ophy of history; see also P. J. Yarrow, *La pensée politique et religieuse de Barbey d'Aurevilly* (Genève, 1961), esp. 200–215.

[1] Cf. Antoine Albalat, *La vie de Jésus d'Ernest Renan* (Paris, 1933) ch. IV.

[2] Vulliaud, *op. cit.*, 179; cf. Albert Guérard, *French Prophets of Yesterday: a Study of Religious Thought under the Second Empire* (London, 1913), 64–67.

[3] Félix-Antoine Dupanloup, *L'athéisme et le présent péril social* (Paris, 1866) and *Les malheurs et les signes du temps* (Paris, 1866); cf. J. Maurain, *La politique ecclésiastique du Second Empire* (Paris, 1930), 757.

time, but it was not written with enough literary talent to stir public opinion.[1]

Other conservative authors attempted to place their reactionary philosophy on a modern, scientific basis. The most successful effort in this direction was undertaken by the well-known sociologist Frédéric Le Play, a rejuvenated, progressive and scientific Bonald, as he has been called.[2] His interpretation of history as presented in *La réforme sociale* (1864) was not, like that of the theocrats, based on belief in a Divine Providence but instead on an analysis of social institutions, especially that of the family. Believing in the alternation of progress and decline rather than in any unilinear development, Le Play warned his complacent compatriots that despite material prosperity and regained international preponderance France continued to be undermined by the erroneous principles of 1789. Like many conservatives and liberals of the nineteenth century, he favored decentralization of government and held the old regime partly responsible for the destruction of local autonomy. The poison, according to Le Play, had started to penetrate the French social system as early as 1661 when the monarchy had triumphed over the French aristocracy. He preached a moral reform based on the Ten Commandments but privately expressed the opinion that a catastrophe was necessary – and inevitable – to cure the national corruption.[3]

A great admirer of English society, Le Play lacked the supreme confidence of the theocrats in the mission of the French people. But in most of his work he presented sociological evidence in favor of the principles of the traditionalist school: respect for social hierarchy and authority, sacredness of family ties, the superiority of the moral principles of Christianity. Opposed to moral and intellectual emancipation of the masses, his system aimed at what Proudhon called "the scientific organization of servitude."[4]

An even more daring attempt to lend the reactionary point of view scientific prestige was made by Comte Arthur de Gobineau, whose well-known *Essai sur l'inégalité des races humaines* (1853–55) was

---

[1] Claude-Marie Raudot, *De la décadence de la France* (4th ed., Paris, 1850); cf. *idem, De la grandeur possible de la France faisant suite a la Décadence de la France* (Paris, 1951); A Mothéré, *Réponse à l'ouvrage de M. Raudot* (Paris, 1850); Ch. Coquelin, "De la prétendue décadence de la France et de l'Angleterre et des ouvrages de MM. Raudot et Ledru-Rollin," *Journal des économistes*, Aug. 15, 1850, 56–58.

[2] Sainte-Beuve, *Nouveaux Lundis* IX, 180.

[3] Frédéric Le Play, *La réforme sociale en France déduite de l'observation comparée des peuples européens* (6th ed., Tours, 1878), I, 92–93, 190; IV, 382; Louis Thomas, *Frédéric Le Play, 1806–1882* (Paris, 1953), 8, 41, 63.

[4] Leroy, *Histoire des idées sociales*, III, 278.

partially written with the purpose to explain the alleged retrogression of France. Rejecting all theories which held moral corruption, religious fanaticism, economic decline, or certain political institutions responsible for the fall of nations, Gobineau came to the conclusion that the sole reason should be seen in racial decay resulting from the mixture of superior races with inferior ones. He was convinced that all that was great, noble, and creative in the world was due to one race, the so-called Aryan race. Applied to France, this theory accounted for the greatness of the country in the past by the dominant position held by Teutonic invaders and explained its gradual decline by the increasingly important role which inferior Celtic and Roman racial stock of Southern France had played since the accession of Henry of Navarre. As a result, the highly centralized form of government, Roman in origin, had gradually broken the influence of the feudal aristocracy and with the Revolution of 1789 the anarchistic South had taken its full revenge.[1] In his own days, Gobineau held, the superior race was obliterated in France to a larger degree than in any other European country, and he predicted that France had only thirty years more to live. The supposedly superior Aryan race was, according to Gobineau, best preserved in England, the only nation that therefore still had a future.[2] Gobineau's racial theories went largely unnoticed in France during his life time but became later on, especially in Germany, the starting point for many speculations on Nordic superiority and Latin degeneration.

II

French reactionaries had been raising their warning voices since the outbreak of the Revolution of 1789, and the events of 1848 and the following years merely intensified their apprehensions. Among liberal intellectuals, on the other hand, pessimism was a new phenomenon – until 1848 most of them had believed in progress and looked upon the political development of their country with confidence.

After 1848 many began to doubt whether free institutions had any future. The anxiety with which they viewed the course of events was

---

[1] Joseph-Arthur de Gobineau, *Essai sur l'inégalité des races humaines* (Paris, 1853–55), I, *passim*, esp. p. 70; cf. Maurice Lange, *Le Comte Arthur de Gobineau* (Strasbourg, 1924).

[2] Gobineau to Alexis de Tocqueville, Nov. 29, 1956, Tocqueville, *Œuvres complètes*, ed. J. P. Mayer, vol. IX (Paris, 1959), 269–275; cf. *ibid.*, 28–33; Michel Mohrt, *Les intellectuels devant la défaite de 1870*, 149; Melvin Richter, "A Debate on Race. The Tocqueville-Gobineau Correspondence," *Commentary*, XXV (1958), 151–160.

perhaps best expressed by Tocqueville; "Ce qui est clair pour moi," he wrote to a friend in 1850, "c'est ce qu'on s'est trompé depuis soixante ans en croyant voir le *bout* de la révolution . . . Il est évident aujourd'hui que le flot continue à marcher, que la mer monte . . . Ce n'est pas d'une modification, mais d'une transformation du corps social qu'il s'agit . . . On sent que l'ancien monde finit: mais quel sera le nouveau? Les plus grands esprits de ce temps ne sont pas . . . en état de le dire . . ."[1]

In addition to fear of socialism and democracy, rancor about the loss of position and influence explains the gloomy views of many liberals. Thus Victor Cousin, who had served as the official philosopher of the July Monarchy, considered the February Revolution a horrible crime that might lead to the dismemberment of France.[2] Guizot attacked the idolatry of the democratic and republican form of government as the major evil of French society, and another former prime minister, the Duc de Broglie, believed that the end of society was at hand. [3]

Some liberals lost their former admiration for the French Revolution now characterized by a "liberal" Catholic, the comte de Montalembert, as "une sanglante inutilité."[4] A more substantiated attack against the principles of French Revolution was launched by the literary critic Emile Montégut in a number of articles in the *Revue des Deux Mondes* of 1848, 1849, and 1850. Although Montégut recognized that the Revolution had brought an end to many abuses, he criticized it for its addiction to utopianism: "C'est de là que datent tous nos malheurs. Le temps approche où la révolution française sera jugée tout autrement qu'on ne l'a fait jusqu'à présent." According to Montégut, the moral malady of his century lay in the predominance of the human principle or the glorification of mankind by itself. He called the pursuit of material welfare the great plague of his time and urged France, if she wanted to be saved, to renounce her chimeras and to give up her ambition to work for humanity. Perhaps no other Frenchman of the period better expressed the mood of disillusionment following the Revolution of 1848: "Nous avons perdu plus d'une illusion. Chaque pas que nous faisons est un désenchantement, chaque

[1] Letter to Eugène Stoffels, April 28, 1850, Tocqueville, *Œuvres complètes* (Paris, 1861–66), V, 460–461; cf. *idem*, *Souvenirs*, 83–84.
[2] Ernest Renan, *La réforme intellectuelle et morale de la France* (1871) in *Œuvres complètes*, I, 342.
[3] Tocqueville, *Souvenirs*, 87; François Guizot, *De la démocratie en France* (Paris, 1849).
[4] Maurain, *op. cit.*, 24.

parole que nous prononçons un regret. Mais je crains que nous léguions aux générations qui suivront des enseignements encore plus terribles. Les derniers voiles tomberont, les dernières illusions seront déchirées, et peut-être que d'ici à un siècle les hommes assisteront à un spectacle dont les annales du monde n'offrent pas d'example."[1]

Under the Second Empire the free expression of critical comments on the state of France was greatly hampered by a strict censorship. But liberals were in a more favorable position than Frenchmen of other political persuasions, for they controlled some highly respectable publications such as the *Revue des Deux Mondes* and the *Journal des débats*, which the government did not dare to suppress, and could also voice their opinion in another liberal stronghold, the Académie française. During the first years of Napoleon III's rule it was not much more than pinpricks which they administered, but toward its end, when the regime was tottering, liberal criticism became devastating. At that time the older liberal generation of the July Monarchy was joined by young intellectuals defending the cause of freedom with more modern ideas.

A talented spokesman of this new generation of liberals, Prévost-Paradol, in his essay *La France nouvelle* (1868), gave an analysis of the existing decadence and made some suggestions for reform. Accusing democracy of leading to anarchy and causing all decent people to turn in disgust from public affairs, he felt that French history since 1789 contained more miserable weaknesses and catastrophes than the history of any other period. Since the decline of religious sentiment, man was no longer inclined to subordinate his private interests to public welfare out of any other motive than "point of honor", and this motive, he feared, was being undermined by the notion that success is all-important and justifies everything. He urged his fellow countrymen to give up their predilection for utopias and to imitate instead the English in their respect for tradition and political compromise.

Viewing the position of France among the great powers, he pointed out that France was gradually falling behind other nations in number of inhabitants and that territorial expansion was required if total decadence was to be avoided. Prévost-Paradol reminded his readers of the historical law that all nations have in turn their periods of growth,

[1] Emile Montégut, "Lettres sur les symptômes du temps," *Revue des Deux Mondes*, April 15, May 1, and July 1, 1848; and esp.: "De la maladie morale du XIXe siècle," *Ibid.*, Aug. 15, 1849, pp. 675, 677, 682, 685; "La première moitié du XIXe siècle," *ibid.*, Febr. 1, 1850, p. 387, 396; cf. R. A. Lochore, *History of the Idea of Civilization in France (1830–1870)* (Bonn, 1935), 125; Pierre Muenier, *Emile Montégut* (Paris, 1925).

maturity, decadence, and death. He held a contest between France and Germany inevitable and a French defeat highly probable. "Il n'y a point de milieu," was his pessimistic comment, "pour une nation qui a connu la grandeur et la gloire entre le maintien de son ancien prestige et la complète impuissance."[1]

Ernest Renan and Hippolyte Taine, the two most brilliant representatives of this younger generation, fully shared the liberal misgivings about the state of their country. Although detested by conservatives as subversive critics of orthodox Christianity they were far from radical in their political philosophy.

In 1848 Renan's views were still highly utopian and his *Avenir de la science* (written in 1848, but not published until 1890) can be regarded as the purest and most intelligent expression of the exalted idealism of the early nineteenth century. At that time he declared: "Il n'y a pas de décadence au point de vue de l'humanité. Décadence est un mot qu'il faut définitivement bannir de l'histoire." Renan attributed to science the leading role in solving man's eternal problems: "Organiser scientifiquement l'humanité, tel est le dernier mot de la science moderne, telle est son audacieuse, mais légitime prétention."[2]

Without ever completely renouncing his youthful idealism and confidence in science, Renan, like so many other young intellectuals of his time, lost his naive faith in the future. "La crise de 1848," wrote Renan later on, "nous émut profondément... elle fut, pour les esprits jeunes et actifs, comme la chute d'un rideau qui dissimulait l'horizon."[3] As early as 1849, contrary to the ideas that he had expressed a few months earlier, he spoke of "la décadence générale" of the civilization of his time. Under the Second Empire Renan further developed his critical views of the development of modern France, tracing its evils back to the late Middle Ages when the ideals of freedom and honor introduced into France by the Germanic tribes had been destroyed by unscrupulous kings like Philip the Fair and

[1] Lucien Anatole Prévost-Paradol, *La France nouvelle* (Paris, 1868) esp. part. III; on Prévost-Paradol, see the authoritative work by Pierre Guiral, *Prévost-Paradol (1829–1870): pensée et action d'un libéral sous le Second Empire* (Paris, 1955). Another liberal, Louis Rambaud had even less hope for a regeneration of France; in his *Testament d'un Latin*, published in 1872, but written before the Franco-Prussian war, this admirer of Tocqueville and Prévost-Paradol asserted that the French lacked any appreciation of political freedom and that nations without liberty were doomed in the modern world. The future, he stated, would belong not to the French, who were proudly enjoying the charms peculiar to a decadent society, but to the freedom-loving, English-speaking nations of the world.

[2] Renan, "Réflexions sur l'état des esprits," (1849) *Œuvres complètes*, I, 231; also in *Avenir de la science* in *Œuvres complètes*, III, 757.

[3] *Souvenirs d'enfance et de jeunesse* in *Œuvres complètes*, II, 889.

Louis XI. He also denounced "the revolutionary philosophy, great and liberating as it was," because it contained "the hidden poison of belief in violence" and was based on a materialistic conception of property and a neglect of individual rights.[1]

In referring to the division of his nation into revolutionaries and conservatives, each unwilling to compromise, Renan reminded his readers of the old Hebrew legend that Rebecca, feeling the two children she was bearing struggling within her, was told on inquiring of the Lord that two nations were struggling within her womb: "Dans le sein de notre pays comme dans celui de Rebecca, se battent deux peuples dont l'un veut étouffer l'autre."[2]

Renan's deepest concern was with the supposed decline in spiritual values. He asserted that France was the least religious, though the most orthodox nation in the world and had become gravely ill by seeking to create a perfect kingdom in this world. He was haunted by the possible triumph of "la sottise, contente d'elle-même, s'épanouissant à son aise au soleil et procédant sans regrets aux funérailles du génie." "Notre siècle," he sighed, "ne va ni vers le bien, ni vers le mal; il va vers le médiocre."[3]

Unlike Renan, Hippolyte Taine never suffered from exaggerated illusions about the perfectibility of mankind. His pessimism was largely temperamental and was merely strengthened and not created by the political events of his time.[4] In *La vie et opinions de M. Frédéric Thomas Graindorge*, a fictional report on French society by a Frenchman who, after having made his fortune in the United States, returned to his country. Taine bitterly assailed the materialistic and hedonistic mentality prevailing in the 1860's, which he contrasted with the idealism of an earlier generation. Like many other writers of his time, he drew ominous comparisons between contemporary Paris and the corrupt societies of ancient Rome and Alexandria.[5] At the end of the Second Empire, he seemed to have lost all confidence in his native country: "Ceux qui veulent chez nous retrouver l'individu oublient que tout ceci est poussière. En dehors du fonctionnaire nous n'avons

[1] "Reflexions sur l'état des esprits," *Œuvres complètes*, I, 218; "La Farce de Patelin," (1856), *ibidem*, II, 211–212.

[2] *Questions contemporaines* (1868), preface in *Œuvres complètes*, I, 27.

[3] "Réflexions sur l'état des esprits," *Œuvres complètes*, I, 228; "La poésie de l'exposition," (1855), *ibid.*, II, 239ff.

[4] Cf. R. Stadelmann, "Taine und das Problem des geschichtlichen Verfalls," *Historische Zeitschrift*, CLXVII (1943), 116–135.

[5] Cf. Carter, *The Idea of Decadence*, 15, 51–55, 128; in 1857, however, Taine pointed out that France was in a much better position than Rome in its period of decline; cf. his *Essais de critique et d'histoire* (11th ed., Paris, 1908), 280.

plus d'éléments d'association, ni d'organisation. A mon avis notre rôle est fini, du moins provisoirement, l'avenir est à la Prusse, à l'Amérique et à l'Angleterre."[1]

The liberals did not go so far as the reactionaries in their despair of modern civilization. Whereas the latter considered modern science and philosophy as the handmaidens of the dangerous revolutionary spirit, the liberals blamed the weakness of the country largely on the obscurantism of the clergy and the backwardness of France's educational system. Moreover, criticizing the Revolution for its methods, rather than for its principles, and basing their opposition to a centralized powerful state on a philosophy of freedom, they did not fully renounce a progressive philosophy. Even one of the most pessimistic liberals, Tocqueville, refused to accept the fatalistic philosophy of his friend Gobineau and rejected the analogy between the state of France and that of the declining Roman Empire: "Nous ne sommes pas une nation décrépite, mais une nation fatiguée et effrayée; mais nous valons mieux que notre destinée actuelle."[2]

Henri de Ferron's *Théorie du progrès* (1867) can be considered a characteristic expression of the compound of hope and despair that pervaded most liberal thought of this period. Influenced by the comte de Saint-Simon, Ferron disagreed with those of his contemporaries who considered the idea of progress a pure illusion. On the other hand, as a great admirer of Benjamin Constant, Madame de Staël, John Stuart Mill, and Tocqueville, he criticized Saint-Simon for believing that the state should play a major role in improving existing conditions.[3] Political freedom was, according to him, the only road to progress. For this reason he felt that in France the progressive movement of modern civilization had come to a standstill with the triumph of royal absolutism in the sixteenth century. The French Revolution represented to him the beginning of a great crisis rather than a definite turn for the better. He believed that in his time the Latin races, in contrast to the Anglo-Saxons and the Germans, were in a state of decadence or, at least, of stagnation.[4] Ferron was one of the first French writers to interpret the course of history in Darwinian terms: "Si l'on y prend garde, la race saxonne, fortifiée par le régime

---

[1] Hippolyte Taine, *Sa vie et sa correspondance* (4 vols., Paris, 1901–1908), II, 332ff.; cf. *idem, Essais de critique et d'histoire*, 294.

[2] Tocqueville to G. de Beaumont, Feb. 27, 1858, *Œuvres complètes*, VII, 487ff.

[3] Henri de Ferron, *Théorie du progrès* (2 vols., Paris, 1867), I, 382, 300, 304.

[4] *Ibid.*, I, 16; II, 364, 374, 437–439.

de la liberté, remplacera les autres races du globe, en vertu du loi de Darwin sur la concurrence vitale."[1]

Unlike most traditionalists, French liberals of this period highly admired the political institutions or cultural achievements of Protestant countries. Almost all liberals were fervent Anglophiles. The Catholic Montalembert was sentenced to a month's imprisonment for his praise of the English constitution, and Renan pointed out that England, without resorting to a revolution, had made more progress in establishing political freedom than had France, which had passed through ten revolutions during the last century.[2] The liberal economist Louis-Gabriel Léonce de Lavergne called England "cette puissance colossale, la plus grande que le monde ait jamais vue, sans en excepter l'Empire romain . . ."[3] The conservative argument that free institutions were only suited to England where they had grown gradually and should not be copied in countries with different political traditions, was refuted by Laboulaye, who pointed to the satisfactory operation of the parliamentary form of government in Belgium, Switzerland, and the Scandinavian countries and who denied that the French were less politically mature than other western nations.[4]

Some of these Anglophiles became the first French advocates of "individualism" a term which, until this time, had been almost exclusively used in a pejorative sense. Whereas prior to the Revolution of 1848 England had been widely detested as the stronghold of modern "individualism," it now began to be admired for exactly the same reason. The economist Dupont-White, it is true, attempted to justify what he called the anti-individualistic, centralistic, and sociable tradition of the French nation, but most censors of the imperial government felt that France needed more of the English and American brand of individualism and that only in this way could an end be made to the system of administrative despotism by which France had been ruled since the days of Louis XIV.[5]

The criticism of France that was implied in the glorification of England was also inferred in the admiration for other foreign countries.

[1] *Ibid.*, II, 448–449.

[2] J. E. C. Bodley, *France* (2d ed., London, 1899); Ernest Renan, *Œuvres complètes*, II, 211–212; cf. Guiral, *op. cit.*, 497.

[3] Louis-Gabriel Léonce G. de Lavergne, "De l'accord de l'économie politique et de la religion," *Revue des Deux Mondes*, sec. periode, vol. XLII (Nov. 15, 1862).

[4] Édouard de Laboulaye, *Le parti libéral, son programme et son avenir* (Paris, 1863).

[5] Charles B. Dupont-White, "De l'esprit des races: l'esprit individualiste et l'esprit centraliste," *Revue des Deux Mondes*, sec. per., vol. XL (Aug. 15, 1862), 871–914; Ernest Renan, *Philosophie de l'histoire contemporaine* (1859) in *Œuvres complètes*, I, 35; Ferron, *op. cit.*, I, 33, 307ff., 329–330, 387–388.

Some liberals went much farther than Tocqueville in praising the political institutions of the United States. Laboulaye's *Paris en Amérique* (1863), a fictional portrayal of the political, religious, and educational freedom of the United States, was at the same time a bitter satire on the despotic centralization of the French government and French pretensions to guide the rest of humanity.[1] Similarly, the greatness of German civilization was extolled by many French liberals, who were convinced that Germany had achieved the same degree of excellence in the cultural fields as England or America in political organization. Germany, in the words of the historian Gabriel Monod, was "cette seconde patrie pour tous les hommes qui étudient et qui pensent."[2] Thus Renan was a staunch advocate of Franco-German cooperation, feeling that France had almost everything to learn from her Eastern neighbor in the way of scholarship, religious liberalism and higher education.[3] Taine was also profoundly impressed by the achievements of German intellectuals: "Au premier aspect, on admire surtout la minutie de leur attention, l'énormité de leur savoir, leur talent d'abstraire, leur aptitude de métaphysique pour les vues d'ensemble. Au second regard, on remarque que si ces facultés ont pu donner leurs fruits c'est que la conscience, la patience, l'abnégation, la sobriété, une quantité de vertus morales y étaient jointes . . ."[4] At least among an elite of French intellectuals it was recognized that during the last two centuries the Germanic element had been in progress and the Romance element losing ground on all sides.[5]

III

The outbreak of the Revolution of 1848 was greeted with enormous enthusiasm by the French Left. The revolutionary days were described by the republican Eugène Pelletan as "le plus grand événement qui ait ébranlé les âmes depuis le jour où le Christ en penchant la tête

[1] Edouard de Laboulaye, *Paris en Amérique* (Paris, 1863); another liberal inspired by the American dream, the comte Agénor de Gasparin, expressed his views in *Les Etats-Unis en 1861: un grand peuple qui se relève* (Paris, 1861); other liberals, however, continued to regard England as the paragon of political wisdom; cf. Guiral, *op. cit.*, 494.

[2] Gabriel Monod, *Allemands et Français* (Paris, 1872), 138.

[3] Renan, "L'instruction supérieure en France," (1864), *Œuvres complètes*, I, 69–97; cf. *ibid.*, I, 14, 23.

[4] Quoted in V. Giraud, *Essai sur Taine, son œuvre et son influence* (Paris, 1912), 241; cf. Stadelmann, *loc. cit.*, 134–135. See also Taine, *Histoire de la littérature anglaise* (5 vols., Paris, 1911), V, 243ff.: "De 1780 à 1830 l'Allemagne a produit toutes les idées de notre âge historique et pendant un siècle, peut-être, notre grande affaire sera de les repenser."

[5] Philarète Chasles, *Études sur l'Allemagne* (2 vols., Paris, 1854–61), I, 5; cf. Saint-René Taillandier, *Histoire et philosophie religieuse* (Paris, 1860).

sur la croix, brisa le vieux monde."[1] The old Jacobin dream of liberating all oppressed European peoples by armed French intervention once again ran high. "Oui, je veux la guerre," declared the representative Joly in the National Assembly, "je la veux plutôt que l'avilissement de mon pays."[2]

The triumph of the forces of reaction in France as well as elsewhere in Europe provoked a bitter disillusionment and forced the Left to revise their naive faith in the democratic instincts of the French people and their illusions as to a speedy regeneration of mankind. Many of the republican leaders, heartbroken, withdrew from the public scene and admitted the error of their youthful idealism. Michelet and George Sand uttered some harsh words about the common people whom they had once glorified.[3] Quinet, who had declared in 1848 that "right, truth, freedom, and brotherhood are the true kings of the earth, the only rulers whom no physical force can overthrow," now wrote: "Idolatry is no longer permissible ... Away with historical fetishes, Caesar or Robespierre, away with the glorification of the French people." "J'ai vu clairement depuis seize ans," he wrote a friend in 1867, "qu'il n'y a rien à attendre de cette nation pourrie pour plusieurs générations."[4] In 1856, Lamartine shocked many of his readers by declaring that not the doctrine of the indefinite perfectibility of mankind, but the old belief in primeval perfection and the fall of man was still the most satisfactory premise upon which to construct a philosophy of history.[5] Numerous leftist publicists, moreover, decried the immorality and corruption of the Second Empire. Thus Eugène Pelletan, in his *Nouvelle Babylone* (1862), contrasted the literary and political idealism that had characterized Parisian society in the 1830's with the suppression of all talent and the moral degradation that prevailed in the French capital under the reign of Napoleon III; in eloquent passages he castigated the chase for money and public offices, the venality of the press, the immorality of literature, and the unrestrained speculation on the stock market.[6]

---

[1] Eugène Pelletan, *Histoire des trois journées de février 1848* (Paris, 1848).

[2] Duveau, *Histoire du peuple français de 1848 à nos jours*, 284ff.; cf. Robert Schnerb, *Ledru-Rollin* (Paris, 1948), 44–46.

[3] M. Leroy, *op. cit.*, III, 67; Irving Babbitt, *Rousseau and Romanticism* (Meridian Books, New York, 1955), 258, quoting George Sand's characterization of humanity as "a large number of knaves, a very large number of lunatics, and an immense number of fools."

[4] H. Monin, "Étude critique sur le texte des *Lettres d'exil* d'Edgar Quinet," *Revue d'histoire littéraire de la France* XV (1908), 484; Albert Guérard, *op. cit.*, 95.

[5] Lamartine, *Cours familier de littérature*, I (Paris, 1856), 161–239; cf. É. Petit, *Lettres à Lamartine. Le monde marche* (Paris, 1857); Etienne Vacherot, "La doctrine de progrès," *Revue de Paris*, XXXIII (1856), 544–559.

[6] Cf. Edouard Petit, *Eugène Pelletan, 1818–1884* (Paris, n.d.), 79–87.

Yet most French leftists, though disappointed in the outcome of the Revolution of 1848 and concerned about France's immediate future, did not recant their belief in eventual progress. Quinet and Michelet, for example, continued to be convinced that mankind was heading for a glorious future, even if they now based their confidence more on the progress of science than on the moral instincts of the common people.[1] How dogmatically the idea of progress was accepted by the French Left might be illustrated by the statements of two diverse, but each in their own way highly representative figures: Victor Hugo declared that "l'éclosion prochaine du bien-être universel est un phénomène divinement fatal,"[2] and Pierre Larousse, the editor of the well-known encyclopedia named after him, gave the following comment in article "Progrès:" "De notre temps, si l'on en excepte des esprits chagrins ou aveugles, absolument ignorants d'histoire ou qui rêvent d'impossibles retours vers un passé définitivement enterré, la croyance universelle est que le progrès est la loi même de la marche du genre humain."[3]

It was especially among the younger generation of French republicans and socialists that a dogmatic belief in progress remained strong.[4] Eugène Pelletan concluded his denunciations of the morals of "modern Babylon" with the words: "J'aime mon siècle, . . . je l'admire . . . Je ne justifie pas le XIXe siècle, je fais mieux, je le glorifie. C'est un siècle prophète. . . . Je ne cherche pas à décourager la France, mais bien à la rappeler à l'œuvre du siècle. . . . Qu'elle rentre en elle-même, et bientôt elle reprendra la tête de la colonne."[5] In name of his generation he rejected "l'interdit que Lamartine jetait du haut de son génie à la marche incessante de l'humanité." The republican philosopher Etienne Vacherot likewise took exception to Lamartine's pessimism: "Nous tenons au dogme du progrès comme un croyant tient à sa foi.

[1] Edgar Quinet, *La création* (Paris, 1870); cf. Tronchon, *Romantisme et préromantisme* 69; Charles Renouvier, *Philosophie analytique de l'histoire* (4 vols., Paris, 1896–97), IV, 478.

[2] Victor Hugo, *Les misérables* (1862), part. 4, VIII, 4; *idem. La légende des siècles* (largely written before 1859), esp. "Plein ciel"; cf. Charles Renouvier, *Victor Hugo, le philosophe* (2d ed., Paris, 1912), 139ff.

[3] Pierre Larousse *Grand dictionnaire universel du XIXe siècle* (Paris, 1867–78), XIII, 225; cf. *ibid.*, I, lxxiv; for other contemporary statements on the universality of the idea of progress see: P. J. Proudhon⸍ *De la justice dans la Révolution et dans l'Église* in *Œuvres complètes* (new ed. Paris, 1923–   ), XI, 511; Ferron, *Théorie du progrès*, I, 162–165, 300.

[4] Cf. M. Dessal, *Charles Delescluze, 1809–1871, un révolutionnaire jacobin* (Paris, 1952); Allain-Targé, *La République sous l'Empire*, ed. S. de La Porte (Paris, 1939); Henri Peyre, *Louis Ménard (1822–1901)* New Haven, 1932), 97, 198; Bodley, *France*, 31.

[5] Eugène Pelletan, *Lettres à Lamartine. Le monde marche* (Paris, 1857) and *La profession de foi du dix-neuvième siècle* (Paris, 1852).

Personne ne nous arrachera. C'est la première vérité de notre religion."[1] Although many young republicans proclaimed the "decadence" of France, they can be suspected of using the term as a polemical weapon against a detested regime. This was, for example, the case with the notorious pamphleteer Henri de Rochefort in his satirical sketches, published under the title Les Français de la décadence (1866). Likewise the republican journalist Edouard Lockroy, in his A bas le progrès (1870), did not so much attack the belief in progress as the complacent statements made by the government officials about the progress achieved under the imperial regime.

Most of the younger republicans, it is true, no longer placed their confidence in high moral aspirations but expected their dreams to be realized as a result of the advance of science and industry. They impressed their elders as materialists. "La nouvelle génération," wrote Mazzini to Quinet in 1869, "n'a pas de foi, elle a des opinions. Elle renie Dieu, l'immortalité, l'amour, promesse eternelle, ... la croyance dans une loi providentielle intelligente, tout ce qu'il y a de bon, de grand, de beau, de saint dans le monde, toute une héroïque tradition de grands penseurs religieux, depuis Prométhée jusqu'au Christ, depuis Socrate jusqu'à Kepler, pour s'agenouiller devant Comte, Büchner et Moleschott."[2] The younger generation, in their turn, looked upon the democratic leaders of the Revolution of 1848 as old fogeys ("vieilles barbes") and reproached them for their religiosity and moral declamations. The men of 1848, according to one of the younger republicans, Auguste Vermorel, had "perdu, trahi, déshonoré, étouffé, égorgé la République, inaugurée magnanimement et glorieusement par le peuple ... tous leurs actes ont été des crimes contre la démocratie et la liberté."[3]

Although some of the younger republicans were affected by the frivolous and cynical spirit of the Second Empire, most of them were more naively idealistic than they were willing to admit. "Laissez-nous fonder la République," exclaimed Eugène Pelletan, "et vous verrez comment nous moraliserons la France."[4] Many of them still believed in the superiority of the French nation and its universal mission,[5] rejecting only the Jacobin view, still so strong in 1848, that it was

[1] Étienne Vacherot, "La doctrine de progrès," Revue de Paris, XXXIII (1856), 544–559; idem, Essais de philosophie critique (Paris, 1864), 415ff., 448.

[2] Giuseppe Mazzini, Scritti editi ed inediti, vol. LXXXVIII (Imola, 1940), 79ff.

[3] J. Tchernoff, Le parti républicain au coup d'État et sous le Second Empire (Paris, 1906), 364; cf. Georges Weill, Histoire du parti républicain en France (new ed., Paris, 1928), 359–362.

[4] Bodley, op. cit., 497.

[5] Lochore, op. cit., 159–161, 166, 168.

part of this mission to make war on the despots of Europe. They expected improvement rather from international cooperation and sought contact with kindred minds in other countries, organizing conferences to prevent the outbreak of war and to hasten the establishment of the social republic. Many of them were under the illusion that aggressive nationalism and wars belonged to the past, and became critical of the old French dream of military glory and territorial aggrandizement. The old nationalism and militarism of the French Left had not yet died out (as the war of 1870 was to prove), but pacifism greatly increased in strength, partly as a form of opposition against a supposedly militaristic government.[1]

In other words, the regenerationist version of the idea of decadence, combining utter pessimism as to the state of existing society with great illusions concerning the future, persisted in considerable vigor among the French Left of the period. It found perhaps its best expression in the political philosophy of Proudhon. On many occasions this leading socialist theorist of the Second Empire voiced his bitter disillusionment with the French nation. He confessed in 1862 that he no longer believed in France: "Son rôle est fini. C'est une nation prostituée; elle est le foyer de toutes les corruptions qui rouillent le vieux monde, et comme elle a tenu le drapeau de la liberté et du droit, elle porte aujourd'hui l'étandard de la dissolution universelle. La France en est aujourd'hui où était l'Espagne après Philippe II: elle déchoit depuis 1830; aujourd'hui sa décadence marche au pas accéléré: conscience, intelligence, caractère, tout périt en elle."[2] "Est-ce que vous comptez sur l'énergie française?" he asked Michelet in 1860, "Je serais sans doute heureux d'entendre un nouveau réveil; mais je n'y compte pas."[3] According to him, the French had some splendid qualities, but they were basically feminine, vain, and credulous, lacking in the elevated sentiments of civil and political freedom. He predicted continued decadence for at least two generations and held it very well possible that the Latin races would, within ten years, be definitively surpassed and, sooner or later, be dominated by the Germanic races.[4]

---

[1] Cf. Duveau, op. cit., 293; Georges Goyau, L'idée de patrie et l'humanitarisme: essai d'histoire française, 1866–1901 (Paris, 1913); Leroy. op. cit., III, 322ff.; Raoul Girardet, La société militaire dans la France contemporaine, 1815–1939 (Paris, 1953), 40.

[2] Proudhon, Correspondance, XI, 453; cf. ibid., XII, 48, and E. Dolléans, Proudhon (Paris, 1948), 7, 25, 275–276.

[3] Dolléans, op. cit., 392.

[4] Proudhon, De la pornocratie ou les femmes dans les temps modernes in Œuvres complètes, XI, 453–455; Proudhon to Langlois, April 2, 1862, Correspondance XII, 48; Alfred Damiron, Le Tiers parti sous le Second Empire (1863–1866) (Paris, 1887), 20–21.

Yet, at the same time, Proudhon repeatedly proclaimed his un-wavering and doctrinaire belief in universal and inevitable progress: "Ce qui domine dans toutes mes études, ce qui en fait le principe et la fin, le sommet et la base ... c'est que j'affirme résolument, irrévo-cablement, tout et partout, le *Progrès*. ... Tout ce que j'ai jamais écrit, tout ce que j'ai nié, affirmé, attaqué, combattu, je l'ai écrit, je l'ai nié ou affirmé au nom d'une unique idée: le Progrès."[1] Even France, though it would no longer take the lead in the progressive development of mankind, would be forced to follow the progress brought about in other countries of the world. Proudhon considered it blasphemy to believe that mankind had not improved upon the stupid, miserable and evil state in which it had been in the first days of creation.[2]

In his major work, *De la justice dans la Révolution et dans l'Eglise* (1858), he developed a philosophy of history which accepted progress as the natural state of mankind, but allowed for fairly protracted periods of decadence. He viewed history as a long conflict between the principle of Revolution embodying the forces of work, science, and justice on the one hand and extravagant idealism as preached by organ-ized religion on the other. He explained the decline of earlier civili-zations (in the Near East, Greece, Rome, and Spain) by the unwhole-some influence of mysticism. "C'est donc l'Eglise, ministre visible de l'idéal absolu et invisible, qui ne parle aux hommes que de l'abondance de son idéalisme, c'est l'Eglise que j'accuse... d'être la grande ma-nœuvrière de la mystification universelle, dont le dernier mot pro-noncé par elle-même, est déchéance."[3] Yet he never doubted that the constructive forces would ultimately prevail, and it was this conviction that saved him from despair: "Si tout ne me démontrait que la société est entrée dans une crise de régénération, qui sera longue et peut-être terrible, je croirais à l'irrévocable décadence et à la fin de la civili-sation."[4]

Proudhon was one of the few French republicans who did not look upon the Russian colossus as the greatest obstacle to the triumph of the forces of progress.[5] Another French anarchist, influenced by Proudhon, Ernest Cœurderoy, contrasted the barbarian but vigorous

---

[1] Proudhon, *Philosophie du progrès* in *Œuvres complètes*, XVI, 43, 45–46; cf. *Correspondance*, V, 247, 249.
[2] Proudhon, *De la justice dans la Révolution et dans l'Église* in *Œuvres complètes*, XI, 511.
[3] *Ibid.*, XI, 547.
[4] Letter to Miller in 1862, Edouard Dolléans, *op. cit.*, 275–276; cf. *ibid.*, 7, 25, 323.
[5] Proudhon, *Si les traités de 1815 ont cessé d'exister? Actes du future Congrès.* (Paris, 1863).

Slavic nations with the more highly civilized but decadent nations of the West. "Nous sommes les races femelles," he wrote in 1854, "pleines de grâce, de délicatesse et de sensualité voluptueuse. Ils sont les races mâles qui poursuivent les races femelles, les violent et les rendent fécondes."[1] He felt that it was not until after the total destruction of the present, corrupt society of the West by an invading Russian army that the cause of the Revolution would have a chance to triumph. A similar point of view was taken by a Slavophile professor of the Collège de France, Cyprien Robert, who expected that the Slavic world would play a major role in regenerating the decadent Old World, which manifestly lacked the strength to bring about its own renewal.[2]

Not all republicans retained this sanguine confidence in regeneration. The disillusionment with the Revolution of 1848 led a number of prominent men of letters to abandon all hopes for the future of civilization. At the beginning of the Revolution many leading authors had shared the popular illusion that utopia was around the corner and had offered their services to the new government. Even writers who were known for their indifference to public affairs like Charles Baudelaire, Gustave Flaubert, and Leconte de Lisle had been affected by the popular enthusiasm. But when this literary elite discovered that their hopes were unfounded, an intense pessimism overpowered them. Some of them withdrew into their ivory towers and vowed to devote their lives to their art alone. "Ne t'occupe de rien que de toi," was Flaubert's advice to a friend, "Laissons l'Empire marcher, fermons notre porte, montons au plus haut de notre tour d'ivoire, sur la dernière marche, la plus près du ciel. Il y fait froid quelquefois, n'est-ce pas? Mais qu'importe! On voit les étoiles briller clair et l'on n'entend pas les dindons."[3]

One of the most bitterly disappointed young republicans was the painter Paul Chenavard, who repeatedly told his friends that progress was an illusion, that faith in science and material prosperity was a fatal weakness, and that mankind was already on the downward path. This somber vision was illustrated in an ambitious series of paintings, called "Philosophie de l'histoire," which was intended to decorate the Panthéon, but which was rejected by the government. In this huge canvas, major episodes of the course of civilization were portrayed

---

[1] Ernest Coeurderoy, *Hurrah ! ! ! ou la révolution par les Cosaques* (Londres, 1854), 66.

[2] Cyprien Robert, *Le monde slave, son passé, son état présent et son avenir* (2 vols., Paris, 1852), I, 1, 3.

[3] Mohrt, *op. cit.*, 25.

from its beginning, which Chenavard set in the year 4200 B.C., until his own time. According to the painter, history consisted in a cycle of 6300 years and displayed in its course exactly the same characteristics as man from birth to death, each century corresponding to one year in man's life. This meant that mankind had arrived in the last period of its existence, comparable to old age, which man experiences between the age of 56 and 63. Mankind had weakened and was approaching its end, but it would not die until after it had pushed scientific and technological discoveries to their utmost limits. In this period the arts were losing their vigor with the exception of music singing the hymn of fraternity in a universal language.[1]

A few men of letters arrived at similar conclusions. As early as April of 1848 the poet Leconte de Lisle had lost his illusions about the Revolution." "Que le peuple est stupide . . . Qu'il crève de faim et de froid, ce peuple facile à tromper, qui va bientôt se mettre à massacrer ses vrais amis."[2] In 1849 he advised his friend Louis Ménard not to waste his youth and intelligence on sterile efforts to regenerate a decadent country. In his preface to his *Poèmes antiques* (1852) he characterized the entire history since the glory of Greek civilization as barbarian or decadent. These were the very opinions which Ménard adopted in the following years, and it was perhaps under Ménard's influence that the philosopher Charles Renouvier, in many respects the sharpest mind of the period, renounced his earlier optimistic philosophy of history and started his vigorous and thoughtful campaign against the doctrine of inevitable and continuous progress.[3] In a number of works partly written under the Second Empire (*Introduction à la philosophie analytique de l'histoire* and *Uchronie*) this eminent thinker subjected the interpretations of history expounded by Saint-Simon, Comte, Hegel, Marx, Spencer, and other nineteenth-century writers to a critical analysis pointing out how progressive forces had frequently been defeated in the past and how a doctrinaire belief in progress, by minimizing the role played by human responsibility and initiative, tended to undermine morality. Without denying that progress had occurred in the past and might take place in the

---

[1] Théophile Silvestre, *Les artistes français; études d'après nature* (Paris, 1878), 311ff.; J. C. Sloane, "Baudelaire, Chenavard, and Philosophic Art," *Journal of Aesthetics and Art Criticism*, XIII (1955), 285–299.

[2] Marius-Ary Leblond (pseud. de Georges Athenos and Aimé Merlo), *Leconte de Lisle* (Paris, 1906), 227–230, 238–246; cf. Irving Potter, *Leconte de Lisle and his Contemporaries* (Berkeley, 1951), 75ff.; Henri Peyre, *op. cit.*, 78.

[3] Peyre, *op. cit.*, 183, 189–190, 367, 371–372, 375–376, 377.

future, Renouvier considered the almost religious faith which many
contemporaries placed in the idea of progress a harmful illusion
impairing the chances of bringing about any real improvement in
man's condition.[1] Renouvier, then, objected to the belief in progress
only in so far as it assumed a deterministic or fatalistic character. It
was for this reason that he was equally opposed to a belief in inexorable
decadence as it was accepted by some of his contemporaries: "The
true law lies in the equal possibility of progress or regress for societies
as well as for individuals."[2]

IV

The political developments of the period were not the sole reason
for the mood of pessimism prevalent among French intellectuals. The
radical transformation of French society under the impact of the rapid
industrialization which took place during the Second Empire was
widely viewed with even greater alarm. Many prominent writers
inveighed against the wild speculations on the stock market, the
widespread corruption in politics, and the commercialization of art and
literature. Manifestations of the new industrial spirit like the Great
Exhibitions of 1855 and 1866 or the modernization of Paris under the
direction of Baron Haussmann often provoked sour comments on their
part.[3] This was not the first time that Frenchmen lamented the enervating effects of industry and luxury, but during the reign of Napoleon
III such jeremiads became more bitter and universal than before.

Reactionaries were, of course, foremost in this denunciation of the
materialistic spirit of modern civilization, but liberals like Renan and
Montégut, republicans like Pelletan and Quinet, and a socialist like
Proudhon also deplored the loss of idealism which the intensified
quest for material possessions seemed to entail.[4] Popular playwrights
such as Emile Augier, Théodore Barrière, and Alexandre Dumas *fils*

[1] Charles Renouvier, *Introduction à la philosophie analytique de l'histoire* (first published as
vol. IV of his *Essais de critique générale*) (Paris, 1864); *Uchronie; esquisse historique apocryphe
du développement de la civilisation européenne tel qu'il n'a pas été, tel qu'il aurait pu être* (Paris, 1876);
O. Hamelin, *Le système de Renouvier* (Paris, 1927), 421ff.; P. Mouy, *L'idée de progrès dans la
philosophie de Renouvier* (Paris, 1927); see also *supra*, 100, note 2.

[2] *Uchronie*, as quoted in Bury, *The Idea of Progress*, 304.

[3] Ernest Renan, "La poésie de l'Exposition," (1855), *Œuvres complètes*, II, 239ff.; Baudelaire, "Exposition universelle," *Œuvres* (ed., Bibl. de la Pléiade, Paris, 1954), 693-695;
Louis Veuillot, *Les odeurs de Paris* (Paris, 1866); G. Duveau, *Histoire du peuple français*, 251.

[4] E. Montégut, "De la maladie morale du XIXe siècle," *Revue des Deux Mondes*, III
(1849), 671-686; Richard H. Powers, *Edgar Quinet, a Study in French Patriotism* (Dallas, 1957),
160-161; E. Pelletan, *La Nouvelle Babylone, lettres d'un provincial en tournée à Paris* (Paris,
1862); Dolléans, *Proudhon*, 321ff., 402.

added their voices to the chorus of critics by exposing the venality of the daily press, the newly won prestige of Parisian courtesans, the dissolution of family ties, and the spirit of scepticism and *blague* of their contemporaries.[1] Finally many eminent philosophers (Emile Saisset, Jules Simon, Elme-Marie Caro) bewailed the frantic search for pleasure that had supposedly taken hold of the French people.[2]

Many of these writers had the feeling, as Renan put it, of living in "un âge de plomb ou d'étain," a period in which man had no longer the time to devote himself to artistic and intellectual pursuits.[3] They were especially afraid that in an increasingly utilitarian society literature, the finest product of French civilization, was losing its *raison d'être*. The misgivings of the literary elite were perhaps best expressed by the critic Edmond Scherer; "L'esprit du public . . . est à la conquête du monde matériel, à l'exploitation, à l'industrie, à la richesse . . . La vie est compliquée, difficile. Chacun a sa place à se faire au soleil. Les loisirs diminuent . . . La démocratie, c'est le niveau général qui s'élève, mais ce sont les sommités qui s'abaissent. La démocratie, c'est la médiocrité . . . Le monde moderne n'a plus de temps que pour deux choses: le travail qui lui donne du pain, et l'amusement qui le distrait du travail. Mais cet amusement n'a pas besoin d'être raffiné, il faut qu'il soit tout ensemble facile et énergique. Nous allons à l'américanisme."[4]

It was at this time that America began to replace England as the nightmare of all who felt that the traditional values of European civilization were threatened by industrialization and mechanization. The anonymous author[5] of *La cité nouvelle* (1868), describing a highly rationalistic and mechanized society A.D. 2000 from which all refinement of civilization had disappeared, presented this anti-utopia as the logical conclusion of contemporary trends in the United States. It was the "gaslight of America," according to Baudelaire, that had

---

[1] Cf. C. H. C. Wright, *The Background of Modern French Literature* (Boston, 1926), 210, 214, 227, 229-230; Henry Gaillard de Champris, *Émile Augier et la comédie sociale* (Paris, 1910), 23ff., 222, 264, 540.

[2] Émile Saisset, *Essai de philosophie religieuse* (Paris, 1860); Jules Simon, *La religion naturelle* (Paris, 1856); Elme-Marie Caro, *Études morales sur le temps* (Paris, 1855).

[3] Renan, *Œuvres complètes*, II, 250.

[4] Edmond Scherer, "L'ère impériale," (1868), *Etudes sur la littérature contemporaine* (Paris, 1885-95), IV, 21-22; cf. Sainte-Beuve, "Essais de critique naturelle par M. Émile Deschanel," *Nouveaux Lundis*, IX, 62ff.

[5] This anonymous work is generally attributed to the Bonapartist journalist Fernand Giraudeau (see Guiral, *op. cit.*, 572-573). An earlier anti-utopia was conceived by Emile Souvestre, whose *Le monde tel qu'il sera* (1845-46) greatly impressed Ernest Renan; cf. Richard Chadbourne, *Renan as an Essayist* (Ithaca, 1957), 96-97.

asphyxiated the genius of Edgar Allen Poe.[1] Likewise Ernest Renan considered the United States a cultural desert and was, for this reason, willing to exchange this entire country for one Italian town like Pisa.[2]

The greatest work of art evoking in lurid colors the corruptions of the Second Empire is undoubtedly Zola's famous novel series, *Les Rougon-Macquart*. Although largely written after 1870, its original conception and much of its inspiration date back to the reign of Napoleon III, and it is this period that the author intended to describe in all its depravity (as indicated by the subtitle: *Histoire naturelle et sociale d'une famille sous le Second Empire*). The principal varieties of degeneracy that are elaborately portrayed (such as sexual aberrations, neuroses, alcoholism, prostitution) are too well known to be in need of any detailed analysis. Although of considerable literary merit, Zola's novels depicted the Second Empire in simplistic terms (''une étrange époque de folie et de honte'') and failed to explain how this corruption originated or how it contributed to Napoleon III's downfall.[3] The only philosophy of history suggested is the conventional view that degeneration is the product of luxury and hereditary predisposition and that an "expiation" like the debacle of Sedan is needed to restore a nation to sanity.

A much sharper analysis of the development of modern civilization is contained in the works of Antoine Cournot, a philosopher whose original insight was not fully appreciated until the twentieth century. He predicted that as the result of increased mechanization and rational organization everything would be reduced to figures and facts, and that man would become a dehumanized robot losing his spontaneity. "Ce qui s'appelle proprement une civilisation progressive n'est pas, comme on l'a dit souvent, le triomphe de l'esprit sur la matière, mais bien plutôt le triomphe des principes rationnels et généraux des choses sur l'énergie et les qualités propres de l'organisme vivant, ce qui a beaucoup d'inconvénients à côté d'avantages."[4] "Du roi de la création

---

[1] Baudelaire, *Œuvres complètes*, ed. J. Crépet (19 vols., Paris, 1920–53), II, viii-ix.

[2] Renan, "Channing et le mouvement unitaire aux États Unis, "*Œuvres complètes*, VII, 279; Lamartine and Proudhon were also highly critical of the United States; cf. Edouard Berth, *Les méfaits des intellectuels* (Paris, 1914), 31ff.; A. B. North Peat, *Gossip from Paris during the Second Empire* (London, 1903), 133–134. In Flaubert's *Bouvard et Pecuchet* the Philistine Pécuchet indulges in prophecies of doom and speculates about the possibility that in the near future all idealism will disappear and that America will conquer the world (Löwith, *Meaning in History*, 97).

[3] Petriconi, *Das Reich des Untergangs*, 37–66; Wright, *op. cit.*, 229.

[4] Antoine A. Cournot, *Traité de l'enchaînement des idées fondamentales dans les sciences et dans l'histoire* (Paris, 1861), par. 330; cf. R. Ruyer, *L'humanité de l'avenir d'après Cournot* (Paris, 1930); Leroy, *op. cit.*, III, 122–124.

qu'il était ou qu'il croyait être, l'homme est monté ou descendu (comme il plaira de l'entendre) au rôle de concessionnaire d'une planète."[1]

There were, of course, dissenting voices. The poet Maxime Du Camp glorified modern industrial society and felt that French literature was decadent because it was oriented toward the past instead of marching forward like a daring pioneer.[2] Most professional economists far from deploring the modernization of French economy expressed their concern about the prevalence of archaic methods in French industry and French agriculture. They criticized the French educational system for training too many lawyers, men of letters, and politicians, but not enough persons qualified to play a productive role in the economy of their country.[3] Yet these views did not represent the opinion of the majority of French intellectuals, who were more alarmed by the disintegrating effects of industrialization than by any possible backwardness of the French economic system.

A social trend closely related to France's economic development that began to perturb a number of French writers at this time was the slow growth in population. The conservatives, who should be given credit for having called the attention of the French public to the dangerous implications of the decline of the French birth rate, were less concerned about the economic implications of a stationary population than about its effects on the military strength of the country and its significance as a reflection of increasing materialism and atheism. In *La décadence de la France* (1850), Raudot, the first author discussing demographic trends in connection with national decline, showed how France, once the most populous European country, now ranked behind Austria, Russia, and England in size of population.[4] A few years later, the distinguished sociologist Le Play developed the theory, anticipated by Balzac, that the low birth rate resulted from the clause in the Code Napoléon prescribing the equal division of an inheritance between all children; this provision, he held, had the effect of encouraging a limitation of the size of the family, notably among peasants, who were interested in leaving their land undivided. Like many later

---

[1] Cournot, *Considérations sur la marche des idées et des événements dans les temps modernes* (Paris, 1872), 230.

[2] Maxime Du Camp, *Chants modernes* (ed. Paris, 1861), 8, 11.

[3] Arthur L. Dunham, *The Anglo-French Treaty of Commerce of 1860*, 125ff., 204; G. Duveau, *La vie ouvrière en France sous le Second Empire* (Paris, 1946), 25; *idem, Histoire du peuple français*, 251.

[4] Raudot, *De la décadence de la France; idem,* articles in the *Correspondant* of May, 1857 and the *Gazette de France* of July 1, 1866.

traditionalists who accepted his explanation, Le Play therefore favored a legal reform.[1]

Raudot's and Le Play's misgivings were not shared by many of their contemporaries. The decline of the birth rate was, of course, a widely known fact, but it continued to be interpreted as a desirable trend. In the early years of the Second Empire it was still customary to award special prizes of "temperance" to "meritorious" working class families of "moderate" size. After the publication of the census figures of 1856, which revealed that in the preceding years the population of France had actually decreased, the problem was for the first time widely discussed in newspapers and periodicals.[2] Liberal economists, however, explained the figures largely by the increase of the death rate as a result of the Crimean war, falling production, and epidemics. Léonce de Lavergne expressed the views of many of his colleagues when he blamed the lack of population growth upon the unsatisfactory state of French agriculture and rejected any legislation to promote natality. He was convinced that the true remedy was to reduce government expenses from two billion to 1,400 or 1,500 million or even less if possible and that Jacques Bonhomme, the French peasant, would do the rest.[3] After the census of 1866 (revealing a further decline of the birth rate in a period of rapid deterioration of France's international position) alarmists once again tried to shake the complacency of the French public.[4] A prominent liberal, Prévost-Paradol, at this time adopted the conservative position and fully supported the Imperial government in its policy of increasing the size of the army. Nevertheless, the argument that "the power of a nation depends on the number of men she can arm," did not make a deep impression. Even those who were concerned about the slow increase of the population opposed the government proposal on the ground that the birth rate would decline even more sharply with a larger number of men away from their homes. On the whole, the French public remained apathetic and tended to share Hippolyte Taine's point of view that a decline of the birth rate was a sign of the "progress of reflection and civilization" among the French nation.[5]

---

[1] Charles de Ribbe, *Le Play d'après sa correspondance* (Paris, 1884), 56–62.

[2] Joseph J. Spengler, "French Population Theory Since 1800", *loc. cit.*

[3] Léonce de Lavergne, "L'agriculture et la population," *Revue des Deux Mondes*, April 1, 1857, 481–501; cf. Tocqueville, *Œuvres complètes*, vol. VII (Paris, 1866), 447; Guiral, *op. cit.*, 158ff.

[4] Cf. J. Spengler, *France Faces Depopulation*, 118–120. Guiral, *op. cit.*, 513ff.

[5] Taine, *Derniers Essais de critique et d'histoire*, (6th ed., Paris, 1923), 119–120.

V

Under the Second Empire the idea of decadence was above all a literary concept. Many arbiters of taste, convinced that literary standards were declining, regarded this phenomenon not as a mere symptom but as the very cause of the decadence of their times. In their view, Romantic literature had enervated the people's minds and was thus largely responsible for the moral and political crisis from which French society was suffering.[1] This attitude was no longer taken only by dignified bourgeois or conservative academicians. At this time the literary *avant-garde* itself criticized Romanticism for its lyric effusions, moral declamations, and vague religious doctrines. As early as 1847 Sainte-Beuve had noted in his diary that Romantic phrase-makers like Lamartine, Michelet, and Guizot were ruining France.[2] His point of view was soon shared by many younger men of letters who came to the conclusion that their elders had failed because of their addiction to Romantic dreams and phraseology.[3] Thus Taine made his literary debut by a sharp criticism of the idealism of Romantic philosophers and characterized the Romantic disease as "partout le dégoût, l'abrutissement et la maladie, l'impuissance, la folie, le suicide: au mieux l'exaltation permanente et la déclamation fébrile."[4] Maxime Du Camp, in his *Mémoires d'un suicide* (1855), described the Romantic melancholy from which he had suffered in his youth and commented: "Si l'on venait me démontrer aujourd'hui que j'ai été un peu fou, je ne serais ni indigné, ni étonné."[5] According to Proudhon, Romanticism by repudiating the principle of justice and by destroying all moral concepts was mainly responsible for the failures of the Revolution of 1848. He fully supported the new school of realism, hoping that it would bring an end to the state of decadence in which French letters had been for the past seventy years.[6] The works of the greatest novelist of the period, Gustave Flaubert, were also intended

[1] Cf. Maxime Du Camp, *Chants modernes*, p. 8.; Ch. Menche de Loisne, *Influence de la littérature française de 1830 à 1850 sur l'esprit public et les mœurs* (Paris, 1852); Eugène Poitou, *Du théâtre et du roman et leur influence sur les mœurs* (Paris, 1851).

[2] Sainte-Beuve, *Mes poisons. Cahiers intimes inédits* (Paris, 1926), 60, 62, 67, 86, 112, 114–116

[3] Thus Baudelaire severely criticized the Romantic conception of art; cf. his "L'école païenne," (1852), *Œuvres* (ed. Bibl. de la Pléiade, Paris, 1954), 980–981; Lautréamont was even more vehement in his indictment of Romanticism; cf. *Œuvres complètes* (Paris, 1953), 361–363.

[4] Quoted in Maigron, *op. cit.*, 96.

[5] *Ibid.*

[6] Proudhon, *Les majorats littéraires* (Paris, 1963); *idem, De la justice dans la Révolution et l'Eglise* in *Œuvres complètes*, XI, 489, 534; Maigron, *op. cit.*, 493; Leroy, *op. cit.*, III, 162–163.

to illustrate the dangers of Romantic idealism. In *Madame Bovary* he created the archtype of the romantic soul who, dissatisfied with her prosaic surroundings, became the victim of her dreams to escape the boredom of life. The same morale was implied in his other novel dealing with problems of contemporary society, *L'éducation sentimentale* (1869). If the French people had understood this novel, Flaubert claimed in 1871, they would never have committed the folly of the Commune.[1]

The disgust with Romantic verbosity and subjectivity led to a vogue of realism and positivism. "Ce qui domine dans notre littérature d'imagination, comme dans la critique moderne, comme dans la science et dans l'histoire," wrote the literary critic Emile Montégut in 1861, "c'est l'amour du fait, de la réalité, de l'expérience."[2] Yet these self-styled realists did not fully overcome Romanticism. Many of them continued to suffer from a disease highly similar to the Romantic *mal du siècle*, though they expressed this sentiment in a more objective, allegedly more scientific form. Thus, Gustave Flaubert was a Romantic at heart, plagued by the same maladies as Madame Bovary, and Emile Zola admitted his preference for "les œuvres de décadence où une sorte de sensibilité maladive remplace la santé plantureuse des époques classiques."[3] The group of famous authors regularly meeting at the "Dîners Magny" (Taine, Flaubert, the brothers Goncourt, Théophile Gautier) shared a keen interest in sexual perversions and the theories of the Marquis de Sade.[4] In an attempt to characterize the mentality of himself and some of his friends, Théophile Gautier used terms like "décadent." "primitif," "bizarre," and "exalté."[5] These writers themselves admitted that they were suffering from a nervous exhaustion and irritability allegedly typical of periods of decadence: "L'anémie nous gagne." it was stated in a novel by the brothers Goncourt, "voilà le fait positif. Il y a dégénérescence du type humain . . . Peut-être cela a-t-il été la maladie de l'empire romain, dont certains empereurs nous montrent une face dont les traits, même dans le bronze, semblent avoir coulé . . . Mais alors il y avait de la ressource. Quand une société était perdue, épuisée au point de vue physiologique, il lui arrivait une invasion de barbares

---

[1] Leroy, *op. cit.*, III, 68.
[2] As quoted in J. Bédier and P. Hazard, *Histoire de la littérature française illustrée* (Paris, 1923), II, 268.
[3] Émile Zola, *Mes haines* (1866) (Paris, 1880), 67–68.
[4] Cf. Praz, *op. cit.*, 152–153; Carter, *op. cit.*, 70.
[5] Lethève, *loc. cit.*, 49.

qui lui transfusait le jeune sang d'Hercule. Qui sauvera le monde de l'anémie du XIXe siècle? Sera-ce dans quelques centaines d'années une invasion d'ouvriers dans la société . . .?"[1]

Many of these authors preoccupied with the corruptions of their time no longer looked upon decadence as an unmitigated evil but as a source of artistic inspiration resulting in works of a beauty unknown to less corrupt societies. With their novels and their poetry they initiated the decadent movement in literature, in which decadence was not rejected with moralistic indignation but cultivated as the breeding ground of a refined civilization. This movement had been anticipated by many Romantic authors who had believed that modern society, allegedly in a state of decline, required new forms of artistic expression. A morbid delight in exposing the vices of their contemporaries had characterized especially the outlook of many later Romantics, admirers of the Marquis de Sade, but it was left to critics of Romanticism to draw a original and formal theory of decadence from these Romantic premises.

Charles Baudelaire is generally considered to have been the leading figure in the literary movement of Decadence, and his reputation as such is largely deserved. It is true that Baudelaire never developed a consistent philosophy of history, for he was a tormented soul torn into different directions in whose work completely contradictory statements on the subject of decadence can be found. A similar inconsistency was a distinguishing characteristic of most Decadents, who felt repelled by, and attracted to, decadence at the same time, and in Baudelaire this conflict attained perhaps its greatest intensity.

An admirer of the doctrines of Joseph de Maistre, Charles Baudelaire had nothing but contempt for the prevailing belief in progress. Embittered, like many of his contemporaries, by the outcome of the Revolution of 1848,[2] he went further than most in venting his disgust with modern civilization. He developed a savage hatred for all men and reserved his bitterest remarks for denouncing France and Paris. In a sketched preface to the *Fleurs du mal*, he characterized Paris as the "centre et rayonnement de bêtise universelle."[3] He called the belief in progress "une erreur fort à la mode, de laquelle je veux me garder comme de l'enfer,. . . une idée grotesque qui a fleuri sur le

---

[1] Edmond and Jules de Goncourt, *Charles Demailly* (1860), ch. LVIII (Paris, 1900), 283.

[2] Cf. Marcel Ruff, *op. cit.*, 224–226.

[3] *Œuvres* (ed. Bibl. de la Pléiade. Paris, 1954). 1380.

terrain pourri de la fatuité moderne . . . Cette infatuation est le diagnostic d'une décadence déjà trop visible."[1] Baudelaire's bleak vision of the future was most explicitly stated in a fragment of a never completed essay on "The End of the World": "Le monde va finir. . . . Nous périrons par où nous avons cru vivre. Le mécanique nous aura tellement américanisé, le progrès aura si bien atrophié en nous toute la partie spirituelle, que rien, parmi les rêves sanguinaires, sacrilèges ou anti-naturelles des utopistes ne pourra être comparé à ces resultats positifs."[2]

In many of his opinions Baudelaire betrayed a conventional nostalgia for the lost virtues of the past: "Ce n'est plus ce monde charmant et amiable que j'ai connu autrefois. Les artistes ne savent rien, les littérateurs ne savent rien, pas même l'orthographie. . . . Je suis un vieillard, une momie, et on m'en veut parce que je suis moins ignorant que le reste des hommes. Quelle décadence! Excepté d'Aurevilly, Flaubert, Sainte-Beuve, je ne peux m'entendre avec personne." "Je deviens tellement l'ennemi de mon siècle," he declared after reading Montesquieu's *Considérations sur la grandeur et la décadence des Romains* and Bossuet's *Discours sur l'histoire universelle*, "que tout sans en excepter une ligne, m'a paru sublime."[3]

Yet Baudelaire, as is known, was more than a conventional *laudator temporis acti*. Modern civilization, which he judged so severely in many of his works, fascinated him at the same time. He was a modernist in the sense that he preferred the artificiality and corruption of a decaying society to the more robust virtues of less degenerate civilizations. "Baudelaire accepta tout l'homme moderne," testified his fellow poet Théodore de Banville in 1867, "avec ses défaillances, avec sa grâce maladive, avec ses aspirations impuissantes."[4] He felt that the modern world had a grandeur of its own which might engender works of greater refinement than the *Iliad* or the *Divine Comedy*. As an admirer of the Satanist individualism of Pétrus Borel and profoundly influenced by the Marquis de Sade, Baudelaire did not consider evil a merely destructive force. This attitude explains that, though he execrated Paris as the center of modern corruption, he also declared his love for the city that had inspired him to write his poetry, "une fleur du mal," as Barbey d'Aurevilly called it, "venue dans les serres chaudes

[1] Baudelaire, "Exposition universelle de 1855," *Œuvres*, 693–694; cf. his *Correspondance générale* (Paris, 1947), IV, 95, 99, 180.
[2] Baudelaire, "Fusées," *Œuvres* (Paris, 1954), 1203–1205.
[3] *Correspondance générale*, II, 300; IV, 99.
[4] Quoted in Carter, *The Idea of Decadence in French Literature*, 55–56.

d'une Décadence."[1] Unlike most critics of his time, Baudelaire was not primarily a moralist denouncing the abuses of society but a gifted poet evoking with a shocking frankness the corruption and moral perversity of his own heart. Although condemning his own evil proclivities from a Christian point of view, he justified them as the mainspring of literary creativity in an age of decadence.

What was decadent, according to Baudelaire, was the society of his time, not the art that tried to express this decadence. He rejected "decadence" as a literary label, calling it a convenient term for ignorant pedagogues, "un mot vague derrière lequel s'abritent notre paresse et notre incuriosité de la loi."[2] The term which best sums up Baudelaire's aristocratic estheticism is not "decadence" but "dandyism." The dandies, Baudelaire felt, were the only heroes in a period of decline, who possessed the lucidity to recognize the omnipotence of evil which was ignored by the masses. "Mais, hélas," he wrote, "la marée montante de la démocratie, qui envahit tout, noie jour à jour ces derniers représentants de l'orgueil humain . . ."[3]

Baudelaire's attitude toward decadence, consisting of a blend of a Christian sense of guilt, morbid delight, and bitter resentment, was highly ambivalent. But the epithet of decadence, which the poet himself always rejected, was attached to his work by his contemporaries, who were more struck by the unconventional aspects of his art than by its traditional elements.[4] As might have been expected, many critics hostile to the new spirit of Baudelaire's poetry applied this derogatory label to his work; some of them denied it any artistic value and regarded the fact that this type of literature was taken seriously as a clear sign of intellectual degeneration.[5] It is more surprising that many of Baudelaire's admirers also emphasized the decadent character of his poetry. By his famous preface to the *Fleurs du mal* (1868), Théophile Gautier greatly contributed to the reputation that Baudelaire acquired later on in the century; he characterized Baudelaire as "un poète de *décadence*," who out of aversion for natural

[1] Characterization of the *Fleurs du mal* by Barbey d'Aurevilly; see William T. Bandy, *Baudelaire Judged by his Contemporaries* (Nashville, 1933), 168.

[2] Letter to Jules Janin, 1865, *Œuvres complètes*, ed. J. Crépet (XII,), 230; cf. Baudelaire's introduction to his translation of Poe's *Tales*, *Œuvres complètes*, ed. Jacquet Crépet, VIII, pp. v-vi.

[3] "Le peintre de la vie moderne," *Œuvres* (Paris, 1954), 908.

[4] A recent attempt to minimize the sadist element in Baudelaire was made by Georges Blin, *Le sadisme de Baudelaire* (Paris, 1948); for a contrary interpretation see Praz, *op. cit.*, 142–152 and Jean Paul Sartre, "Introduction" to Baudelaire, *Écrits intimes* (Paris, 1947).

[5] Cf. William T. Bandy, *op. cit.*, 35–36, 38, 53, 126; Edmond Scherer, *Études sur la littérature contemporaine*, IV, 280–281, 291.

simplicity had shown an indulgence for moral depravity and chosen the artificial "style de décadence." [1] The poets of the *fin de siècle* went even further in minimizing the traditional elements in Baudelaire's poetry and philosophy of life. Taking Baudelaire's profession of Satanism more seriously than it had been intended, they proclaimed him "le prince des décadents." "Baudelaire," according to one of the minor Decadent poets, Georges Rodenbach," entraîna la poésie dans une décadence . . . noble et glorieuse . . ."[2]

In a similar way later French authors enlarged upon Baudelaire's professions of modernity. "Poètes maudits" like Rimbaud and Lautréamont, whose poetry, written at the end of the Second Empire, was pervaded by "decadent" sentiments devoid of any Christian sense of guilt, broke even more radically with tradition than Baudelaire. Rimbaud's pronouncement "Il faut être absolument moderne" did not, of course, imply a high appreciation of the modern world, which, on the contrary, he detested as vehemently as any Romantic poet.[3] But it did imply that this corrupt modern world was so utterly different from earlier societies that the artist was doomed to sterility unless he created new forms of expression adapted to the temper of his age.

VI

Under the Second Empire the mood of French intellectuals was much more pessimistic than it had been in the first half of the nineteenth century. Of course, not all of the declamations about the decadence and corruption of France corresponded to deeply rooted convictions. Many of the derogatory remarks about the state of the country were merely a form of political agitation against a detested regime. The Second Empire deprived many intellectuals of the influence they had exercised during the July Monarchy; it curtailed intellectual freedom; it imprisoned some authors and forced others into exile. It was therefore not surprising that, as Napoleon III remarked to a British ambassador, there existed a conspiracy among men of letters against his regime.[4] Yet one would greatly underestimate the signifi-

---

[1] Cf. Carter, *op. cit.*, 13–15.

[2] Quoted in Carter, *op. cit.*, 138.

[3] Arthur Rimbaud, *Une saison en enfer*, Adieu in *Œuvres complètes* (ed. Bibl. de la Pléiade, Paris, 1954), 243; cf. Charles Baudouin, *The Myth of Modernity* (London, 1954). On Lautréamont's disgust of the modern world see his *Poésies*, *préface à un livre future* in *Œuvres complètes* (Paris, 1953), 361–363.

[4] Charles C. F. Greville, *Memoirs, 1816–1860* (London, 1938), VII, 385; cf. Sainte-Beuve, "Les regrets," *Causeries du lundi*, VI, 397–413; Mohrt, *op. cit.*, 225.

cance of the new pessimism by merely regarding it as a form of political propaganda. A mood of despondency was also common among writers who were politically indifferent or even in sympathy with the Empire, whereas many opponents of the regime like Victor Hugo retained their robust belief in progress. Not only political pamphleteers but also clear-headed scholars like Renan and Tocqueville and profound philosophers like Cournot and Renouvier expressed their misgivings about the trends of their times.

The gloomy outlook of many French littérateurs, scholars, and philosophers sharply contrasted not only with the more sanguine views which many of these same men of letters had held prior to the Revolution of 1848, but also with the optimism and the complacency of the general public. The Second Empire was a period of rising prosperity and of spectacular technological inventions which were accepted by many as convincing evidence of the idea of progress. The belief in the indefinite perfectibility of mankind, although it was subjected to serious criticism by many French intellectuals, became more popular than ever before among the masses of the population, who, breaking away from Catholicism, eagerly accepted a secular substitute for the lost belief in the world hereafter. Indeed, many Catholics themselves became fervent adepts of the belief in progress maintaining that this idea, far from being in conflict with Christian doctrine, was in essence a concept of Christian origin.[1] "Gardez-vous surtout," exhorted the abbé Michon his fellow Catholics, "de toute parole amère contre ce progrès humain que notre siècle peut s'exagérer, mais dont il est légitime fier."[2]

Even most writers fully convinced of the degeneration of their own time did not actually despair of the future. With some notable exceptions, French intellectuals of the Second Empire continued to believe in a turn for the better. But the naive utopianism of the preceding period had lost most of its intellectual respectability. Romantic illusions as to a speedy regeneration of mankind were sharply criticized not only by traditionalists but by many "progressive" thinkers as well. Affected by the new vogue for positivism, many members of the younger generation presented their views of history as the result of a

---

[1] Cf. Auguste Ott, *Dictionnaire des sciences politiques et sociales* (Paris, 1854–55), articles "Décadence" (II, 54–55) and "Progrès" (III, 527, 544); Jean-Hippolyte Michon, *Apologie chrétienne au XIXe siècle. Le dogme chrétien dans ses rapports avec la doctrine moderne du progrès et de la perfectibilité* (Paris, 1863); Alphonse Gratry, *La morale et la loi de l'histoire* (Paris, 1868), ch. XIV; Charles F. Montalembert, "L'Espagne et la liberté," (1868), *Bibliothèque universelle*, LVI (1876), 112–113.

[2] Michon, *op. cit.*, 279.

scientific, realistic study of society. More than ever before, speculations on the past, the present, and the future were based on a relatively accurate and detailed knowledge of history and a fairly sharp analysis of contemporary social and political trends. Even reactionaries adduced the findings of some solid research on the Old Regime in support of their glorification of the past. The new respect for science is also evident in the first use made of Darwinian theories in explaining the course of history.

Whereas the majority of French intellectuals continued to believe, with more or less serious reservations, in the possibility of progress, a small but increasing number of prominent writers became convinced that no improvement whatever could be expected. A reactionary like Gobineau, republicans like Ménard, Chenavard, and Leconte de Lisle felt that the existing decadence was irrevocable. Among these embittered idealists Schopenhauer's philosophy found its first French devotees.[1] The first literary "decadents" like Baudelaire and his admirers also accepted the corruption of their time as irremediable, but they went still a step further in breaking with regenerationist aspirations: they began to appreciate the decadence of their period as a source of beauty unknown to the past.

Yet such philosophies preaching the inevitability or even the desirability of evil were denounced by some of the most distinguished French writers of the period (Renouvier, Quinet, Tocqueville, and even Proudhon) who rejected any doctrine infringing on man's responsibility to shape his own destiny. It is the strength of this liberal tradition in nineteenth-century France, opposed to determinism and fatalism, that perhaps more than anything else explains that no French writer of distinction developed a formal pessimistic philosophy comparable to the ambitious constructions which were conceived by German or Russian writers of the period.

As in the first half of the nineteenth century, it was the trends of Western civilization *in general* (the increase in materialism, atheism, etc.) that was at the source of most of the pessimism in the Second Empire. In this period, however, more than before, Frenchmen became concerned about national decadence. It was certain disturbing phenomena special to their own country, or at least not as manifest in other highly developed countries, that caused some French

---

[1] Cf. A. Baillot, "Schopenhauer im Urteil seiner französischen Zeitgenossen. Frühe Dokumente," *Jahrbuch der Schopenhauer-Gesellschaft*, XIX (1932), 252–279; idem. *L'influence de la philosophie de Schopenhauer en France (1860–1890)* (Paris, 1927).

writers to view the future of their country with anxiety. In the Second Empire the slow growth of the French population led French writers for the first time to the pessimistic conclusion that the future would belong to the more procreative nations of the world. Moreover, as a result of the behavior of the French populace in 1848 and the following years, many French liberals, republicans, and socialists became convinced that their nation, in contrast to the English, lacked any political talent. French liberals were the most outspoken in their praise of England, but even many writers with more radical political opinions who, prior to 1848, had denounced the corrupt and plutocratic government of Great Britain, now began to look with admiration upon English free institutions. Louis Blanc omitted the anti-English passages from the new edition of his *Organisation du travail*, and Michelet, one of the most vehement Anglohobes in the 1840's, now preferred England to the France of Napoleon III and came out in favor of constructing a tunnel under the Channel.[1] Even French socialists visiting England were impressed by the strong trade union movement and the many facilities for popular education.[2] Anglo-Saxon individualism was no longer viewed with such horror as it had been during the July Monarchy but was regarded as the underlying cause of the political successes of the English speaking nations, whereas the contrasing political tradition of centralization and statism was seen as the major reason for French failure.

This alarm over the future of France, just as the concern about the evils of modern technology and industrialization, was not shared by the majority of the French people. Under the Second Empire, when France once again played a leading role in European politics and modernized Paris acquired an international reputation as a center of amusement, finance, art, and literature, the prevailing mood of the French nation was rather one of increased self-confidence and pride. At least during the first ten years of the Empire, few questioned the invincibility of the French army. Ratapoil, a creation of Daumier, became the personification of chauvinism from which even many intellectuals were not exempt. "Nous sommes ce peuple," wrote the poet Maxime Du Camp in 1855, "qui, traversant l'Europe au bruit du canon, va porter à toutes les nations les germes d'une liberté encore endormie peut-être, mais que j'entend sourdre sous la terre; nous

---

[1] Cf. Louis Blanc, *Lettres sur l'Angleterre* (Paris, 1865); Guiral *op. cit.*, 496; Jeanlouis Cornuz, *Jules Michelet. Un aspect de la pensée religieuse au XIXe siècle* (Genève, 1955), 148–154.
[2] Duveau, *Pensée ouvrière sous le Second Empire*, 180.

sommes ce peuple . . . qui force, par sa défaite même, toutes les races à venir s'asseoir chez lui au banquet de la civilisation."[1]

The belief in the superiority of French civilization and in the mission of France to spread liberty and equality around the world remained very strong among the French Left. Antoine Aragon, among other republicans, still indulged in schemes in which France "the brain of the world" and "the Queen of Western civilization," would exercise a "moral and political presidency" over a great federation of European peoples.[2] Likewise the old belief that France, as the eldest daughter of the Church, was chosen by God to save the world continued to fascinate Roman Catholics.[3] Even many liberals, although less inclined to chauvinism than other Frenchmen, occasionally expressed their belief in the unique and great qualities of their nation. In 1863 Montalembert, pleading for French aid to the Polish insurgents, asserted that France had only to declare herself with vigor, and she would be obeyed since her armies were known to be invincible.[4] Renan characterized the French as a nation that could never be mediocre and Tocqueville called them "la plus brillante et la plus dangereuse des nations de l'Europe, et la mieux faite pour y devenir tour à tour un objet d'admiration, de haine, de pitié, de terreur, mais jamais d'indifférence."[5]

National complacency was somewhat shaken by the battle of Sadowa in 1866 revealing the military power of modern Prussia.[6] Republicans and liberals alike interpreted the Prussian victory over Austria as the triumph of an enlightened, Protestant nation over a backward Catholic one. "Le vanqueur de Sadowa," stated Jules Simon, "est l'instituteur allemand."[7] At this time a French general, Louis Trochu, created a sensation with his book *L'armée française en 1867*, pointing out that the French army was gradually falling behind that of other nations because its officers were inadequately educated and its soldiers excessively individualistic. He argued that the traditional French *élan* would not be sufficient to win a war against a well-disciplin-

---

[1] *Chants modernes*, 12–13; cf. Claude Digeon, *La crise allemande de la pensée française (1870–1914)* (Paris, 1959), 9–12; C. H. C. Wright, *Background of Modern French Literature*, 180–181.

[2] Lochore, *History of the Idea of Civilization in France*, 168.

[3] *Ibid.*, 159–161, 166.

[4] Duveau, *Histoire du peuple français*, 292; cf. Emile Ollivier, *L'Empire libéral, études, récits, souvenirs*, vol. VI (Paris, 1902), 159–160.

[5] Renan, *Questions contemporaines* (1868), *Œuvres complètes*, I, 26; Tocqueville, *L'ancien régime et la Révolution* (4th ed. Paris, 1860), 334–336.

[6] Cf. Digeon, *op. cit.*, 24–47.

[7] Duveau, *La pensée ouvrière*, 179–180.

ed enemy and that the belief in the invincibility of the French army
was a dangerous legend.[1]

The French government received even more urgent warnings from
its military attaché in Berlin, Baron Eugène Stoffel, who wished that
France would have an open mind for the great qualities of Prussia:
"une nation sérieuse, rude et forte; dépourvue, il est vrai, de tout don
attrayant, de tout charme, de tout sentiment délicat et généreux,
mais douée, en revanche, des qualités les plus estimables, l'amour du
travail et de l'étude, l'application, l'esprit d'ordre et d'économie, le
patriotisme, le sentiment du devoir et celui de la dignité individuelle,
enfin le respect de l'autorité et l'obéissance aux lois." He considered
ignorance and presumption the gravest shortcomings of the French
nation, defects perpetuated by a system of education "qui nous donne
l'admiration exclusive de nous-mêmes et de la France, qui surexcite
et développe nos défauts naturels et éteint en nous le désir de nous
instruire et de nous perfectionner."[2] Other French writers of the time
began to question the accuracy of the idyllic image of Germany
that had been current in France since the days of Mme de Staël:
"C'est la vieille devise des Teutons and des Goths," wrote the socialist
Armand Barbès to George Sand in 1867, "que reprennent Bismarck
et les siens: Marchez au Midi! C'est bien le barbare qui menace de se
précipiter sur nous! Pauvre chère France! Et nous avons été assez
bêtes, depuis Mme de Staël, pour vanter les œuvres d'au-delà du
Rhin!"[3]

But even at this late hour the French nation did not fully realize the
seriousness of the situation. The urgently needed army reform was not
carried out. Even those who were aware of the weakness of France were
opposed to increasing the budget since they feared that this would
bolster a tottering regime. Many shared the surprising opinion of the
Journal des Economistes: "Une intelligente et franche politique de
désarmement aurait, à notre avis, pour effet d'accroître la force et la
sécurité du pays."[4] But at the same time, public opinion reproached
the government for its various diplomatic defeats and called for a more
aggressive foreign policy. Thus Emile de Girardin, an influential
newspaper editor, preached the necessity of war against Prussia in order

---

[1] Louis Jules Trochu, *L'armée française en 1867* (Paris, 1867).
[2] Eugène G. H. C. Stoffel, *Rapports militaires écrits de Berlin de 1866 à 1870* (Paris, 1871),
p. XVII, 321–322.
[3] Quoted in Maurice A. Souriau, *Histoire du Romantisme en France*, I, 292.
[4] *Journal des économistes*, 3e série, vol. IX (March 15, 1868), 358.

to reconquer France's natural frontiers: "N'ayons qu'un seul cri: le Rhin! Rien de plus, rien de moins."[1]

Although it is hazardous to gauge public opinion, there is much to be said for the conclusion based on the reports of the solicitors general of the Second Empire that war was declared on Prussia in order to satisfy the popular demand for a Prussian humiliation.[2] When the government asked for a declaration of war, only very few deputies voted against, and these opposed the war not so much because they feared that France might be defeated, but because they were afraid that a French victory would greatly strengthen the regime of Napoleon III. Ernest Renan, one the few French authors who wholeheartedly detested the war, had written in 1869: "Quelques erreurs énormes entraînent notre pays aux abîmes; ceux à qui on les signale sourient." Even Renan did not fully anticipate the catastrophe of the *année terrible*.[3]

---

[1] M. Dessal, *Charles Delescluze*, 225.

[2] Lynn M. Case, *French Opinion on War and Diplomacy during the Second Empire* (Philadelphia, 1954), 269.

[3] Renan, *Saint-Paul*, dedication, *Œuvres complètes*, IV, 708.

CHAPTER V

THE YEAR OF DISASTER

Nous assistons à la fin du monde latin.

FLAUBERT[1]

C'est le moment pour tout Français de s'emprisonner volontairement dans son pays.

MONTÉGUT[2]

The French people were utterly unprepared for the national disasters
that befell them during the lightheartedly undertaken war against
Prussia. The unexpected tidings of evil which followed one another in
rapid succession left public opinion in a state of despair, fear, and rage.
First the German victory destroyed the widely accepted legend of the
invincibility of the French army. The defeat of France was the more
humiliating as this time it was inflicted by a single European nation,
and not, as in 1814 and 1815, by a coalition of European powers.
The subsequent civil war added greatly to the national bewilderment.
The fratricidal conflict in which the French engaged under the eyes
of the enemy was widely seen as another indication of the political
immaturity of the French nation. After the Commune, neither the
property-owning classes, alarmed by this renewed attack on the
existing social order, nor the extreme Left, embittered by the ruthless
suppression of the uprising, were able to face the future with equanimity. The third major event of the *année terrible* that made a deep
impression on the French mind was the loss of temporal power by the
papacy, which came to many French Catholics as an even greater
shock than the dramatic occurrences in their own country.

The sense of anxiety caused by these disastrous events was expressed
in a large number of pamphlets, political treatises, periodical articles,

---

[1] Gustave Flaubert, *Correspondance* (4 vols., Paris, 1884–92), VI, 201.

[2] Quoted in Claude Digeon, *La crise allemande de la pensée française, 1870–1914* (Paris,
1959), 89; Digeon's perceptive study of the impact of the year of disaster is particularly
illuminating in its analysis of the response of prominent men of letters. According to Digeon
(*op. cit.*, 352), the national defeat did not immediately foster a sense of decadence. This
seems, however, to be true only of the literary, fatalistic sense of decadence as it became
current in the 1880's, not, as this chapter intends to demonstrate, of the idea of decadence
taken in a broader sense.

and private letters. The titles of some of these publications are reve-
latory of the pessimistic mood which was rampant at the time: *La
chute de la France, La fin du monde, De la décadence de nos mœurs, La France
dégénérée, Mépris et décadence, Le testament d'un Latin, La catastrophe de la
France, 1871! Les premières phases d'une décadence*, etc.[1] Pessimism had been
far from uncommon among French intellectuals before the war, but
it now seemed to affect also large groups of the population which
thus far had unquestionably accepted the dogma of indefinite progress
and had indulged in dreams of national grandeur. Even the elite who
had not shared the popular optimism, was not fully prepared for the
disaster. "Quelle barbarie! Quelle reculade!," wrote Gustave Flaubert
on March 11, 1871, "Je n'étais guère progressiste et humanitaire
cependant. N'importe, j'avais des illusions! Et je ne croyais pas voir
arriver la fin du monde. Car c'est cela. Nous assistons à la fin du monde
latin."[2]

Flaubert's views represented an extremist version of national
despondency. The prevalent mood was somber but not one of utter
despair of the future. Most writers admitted that for some time (since
1789, 1792, 1830, or 1848, depending on the author's political convictions) France had been suffering from serious maladies; but they
did not give up hope for a regeneration, renaissance, or salvation of
their country. Many Frenchmen continued to believe in progress
even if they were now less assured than before that their nation would
lead humanity on the road to greater happiness and enlightenment.
Few, in other words, accepted continued decline as inevitable and no
writer attempted to glorify the state of decadence as was done by
later men of letters of the *fin de siècle*.

The pessimism of many publicists did not, moreover, go very
deep. They often handled the term "decadence" as an ideological
weapon in the heated controversy about the new political order of
their nation. They indulged in slogans as "the Republic or Decadence,"
"Religion or Decadence," making little or no attempt to substantiate
their statements with a well-elaborated philosophy of history. The

---

[1] Etienne Baudry, *La fin du monde latin* (Paris, 1870); Auguste Dalichoux, *1871! Les premières phases d'une décadence* (Paris, 1871); anon., *Des causes de la décadence française* (Bordeaux
1871); D. Gesta, *La chute de la France* (Paris, 1871); anon., *République ou décadence* (Paris
1871); Jules Patenotre, *La France dégénérée* (Paris, 1871); Alfred de La Guéronnière, *La
catastrophe de la France. L'anarchie démagogique* (Bruxelles, 1871); Louis Rambaud, *Le testament
d'un Latin* (Paris, 1872); J. Flayat, *Mépris et décadence* (Agen, 1873).
[2] Flaubert, *Correspondance*, VI, 201; cf. *ibid.*, VI, 159ff., 183, 184; Flaubert seems to have
been influenced by the pessimistic views of his friend Maxime Du Camp; see the latter's
Souvenirs littéraires (Paris, 1892), II, 363.

speculations of even the most scholarly commentators of the time were colored by their political or religious views.

Given the great variety of political and religious views of the period, it can be expected that there existed little consensus as to the causes of French "decadence." The Catholics attributed the national disasters to the decline of faith, blaming Comte, Renan, Taine, and other modern intellectuals for the growth of materialism and atheism.[1] "Nous périssons," wrote the most eloquent spokesman for the Ultramontanist point of view, Louis Veuillot, "faute de foi, faute de loi, faute de justice en nous et entre nous."[2] The young historian Gabriel Monod, on the other hand, asserted that France had not sinned against faith but against science, and Gustave Flaubert proclaimed that the French would never succeed in putting their house in order as long as the Academy of Sciences had not superseded the papacy as the supreme spiritual authority.[3]

The opinions were equally divided as to the part which foreign, especially German, influences had played in the national downfall. Whereas Catholics and traditionalist philosophers and men of letters complained that Protestantism, German philosophy and Romanticism had enervated the French Latin mind,[4] their modernist opponents maintained that France had failed because it had not kept up with German educational, religious, and scientific progress.[5] Least agreement of all, as might have been expected, existed on the political principles responsible for the downfall of France. Depending on the political persuasion of the writer, the revolutionary and democratic spirit, centralization of political power, or reactionary attachment to the principles of the Old Regime was seen as having undermined the strength of the nation.

The diagnosticians of the French crisis, however, did not disagree on

[1] Cf. Jean-Baptiste Causette, *Dieu et les malheurs de la France* (Toulouse, 1871); Louis Veuillot, *Paris pendant les deux sièges* (2 vols., Paris, 1871); Guillaume Alfred Heinrich, *La France, l'étranger et les partis* (Paris, 1873), Antoine Blanc de Saint Bonnet, *La légitimité* (Paris, 1873).

[2] Veuillot, *op. cit.*, II, 160.

[3] Gabriel Monod, *Allemands et Français* (Paris, 1872), 21; Flaubert, *Correspondance*, VI, 281; Emile Zola also expected French regeneration only from a greater respect for positivist science; on the philosophy underlying his well-known statement "La République sera naturaliste ou elle ne sera pas," see Digeon, *op. cit.*, 271ff.

[4] This point of view was, for example, taken by Louis Veuillot, Désiré Nisard, and Elme-Marie Caro; see Digeon, *op. cit.*, 115–117, 119, 157–163.

[5] This was, for example, the opinion of Renan, Gasparin, Quinet, Michelet, Flaubert, Renouvier, Emile Zola, and many other liberals and radicals. Edme Champion declared: "La pente qui éloigne de Voltaire aboutit à Sedan"; see E. Faguet, *L'anticléricalisme* (Paris, 1905), 185–187. Antoine Rocher (pseud.), in *Messieurs les capitulards et les citoyens communards* (Genève, 1873), p. 8, asserted "Le salut de la France est dans l'athéisme et la révolution."

all questions. In the first place, almost all of them severely criticized the Emperor, his generals, and his ministers for the inefficiency and irresponsibility of their policies.[1] The National Assembly itself subscribed to this view when, on March 1, 1871, it officially declared that Napoleon III was responsible for "the ruin, the invasion, and the dismemberment of France."[2] In a less personal point of view, many Frenchmen of varied political persuasion inveighed against the frivolity, the materialism, and the corruption of the Second Empire, sharply contrasting them with the serious and frugal spirit of victorious Germany. With few exceptions the writers of this period, not improperly called "l'ordre moral," criticized the *blague* and the spirit of easy living of pre-war society. As Hippolyte Taine put it: "Notre grande faute, c'est d'avoir voulu que tout fût amusant; l'art et le talent de s'ennuyer ont fait la force des Allemands."[3]

Of a more lasting impact was the general conviction that the national disaster was due to an exaggerated estimate of the strength of the nation, resulting in an overambitious foreign policy. France, it was believed, had held herself too much responsible for the welfare of humanity and had not enough concentrated on her own problems and interests. It was for this reason that Louis Veuillot urged the French to dissociate themselves completely from what took place in the rest of the world, to the point of dispensing with international treaties and diplomatic relations.[4] This isolationist view, in a less extreme form, is found in almost all publications of the period, conservative, liberal, and republican alike. "C'est le moment," wrote Montégut, an author who had once tried to awaken the French to the value of foreign civilizations, "pour tout Français de s'emprisonner volontairement dans son pays."[5] The Republic, declared Gambetta in 1876, had absolutely renounced "prosélytisme et cosmopolitisme, comprenant très bien que ... la politique extérieure d'une République française ... impose la nécessité de respecter la constitution des autres peuples quelqu'elle soit."[6] The early nineteenth-century nationalism that had called for spreading liberty, equality,

---

[1] Cf. Émile de Girardin, *Grandeur ou déclin de la France. Questions des années 1874 et 1875* (Paris, 1876), 177; Emile Littré, "De la situation que les derniers événements ont faite à l'Europe, au socialisme, et à la France," (1871), *De l'établissement de la Troisième République* (Paris, 1881), 133ff.; Digeon, *op. cit.*, 101, 141.

[2] E. R. Curtius, *The Civilization of France* (New York, 1962), 86.

[3] Taine, *Sa vie et sa correspondance*, II, 49; cf. Digeon, *op. cit.*, 78–79, 133, 281.

[4] Mohrt, *Les intellectuels devant la défaite*, 152–153; cf. Heinrich, *op. cit.*, 25.

[5] Quoted in Digeon, *op. cit.*, 89.

[6] Léon Gambetta, *Discours et plaidoyers politiques*, ed. J. Reinach (Paris, 1881), V, 181.

and fraternity around the world, lost almost all support. This contraction of French nationalism, implying a belief, if not in decadence, at least in a diminished position of France in the world, was one of the most important effects of the War of 1870 on the French mind.[1]

The image that Frenchmen formed of their nation underwent another important change as a result of the defeat. Although most publicists were extremely reluctant to explain the German victory by any basic superior qualities of the German people, they readily conceded a German superiority in the fields of discipline, organization, and national unity. The French weaknesses in these areas were, on the other hand, frequently summed up in the highly ambiguous term "individualism."[2] This interpretation of the German and French national characteristics, which became something of a cliché from this time onward, constituted a radical reversal of the views on German and French national traits that had been common before the war, when the Germans had generally been singled out as being excessively individualistic and the French, on the other hand, had been regarded as possessing a special gift for cooperative enterprise.[3]

Since the war of 1870 the indictment of French "individualism" as one of the principal sources of French "decadence" and the advocacy of an "organic," corporative order allowing for the kind of social cohesion and national discipline as allegedly existing in Germany became favorite themes of many French conservatives. The uncontested master of this school of thought was the sociologist Frédéric Le Play, who felt that the misgivings with which he had viewed the state of his country under the Second Empire were fully borne out by the events of the *année terrible*.[4] It was among his Catholic admirers that the individualistic spirit of the Revolution found some of its severest critics. "La Révolution," asserted one of the leaders of the new social Catholic movement, Albert de Mun, in 1875, "n'est pas seulement le crime d'un jour et d'une époque; elle est une idée dont les sources sont anciennes et qui s'appuie sur des racines aussi vieilles que le monde: elle est l'esprit de négation qui repousse toute doctrine, l'esprit

---

[1] Cf. Digeon, *op. cit.*, 99, 234, 252–253, 537–538, 540.

[2] Cf. Vicomte de P. Épigny, *La France, hier, aujourd'hui, demain* (Paris, 1871), preface: Digeon, *op. cit.*, 109, 238, 281.

[3] Cf. my article, "The French: Are They Individualists?" *The South Atlantic Quarterly*, LXI (1962), 1–12; Digeon, *op. cit.*, 58.

[4] Louis Thomas, *Frédéric Le Play, 1806–1882* (Paris, 1943), 16; cf. Paul Ribot, *Du rôle social des idées chrétiennes, suivi d'un exposé critique des doctrines sociales de M. Le Play* (2 vols., Paris, 1879).

d'indépendance et d'orgueil qui refuse toute obéissance et sa devise est: *Non serviam.*" [1]

Many writers who did not sympathize with the reactionary views of such Catholics did share their concern about the lack of social and political unity from which the French had been suffering since the Revolution of 1789. Many self-styled liberals pointed to the individualistic spirit of the French Revolution as the primary source of France's misfortunes in the nineteenth century. Emile Montégut's influential articles in the *Revue des Deux Mondes* blamed the Revolution for having created "cet état monstrueux de l'individualisme où l'homme, atome égoïste autant que faible, libre, mais impuissant, sans autre loi que lui-même, mais sans secours contre lui-même tourbillonne autour des autres atomes." [2] Even republicans admitted the necessity for greater social discipline. One of their most distinguished spokesmen, the philosopher Charles Renouvier, although in almost all respects an unqualified admirer of the great Revolution, conceded that since 1789 Frenchmen had been uprooted from their traditional way of life and that they had much to learn from Germany in the way of social discipline. [3]

There is no need to comment on the many publications of this time that merely repeated the ideas already presented by previous critics of modern France. Most conservatives adopted the clerical point of view and restated the views of early nineteenth-century reactionaries like Joseph de Maistre and Donoso Cortés. Many Catholics saw in the national disaster a form of divine punishment for the many aberrations of the French people such as lack of faith, disintegration of the family, decline of the birth rate, and secularism in Church and State. [4] Some of them predicted a miraculous turn of events including a resto-

[1] As quoted in Georges Weill, *Histoire du mouvement social en France, 1852–1924* (3d ed., Paris, 1924), 182. Anti-individualism remained very strong among the leaders of Social Catholic movements organized under Le Play's influence; see Matthew H. Elbow, *French Cooperative Theories, 1789–1948* (New York, 1953), 57–58; Marquis de La Tour-du-Pin, art. "Individualisme," in *Dictionnaire apologétique de la foi catholique* (Paris, 1911–1915), II, 716–718.

[2] Émile Montégut, "Où en est la Révolution française?" *Revue des Deux Mondes*, sec. période, XCIV (Aug. 15, 1871), 885; cf. *idem*, "Les transformations de l'idée de patrie," *ibid.*, XCVI (Nov. 15, 1871), 415–442. Edmond de Goncourt expressed a similar opinion: " . . . la Révolution française a tué la discipline de la nation, a tué l'abnégation de l'individu . . . ." (Digeon, *op. cit.*, 171).

[3] Charles Renouvier, "La décadence de la France," *Critique philosophique*, I (April 11, 1872), 152–156; *ibid.* (April 18, 1870), 164.

[4] Cf. Eugène Villedieu, *L'expiation* (Paris, 1871); Amédée de Margerie, *La Restauration de la France* (Paris, 1871); A. de Richecour, *Ce que doit être l'alliance des races latines* (Paris, 1871); *Grandeur ou décadence*, par un électeur rural; (Auch, 1871); Martial Delpit, *Le dix-huit mars; récit des faits et recherche des causes de l'insurrection. Rapport fait à l'Assemblée nationale* (Paris, 1871);

ration of pope and king to their legitimate positions if the French people were willing to expiate their sins.[1] At least one prominent Catholic publicist, Monseigneur Gaume, regarded the contemporary events as a clear indication that the latter days had arrived and that Old Europe would fall under Russian domination.[2] On a popular level, many priests and abbots, freely interpreting obscure scriptural passages about Gog and Magog and the Beast with the mysterious figure of 666[3] and attributing the national misfortunes to the sinister intrigues of the Freemasons and other secret societies,[4] indulged in speculations about a coming millenium after the present catastrophes had run their due course.

The voices of French ultraconservatives who lacked sympathy with the Catholic point of view and were less concerned about the growth of atheism and the loss of temporal power of the papacy than about the growing strength of democracy and socialism, were silenced by the wave of religious enthusiasm which followed the national defeat and the suppression of the Commune. The most orginal exponent of secular reactionarism, the Comte de Gobineau saw in the events of 1870–71 the full confirmation of his racial theories and now stated that the bells of doom had tolled for France, whereas a glorious future was still in store for Northern European countries.[5] It is, however, symptomatic of the lack of popularity of this point of view that Gobineau's writings of these years were not published during his lifetime.

Many prominent liberals shared Gobineau's admiration for the Germanic nations without, however, accepting his fatalistic racialism and his utter denigration of the French nation. The political, if not religious, views of these liberals, already highly conservative in the Second Empire, became even less progressive after the Franco-Prus-

---

Auguste Nicolas, *l'État sans Dieu, mal social de la France* (Paris, 1872); Joseph-Élie Méric, "Du scepticisme et de la décadence nationale en France," *Revue politique et littéraire: Revue bleue*, III (1872), 51–55; see also the works, cited *supra*, 125, note 1.

[1] Pierre-François Richaudeau, *La prophétie de Blois* (Tours, 1870); for other prophecies made at this time, see the works listed in the *Catalogue de l'histoire de la France* (Paris, 1855–1895), XI, 495, 510.

[2] Jean-Joseph Gaume, *Où en sommes-nous? Étude sur les événements actuels, 1870 et 1871* (Paris, 1871).

[3] Marquise Anna Godefroy-Ménilglaise, *Sodome, Ninive, Jérusalem, admonestation à Paris* (Paris, 1872); Gustave Louis, *Gog et Magog* (Paris, 1873); cf. Rémond, *La droite en France*, 133–134; Jacques Chastenet, *Histoire de la Troisième République* (Paris, 1952–   ), I, 153–155.

[4] E. A. Chabauty, *Lettres sur les prophètes modernes* (Poitiers, 1872), 126ff.; Nicolas Deschamps, *Les sociétés sécrètes et la société* (Paris, 1873–76); cf. Robert F. Byrnes, *Antisemitism in Modern France* (New–Brunswick, 1950), I, 126ff., 199–200.

[5] Gobineau, *Frankreichs Schicksale im Jahre 1870* (Leipzig, 1917), 18.

sian War. Yet their works, written with considerable literary talent and based on impressive scholarship left a lasting impression on the French mind. This was especially true of the works of Ernest Renan and Hippolyte Taine, who came to be accepted as spiritual guides by an influential part of the rising generation and whose pessimism lent great prestige to the opposition to the revolutionary principles upon which modern France was built.

Ernest Renan was shocked by the war primarily because it rudely disturbed his dream of Franco-German cooperation. His provocative and forceful essay, *La réforme intellectuelle et morale de la France* (1871), was his bitterest attack on contemporary French society, but it added little to the ideas which the author had already outlined in his earlier publications: a distrust of radical ideologies, a condemnation of French frivolity, and a hatred of the mediocrity and the materialism of modern civilization. Urging his fellow countrymen to model France's religious and educational institutions after those of Germany and to follow England's example in building a political order in which tradition and innovation were harmoniously blended, he lacked the confidence that his suggestions would be heeded. More bitterly than in any of his previous writings, Renan inveighed against the equalitarian and utopian mentality of the Revolution. He called democracy "le plus énergique dissolvant de toute vertu que le monde ait connue jusqu'ici." and asserted that "le jour où la France coupa la tête à son roi, elle commit un suicide."[1] Exclaiming "Finis Franciae," he envisaged a future in which world leadership would belong to the nations that had not yet suffered from the weakening of the military spirit, namely Germany and the Slavic races, whereas France might become a German satellite and even England a state of secondary rank.[2] His lack of confidence in the future of France was best revealed in a statement, reputedly made to the nationalist leader Paul Déroulède: "Jeune homme, la France se meurt, ne troublez pas son agonie."[3] It is not surprising that statements of this kind earned Renan the reputation of being one of the major exponents of the idea of French decadence.[4] Actually, Renan, constantly wavering between the prin-

[1] *Réforme intellectuelle* in *Œuvres complètes*, I, 338, 385; Renan's criticism of French society was shared by Michel Bréal in his *Quelques mots sur l'instruction publique* (Paris, 1872); see Daniel Halévy, *Trois épreuves, 1815, 1870, 1940* (Paris, 1941), 40–41, 83–85.

[2] *Œuvres complètes*, I, 350–351. 405–406; cf. Richard Chadbourne, *Renan as an Essayist* and Digeon, *op. cit.*, 179–215.

[3] A. Bellesort, *Les intellectuels et l'avènement de la Troisième République (1871–75)* (Paris, 1931), 159.

[4] Cf. Louis Vié, *Renan, la guerre de 70 et la "Réforme" de la France* (Paris, 1949).

ciples of conservatism and innovation, never developed a fully consistent political philosophy. In his later years he stripped himself of most of his illusions about modern Germany and lukewarmly accepted the Third Republic.[1]

Taine, on the other hand, slowly but consistently worked out a highly pessimistic interpretation of modern French history to which he clung until the end of his life. Taine's usually so well-balanced mind lost its bearings in the year of disaster.[2] In his bewilderment and anxiety about the fate of his nation he decided to undertake an historical investigation into the causes of the national failure. The result of this vast enterprise, to which he devoted most of the energy of his remaining years, was his monumental *Origines de la France contemporaine* (1876–1894). Whatever its merits as a study of the French Revolution, this work constitutes a valuable testimony to the anxiety current at the time: "Si l'avenir veut connaître l'état d'âme de la France au lendemain de la guerre," commented a fellow historian, Gabriel Hanotaux, "il ouvrira ce livre qui prolonge et renouvelle, en ses pages désespérées, la plainte des vaincus."[3]

Outstanding for its literary qualities rather than for its balanced judgment or sound scholarship, Taine's *magnum opus* was influential as no other work in discrediting the Great Revolution of 1789 among French intellectuals.[4] Like many reactionaries, Taine considered the Revolution the logical outcome of the philosophy of the Enlightenment, which had been taken more seriously in France than anywhere else. On the other hand, he did not make an attempt to hide the many serious abuses from which the *ancien régime* had been suffering and expressed unqualified admiration for the new scientific spirit. His real originality consisted in blaming the "classical spirit" so prevalent among the French educated classes for the undesirable turn that the introduction of modern science had taken in France.[5] This classical spirit, as it had been dominant in France during the last two centuries of the *ancien régime*, he asserted, excelled in deductive analyses and abstract generalizations, preferring clarity and elegance of expression

[1] Cf. Renan, "Discours de réception à l'Académie française," *Œuvres complètes*, I, 728; cf. Digeon, *op. cit.*, 213–214.

[2] Gabriel Hanotaux, *Histoire de la France contemporaine* (1871–1900) (4 vols., Paris, 1903–06), II, 549–555.

[3] *Ibid.*, II, 555.

[4] "Son œuvre est l'arme la plus meurtrière qui ait été forgée depuis cent ans contre l'erreur funeste de 89." (Paul Bourget, *Études et portraits*, vol. III, *Sociologie et littérature*, Paris, 1906, 113).

[5] Taine, *L'ancien régime* (Paris, 1887), 266.

to solid erudition and observation of social and political realities. He was willing to admit that this classical mentality had produced great works in literature and philosophy but argued that it had had disastrous consequences in the fields of practical politics because it had made the French mind receptive to utopian abstractions and radical revolutions and impatient with concrete and gradual reforms. According to Taine, this classical mentality had found its true incarnation in the Jacobin, whom he described as a gorilla driven by a naive belief in progress, full of resentment and completely ignorant of political science.[1]

Taine's historical study was characterized by extreme pessimism. He failed to discover any genius for politics among the French, even in the periods in which the country had dominated Europe. His point of view is not unfairly summed up in the aphorism: "L'Ancien Régime a été un fiasco, la Révolution un fiasco, l'Empire un fiasco, c'est pour cela que nous pataugeons dans la boue."[2] His work was therefore less a study in French decadence (which implies a period of greatness) than a brilliant and vehement indictment of French political behavior. Intentionally written to discredit radical political experiments in the name of tradition and historical continuity, it actually amounted to a condemnation of the political traditions of France and a glorification of the political wisdom of Germanic nations, especially that of England.

Renan, Taine, and many other French intellectuals of this time (Renouvier, Nefftzer, Secrétan, Quinet) were inclined to view the failure of the Protestant Reformation in France as one of the most fateful events in the national development.[3] "Heureux les pays protestants," wrote Renouvier to Secrétan in 1871, "La France a, comme on dit, manqué le coche au XVIe siècle."[4] This point of view was the main theme of La France, nos fautes, nos périls, notre avenir (1872), by a prominent French Protestant, the Comte Agénor de Gasparin. The major cause of French decadence was, according to him, the strongly developed tendency toward political centralization which, introduced by the Romans, had become ingrained in French society under the influence of the Catholic Church. It was not the defeat

---

[1] Cf. Rudolf Stadelmann, "Taine und das Problem des geschichtlichen Verfalls," Historische Zeitschrift, CLXVII (1943), 116–153; F. C. Roe, Taine et l'Angleterre (Paris, 1923), 94ff.

[2] Digeon, op. cit., 224.

[3] Cf. A. Billy, Les frères Goncourt, la vie littéraire à Paris pendant la deuxième moitié du XIXe siècle (Paris, 1954), 265.

[4] Mouy, L'idée de progrès, 71; Digeon, op. cit., 274, 277.

on the battlefield, he argued, but the weakening of the intellectual and moral fiber of the nation that was the reason for the loss of French leadership in European affairs. Gasparin severely criticized the French for their unwillingness to recognize their shortcomings, among which he included boastfulness, vanity, frivolity, mendaciousness, and false patriotism, and he was one of the few intellectuals who continued to depict the Germans as morally superior in every respect. The Latin civilization, he concluded, is affected by an irremediable evil: being the first born, it is the oldest and will therefore be the first to die.[1]

Whereas concern, alarm, and even despair was characteristic of most, if not all conservative and liberal publicists, such a pessimistic attitude was much less common among those who still firmly believed in the principles of the French Revolution. The tragic events of these years, however, also undermined the confidence of a number of republicans. In the beginning of the war few of them had wished for a victory as this would have strengthened the imperial regime. They almost rejoiced in the debacle of Sedan, because it led to the downfall of the hated Empire. It was rather the failure of the new regime to turn the course of events in favor of France that led some republicans to despair. They could not fail to make invidious comparisons between the successful manner in which the First Republic had expelled the invading armies from French soil and the failure of the new Republic to do the same. France, complained a republican author, Auguste Dalichoux, did no longer produce giants like Mirabeau, Danton, and Robespierre who could save the country. In 1792, he stated, only the nobility had been decadent, this time the bourgeoisie and even the lower classes had become profoundly corrupt.[2]

An additional reason for republican pessimism was that the defeat had been inflicted by Germany, a nation, which most republicans as well as liberals had admired for its idealistic and progressive civilization but which now stood revealed as a state of blood and iron, seemingly destined to dominate the European continent. Disillusionment with Germany was one of the reasons that Jules Michelet lost the firm confidence in the future which he had still expressed in the last year before the war. He was forced to recognize that the Germany of his dreams no longer existed or was at least taken captive by the "Slavic" nation of Prussia. The change in Germany, he feared, was

---

[1] Gasparin, La France, nos fautes, nos périls, notre avenir (Paris, 1872), II, 55; Mohrt, op. cit., 171ff.

[2] Auguste Dalichoux, 1871! Les premières phases d'une décadence (Paris, 1871), 15, 31.

indicative of the general development of his century from a freedom loving mentality to a nihilistic and fatalistic philosophy in which man was reduced to a position of cog in a military and industrial machine.[1]

An even more important reason for republican despondency in the years immediately following the defeat was the existence of a royalist majority in the National Assembly. In 1872 a republican, Emile Second, indulged in a fictitious account of what the history of France during the remaining part of the century might be if the monarchy were restored (*Histoire de la décadence d'un peuple, 1872-1900*). He anticipated economic and financial decline, cultural decadence, and social unrest, finally leading to another war against Germany, another defeat and further cession of territory this time followed by a Bonapartist restoration, civil war and partition of the country by neighboring powers. In 1900, he predicted, the statement might be made: "La France n'existe plus aujourd'hui que de nom, et elle est destinée à disparaître complètement, comme la Pologne."

The poet and scholar Louis Ménard was another fervent republican whose pessimism far from decreasing after the downfall of the Empire, became more pronounced than ever. "Notre décadence," he stated in a letter to his friend Renouvier in 1875, "est plus absolue et plus irrémédiable que celle de l'Espagne." It made little difference, according to him, whether Thiers or Napoleon III occupied the palace of the Élysée. Convinced that civilization had reached its peak in the Greek democracies and that the course of events since that time had largely consisted in a process of degeneration, only temporarily interrupted by the Renaissance and the Reformation, he had no sympathy for the current "adoration of progress," which reminded him of the messianism of Jewish fanatics compensating for the successive downfalls of their own nationality by stubborn dreams of universal domination.[2]

Pessimism was, however, not the dominant mood among republican ranks. Renouvier, who so profoundly influenced the new republican ideology, fully shared Menard's misgiving about the pernicious effect of the current belief in progress, but felt that a fatalistic belief in decadence was at least equally detrimental to morality as dogmatic optimism and that as far as France was concerned the situation had improved rather than deteriorated as a result of the war. He held that the fall of the imperial regime could not have been bought too

[1] See Digeon, *op. cit.*, 129ff.
[2] Henri Peyre, *Louis Ménard*, 367ff.; cf. *ibid.*, 183.

dearly and that "le malheur, source de réflexion et de progrès, est préférable à l'enflure de la fausse gloire qui tue toutes les vertus, et jusqu'à l'intelligence, . . ." Although feeling that the French defeat was deserved and that France could still learn much from her enemy's liberal religious policy and superior educational system, Renouvier became convinced that the German cult of violence and fatalism rather than any French shortcomings constituted the greatest threat to the future of European civilization.[1]

Most republicans felt even more sanguine about the future of a Republican France. The national defeat left hardly any mark on the robust optimism of Victor Hugo who continued to dream of a United States of Europe with Paris as its capital.[2] Edgar Quinet, who had lost almost all confidence in his fellow countrymen during the Second Empire, regained much of his earlier belief in his nation after the Republic was established. He admitted that the spirit of true freedom was virtually nonexistent in France, but he denied that France was an old nation and urged his fellow countrymen to avoid pessimism like a plague.[3] Another prominent intellectual who became one of the spiritual mentors of the new Republic, Emile Littré, was even more optimistic. Although conceding that his youthful, Comtian belief in the coming of an era of universal peace had been an illusion, and criticizing the French for their political immaturity, he blamed the downfall of France on Napoleon III and clericalism and rejected the idea of French decadence. He pointed to the economic prosperity of the country and the flourishing state of arts, sciences and philosophy, and never doubted that France would continue to play a leading role in the progressive development of mankind.[4]

Pessimistic views as to the future of France, far from universal among French intellectuals, were even less widely accepted by the rest of the nation. The popular attitude, as revealed by novels, poems, and political speeches, seemed to have a refusal to admit that the

---

[1] Cf. *Ibid.*, 371ff., Mouy, *L'idée de progrès dans la philosophie de Renouvier*, 70ff,; *Critique philosophique*, I (1872), 3–9, 152–156, 169, 225–229, 257–262.

[2] Victor Hugo, *Actes et paroles depuis l'exil (1870–1876)* (Paris, 1876); Digeon, *op. cit.*, 147–153. Cf. Victor Hugo's injunction to the periodical *Renaissance* in 1872: "Vous ne parlerez jamais . . . de décadence"; Michel Mansuy, *Un moderne. Paul Bourget de l'enfance au Disciple* (Besançon, 1961), 188.

[3] Quinet, *La République. Conditions de la régénération de la France* (1872), *Œuvres complètes*, vol. XXV (1881), 143, 278–279; *idem, Esprit nouveau* (1874) *Œuvres complètes*, vol. XXIII, preface; cf. Digeon, *op. cit.*, 138–147.

[4] Littré, "De la situation que les derniers événements ont faite à l'Europe, au socialisme et à la France," (1871), *De l'établissement de la Troisième République*, 129. 135; *idem, Conservation, révolution et positivisme* (2d ed., Paris, 1879); cf. Stanislas Aquarone, *The Life and Works of Emile Littré (1801–1881)* Leyden, 1958), 157–158.

French army had been beaten in an honorable battle by superior forces.[1] As in similar instances of sudden, unexpected military collapse (France in 1940; Germany in 1918) the people were inclined to believe that spies, fifth columnists, Freemasons, or Jews rather than any national deficiences were to blame for their disasters. The German victory was attributed not so much to any German virtues as to their barbarian and perfidious way of warfare. Contrary to what might have been expected, public opinion became even more convinced than before of the superiority of the French people, especially in relation to the Germans. The prediction made by Maxime du Camp in September, 1870 came true in part: "On va s'expliquer au peuple français qu'il est le premier peuple du monde, qu'il a été trahi, qu'il a été livré, en un mot qu'il est indemne."[2] The unlimited confidence in the strength and resources of France, complained another writer, Guillaume Heinrich, constitutes the greatest obstacle to national regeneration.[3] The popularity of the conviction that the defeat was not the result of any basic national weaknesses, is also attested by the vogue of the idea of revenge, implying the belief in the ability to defeat Germany in the near future.

Even may intellectuals subscribed to this view of the fundamental superiority of the French nation. Louis Veuillot stated that Prussia would never have been able to vanquish a nation ten times stronger and richer than herself, if God had not wanted to punish France.[4] Many scholars, reacting against the relative cosmopolitanism that had been characteristic of the French mind before the war, began to emphasize the superior qualities of French civilization. The tone for this cultural nationalism was set by the historian Fustel de Coulagnes in a famous article in the *Revue des Deux Mondes* of 1872, deploring that in the bottom of their heart Frenchmen nourished a certain hatred of themselves that expressed itself in a glorification of other nations. He maintained that since 1815 "on se figura une Angleterre qui avait toujours été sage, toujours libre, toujours prospère; on se representa une Allemagne toujours laborieuse, vertueuse, intelligente."[5]

---

[1] E. Koschwitz, *Les Français avant, pendant et après la guerre de 1870–71. Etude psychologique basée sur des documents français* (Paris, 1897); In his *Dictionnaire des idées reçues*, Flaubert noted: "Allemands ... ce n'est pas étonnant qu'ils nous aient battus, nous n'étions pas prêts!" Digeon, *op. cit.*, 17; cf. *ibid.*, 57–72.

[2] Maxime Du Camp, *Souvenirs littéraires* (Paris, 1892), II, 363.

[3] Heinrich, *op. cit.*, 25.

[4] E. Malcolm Carroll, *French Public Opinion and Foreign Affairs, 1870–1914* (New York, 1931), 69.

[5] Fustel de Coulanges, "De la manière d'écrire l'histoire en France et en Allemagne depuis cinquante ans, "*Revue des Deux Mondes*, Sept. 1, 1872; Digeon, *op. cit.*, 235–253. Cf.

Many of the intellectuals who had despaired of their country at the time of the defeat and the Commune, moreover, soon realized that their fears had been excessive. When shortly after the war France displayed a surprising recuperative power, paid off its huge war indemnity earlier than anyone had anticipated, reorganized its educational system and its army, and showed a greater sense of national unity and political wisdom than at any time since 1789, national confidence began to recover some of its former strength. In 1878 the Third World Exhibition in Paris and the French participation in the Congress of Berlin convinced many that France again counted as an important economic and political power and that the worst crisis belonged to the past.[1] Republicans more than any other political group regained confidence in the future as the political tide turned into their favor. But even some liberals like Ernest Renan were willing to admit that their fears of a republican regime had been unreasonable and that the Republic was the form of government that divided Frenchmen least.

The triumph of the Republic, on the other hand, deepened the pessimism of many conservatives. In 1879 Barbey d'Aurevilly, in his new preface to his *Prophètes du passé*, stated: "En 1851, malgré tout ce qui s'était accompli de leurs prophéties, il y avait encore pour les nations de l'espérance. En 1879, il n'y en a plus. Tout est consommé . . .;" in the same year another French monarchist, F. Lorrain, indicted democracy as the major cause of French weakness: "La République achève parfaitement ce que les Allemands avaient si bien commencé;" and Arthur de Gobineau confided to a friend: "Je tiens pour incontestable que la France est un pays perdu, comme l'Empire romain son type a été un pays perdu . . . La population y va diminuant, les opinions s'y énervant, les instincts s'y pulvérisant. C'est une race souillée, trop bâtarde; elle ne sait plus ni ce qu'elle veut ni ce qu'elle fait."[2]

In spite of the popular refusal to believe in any essential national deficiencies and in spite of the waning of an attitude of utter despair on the part of many intellectuals, the experiences of the *année terrible*

Emmanuel Liais, *Suprématie intelectuelle de la France. Réponse aux allégations germaniques* (Paris, 1872); Jacques Barzun, *Race, a study in Modern Superstition* (New York, 1937), 236; Ruth Benedict, *Race* (New York, 1940), 129–130, 202–204. Many Saint-Simonians also reaffirmed their belief in the superiority of French civilization; cf. "Le grand coupable dans les malheurs de la France," *Œuvres de Saint-Simon et d'Enfantin*, vol. XXVI (Paris, 1872), preface.

[1] Chastenet, *Histoire de la Troisième République*, I, 247.

[2] Barbey d'Aurevilly, *Prophètes du passé*, new conclusion written in 1879 (Paris, 1880), 233; Digeon, *op. cit.*, 93, 356–357.

left a lasting mark on the French mind. In the next chapter it will be seen that the pessimism and the feeling of decadence which was so characteristic of the new literary generation that reached maturity after the war had its origin at least partly in the tragic experiences of the national defeat. More generally, it can be stated that the national downfall dealt a decisive blow to the sentiments of national complacency and grandeur. French nationalism abandoned the generous and idealistic orientation which had characterized it earlier in the century and became more modest in its aspirations. Since the war a sense of national inferiority haunted an influential segment of the French population; the loss of Alsace-Lorraine, for instance, served as a constant reminder of the decline of French power. Around 1900 France might still be widely considered "le plus beau royaume sous le ciel," but French claims that the world's future would belong to their nation sounded less self-assured and were less numerous than similar statements made by German, Russian and English writers of the time. If Frenchmen still talked about the greatness of their nation, they had the past rather than the future in mind. French nationalism lost its expansive and dynamic character and became increasingly historically minded. 1870 more than any other date in French history constituted the end of the prevalent belief in "la grande nation."

CHAPTER VI

FIN DE SIECLE
1877–1905

Je crois à la fatale et imminente putréfaction d'une latinité
sans Dieu et sans symbole . . . Je juge que la fin de la France
n'est plus qu'une question d'années.

JOSEPHIN PÉLADAN, in 1890[1]

A country is not without honor save in its own prophets.

SAMUEL BUTLER, 1835–1902[2]

No other period in French history has such a well-established reputation for pessimism as the so-called *fin de siècle*. As early as 1878 Joseph
Reinach noticed with deep concern the influence which Arthur
Schopenhauer and Eduard von Hartmann exerted on French intellectuals.[3] In 1881 the republican journalist Raoul Frary complained:
"La décadence, ce mot nous poursuit. Nous le trouvons sur les lèvres
des indifférents, des égoïstes, comme dans la bouche des philosophes
pessimistes, des vieillards moroses, des vaincus de la bataille politique."[4] Foreign observers came to similar conclusions. The English-
man John Bodley, who spent the years 1890–1897 on French soil to
collect material for his perceptive study on contemporary France,
remarked that an acute and contagious pessimism had infected a
large proportion of the French nation.[5] A few years later his com-
patriot Charles Dawbarn asserted that the French had lost their lightheartedness and gaiety at Sedan and had not recovered them since.[6]

Such diagnosticians of the French mind were undoubtedly guilty
of exaggeration. As will be pointed out below, the great majority of
the French nation and even a large part of the intellectuals did not
suffer from excessive gloom, but it is true that during the last decades
of the nineteenth century a vocal, if not necessarily representative

---

[1] Jules Huret, *Enquête sur l'évolution littéraire* (Paris, 1891), 37.
[2] As quoted by Arnold Toynbee, *A Study of History*, abridged ed. by D. C. Somervell
(Oxford, 1946), 330.
[3] Joseph Reinach, "De l'influence de l'Allemagne en France," *Revue bleue*, May 4,
1878, as quoted by Digeon, *La crise allemande de la pensée française*, 338.
[4] Raoul Frary, *Le péril national* (5th ed., Paris, 1881), 221.
[5] Bodley, *France*, 19ff.
[6] Charles Dawbarn, *France and the French* (London, 1911), 29.

segment of the French population consciously and often proudly adopted a pessimistic philosophy of life.

I

Much of the *fin de siècle* pessimism had its origin in the political conditions of the time. It was in the first place the international situation of France that continued to fill many Frenchmen with anxiety. Although France had recovered from many of the wounds inflicted by the War of 1870, its rank among the nations of the world was no longer as high as it had been in preceding centuries. Numerous French patriots were convinced that under the new republic the position of France, far from improving, was becoming progressively worse. Even many Frenchmen who had initially welcomed the establishment of the Third Republic lost their confidence in the new regime when the government seemed to abandon any thought of a war of revenge. They reproached the republican leaders for playing into the hands of Germany by wasting French military strength on futile colonial expeditions instead of concentrating on the recovery of Alsace-Lorraine. The opinion that France was a declining power probably gained widest currency around the turn of the century when serious reverses in French foreign policy (the Fashoda and Tangiers crises) caused many Frenchmen once again to despair of their country's future. At this time a large number of books, pamphlets, and articles as well as various opinion polls discussed the topic of the decadence of France. Many critics compared the deplorable condition of their country with that of other "Latin" countries like Italy and Spain, which also suffered defeat in their foreign policies at the end of nineteenth century.[1] The entire Latin world, it seemed to many, was no longer able to compete with the more enterprising and superiorly organized nations of Northern Europe and the United States and was therefore doomed to decadence.

One of the most persistent critics of the Third Republic's foreign policy was Madame Juliette Adam, a fervent patriot and republican, who reproached even her friend Gambetta for his lack of nationalism and became known as "la grande désabusée."[2] Such was also the political development of Paul Déroulède, the founder of the Ligue des patriotes,

---

[1] N. Colajanni, *Latins et Anglo-Saxons* (Paris, 1905); R. Altamira y Crevea, *Psicología del pueblo español* (2d ed. Barcelona, 1917).

[2] Cf. Winifred Stephens, *Madame Adam (Juliette Lamber)* (New York, 1917, 202, 224; Alcide Ebray, *La France qui meurt* (Paris, 1910), 346.

a mass movement initially sponsored by Gambetta. In his later years Déroulède became convinced that nothing could be expected from the existing regime and began to favor an authoritarian form of government. After having made a number of unsuccessful attempts to overthrow the Republic, he died a bitterly disappointed man.[1]

The deep concern which many ardent republicans felt about the lack of French preparation for a possible new conflict with Germany was most forcefully expressed by Raoul Frary in his book *Le péril national* (1881), warning against the general tendency to underestimate German power and to believe that France was still "la grande nation." The state of the nation, he asserted, had deteriorated since the War of 1870: Whereas in the years immediately following the defeat a strong nationalism had animated the French people, still intent on revenge, ten years afterwards the national humiliation seemed to have been forgotten and a complacent pacifism was gaining ground; in the mean time the decline of the birth rate, vehement political strife, and religious scepticism continued to undermine the strength of the nation. The author felt that the situation of France was serious, but not hopeless and that further decadence could be avoided if the French made a determined effort to overcome their weaknesses.[2]

It was Great Britain as well as Germany that, according to many nationalists, threatened the continued existence of France as a great power, and on numerous occasions Anglophobes accused the French government of having capitulated to a country that was still widely regarded as France's hereditary enemy. In his best seller, *La France conquise* (1906), Gustave Flourens, a former republican minister of foreign affairs, complained that France had become an English satellite and was no more than a wreck aimlessly pushed around by revolutionary currents. Like so many other old time republicans, he was bewildered by the antimilitarist and internationalist illusions that seemed to have taken hold of a large part of the French people.[3]

It was the domestic development even more than the precarious international situation of France that fostered a sense of disillusionment and gloom.[4] Ministerial instability and a number of widely publicized scandals involving government officials and members of

---

[1] Cf. Walter Frank, *Nationalismus und Demokratie im Frankreich der dritten Republik* (Hamburg, 1933), 142ff.

[2] *Le péril national*, 199–200, 202–203, 227, 263; cf. Digeon, *op. cit.*, 358–359.

[3] Gustave Flourens, *La France conquise* (Paris, 1906), 92, 178; cf. Stephans, *op. cit.*; Eugen Weber, *The Nationalist Revival in France, 1905–1914* (Berkeley, 1959), 33–34.

[4] Cf. Bodley, *op. cit.*, 19ff., 412.

the legislative assemblies earned the new regime the reputation of being corrupt and inefficient. The numerous Frenchmen who had opposed the Third Republic from the very beginning, convinced as they were that such a regime could bring only disaster to their country, were greatly strengthened in their convictions by the unedifying spectacle of French parliamentary democracy. Their unfavorable opinion was soon shared by other Frenchmen who had been among the supporters of the original, still conservative Constitution of 1875, but who lost all confidence in parliamentary institutions when Radical politicians began to carry out their anticlerical and democratic program. Thus a former collaborator of Gambetta, the comte de Chaudordy, asserted in 1889 that the past ten years had been the most disastrous that France had ever experienced, and he doubted whether there was still enough force and political courage left for restoring the country's strength.[1] In the same year, Eugène de Vogüé, the gifted essayist who was largely responsible for the discovery of the great Russian novelists by the French public, professed his complete disillusionment with the Republic: "1870 marque du même coup le dernier degré de nos misères et le triomphe définitif des principes dissolvants."[2] An even more devastating judgment was passed by Jules Roche, a former minister of the Republic, in 1897: "Nous sommes le pays le plus mal gouverné, ou dirai-je pour n'humilier personne, l'un des plus mal gouvernés qu'on puisse voir dans le monde."[3]

Such critical views of French democracy were shared by many other leading men of letters, who began to regret their earlier support of the republican regime. Thus Jules Lemaître concluded in 1885 that the Republic had frustrated all his hopes. By the close of the century his pessimism had deepened. "Il me semble," he remarked in 1897, "que la décadence française se distingue des autres décadences historiques en ceci, qu'elle se connaît parfaitement . . . Jamais peuple malheureux n'a été plus conscient de ses maux."[4] Feeling that France was going to her doom with her eyes open, he began to see in the new royalist movement of the Action française the only chance of salvation.[5] About the same time the eminent literary historian Ferdinand Brunetière developed into an unqualified opponent of political "individu-

---

[1] J. B. A. Damaze, comte de Chaudordy, *La France en 1889* (Paris, 1889), 129.
[2] Eugène de Vogüé, *Remarques sur l'Exposition du Centenaire* (1889) as quoted in Digeon, *op. cit.*, 299; cf. R. F. Byrnes, *Antisemitism in Modern France*, 106.
[3] *Figaro*, June 11, 1897.
[4] Jules Lemaître, *Opinions à répandre* (4th ed. Paris, 1901), 10; cf. Digeon, *op. cit.*, 339.
[5] Cf. Victor Giraud, *Les maîtres de l'heure* (Paris, 1914), II, 60–74.

alism" and began to look upon the Catholic Church as the only possible bulwark against the disintegration of the social order.[1] The conversions of Maurice Barrès and Paul Bourget to conservative nationalism are additional instances of a strong antidemocratic trend among the leading authors of the period.

The leftist ideology, it is true, had not lost all its support among the literary "elite." But even many devotees of the principles of the French Revolution were perturbed by the mediocrity of political life in the Young Republic. Thus numerous young writers vehemently assailed a regime from which they had expected too much. Although the founders of the Third Republic, unlike those of earlier republics, had not entertained naive illusions as to a complete regeneration of society, many of them had been confident that a kind of republican puritanism would sweep away the moral and political corruption that had been rampant under the Second Empire. They soon recognized their mistake. Exasperated at the slow pace at which democratic and social legislation was introduced, they reproached the leading politicians for their opportunism. In their disgust with the sordidness of the new parliamentary regime, many moralists sighed: "Ah! que la République était belle sous l'Empire."[2]

The discredit into which the Republic had fallen in the eyes of many leftist intellectuals is reflected in Jules Vallès' remark in 1883 that, though he wished no one evil, he looked forward to the day that a general would make short work of all intrigue and cowardice of French parliamentarians.[3] The prevalence of such feelings explains that many radicals readily sympathized with General Boulanger's attempt to establish a plebisciterian dictatorship. This same mentality also fostered a widespread attitude of indifference and cyncism toward politics. In view of the low standards of political life many men of letters considered it below their dignity to take any interest in public affairs.[4] "Aucune époque, semble-t-il," stated the leading Symbolist magazine, the *Mercure de France*, "ne fut plus propice que la nôtre à

[1] Ferdinand Brunetière, "Après le procès," *Revue des Deux Mondes*, March 15, 1898; A. Darlu, *M. Brunetière et l'individualisme: à propos de l'article "Après le procès"* (Paris, 1898).

[2] Guerlac, *Citations françaises*, 286; E. de La Ravine, *Le progrès, satire* (Paris, 1883); Edmond de Goncourt, *A bas le progrès* (Paris, 1893); cf. Bodley, *France*, 24ff., 385, 497; André Dansette, *Le Boulangisme*, 144–145.

[3] André Billy. *L'époque 1900* (Paris, 1951), 403–404, 410; cf. Edward "The Third Force, 1897–1939," in *Modern France*, ed. Edward M. Earle (Princeton, 1951), 127.

[4] In 1892 this increasing sense of political apathy and social irresponsibility aroused the alarm of the future leader of the Socialist party, Léon Blum, who attributed it to the failure of the nineteenth-century revolutions to live up to the high expectations which they had raised ("Progrès de l'apolitique en France," *Revue blanche*, July 1, 1892).

se croiser les bras et à attendre. Nous sommes du monde qui s'en
va et il est séant de s'en aller avec lui . . . La seule chose convenable
est donc plus que jamais de remonter dans les tours d'ivoire, pendant
qu'elles sont encore debout . . ."[1] The only political ideology upon
which many littérateurs looked with sympathy was anarchism.
Even love for one's country was held in suspicion as a vulgar sentiment,
unworthy of the enlightened mind. "Le patriotisme," it was stated
in one of the literary periodicals in 1899, "est un sentiment déraiso-
nable, source funeste de la plupart des maux qui désolent l'humanité."
The leading Symbolist critic, Rémy de Gourmont, remarked that
his generation was no longer dreaming of dying for their country:
"Nous chantons d'autres romances, nous cultivons un autre genre
de poésie. S'il faut le dire nettement les choses, eh bien! Nous ne
sommes pas de patriotes."[2]

Whereas in the past young Frenchmen had played an important
role in the fight for democracy, they now displayed their revolutionary
ardor mainly in literary movements publishing modernistic manifestoes instead of political platforms. An esthetic individualism became
more than before part of the creed of all men of letters. This individualism, as clearly pointed out by one of the most articulate advocates
of nonconformity, Georges Palante, had nothing in common with the
individualistic ideals of French republicans or *laissez-faire* economists.
It rejected any idea of social responsibility and was the opposite of
the gregarious spirit that was supposed to be characteristic of democracy. Unlike a liberal or a democrat, Palante argued, the true individualist was not an optimist, but a pessimist, for he believed in the inevitability of a conflict between the individual and society, a conflict
that tended to become more acrimonious in the modern age of mass
vulgarity.[3]

II

Of all the censors of the political morality of the Third Republic,
the ultraconservatives glorifying the old regime were the most virulent
in their criticism. With exasperation they watched the gradual
strengthening of democratic and socialist principles. All their attempts

[1] As quoted in Alfred de Tarde and Henri Massis, *Les jeunes gens d'aujourd'hui* (Paris,
1912), 10–11.
[2] Jacques Chastenet, *Histoire de la Troisième République*, III, 16; cf Girardet, *La société
militaire en France*, 213–222.
[3] Georges Palante, *Individualisme et pessimisme* (Paris, 1913), 3, 163–164.

to discredit the new regime at the time of the Boulanger crisis, the Panama scandal, or the Dreyfus case came to naught. It became manifest that the trend of the times was running against them and that the "beast of the Revolution," instead of being put to shame, reigned more supremely than ever.

The sharp contrast which these traditionalists made between the greatness of old France and the deplorable state of contemporary France could have served as a perfect basis for the elaboration of a theory of national decadence. Yet they did not succeed in producing any significant pessimistic philosophy of history. This was partly because most of them lacked the scholarly training or the perceptive insight required for making a rational analysis of the development of their country. But a more important reason for their failure was that out of political considerations they were unwilling to admit that the French people had radically changed since the end of the old regime. Although describing the present state of affairs in the darkest colors, they maintained that the nation itself was not decadent. Making an artificial distinction between true France and the existing political regime, they attributed the prevailing corruption to a few selfish politicians and some small groups of subversive elements like the Jews and the Freemasons. This enabled them to uphold their confidence in the superior qualities of the French nation and in its speedy, miraculous regeneration once the democratic system had been swept away.

A good example of this type of thinking is *La France vraie* (1887) the work by an obscure author, Saint Yves d'Alveydre. He maintained that the true France continued to exist in spite of all appearances to the contrary. According to him, the history of France demonstrated the falsity of all lamentations that France was a modern Sodom and Gomorrah. "Le vrai Paris, la vraie France n'en demeurent pas moins la Ville sacrée de la terre sainte de l'Occident ... C'est là encore, c'est là toujours que s'élabore le grand mystère social pour toutes les cités, pour toutes les nations." The author believed that the French possessed the mystical gift of political unity, the so-called "synarchie," which consisted in the harmonious co-operation of the three estates, the clergy, the nobility, and the bourgeoisie, as most spectacularly displayed in the States General of 1302. As a true theocrat, he saw in the military order of the Templars the purest embodiment of his political ideal, and he blamed the Latin tradition of Caesarism for the deviation of the French monarchy from its original, medieval function. Like many other traditionalists of his time, he believed in the Celtic nature of the French people and considered a Celtic revival essential to the regeneration of his country. These fantastic views did not leave any impact on his contemporaries but came to be seriously discussed as the basis of a new political and social order after the fall of France in 1940.[1]

In the years of the triumph of the republican credo the extreme Right might have disappeared altogether as a political force if it had not renewed its program so that it could appeal to larger segments of the population. The first attempt to organize a reactionary movement based on popular support was made by the notorious Jew-baiter, Edouard Drumont, who, with the publication of his best seller, *La France juive* (1886), established his reputation as a leading spokesman of the reactionary point of view. This was not the first time that anti-Semitism was exploited for political purposes. Earlier in the nineteenth century, French socialists like Fourier and Proudhon had denounced the Jews as ruthless exploiters of the working class. But Drumont was the first publicist to use anti-Semitism in defense of a reactionary and nationalist ideology and to make it the central part of a political philosophy.[2]

Drumont had a sentimental love for the past of France and his native city, Paris (no other author fulminated more vehemently against the building of the Eiffel tower), and posed as a gallant knight fighting modern greed and materialism, for which Jews, besides Freemasons and Protestants, were held responsible. His study, though lacking completely in historical objectivity and balanced judgment, was written with considerable literary skill. It satisfied the public's interest in shocking anecdotes about prominent personalities and impressed even many scholars by its display of erudition. The impact of *La France juive* on public opinion was also furthered by the circumstance that it was published at a time when Jews had begun to occupy some important positions in French society and the first wave of anticlerical legislation had intensified the conservatives' hatred for the Republic.

La France juive was followed up, in 1890, by the foundation of the

---

[1] Joseph-Alexandre Saint Yves d'Alveydre, *La France vraie* (2 vols., Paris, 1887), p. viii, 147, 153, 154, 540–541; cf. Epting, *Das französische Sendungsbewusstsein*, 41. On the current "Celtomania", see E. R. Curtius, *The Civilization of France* (Vintage Books ed., New York, 1962), 65–66; Byrnes, *op. cit.*, 145, 273–274.

[2] Cf. Georges Bernanos, *La grande peur des bien-pensants* (Paris, 1931); Byrnes, *op. cit.*, 118–125, 137ff.

French National Anti-Semitic Lague, and, in 1892, by the publication of a newspaper, *La libre parole*, which continued on an even more vulgar level the campaign against the Jews and the corruption of the Third Republic.

The weakness of Drumont's movement consisted in the absence of any other program than that of confiscating Jewish property, remaining even noncommittal on the question of the restoration of the monarchy. Although Drumont had considerable popular support, he antagonized many prominent conservatives, his only possible source for financial support, by denouncing them as henchmen of Jewish financiers. Actually Drumont cannot be fully classified as a conservative, for he was very critical of the upper bourgeoisie, the aristocracy, and the higher clergy, whereas he spoke highly appreciatively of many socialist leaders and sympathized with the lot of the poverty-stricken masses. His pessimism was the more bitter because it combined leftist indignation about capitalistic exploitation with rightist alarm at the loss of spiritual values.

Although Drumont continued his campaign until his death in 1917, he soon realized that he was fighting for a lost cause, and the statements made in his later books (the titles of which are revealing in themselves: *La fin d'un monde* 1888, *Le testament d'un antisémite*, 1891) became increasingly pessimistic. "Mon erreur fondamentale," he confessed, "a été de croire qu'il existait encore une vieille France, un ensemble de braves gens, gentilhommes, bourgeois, petits propriétaires fidèles aux traditions de leur race, et qui, égarés, affolés par les turlutaines qu'on leur débite depuis cent ans, reprendraient conscience d'eux-mêmes si on leur montrait la situation telle qu'elle est, se réuniraient pour sauver leur pays." The French, he concluded, were not even capable of true pessimism but were affected by a lassitude which was the prelude of death, whereas pessimism was a characteristic of superior races.[1]

The same gloomy conclusion was reached by one of Drumont's admirers, Gaston Routier in his *Grandeur et décadence des Français*, written at the time of the Dreyfus crisis. France, he complained, had become the laughing stock of the world, a nation of comedians and courtesans. "Jamais pays n'a offert au monde un plus écœurant spectacle." As a good Catholic traditionalist, he did not sympathize with the current Anglomania but held that the Anglo-Saxons, in spite of certain eminent qualities, were even closer to their downfall than the French.

---

[1] Drumont, *Le testament d'un antisémite* (Paris, 1891), 45, 172–173; Byrnes, *op. cit.* 165.

This true admirer of the old regime found his ideals best represented in Spain, the least modern country in Western Europe, and it is there that he sought refuge from the corruption of modern civilization during the last years of his life.[1]

It was not until after adopting nationalism as an integral part of their political program that the reactionaries recovered some of their lost strength. Until the end of the nineteenth century, militarism and nationalism had been favored by the Left rather than by the Right. Even after the war of 1870 the policy of revenge against Germany had found most of its advocates among the republicans. The first large nationalistic organization under the leadership of Déroulède, an admirer of Gambetta, had initially had a republican and not a conservative character. The process of changing attitudes started with the Boulanger crisis (1887–89), which began as an attempt made by the Radicals to revise the constitution and to carry on a more aggressive policy against Germany but which, in its later phase, came increasingly under the control of the royalists, who now adopted a nationalistic and militaristic program, whereas the Left began to show its distrust of the army and of a bellicose policy.[2] The new positions were consolidated by the Dreyfus affair, aligning the nationalist Right, defending the army, against the majority of the Left, convinced of the innocence of Dreyfus.

The Dreyfus affair ended in another of the many disappointments that the French Right experienced during the nineteenth century. The party of "Anti-France" triumphed, despoiling the clergy of more of its ancient rights, purging the army of its anti-republican elements, and creating new enthusiasm for the "detested" principles of 1789. The despondency among French conservatives was greater than ever before. Yet, at the same time, the extreme Right found a new leader in the person of Charles Maurras, who gave it a new political philosophy and restored some of its confidence.

The rise of the royalist movement of integral nationalism, also known as the Action française, had been prepared by a number of leading men of letters during the 1890's: Bourget, Brunetière, above all Barrès, the first author to use the term "nationalist" with the new conservative connotation.[3] It was, however, Maurras who gave the

---

[1] Gaston Routier, *Grandeur et décadence des Français* (Paris, 1898), p. v, ix, x, 54–57, 92, 22, 311, 318ff., 370, 380; similar ideas in Isidore Bertrand, *Un monde fin-de-siècle* (Paris, 1891).

[2] Cf. A. Dansette, *Le Boulangisme* (Paris, 1946), 374–375; Girardet, *La société militaire dans la France contemporaine*, 213–233.

[3] William C. Buthman, *The Rise of Integral Nationalism in France, with Special Reference to the Ideas and Activities of Charles Maurras* (New York, 1939), 61–62.

various elements disgusted with the republican regime a definite program and who, after his conversion to royalism in 1896, single-mindedly dedicated himself to the propagation of this political creed.

Maurras' political philosophy was simplicity itself and can be summed up in the antithesis "Republic versus Monarchy." One was the "Beast," the party of "Anti-France," that was leading the country to its ruin; the other represented the only possible salvation. Theoretically Maurras advocated the temperate, not the absolute monarchy. He held that France had reached the height of its glory under the reigns of the first two Bourbon kings, who had still respected local autonomy and corporate privileges. Even Richelieu, according to this view, had never had the design of suppressing all freedoms since the only purpose of the great Cardinal in strengthening royal authority had been to crush France's enemies. The first step in the decline of France was seen in the absolutist policies of Mazarin and Louis XIV, who had discontinued the practice of asking the nation for advice and who had centralized the form of government. The second and more radical deviation from sound political principles had occurred during the French Revolution when the nation had needlessly broken with the monarchy. Like Maistre and Le Play, Maurras considered this event the greatest calamity that had ever befallen the country.[1] Henceforth the situation had rapidly deteriorated, and the country had never been weaker than at the time of the Dreyfus affair, after it had been ruled by "foreign thieves and villains" for several decades. The final step, meaning the complete suppression of France, would be unavoidable unless the nation acted upon the program of the Action française. The greatest political error was, according to Maurras, the democratic principle of equality. The dilemma was: "L'inégalité ou la décadence! L'inégalité ou l'anarchie! L'inégalité ou la mort!"[2]

In spite of his bitter criticism of the existing regime, Maurras professed to be an optimist. He denied that the French nation was decadent. All that was wrong was the present political system and by merely accepting the monarchy the nation would once again become as powerful as it had been in the past.[3] Maurras entertained the simplistic, chiliastic belief that in the present the world was worse than

---

[1] Charles Maurras, *Enquête sur la monarchie* (Paris, 1925), 334ff., 496–497; Maurras borrowed this interpretation of French history largely from the journalist Frédéric Amouretti.

[2] *Ibid.*, 38–39, 79.

[3] *Ibid.* p. xlv; Maurras, *Dictionnaire politique et critique* (Paris, 1931), article "Décadence" and "Pessimisme;" *idem, Mes idées politiques* (Paris, 1937), 85ff.

it had ever been, but that by a miraculous turn of events all evil would vanish.

In his political thinking Maurras broke sharply with the kind of Christian idealism that had permeated most French traditionalism of the nineteenth century. Although looking with favor upon the Catholic Church as a prop of an aristocratic social order, he professed utter contempt for the revolutionary principles of Christ.[1] As a pagan, agnostic admirer of Comte's secular positivism, Maurras lacked any sympathy with the mystical and religious aspirations of many of his conservative contemporaries. He was the first traditionalist who was exclusively concerned with the interests of France, "la France seule," and denounced any loyalty to Christian or other supranational ideals.

Maurras fully endorsed the anti-Semitism and the other phobias that had proven their values in the hands of Drumont, but he went much further in his xenophobia than earlier Frenchmen by denouncing also the culture of foreign nations. His nationalism, as he himself admitted, had originated as an esthetic theory;[2] even before his conversion to royalism, Maurras had taken up arms in defense of French literary tradition by supporting the Ecole romane, founded in 1891 to combat the new cosmopolitan spirit in French literature. In his later career as a polemicist, Maurras widened his attack on foreign, especially Germanic influences, among which he counted Protestantism, democracy, individualism, and Romanticism. Madame de Staël, more than any other writer, was accused of having perverted the French mind by the idyllic picture she had presented of German civilization. With the treatise *De l'Allemagne*, he wrote, "le désordre, l'impropriété, l'inconséquence ont tout à fait pris possession de la pensée française."[3] In the course of the nineteenth century – "the stupid century," as Maurras's disciple, Léon Daudet put it – the admiration of foreign civilizations had reached its peak and French intellectuals, with only few exceptions (Maistre, Bonald, Comte, Le Play, and Fustel de Coulanges) had yielded to the alien and the barbarous.[4] France, he urged, should forsake its infatuation with vague, romantic, and idealist chimeras of foreign origin and return to the sound values of the *grand siècle*: reason, order, and discipline. France should seek its inspiration not in the confused genius of Teutonic

---

[1] Edward R. Tannenbaum, *The Action Française* (New York, 1962), 83–85.
[2] Maurras, *Quand les Français ne s'aimaient pas* (Paris, 1926), p. xiii.
[3] *Ibid.*, 36–37.
[4] Maurras, *La contre-révolution spontanée* (Lyon, 1943); Léon Daudet, *Le stupide XIXe siècle* (Paris, 1922).

Europe but in the clear, balanced thought of classical antiquity. A restoration of the monarchy would have to go hand in hand with "a Latin Renaissance."

In his attitude toward Germany, Maurras was not fully consistent. In principle he hated this country, not only as representing France's most dangerous opponent in the world, but even more as the alleged cradle of all subversive ideas in modern civilization. On the other hand, like most other conservatives, he could not help but envy the Germans for their traditionalist, monarchial form of government. But even in his praise of the German political system, Maurras betrayed his nationalist bias: "Les Hohenzollern," he wrote, "ne sont que les heureux et brillants imitateurs de nos Capétiens."[1]

Maurras was too much of a littérateur devoid of insight in the political and social realities of his time to become the leader of a strong popular movement. But he did attract a considerable number of gifted writers, who, like Maurras himself, were disgusted with the parliamentary form of government. By one-sided, but suggestive and often brilliant works on French history and literature many of his followers left their mark on the cultural development of their time. Jacques Bainville and a number of other historians influenced by Maurras were instrumental in creating a new interest in the history of pre-revolutionary France.[2] Similarly, the classical revival in French literature of the early twentieth century owed much to the virulent diatribes that Pierre Lasserre and other young royalists directed against the sentimentality, the vague verbosity, and the utopian idealism of prominent Romantic authors like Chateaubriand, George Sand, and Michelet.[3]

An unqualified rejection of Romanticism was also the basic theme of the scholarly studies on the cultural development of modern Europe written by Ernest de Seillière.[4] A conservative in the tradition of Le Play, but not a nationalist or a reactionary, Seillière had no admiration for either Maistre or Maurras, whose doctrinaire fanaticism, he felt, was actually completely foreign to the classical tradition of balance and reason.[5] Their outlook was rather akin to the mentality

---

[1] Maurras, *Kiel et Tanger* (2d ed., Paris, 1910), 169.

[2] Curtius, *op. cit.*, 82–83.

[3] Cf. Pierre Lasserre, *Le Romantisme français. Essai sur la Révolution dans les sentiments et dans les idées au XIXe siècle* (Paris, 1907); Léon Daudet, *op. cit.*, Henri Clouard, *Histoire de la littérature française du symbolisme à nos jours* (2 vols., Paris, 1947–49), I. 343–344; Eugen Weber, *Action Française* (Stanford, 1962), 78ff.

[4] René Gillouin, *Une nouvelle philosophie de l'histoire moderne et française. Les bases historiques et critiques d'une éducation nationale* (Paris, 1921); J. Huizinga, "Ernest Seillière," *Verzamelde werken* (9 vols., Haarlem, 1948–53), IV, 370ff.

[5] Seillière, *Le mal romantique* (Paris, 1908), pp. lx, lxi.

of irrational enthusiasm that Seillière considered the most destructive force in modern civilization and that he designated as "mysticism." The most common form of this state of mind in the modern world was Romanticism, which consisted in the subordination of judgment to instinct and sensibility (and therefore often designated as *passionate* and *esthetic* mysticism).[1] Seillière further distinguished *social* mysticism, best exemplified by the abstract utopianism of the Jacobin and socialist varieties, and finally a *racial* mysticism, which was at the root of the aggressive nationalism of modern times.

In all these instances "mysticism" had, according to Seillière, the effect of intensifying "imperialism." By this he meant the fundamental human desire to rule and expand (what Nietzsche called "the will to power"). Seillière held that in itself this human aspiration was not an evil for it was the mainspring of all cultural achievements, but that it became a disintegrating force in society if it were no longer controlled by reason and experience.

In a large number of works, partly written prior to the First World War,[2] Seillière showed how many prominent French and other European authors (Stendhal, Fourier, and Flaubert being some of his *bêtes noires*) had been infected by the dangerous mystical mentality. Like other anti-Romanticists, he reserved his sharpest criticism for Rousseau, the exponent of social as well as of esthetic and passionate mysticism. He was more original in tracing the disease of mysticism back to earlier times, stressing its strength in Fénelon, describing its manifestations in medieval romances, and indicating its presence even in ancient literature. His interpretation of modern utopian mentality as a secularized version of Christian mysticism was formulated in direct contradistinction to Hippolyte Taine's theory that the Jacobin spirit was the logical product of the "classical spirit."[3] In order to counteract the dangerous trend toward mysticism in the modern world, Ernest Seillière preached a rational but not a rationalistic reaction, by which he meant a respect for the wisdom and experience of the past and a rejection of the modern glorification of the human passions.[4]

---

[1] *Ibid.*, p. ix.

[2] *Philosophie de l'impérialisme* (3 vols., Paris, 1903–1907); *Le mal romantique. Essai sur l'impérialisme irrationnel* (Paris, 1908); *Introduction à la philosophie de l'impérialisme* (Paris, 1911); *Les mystiques du néo-romantisme* (Paris, 1911).

[3] Seillière, "Une théorie de Taine sur la Révolution française," *Revue des Deux Mondes*, XLIII (Jan. 15, 1918).

[4] *Philosophie de l'impérialisme*, III, 327–328.

III

At the end of the nineteenth century French liberals shared many of the misgivings about the state of France that were entertained by the extreme Right. Advocating either a constitutional monarchy or a conservative republic, they bitterly denounced democracy as well as socialism and abandoned their former objections to a strong army. It might be questioned as to whether any real "liberalism" was left in the political outlook of these self-styled liberals. In some questions, however, they continued to distinguish themselves from traditionalists. They held a high opinion of modern science and, though not in favor of anticlerical legislation, were not in sympathy with a policy of restoring the Catholic Church to its former influential position in society. Unlike the ultraconservatives, they were relatively well informed about the civilizations of other European countries and did not indulge in political and cultural chauvinism. After 1870, it is true, German civilization lost much of its prestige for them, but England continued to be held up by the liberals as the country that France should imitate in its social and political institutions if it wanted to survive as a prosperous and stable nation. Whereas the traditionalists accepted Joseph de Maistre, Louis Veuillot, and Frédéric Le Play as their masters, the liberals followed in the footsteps of Tocqueville, Taine, and Renan.

French liberals, who had viewed the state of their country with alarm at the time of the Second Empire, recovered some of their confidence with the adoption of the Constitution of 1875, which embodied many of the principles that their spokesman Prévost-Paradol had advocated in his *La France nouvelle* (1868). But much of their former gloom returned, often in intensified form, during the subsequent three decades, when the lower middle classes rose to positions of power and Radical and socialist ideas began to influence government policies. This new liberal concern about the advent of democracy found its first thoughtful expression in Edmond Scherer's *La démocratie et la France* (1883). In this political treatise the distinguished literary critic asserted that public affairs could not be adequately managed by the popular classes, "si arriérées, si ignorantes, si égoïstes, souvent si corrompues, – dépourvues d'esprit public, étrangères aux idées générales et généreuses." Influenced by Renan, he held the loss of religious faith responsible for the growing spirit of materialism and agnosticism and complained about the disappearance of "une grande partie de ce que l'humanité tenait jadis pour ses titres de noblesse." "On prend trop facilement aujourd'hui," he added, "tout change- ment pour une amélioration; on confond l'évolution et le progrès; mais le déclin, la sénilité, la mort même, c'est encore de l'évolution, et les sociétés n'échappent pas plus que les individus à la loi de la décadence."[1]

Around the turn of the century liberalism found another talented spokesman in the person of Emile Faguet.[2] In a large number of suggestive works this soft-spoken, undogmatic author criticized the republican regime for having promoted a cult of incompetence and a horror of responsibility. Concerned about the decline of the birth rate and the lack of any spirit of initiative, he felt that France, for the time being at least, was in a state of decadence.[3] Like many liberals of his time, he complained that the old patriotism was losing its strength. Highly critical of the "individualistic," negative philosophy of the eighteenth century, he approvingly quoted Nietzsche's definition of democracy as a form of decadence.[4] "La France," he asserted, "se sent nation de second rang; elle ne rêve d'aucune conquête, ne se sent plus appelée par les peuples asservis, ou ne peut pas raisonnable- ment s'imaginer qu'elle soit appelée par eux ... Après avoir été la nation mégalomane, la France est devenue la nation, non seulement prudente, mais timorée et parlant bas."[5]

In 1899 this conservative liberal made a prognosis of the coming century, which shows that he was neither an unqualified pessimist nor an altogether false prophet. He predicted that the small nations of the world would gradually be reduced to a status of satellites and that democracies would tend to develop either into plutocracies or military despotisms with socialist velleities; he also anticipated scientific activity to become more brillant than ever, but superior art and literature to vanish, together with religion and all the habits on which the religious spirit had left its mark, such as the indissolubility of marriage and the subordination of women to men.[6]

One of the bitterest remarks made by Faguet was that he had never met a real liberal in France.[7] This alleged absence of liberalism in

---

[1] Edmond Scherer, *La démocratie et la France* (Paris, 1883), 20; *idem* "La crise actuelle de la morale," *Etudes sur la littérature contemporaine*, vol. VIII (Paris, 1885), 184.

[2] Giraud, *Maîtres de l'heure*, vol. I.

[3] Faguet, in *Revue latine*, I (1902), 29ff.

[4] Faguet, *Le culte de l'incompétence* (Paris, 1910), 29ff.

[5] Faguet, *L'anticléricalisme* (Paris, 1905), 307–308.

[6] Faguet, "Que sera le XXe siècle," *Questions politiques* (Paris, 1899), 245–336.

[7] Faguet, *Le libéralisme* (Paris, 1902), 306; *Revue latine*, IV (1905), 643.

France was the main theme of the well-known study *Les deux France* (1904)
of Paul Seippel, a Swiss Protestant, who enlarged upon Quinet's
and Gasparin's criticisms of French cultural and political traditions
and upon Taine's denunciation of the French "classical spirit."
In a highly schematic survey of French history he attempted to show
how an authoritarian mentality introduced by the Romans, and therefore called "mentalité romaine," had been dominant all through
French history. This illiberal attitude had been fully adopted by the
Roman Catholic Church, which, during the Middle Ages, had success-
fully suppressed all manifestations of the critical and naturalist spirit
of the French people (the so-called "esprit gaulois"). Similarly the
strongly entrenched "mentalité romaine" had curtailed the liberating
tendencies of the Renaissance and caused the failure of the Reformation, of which the French variety, Calvinism, showed many authoritarian characteristics. The French *philosophes* of the eighteenth century
had stressed reform from above rather than individual freedom, and
the French Revolution had merely paid lip service to liberalism.
French republicans, such as the Jacobins and the anticlericals of the
Third Republic, had adopted all the methods and aims of their
opponents: excessive political centralization, ideological fanaticism
and intolerance. In modern times there had been two Frances: the
revolutionary, red France and the conservative, black France, fighting
one another as irreconcilable enemies, but both bearing the imprint
of the same dogmatic authoritarianism. The author did not deny
the existence of a third, more liberal France but felt that it had never
been strong enough to assert itself, largely because it had been too
negative and critical in its attitude. The book ended on a pessimistic
note; the author feared that a triumphant socialism would inherit
the authoritarian bent of the French mind and would develop it to
even greater perfection than ever before.[1]

A similar view of French history was developed by a number of
liberal Roman Catholics belonging to the so-called school of Tourville,
a progressive offshoot of Frédéric Le Play's movement of Social
Catholicism. Being mainly interested in the organization of the family,
to which they attributed a decisive influence on all other social
relations, they distinguished three major varieties: (1) a patriarchal,
(2) an individualistic or "particularistic," and (3) a collective or

---

[1] The absence of a strongly rooted feeling for liberty was also the main theme of Maurice
Caudel, *Nos libertés politiques: origines, évolution, état actuel* (Paris, 1910). Seippel's thesis was
criticized in Victor Giraud, *La troisième France* (Paris, 1917).

"communistic" type of family. The first of these, which once had been universal all over Europe, was gradually dying out; the second one, originating in Northern Europe, had replaced the patriarchal family in Scandinavian and Anglo-Saxon countries and also temporarily in France, where, however, due to unfortunate circumstances, the third unstable, "communistic" type of family organization had largely taken over.[1]

The Anglophilism of this school of thought attained its most explicit expression in Edmond Demolins' *D'où vient la supériorité des Anglo-Saxons?* (1897), a work that found many readers not only in France but also in several other countries (Spain, Turkey, England). The author was primarily concerned with the different effects which the various forms of family organization had on the manner of raising children. The English individualistic family, according to him, excelled in character building. At an early age English children were treated as mature persons who could not depend on others to solve their problems and who thus developed a sense of responsibility and self-reliance. In France, on the other hand, children expected their parents to make most decisions, and the educational system encouraged mechanical drill and conformity instead of a spirit of initiative. This "communist" mentality was most pronounced in Southern France, which threatened to drag the rest of the country behind it on the road of decline. The individualistic mentality was even weaker in Italy and Spain, and Demolins considered the decadence of these countries a warning example of what might happen to his own country if it did not reform its system of education.[2]

A pessimistic interpretation of Darwinism evident in Demolins' comparison between the French and English educational systems was also accepted by numerous other French social scientists. The most popular author pointing out how natural selection had led to a decline of France was Gustave Le Bon, a physician by training who turned his attention to the problems of social psychology.[3] His

---

[1] Cf. Edmond Demolins, "La maladie du siècle," *La réforme*, II (1882), 153–158; Henri Tourville, *The Growth of Modern Nations; a History of the Particularistic Form of Society* (New York, 1907); Paul de Rousiers, "La fonction de l'élite dans la société moderne," *Science sociale*, Oct., 1912; Jan., 1914; Demolins, *Les Français d'aujourd'hui: les types sociaux du Midi* (Paris, 1898).

[2] Demolins' thesis was pertinently criticized by Charles Gide in the *Revue d'économie politique*, XII (1898), 345–348, and by Maurice Spronck in the *Revue politique et littéraire: Revue Bleu*, 4e série, vol. VIII (1897).

[3] Cf. H. E. Barnes, "A Psychological Interpretation of Modern Social Problems: A Survey of the Contributions of Gustave Le Bon to Social Psychiatry," *American Journal of Psychology*, XXXI (1920), 333–369.

best known works, *Lois psychologiques de l'évolution des peuples* (1894), *La psychologie des foules* (1895), and *La psychologie du socialisme* (1898), in many ways constituted investigations into the causes of the decadence of the Latin peoples. Lacking individualism, burdened with an antiquated systen of education, inclined to collectivism and mob rule, easily influenced by slogans and phrases coined by irresponsible men of letters, these nations, Gustave Le Bon held, could no longer compete with the Anglo-Saxons and other progressive peoples of the world:[1] "Elles perdent chaque jour leur initiative, leur énergie, leur volonté et leur aptitude à agir. La satisfaction de besoins matériels toujours croissants tend à devenir leur unique idéal. La famille se dissocie, les ressorts sociaux se détendent."[2] He called "cette effroyable décadence de la race latine" "une des plus sombres, des plus tristes, et, en même temps, des plus instructives expériences que l'on peut citer à l'appui des lois psychologiques que j'ai exposées."[3] Like many anthropologists and sociologists of his time, Le Bon came to the conclusion that modern science demonstrated the fallacy of democratic principles. Believing that aristocracy was the law of human society, Le Bon maintained that the findings of sociology were as irreconcilable with democratic illusions as the discoveries of geology were with the story of Creation in Genesis.[4]

Gustave Le Bon still implied that the struggle for survival ends with the triumph of the superior race. Other Social Darwinists arrived at even more pessimistic conclusions.[5] They felt that in the modern world inferior racial groups, by the sheer force of their numbers, tend to defeat the less numerous representatives of superior races so that evolution results in retrogression rather than in progress. This point of view was taken by the anthropologist Georges Vacher de Lapouge, who believed to have found additional evidence in support of Gobineau's theory of the superiority of the Aryan race.[6] The history of France, according to him, consisted in a long struggle between the superior, dolichocephalic race and the inferior, brachycephalic part of the nation. Unfortunately for France, and in contrast to what had happened in England, the superior racial group had been decimated,

[1] Le Bon, *Psychology of Socialism* (New York, 1899), 25, 55, 154–157.
[2] Le Bon, *Lois psychologiques de l'évolution des peuples* (10th ed., Paris, 1911), 165.
[3] *Ibid.*, 116.
[4] Le Bon, *Psychology of Socialism*, 282–283.
[5] Cf. N. Colajanni, *Le socialisme* (Paris, 1900); A Fouillée, *Psychologie du peuple français* (Paris, 1898), 31, 130ff., 136; M. Closson. "La dissociation par déplacement," *Revue de sociologie*, 1895.
[6] Cf. Jean Colombat, *La fin du monde civilisé; les prophéties de Vacher de Lapouge* (Paris, 1946).

first by the persecution of the Protestants, later by the Revolution, "le désastre le plus grand qui ait frappé la nation depuis qu'elle soit constituée. "The age of the Enlightenment, which had produced the Revolution, was in his eyes "le plus songe-creux, le plus anti-scientifique de tous les siècles." In modern France social selection had assured the triumph of the bourgeoisie, which Lapouge called "un champignon vénéneux grandi à l'ombre de la guillotine, grâce au sang des nobles et des prêtres," a class which had become even more powerful by exploiting the working classes and by speculating on the stock market; in short had triumphed by way of cruelty, cheating, and selfishness. The situation was all the more serious because of the higher birth rate of the inferior racial group. Lapouge, of course, entirely rejected the law of progress, stating that "cette chimère de notre temps se sera évanouie demain." "L'analyse des sélections sociales aboutit en définitive aux conclusions du pessimisme le plus absolu. L'avenir n'est pas aux meilleurs, tout au plus aux médiocres."[1]

Although such utter gloom was not shared by most French social scientists, many of them viewed the course of modern civilization with alarm. A number of French sociologists, pioneering in the study of social disorganization, were the first scholars who methodically studied such disconcerting phenomena as the increasing rates of crime, divorce, and suicide. Thus André Lalande rejected the current equation of evolution and progress and introduced the concept of "social dissolution" as a more satisfactory explanation of many features of modern society.[2] Other systematic students of social change, became known as the first "social pathologists" comparing society and its disintegration with the human organism and its maladies.[3] The uncontested master of French sociologists, Emile Durkheim, acquired his reputation partly by a thorough study of suicide and other social evils of the nineteenth century, which he attributed to the circumstance that in modern societies men are no longer bound together by common beliefs. His concept of "anomie," as he characterized this state of atomistic individualism, has perhaps been his most fruitful contribution to modern sociological thought.[4]

[1] Vacher de Lapouge, Les selections sociales (Paris, 1896), 443. 445; Colajanni, Le socialisme, 309–310; cf. Fouillée, op. cit., 118.
[2] André Lalande, La dissolution opposée à l'évolution dans les sciences physiques et morales (Paris, 1899).
[3] Paul de Lilienfeld, La pathologie sociale (Paris, 1896).
[4] Cf. Emile Durkheim, Le suicide (Paris, 1897), 282–288; H. Stuart Hughes, Consciousness and Society. The Reorientation of European Social Thought, 1890–1930 (Vintage Books, New York, 1961), 282–283; Digeon, op. cit., 380–381.

Some other scientific theories of the time also led to a questioning of an optimistic interpretation of man's historical destiny. The new naturalistic view of the universe deprived the course of human history of much of the significance which it had had in earlier religious cosmologies and implied that, in the long run at least, man would meet with disaster in his attempt to control his surroundings. According to Alphonse Candolle, the changes to be expected in the physical conditions of our planet would sooner or later lead to a disappearance of all higher forms of civilization.[1] Other Frenchmen viewed the spectacular discoveries of modern science with serious misgivings. Thus the brothers Goncourt, hearing scientists predict that over a hundred years man would have mastered the mysteries of the atom and have succeeded in creating life, believed "qu'à ce moment-là du monde, le vieux bon Dieu à barbe blanche arrivera sur la terre avec son trousseau de clefs et dira à l'humanité, comme on dit au Salon: 'Messieurs, on ferme.'"[2]

In France many scientists were also impressed by the theories of the German physicist Rudolf Clausius (1822–88), asserting that all matter and energy have a natural tendency to lose their specific characteristics so that ultimately a state of inert uniformity or entropy would ensue. Reversing Herbert Spencer's view that the development of the world is from homogeneity to heterogeneity, they believed that the trend of the universe was in the direction of death and disorder.[3] Such somber views of the final destiny of mankind found a distinguished exponent in the great leader of the Radical-Socialists, Georges Clemenceau, whose philosophy of life consisted of a mixture of Social Darwinism and Nietzscheanism. In his *Mêlée sociale* (1894) he evoked the depressing future in which evolution would have taken the form of retrogression. "Qui dit évolution, dit courbe, hélas. Après le sommet atteint, c'est la descente, la chute lente ou rapide dans la vertigineuse nuit ... Ainsi s'achèvera, dans la suprême misère, la lutte commencée pour la vie aux jours de la naissance heureuse dans le monde enchanté."[4]

---

[1] Alphonse L. P. P. de Candolle, "De l'avenir possible de l'espèce humaine," *Histoire des sciences et des savants depuis deux siècles* (Genève, 1873), 376, 411; cf. Colajanni, *Le socialisme*, 288.

[2] Edmond and Jules de Goncourt, *Journal, Mémoires de la vie littéraire* ed. Robert Ricatte (22 vols., Paris, 1956), VIII, 192–193.

[3] D. Parodi, "L'idée de progrès universel," *Bibliothèque du Congrès international de philosophie. 1900* (Paris, 1903), II, 201–203.

[4] Clemenceau, *La mêlée sociale* (1895) (Paris, 1919), pp. xxxii–xxxiv.

IV

In most periods of history poets and novelists have inveighed against the evils of their times. But at the end of the nineteenth century the corruption of society was more than a favorite theme, it became an obsession. Realistic and naturalistic novelists portrayed the degenerations of their age in the most somber colors and authors belonging to the Decadent and Symbolist movements took an even gloomier view of the world in which they lived. "Notre littérature . . . des vingt ou trente dernières années," declared a literary critic, Georges Pellissier, in 1890, "est tout entière empreinte de pessimisme. Si nous jugeons la génération contemporaine d'après ses interprètes naturels, c'est-à-dire d'après ses romanciers, ses poètes, ses auteurs dramatiques les plus aimés . . . elle nous apparaît comme atteinte jusqu'aux moelles de ce pessimisme universel où les moralistes les plus avisés voyaient, il y a peu de temps encore, une maladie particulière à la race germanique et contre laquelle ils assuraient le tempérament de la nôtre, mieux pondérée et plus rassise devait par lui-même nous garantir."[1]

Many contemporaries explained the pessimism of the younger literary generation by the painful experiences of the *année terrible* and the following disenchantment with the Third Republic. "Nous sommes entrés dans la vie," wrote Paul Bourget, "par cette terrible année de la guerre et de la Commune, et cet année terrible n'a pas mutilé que la carte de notre cher pays; . . . quelque chose nous en est demeuré, à tous, comme un premier empoisonnement qui nous a laissés plus dépourvus, plus incapables de résister à la maladie intellectuelle où il nous a fallu grandir."[2] Many young Frenchmen, according to another literary critic, Jules Lemaître, had been so disturbed by the misfortunes of their country that their hearts had been filled with a fund of bitterness that made them incapable of the exuberance and gaiety of their elders.[3]

But the despondency of many French men of letters was more than a specific response to the political misfortunes of their country. It was not in France alone that a profound melancholy pervaded much of the literary production at the end of the nineteenth century.

---

[1] Georges Pellissier, "Le pessimisme dans la littérature contemporaine," (1890) *Essais de littérature contemporaine* (Paris, 1893), 1–2.

[2] Bourget, *Nouveaux essais de psychologie contemporaine* (Paris, 1896), p.vi; cf. A. Feuillerat, *Paul Bourget, histoire d'un esprit sous la Troisième République* (Paris, 1937); Digeon, *op. cit.*, 304–305, 309.

[3] Giraud, *Les maîtres de l'heure*, II, 14.

As Romantic gloom, with which it had much in common, the pessimism of the *fin de siècle* was a European-wide phenomenon that should rather be seen as a renewed protest on the part of highly sensitive minds against the complacency and vulgarity of their contemporaries and as a form of anxiety about the loss of religious assurances.

The new sense of decadence was not an exact replica of the old Romantic despair. At the end of the nineteenth century many men of letters went even further than their predecessors in proclaiming the degeneracy of modern civilization. "Je suis un homme né sur le tard d'une race," sang Paul Bourget in his early years.[1] In a similar vein Paul Verlaine proclaimed: "Je suis l'Empire à la fin de a décadence."[2] Existing society was even more categorically condemned by one of the leading young Decadents, Anatole Baju: "Se dissimuler l'état de décadence où nous sommes arrivés serait le comble de l'insenséisme. Religion, mœurs, justice, tout décade... La société se désagrège sous l'action corrosive d'une civilisation déliquescente."[3] Whereas most Romantics had still cherished the hope that a new idealism would regenerate the world, the writers of the *fin de siècle* no longer entertained such illusions. They tended to be sceptics, cynics, and nihilists, denying the validity of any social or political idealism.

On the other hand, this firm conviction that modern civilization was in a state of irremediable decay did not necessarily foster a mood of utter depression and bewilderment. In contrast to the Romantics, most Decadents accepted the degeneracy of their time with a sense of equanimity, or even delight. They were fascinated as well as repelled by the corruption of their contemporaries and made a desparate attempt to discover beauty in what the "unenlightened" public denounced as corrupt and repulsive. Looking upon themselves as the product of an age of decline, they did not merely lament their lot but also took pride in it; and instead of disassociating themselves from the evils of their period, they concentrated their imagination on all its perversions. As such they were greatly inspired by some earlier authors who had already broken with the traditional moralistic attitude toward decadence and evil: Sade and Baudelaire as well as the realistic and naturalistic novelists. But the Decadents went further than any of their predecessors in viewing contemporary corruption without any moral indignation. Cerebral and passive,

---

[1] "Edel" (1878), *Poésies, 1876–82* (Paris, 1887), 34.
[2] Sonnet "Langueur," *Jadis et naguère* (1884).
[3] *Le décadent littéraire et artistique*, I (April 10, 1886), 1.

many authors of the *fin de siècle* suffered from a singular deficiency of will power. It was this so-called abulia that, more than anything else, earned them the reputation of "decadents."

The Decadent movement found its first important theorist in Paul Bourget. In his *Essais de psychologie contemporaine* (1880–1883) he called the attention of the public to a number of European authors of an older generation (Baudelaire, Renan, Taine, the brothers Goncourt, and others) who had developed a specific style suited to what he considered a decaying society. In the analysis of their works Bourget referred to the irresistible wave of nihilism which was engulfing European civilization: "D'un bout à l'autre de l'Europe la société contemporaine présente les mêmes symptômes, nuancés suivant les races . . . Lentement, sûrement, s'élabore la croyance à la banque-route de la nature, qui promet de devenir la foi sinistre du XXe siècle, si la science ou une invasion de barbares ne sauve pas l'humanité trop réfléchie de la lassitude de sa propre pensée." "Ce serait," he added, "un chapitre de psychologie comparée aussi intéressant qu'inédit que celui qui noterait, étape par étape, la marche des différentes races européennes vers cette tragique négation de tous les efforts de tous les siècles."[1] Like many French conservatives he regarded the growth of individualism and the resulting disintegration of society as the major symptoms of the prevailing decadence. The most significant part of Bourget's analysis is that instead of deploring the late arrival of his contemporaries in the course of history as most Romantics had done, he considered it a privilege and defended the attitude of "decadence" as intellectually and esthetically, if not ethically and socially, superior to the robust but unrefined mentality of healthier, more primitive societies. "Si les citoyens de la décadence sont inférieurs comme ouvriers de la grandeur du pays," he asked, "ne sont-ils pas très supérieurs comme artistes de l'intérieur de leur âme?"[2] And Bourget answered in the affirmative, at least during the early years of his career, when he aspired to be an artist above anything else. Bourget's essays were instrumental in making the attitude of decadence a respectable literary pose. He found an audience among men of letters in Germany and England as well as in France. The most important effect of his ideas was on Nietzsche, who largely accepted Bourget's analysis of the development of European civilization into

[1] *Essais de psychologie contemporaine* (Paris, 1884), 15–16; cf. Michel Mansuy, *Un moderne. Paul Bourget de l'enfance au* Disciple (Besançon, 1961), 319–376.

[2] *Essais de psychologie contemporaine*, 27; in 1876 Bourget declared "Nous acceptons sans humilité comme sans orgueil ce terrible mot de décadence . . ." (Lethève, *loc. cit.*, 51).

the direction of nihilism and decadence and who, in his turn, greatly influenced Oswald Spengler's conception of the *Decline of the West*.[1]

Bourget, though highly influential as a theorist of literary and cultural decline, belonged too much to an earlier generation to identify himself fully with the literary tends which he analyzed. Even in his earlier works he expressed some serious misgivings about the breakdown of the traditional order, and in his later publications he fully adopted the attitude of a conservative censor of modern democratic, individualistic civilization.[2]

A much less ambiguous statement of the Decadent creed was presented in Joris-Karl Huysmans' *A rebours (Against the Grain)* (1884).[3] This novel was the greatest literary sensation in many years and became the real breviary of the Decadent movement. Huysmans' book became, in the words of a devotee of the new literary gospel, "un programme involontaire, la loi et le code, le texte de ralliement, l'hymne des enrôlés pour l'art neuf."[4] The protagonist of *A rebours*, the Duc des Esseintes was the perfect type of an ultrarefined, artistic soul, socially completely irresponsible, living in utter seclusion, and taking delight in the perverse and the artificial. Many people served as a model for this decadent aristocrat: Baudelaire, Edmond de Goncourt, some of Huysmans' eccentric contemporaries like the Comte de Montesquiou-Fesenzac, and, above all, the author himself. Barbey d'Aurevilly, a connoisseur in the genre of literary decadence, called this novel "l'un des plus décadents que nous puissions compter parmi les livres décadents de ce siècle de décadence. Pour qu'un décadent de cette force pût se produire ... il fallait vraiment que nous fussions devenus ce que nous sommes – une race à sa dernière heure."[5] Severely criticized by writers upholding traditional literary taste, it was given an enthusiastic reception by the *avant-garde* in France and other countries. It left a deep impression on many authors who later on acquired a solid literary reputation, such as Mallarmé and Paul Valéry in France, and George Moore and Oscar Wilde in England.

Besides *A rebours*, many other, literarily less significant novels of the

---

[1] E. Stauber, "Die *Essais de psychologie contemporaine* von Paul Bourget und Spenglers *Untergang des Abendlandes*," *Germanisch-Romanische Monatsschrift*, XIII (1925), 141–145.

[2] Cf. *Essais de psychologie contemporaine*, 24, 202; Bourget, *Le disciple* (Paris, 1889), 3–5; Lloyd J. Austin, *Paul Bourget et son œuvre jusqu'en 1889* (Paris, 1940).

[3] Cf. Robert Baldick, *The Life of J. K. Huysmans* (Oxford, 1955), 80–81, 87ff.; Carter, *The Idea of Decadence*, 81ff.

[4] Georges Rodenbach, as quoted in Carter, *op. cit.*, 135.

[5] Quoted in Carter, *op. cit.*, 86.

period were based on the theme of decadence.[1] Some of these presented
lurid descriptions of the sexual depravity and the corrupting luxury of
decaying societies such as Imperial Rome and the Byzantine Empire.[2]
Other novels were set in modern times and portrayed the degeneracy
of aristocratic families, their homosexuality, their scepticism, and their
inability to action. Most of the authors displayed a pronounced
sympathy for occult or mystical doctrines such as spiritism, black
magic, or Rosicrucianism, which they welcomed as a form of salvation
for the depravity and the materialism of their times. One of the most
representative productions of this school was the fifteen-volume novel
cycle, published under the ambitious title, *La décadence latine* (1884–
1900) by Joséphin Péladan, better known by his pen name, the Great
Mage Sâr Mérodack J. Péladan.[4] Barbey d'Aurevilly characterized
this work as "la synthèse de toute une race – de la plus belle race qui
ait jamais existé sur la terre – de la race latine qui se meurt." The
author himself interspersed the story of his decadent heroes with
vehement indictments of the equalitarian, atheistic spirit of republican
France and ended the first volume with the ominous words "FINIS
LATINORUM."[5] In 1891 Sâr Péladan wrote: "Je crois à la fatale et
imminente putréfaction d'une latinité sans Dieu et sans symbole . . .
Je juge que la fin de la France n'est plus qu'une question d'années."[6]
But our Mage could hold out the consolation that the Slavic race
would regenerate Europe and that even France would be given another
important role in the building of a new, more idealistic civilization.

Another representative author of the Decadent school of literature,
Elémir Bourges, fully revealed his disgust with modern civilization
in his novel significantly entitled *Le crépuscule des Dieux* (1884). Its
decadent hero, a degenerate scion of a German aristocratic family,
served as the author's spokesman in declaring that the fatal hour
of the world's destruction was approaching, for the same angels of
fury that had appeared above Gomorrah were already visible in

---

[1] See Praz, *Romantic Agony*, ch. V; Carter, *The Idea of Decadence*, ch. IV.

[2] Jean Lombard, *L'agonie* (1888); *idem, Byzance* (1890); Paul Adam, *Irène et les eunuques*
(1907); cf. Huysmans' statement: "Je rêve à Byzance. Ah! quel livre, si l'on pouvait le
faire sur cette exquise décadence" (Estève, *op. cit.*, 53).

[3] Jean Lorrain, *Le vice errant* (1899); *idem, Monsieur de Phocas* (1901); Octave Mirbeau,
Le Jardin des Supplices (1899); Catille Mendès, *Méphistophéla* (1891); Rachilde (pseud. of
Marguérite Eymery), *Les hors nature* (1897); *idem, Monsieur Vénus* (1889).

[4] Cf. Ed. Bertholet, *La pensée et les secrets du Sar Joséphin Péladan* (4 vols., Neuchâtel,
1952–58); cf. Praz, *op. cit.*, 316ff; Carter., *op. cit.*, 100–104.

[5] Preface of Barbey d'Aurevilly to Péladan's *La décadence latine*, I, *Le vice suprême* (Paris,
1884).

[6] Jules Huret, *Enquête sur l'évolution littéraire* (Paris, 1891), 37.

Europe's sky. The author believed that a new society was arising; it was not, however, the Kingdom of Heaven, but a world hideous by its worship of materialism and mechanization, a world without any artistic refinement and beauty. In 1900 this admirer of Baudelaire and Barbey d'Aurevilly contrasted the creative ages of the past in which "tout un peuple inventait l'Iliade, le Romancero et les Eddas" with his own period, in which the world became "de plus en plus stupide avec ses fariboles de progrès et de fraternité."[1]

Most of these novelists indulging in the portrayal of the corruption of decaying societies were not directly associated with the movement known as "Décadentisme" or "Décadisme".[2] With the poet Paul Verlaine as its major literary sponsor, this short-lived literary school published a number of manifestoes and its own periodical, Le décadent (1886–1889). Its supporters belonged to a younger literary generation than Bourget and Huysmans, and their political and philosophical ideas were more radical and modernistic, many of them being atheists and flirting with anarchism. The older literary critic, Edmond Scherer, characterized them as addicted to intellectual, moral, and religious nihilism, and the Catholic politician Albert de Mun called this generation "fille de la défaite invengée. Elle n'avait plus au cœur l'âpre tourment de la revanche, elle marchait vers la décadence, comme un voyageur sur le vide, orgueilleuse de son audace mortelle."[3]

The pessimism of these young authors should not be taken too seriously. They took a delight in mystifying the bourgeois public, and their "decadence" was often no more than a literary pose. They called themselves "décadents" largely to defy hostile critics who had branded their literary productions with that term. The choice of the term "Décadisme," declared Verlaine, was "un coup de génie." "J'aime le mot de décadence, tout miroitant de pourpre et d'ors. . . . Ce mot . . . suppose des pensées raffinées d'extrême civilisation, une haute culture littéraire, une âme capable d'intensives voluptés. . . . Il est fait d'un mélange d'esprit charnel et de chair triste et de toutes les splendeurs violents du bas-empire; il respire le fard des courtisanes, les jeux du cirque, le souffle des belluaires, le bondissement des fauves, l'écroule-

---

[1] André Lebois, La genèse du Crépuscule des Dieux (Paris, 1954), 238; cf. Praz, op. cit., 327–329; Carter, op. cit., 94–95.

[2] Cf. Gustave Kahn, Symbolistes et décadents (Paris, 1902); Ernest Raynaud, La mêlée symboliste (1870–1890). Portraits et souvenirs (Paris, 1918), I, 70ff., 115, 118; André Barre, Le symbolisme (Paris, 1911).

[3] Edmond Scherer, "La crise actuelle de la morale," (1884) Études sur la littérature contemporaine, VIII, 155ff.; Carré Les écrivains français et le mirage allemand, 114.

ment dans les flammes des races épuisées par la force de sentir, au bruit envahisseur des trompettes ennemies."[1]

Actually most "decadents" did not consider themselves decadent at all, but daring innovators intent on destroying the existing social and religious institutions in order to pave the way for a new and superior form of society. According to one of the leaders of the new literary movement, Anatole Baju, "le Décadent est un homme de progrès. Il est soigneux, économe, laborieux et réglé dans toutes ses habitudes. Simple dans sa mise, correct dans ses mœurs, il a pour idéal le Beau dans le Bien et cherche à conformer ses actes avec ses théories. . . . Maître de ses sens, qu'il a domestiqué, il a le calme, la placidité d'un sage, la vertu d'un stoïcien."[2]

For many young writers "decadent" was only another name for Baudelaire's dandy. "Décadent pour moi," stated Paul Valéry in 1890, "veut dire artiste ultra-raffiné."[3] Some of the authors idolized by the Decadents objected to the new use of the term. Mallarmé, whose poetry Huysmans had, not entirely inappropriately, characterized as the summit of decadence, held that "decadence" was a horrible label and that it was high time to renounce anything resembling it.[4] Similarly most other devotees of the new estheticism became convinced that the term "decadence" contributed to a misunderstanding of their literary creed and therefore preferred to be known as "Symbolists." Verlaine himself, although more than any other major literary figure, responsible for the school's name, later on declared that the term had no meaning whatsoever.[5] The most distinguished critic among the young literary innovators, Rémy de Gourmont, passed the final judgment on the term when he asserted that its only significant meaning was that of literary imitation and that in this sense the term should be applied not to the men of letters who experimented with new forms of expression but to their literary opponents, who continued to write in the outworn style of classicism.[6] Or, as an English admirer of the new trends in French literature, Havelock Ellis put it, "there seems to be no more pronounced mark of the

---

[1] Raynaud, *La melée symboliste*, I, 64–65.

[2] Billy, *L'époque 1900*, 422–423, 444.

[3] Lethève, *op. cit.*, 59.

[4] Henri Mondor, *Vie de Mallarmé* (15th ed., Paris, 1946), 401; cf. René Etiemble, *Le mythe de Rimbaud. Structure du mythe* (Paris, 1952), II, 67.

[5] Jules Huret, *Enquête sur l'évolution littéraire*, 90; Etiemble, *op. cit.*, 71.

[6] Gourmont, "Stéphane Mallarmé and the Idea of Decadence," (1898) *Decadence and Other Essays on the Culture of Ideas* (New York, 1921), 139–155; in 1886, Léo d'Orfer and Jean Moréas made a similar point (Lethève, *loc. cit.*, 56).

decadence of a people and its literature than a servile and rigid subserviency to rule."[1]

Literary decadence in its purest form was the creed of a number of esthetes who believed that by giving an artistic expression to the evil which haunted them they would be able to deliver themselves from their obsessions. Although they lacked any desire or hope to reform society, they were still longing for a regeneration of their own soul. In their search for overcoming their anxieties, most of the prominent authors of the Decadent movement (Huysmans, Verlaine, Oscar Wilde, D'Annunzio) sooner or later renounced their nihilistic ideas and embraced Catholicism or a secular creed like nationalism. But this conversion, even if sincere, was seldom complete and traces of their original decadent individualism can still be detected in the later political or religious views of these writers. For our purpose the most interesting author who, after rejecting Decadence, still remained under its influence is Maurice Barrès, who became the literary mentor of an influential part of the French youth in the first decade of the twentieth century.[2]

Barrès started his literary career as an individualist, a literary dandy, and an anarchist, cultivating his precious ego threatened by the vulgarity of society. An admirer of Wagner and Schopenhauer, he proudly defended the pessimism of his generation against bourgeois complacency.[3] "Ce fut une triste époque," he wrote later about this period," où nous acceptions d'être les représentants de la décadence."[4] When this egotism left him unsatisfied, he became a nationalist, not so much out of a sense of social responsibility as because he was in need of a spiritual lift. He felt that the French nation was the very substance which supported him and that without it he would perish. In other words, Barrès became a nationalist without being really converted just as he became a supporter of the Catholic Church without renouncing his scepticism. He remained all his life an epicurean, who once said that all what he cared for in this world were a few paintings and a few cemeteries.[5] Barrès' nationalism betrayed its origin in a decadent

---

[1] Cf. Havelock Ellis in his introduction to J. K. Huysmans, *Against the Grain* (New York 1931).

[2] Cf. E. R. Curtius, *Maurice Barrès und die geistige Grundlagen des französischen Nationalismus* (Bonn, 1921).

[3] Digeon, *op. cit.*, 338–339.

[4] Barrès, *Cahiers*, IX (1911–1912) (Paris, 1935), 27; cf. Jean-Marie Domenach, *Barrès par lui-même* (Paris, 1954), 14, 20–21.

[5] Julien Benda, *Précisions* (Paris, 1937), 179; R. Valeur in *Democratic Governments in Europe*, ed. E. P. Chase and others (New York, 1935), 516.

mentality. It sprang from a sense of weakness, not from a sense of strength. Aiming at conservation and protection, it concentrated on defending the French farmer and laborer against competition by Jews and foreigners. Preaching the cult of the dead, it was turned toward the past, not toward the future. The only important task assigned to the French people was the revenge of the War of 1870 and the recovery of Alsace-Lorraine. Blood and soil were important slogans of this nationalism, which lacked the generous aspirations of the liberalism of the early nineteenth century and foreshadowed fascism. Barrès' nationalism, an extended egotism, can be called the nationalism of the Decadents.

The so-called decadent sensibility has obviously little in common with the ideas of decadence that had been held by most writers in earlier periods. Cultivating as well as abhorring the corruptions of their times, the Decadents were too ambiguous and too purely emotional in their attitude to produce any consistent theories of historical decline. Many of them, influenced by Schopenhauer, rejected the idea of the Golden Age altogether, either in the past or in the future, and were philosophical, but not historical pessimists. Considering the world irremediably corrupt, they deemed all efforts to improve it utterly senseless. The contemporary world was base, but not decadent, since it had always been, and always would be, in the same hopeless state. The only recourse open to the individual was to escape into the world of art and beauty. The philosophical pessimism of Eduard von Hartmann, another German writer who inspired many Frenchmen of the period, can be characterized even as historical optimism, since his system allowed for a progressive strengthening of otherwordly spiritualism, ultimately leading to the end of the world.[1]

It is as a purely literary and artistic trend carrying the Romantic cult of modernism, estheticism, and individualism to greater extremes that the Decadent movement left its greatest impact. Reacting against the positivistic, deterministic scientism of an earlier literary generation and against the materialism and the standardization of the modern world, the Decadents aimed at a revolution in art and literature. They looked upon themselves as literary, if not social and political, innovators and were as such still optimistic in their hope of bringing on a spiritual regeneration. Although critical of existing society,

---

[1] Eduard von Hartmann, *Philosophy of the Unconscious* (3 vols., London, 1893), II, 1ff.

they seldom suffered from excessive gloom. After all, France, more than ever before, was an intellectuals' paradise, in which littérateurs had less reason for feeling themselves alienated than in any other country. Much of the modernism, nihilism, and hyperindividualism of the Decadent movement survived in later literary movements such as Symbolism, Dadaism, and surrealism. The decadent sensibility was, moreover, an important factor in stimulating a similar state of mind among men of letters in other European countries and brought a vague concept of decadence, in addition to the term itself, to the attention of a larger public.[1]

The Decadents and the Symbolists were not the only French intellectuals of their time reacting against the scientism and positivism of the preceding generation. Their views can be seen as a part of a general idealistic reaction against science that gained impetus in France as well as in other European countries at the end of the nineteenth century.[2] In the 1890's the cult of scientific methods and material progress was attacked by many French writers who were not in sympathy with the new esthetes and their delight in perversion and artificiality. Thus a leading literary critic, Brunetière, who was one of the most unqualified opponents of modern individualism, caused a sensation by proclaiming "la banqueroute de la science."[3] Many other authors with conservative or Catholic inclinations denounced science as undermining the moral and social order.

The best case against the pretensions of prevailing scientism was made by a number of eminent French philosophers.[4] Of these Henri Bergson was the most important because of the radicalism of his antirationalism as well as of the great impact of his theories on his contemporaries. In France and in many other countries his new mysticism was hailed as a liberation from the nightmare of deterministic science. [5] Some of his followers interpreted his theory of creative

---

[1] Cf. *infra*, 248–251, 253.

[2] Cf. Antonio Aliotta, *The Idealistic Reaction Against Science* (London, 1914); Georg Lukács, *Die Zerstörung der Vernunft* (Berlin, 1954); Alfred Kämpf, *Die Revolte der Instinkte* (Berlin, 1948); H. Stuart Hughes, *Consciousness and Society*.

[3] Brunetière, "Après une visite au Vatican," *Revue des Deux Mondes*, CXXVII (Jan. 1, 1895), 91–119.

[4] Edward G. Ballard, "Jules Lachelier's Idealism," *Review of Metaphysics* VIII (1955), 615ff.; Émile Boutroux, *De la contingence des lois de la nature* (Paris, 1879); *idem*, *Science et religion* (Paris, 1908); Alfred Fouillée, *Le mouvement idéaliste et la réaction contre la science* (Paris, 1896); *idem*, *La pensée et les nouvelles écoles anti-intellectualistes* (Paris, 1911); A. Billy, *op. cit.*, 142ff.

[5] Cf. *infra*, 202; Romain Rolland, *Péguy* (2 vols., Paris, 1944), I, 38–39, 300; Julien Benda, *Sur le succès du Bergsonisme* (Paris, 1929); Romeo Arbour, *Henri Bergson et les lettres françaises* (Paris, 1956).

evolution as new doctrine of progress,[1] Bergson himself never developed a formal philosophy of history, but his high regard for creative spirituality, which brought him close to Roman Catholicism at the end of his life, explains that he took a dim view of modern civilization, increasingly dominated by the triumps of scientific technology. "L'humanité," he stated in one of his later works, "gémit, à demi écrasée sous le poids des progrès qu'elle a faits."[2]

The same pessimistic note was struck by some of Bergson's disciples. Georges Sorel and Charles Péguy, as we will see, were obsessed with the decadence of modern society, although, in accordance with Bergson's rejection of any form of determinism, they never fully despaired of the future.[3] A truly Bergsonian mixture of pessimism and optimism also pervades the work of the noted English historian Arnold Toynbee, who has never made a secret of the great debt that he owed to the French philosopher.[4] Like Bergson, Arnold Toynbee has been highly critical of "mechanistic rationalism" and attempted to sustain an essentially mystic philosophy of life with the data of experimental science. On many occasions Toynbee has stated as his belief that since the Renaissance Western civilization has been in a state of breakdown if not collapse.[5] Yet because of his strong, Bergsonian faith in creativity and the freedom of the will, he has always refused to subscribe to any fatalistic belief in decadence à la Spengler.

The new trend toward mysticism and irrationalism did not go unchallenged. Both positivistic and idealistic rationalists discerned in the new vogue of the philosophies of Schopenhauer, Nietzsche, and Bergson as well as in the popularity of the works of Baudelaire, the Decadents, Dostoevsky and Ibsen a serious symptom of cultural decline. A number of distinguished French thinkers (Frédéric Paulhan, Jules Sageret, Alfred Fouillée, B. Jacob, and Julien Benda among

[1] L. Abbott, "Henri Bergson: the Philosophy of Progress," *Outlook*, CIII 388–391.
[2] *Les deux sources de la morale et de la religion* (58th ed., Paris, 1948), 338; cf. Raymond Polin, "Y a-t-il chez Bergson une philosophie de l'histoire," *Les études bergsoniennes*, IV (1956), 7–40; Raymond Aron, "Note sur Bergson et l'histoire," *ibid.*, 44–51.
[3] Cf. *infra*, 203–209
[4] Cf. Tangye Lean, "Study of Toynbee," in *Toynbee and History, Critical Essays and Reviews*, ed. M. F. Ashley Montague (Boston, 1956), 12–13; Rushton Coulborn, "The Individual and the Growth of Civilizations: an Answer to Arnold Toynbee and Henri Bergson," *Phylon*, I (1940), 69–89; 136–148; 243–264.
[5] Toynbee, *A Study of History*, (10 vols., New York, 1934–54); IV, 23–24; Bergsonism might also lead to an extremely relativistic, almost Nietzschean concept of decadence. Thus V. Jankélévitch, a French admirer of Bergson, in his article "Décadence" in the *Revue de métaphysique et de morale*, 1950, 337–369, after having defined decadence as the sterile and narcistic mentality of self-examination that befalls all great ideas and movements born in a creative impulse, concluded his remarks by declaring that decadence is necessary and that decadence is a form of progress.

others) analyzed the inconsistencies of the new philosophical systems.[1] Numerous arbiters of taste took up arms against the alleged aberrations of modernism in art and literature. The most notorious of all these indictments of the new spirit in literature and philosophy was delivered by a cosmopolitan man of letters of Jewish descent living in Paris, Max Nordau. His *Degeneration* (1892–1893) – originally published in German, but soon translated in many other languages – led to heated controversies, in which Bernard Shaw among others came to the defense of the attacked authors.[2] In his work Nordau berated many prominent European writers such as Ibsen, Tolstoy, Richard Wagner, and Nietzsche for their irrationalism and egomania, but reserved his most severe strictures for the literary innovations of French naturalists, Decadents, and Symbolists. He was convinced that modern degeneracy was more widespread in France than in any other nation, because it was there that the *fin-de-siècle* disease of mysticism and perversion had made its first appearance and assumed its most genuine form.[3]

Max Nordau contended that the modern world was passing through a serious crisis. "We now stand in the midst of a severe mental epidemic, of a sort of black death of degeneration and hysteria," and this hysteria, he added, "may not have yet attained its culmination point."[4] He attributed the mental aberrations of his contemporaries to the increased consumption of liquor and tobacco and, in a general way, to the nervous strain resulting from rapid industrialization and urbanization. Yet Nordau was not a pessimist. Unlike many authors whose views he criticized, he did not think that the world was tottering in its old age. As is especially evident from his other publications, he never wavered in a firm, almost naive belief in continuous, rational progress.[5] Convinced that the existing mood of irrationality and despair was limited to the upper classes, he was confident that the sound instincts of the overwhelming majority of the population would

[1] Frédéric Paulhan, *Le nouveau mysticisme* (Paris, 1891); Alfred Fouillée, works cited *supra*, 169, n. 4, B. Jacob, "La philosophie d'hier et celle d'aujourd'hui," *Revue de métaphysique et de morale*, March, 1898; Julien Benda, *Le bergsonisme ou une philosophie de mobilité* (Paris, 1912).

[2] Cf. Georgette Donchin, *The Influence of French Symbolism on Russian Poetry* (The Hague, 1958), 15–17; Milton P. Foster, "The Reception of Max Nordau's *Degeneration* in England and America," *Dissertation Abstracts*, XIV, 1078–1079; G. B. Shaw, *The Sanity of Art. An Exposure of the Current Nonsense About Artists Being Degenerate* in *Collected Works* (New York, 1931), XIX, 293ff.

[3] Max Nordau, *Entartung* (Berlin, 1893), I 3ff.

[4] *Ibid.*, II, 523.

[5] A good specimen of Nordau's utopianism is to be found in his *Interpretation of History* (New York, 1910), 389ff.

ultimately prevail. He felt, moreover, that the process of mankind's recovery would be greatly accelerated if men of science and scholarship were willing to participate in exposing the current trends in art as a form of insanity of a degenerate elite.

Nordau's attack on modern art miscarried because it was marred by a too simplistic conception of artistic creation. Believing that only science was capable of satisfying all of mankind's higher needs, Nordau did not recognize the legitimate roles of metaphysical speculation or of literary imagination and saw in the reaction of the younger generation against the exaggerated pretensions of the experimental method nothing but obscurantism. He further weakened his case by applying the terminology of criminal psychology as used by the Italian Cesare Lombroso to the mentality of modern men of letters, forgetting that sanity and normality are highly relative terms and that many of the great authors of the past, admired by Nordau himself, had not been perfectly balanced personalities.

V

The *fin-de-siècle* notion that France was a decadent country was often based upon the fact of the slow growth of population. The decline in natality, which had been denounced by not more than a few Frenchmen of the Second Empire and had hardly been mentioned by the authors investigating the causes of the defeat of 1870, became a widely discussed aspect of national decline after the establishment of the Third Republic.[1] The concern led to a vast number of publications on the subject, ranging from solid scientific investigations to pamphlets written for the general public. Learned societies debated the question, periodicals polled prominent men of letters, and a large organization (Alliance nationale pour l'accroissement de la population française) was founded in 1896 to act as a pressure group. The fight against depopulation was carried on even in works of fiction. In *La fécondité* (1899) Emile Zola denounced the Malthusian practices of the French public, contrasting them with the responsible attitude of his hero, an industrial worker who ended his life as a farmer surrounded by one hundred and fifty-eight direct descendants.[2] Another widely read novelist, René Bazin, fought for the same cause in his

---

[1] On the subject in general, see Joseph J. Spengler, *France Faces Depopulation.*

[2] F. W. J. Hemmings, *Emile Zola* (Oxford, 1953), 277–282; Eugène Brieux' *Maternité* was also written to fight against depopulation.

popular work, *La terre qui meurt* (1899), evoking the depressing atmosphere of deserted rural districts.

The decline of the birth rate, more than any other trend in modern France, seemed to indicate that the nation was declining in vitality and might be approaching its downfall. Had not Rome struggled in vain with the same problem? "La stérilité croissante et volontaire de la France," proclaimed a foremost statistician Alfred de Foville, "est un mal dont il est probable qu'elle mourra."[1] The military and political implications of the demographic development seemed particularly serious. It was considered to be alarming that in Germany the population increased much more rapidly than in France. In 1876 the economist Léonce de Lavergne pointed out that the population of Germany and England grew each year by more than 400,000, whereas that of France remained stationary. "Il y va de l'existence même de notre nation," he warned," car il n'y pas, comme disait Rousseau, . . . de pire disette pour un Etat que celle des hommes."[2] A few years later another leading critic of French "depopulation," Paul Leroy-Beaulieu, asserted that Germany's increasing demographic ascendancy would prevent France from recovering Alsace-Lorraine, and in 1897 Jacques Bertillon, an active fighter in the cause of repopulation, even predicted: "Dans quatorze ans l'Allemagne aura deux fois plus de conscrits. Alors ce peuple qui nous hait nous dévorera! Les Allemands le disent, l'impriment et ils le feront!"[3]

Besides being held responsible for the weakening of France's military strength, the slow growth of the population was deplored because it stemmed the flow of French settlers to the colonial empire, thus reducing the influence of French nationality and civilization in the world. Moreover, by creating a labor shortage in France, it induced a large scale immigration of Italians, Belgians, and other foreigners into France. This influx of foreign laborers, it was held, threatened to lower the living standards of the French working man, to change French racial stock, and to create cultural heterogeneity. The social psychologist Gustave Le Bon feared that within a very short time a third of the population would be German and another third Italian and maintained that "les pires désastres sur les champs de bataille seraient infinement moins redoutables que de telles invasions."[4]

---

[1] Paul Bureau, *L'indiscipline des mœurs* (Paris, 1920), 235.
[2] E. Levasseur, *La population française* (3 vols., Paris, 1889-92), III, 213.
[3] J. Bertillon, "Le problème de la dépopulation," *Revue politique et parlementaire*, XII (1897), 538-539.
[4] Le Bon, *Lois psychologiques de l'évolution des peuples*, 125.

Agitations against the influence exercised by foreigners became, as we have seen, one of the specialties of the new nationalistic party, the Action française.

Conservatives and Catholics were leading in the crusade against depopulation, but many liberals, Radicals, and socialists shared their anxiety. Such "liberal" philosophers as Alfred Fouillée and Jean-Marie Guyau expressed their deep concern about the decline of the birth rate.[1] "La France est menacée de mort," warned the Radical politician Ferdinand Buisson, "et de toutes la plus honteuse, la mort par incapacité de vivre. "Charles Gide, a distinguished economist with socialist leanings, concluded: "La France est un îlot de sucre qui fond."[2]

Despite the warning voices raised by many social scientists, public opinion remained largely apathetic, and prior to the First World War the French Parliament did not pass any of the major bills proposed to remedy the situation. The opposition came in the first place from liberal economists, who still held to the Malthusian view that the size of the population was mainly dependent on economic productivity. Although concerned about the decrease of the birth rate, they felt that any government measure to promote natality would defeat its purpose since it would lead to more state intervention in private affairs, which in their eyes constituted the major malady of the nation. One of the few leading economists, Leroy-Beaulieu, who advocated some populationist measures, was for this reason seriously taken to task by his colleagues.[3]

Leftist politicians also opposed the repopulationist program, which they distrusted as a clever move on the part of conservatives to secure more votes among large-sized families. The cause of repopulation was further discredited by the fact that the alarmist writers did not practice the doctrine which they preached. Out of the 445 married sponsors of a propopulationist campaign only 74 had more than two children. This is hardly surprising as the critics of depopulation generally belonged to the well-to-do classes, among which the birth rate was below the national average.[4]

[1] Cf. Marie-Jean Guyau, L'irreligion de l'avenir (Paris 1887) and Alfred Fouillée, Psychologie du peuple français.

[2] Bureau, op. cit., 235.

[3] Paul Leroy-Beaulieu, La question de la population (Paris, 1913), 343; Jean Bourdon, "Remarques sur les doctrines de la population," Population, II (1947), 481–495; Spengler, op. cit., 127.

[4] Spengler, op. cit., 127; Sébastien Faure, Le problème de la population (Paris, 1908); Pax Salvat, La dépopulation de la France (Lyon, 1903).

Neo-Malthusianism, furthermore, found many spokesmen among intellectuals more concerned with alleviating the misery of the lower classes than with national grandeur. In 1896 an organization promoting birth control, the Ligue de la régénération humaine, was founded under the leadership of Paul Robin, one of the members of the First International. Their program was supported by many socialists who felt that the populationist propaganda was nothing more than an attempt on the part of the bourgeoisie to secure a continued flow of cheap labor.[1] Most socialists, even if willing to admit that depopulation constituted a serious problem for France, asserted that the trend could only be reversed by a complete abolition of the capitalistic system. It was not until the years immediately preceding World War I that some French socialists began to revise their opinion on this question. At that time Victor Griffuelhes, the syndicalist leader, after having made a tour through the depopulated French countryside, exclaimed: "Les Malthusiens vont trop loin. Tant d'efforts pour bâtir une cité juste et fraternelle dans laquelle personne n'habitera."[2] One of the most logical, if highly chimerical, solutions was proposed by Charles Gide, who stated that the ideal plan would be that each worker should have no more than two children and each bourgeois should at least have four.

A great number of theories reflecting the political views of their exponents were advanced to explain the low French birth rate and to serve as a guiding principle for remedying the undesirable situation. An opinion widely accepted by French conservatives was the view first presented by the sociologist Frédéric Le Play and after his death propagated by his many disciples. According to this interpretation, the decline in the birth rate was attributable to the hereditary provision of the *Code Napoléon*, which forced French parents to leave each of their children a specified proportion of their property and which had supposedly made the French farmer inclined to limit the number of his offspring in order to prevent the splitting up of his land into too many small holdings unable to support any of their owners. This theory, generally combined with an indictment of the individualistic principles of 1789 of which the *Code Napoléon* was held to be an expression, implied that the natality would increase after testamentary freedom had been restored.[3]

[1] Cf. Georges Deherme, *Croître ou disparaître* (Paris, 1910), R. Hertz, *Socialisme et dépopulation* (Paris, 1910); Marius-Ary Le Blond, *La France devant l'Europe* (Paris, 1913), 120ff.

[2] Georges Duveau, *Histoire du peuple français*, 331.

[3] Cf. *supra*, 109; Paul Ribot, *Rôle social des idées chrétiennes*, I, 203ff.

Most experts rejected the Le Play thesis as being too simplistic and as inspired by reactionary principles. An explanation that found more favor among the students of demography was the theory advanced by Arsène Dumont, an author with socialist and anticlerical views.[1] Although deploring the low natality of the French people, Dumont denied that the country was in a state of decadence. He ascribed the low birth rate to what he called social capillarity; that is, the desire and opportunity to rise in socio-economic rank. This social ambition had, according to Dumont, become very strong since the French Revolution, which had created equal political rights but which had still kept the nation divided into groups of highly different economic standings. These new circumstances, he argued, had induced many parents who had aspirations for themselves and their children to practice birth control. Dumont felt that nothing but a radical reorganization of the social order, providing for a larger degree of economic equality and social security, would be able to lessen the degree of social capillarity and thus to end the downward trend of France's birth rate.

Many French social scientists, partly agreeing with Dumont, attributed the low birth rate to a complex of factors which they called the "progress of civilization." In this phrase they included such phenomena as the rise of cities and of the middle classes, the soaring of individual and family ambition, the development of a kind of neo-paganism, expressing itself in selfishness and excessive pursuit of pleasure. According to this interpretation, "progress" might easily lead to retrogression, and France, supposedly the first European nation to reach a high level of civilization, might therefore become the first one to decline.[2] The proponents of this theory were inclined to accept a cyclical theory of history with highly pessimistic implications for their country: Increase of population leads to civilization, which promotes a spirit of foresight, egoism, ambition, and sexual pleasure; this situation in the long run results in a demographic and cultural decline, which continues until arrested by an influx of a young conquering people, by a retrogression to foresightless barbarism, or by the establishment of iron discipline under a despotism. Or, to quote from Gustave Le Bon: "Passer de la barbarie à la civilisation en poursuivant un rêve, puis décliner et mourir dès que ce rêve a perdu sa force, tel est le cycle de la vie des peuples."[3]

---

[1] Arsène Dumont, *Dépopulation et civilisation; étude démographique* (Paris, 1890).
[2] Paul Leroy-Beaulieu, *op. cit.*, 237ff.
[3] Spengler, *op. cit.*, 167–168; Le Bon, *Psychologie des foules* (Paris 1895), 191.

The alarm at the declining French birth rate was hardly lessened by the observation that the natality was also decreasing in other European countries, in most countries actually even more rapidly than in France. In all these countries, however, the birth rate remained still higher than in France and, moreover, the death rate in France, though dropping, did less so than elsewhere and became one of the highest in Europe. The end result was that during the period from 1870 to 1914 the rate of natural increase was much lower in France than in any other European country with the exception of Ireland and that during a number of years the deaths outnumbered the births.

The high death rate, its causes, and the measures to reduce it were less widely discussed than the low birth rate. Yet after attention had been called to the necessity of improving medical care for young mothers and infants, some legislation to that effect was passed. One alleged cause of the high death rate that did cause passionate debates was the large amount of alcoholic beverages consumed by the French population. It was pointed out that the number of licenses for selling liquor and wine had rapidly increased since 1870 and was the highest in Europe. "Le pis est," wrote Jacques Bertillon, "que la France mourra déshonorée. L'histoire aura le droit de dire qu'elle sera morte de deux vices ignobles: le crime d'Onan et l'ivrognerie."[1] Two organizations, L'union française anti-alcoolique and the Alliance d'hygiène sociale, were founded to fight against the excessive consumption of alcohol. This temperance movement urged the French Parliament to reduce the number of licenses, but was completely unsuccessful, for it was up against a much more powerful pressure group, that of the vine growers. Even the majority of the Socialist representatives in the Chamber of Deputies did not dare to take up the fight against the liquor forces, though in principle they sided on this issue with the repopulationists.[2]

There were a number of other social problems related to the slow growth of the population that aroused the alarm of some Frenchmen. The wide distribution of so-called pornographic literature, including the material of the neo-Malthusian League, was the special target of the Senator René Bérenger, but his campaign for the suppression of all obscene literature led to nothing but demonstrations of the Paris

---

[1] Jacques Bertillon. *L'alcoolisme* (Paris, 1904), 229.

[2] G. Mauranges, "L'alcoolisme et le parti socialiste," *Revue socialiste*, LV (1912), 219–226.

student body and the unpopularity of the Senator.[1] The emancipation of women and their participation in economic life, greater in France than in any other European country, was also widely criticized as contributing to the decline of the birth rate. Conservatives, as might have been expected, were leading in the attack on the feminist movement, but after the turn of the century they met with increasing opposition from the socialists and other progressive elements who felt that the status of women should be raised, not lowered.[2]

<h2 style="text-align:center">VI</h2>

French public opinion, easily stirred by issues with ideological implications has seldom shown much interest in purely economic questions. During the greater part of the nineteenth century, the discussion of French economic policy remained the almost exclusive domain of professional economists. Most of these, adhering to the doctrine of *laissez faire*, were sharply critical of the prevailing practices of protectionism, political centralization, and bureaucratization. They held the government intervention in economic affairs responsible not only for the slow pace of economic progress, but also for the low birth rate and the political instability.[3] Their unfavorable view of the French political system was tersely expressed by one of the most uncompromising French liberal economists, Yves Guyot: "Le citoyen est libre de tout faire, mais sous la surveillance de la police."[4]

Most Frenchmen, however, were hardly concerned about the economic situation of their country, which seemed to be far more prosperous than almost any other Continental state. They realized, it is true, that in commerce and industry France was far inferior to Great Britain, but it was widely felt that from a more general point of view this state of affairs was not unfortunate since excessive industrialization supposedly led to materialism, moral decadence, and social unrest.

[1] Gaston Deschamps, *La misère de la démocratie* (Paris, 1899); M. Prévost, art. "René Bérenger" in *Dictionnaire de biographie française*, IV (Paris, 1951), 1498; André Chéradame, *La crise française* (New ed., Paris, 1925), 386–392.

[2] Cf. Jean Larnac, *Histoire de la littérature féminine en France* (Paris, 1929), cf. Billy, *op. cit.*, 230.

[3] This was the point of view consistently presented in the leading organ of French liberal economists, the *Journal des économistes* (see, for example, the articles by Fleury E. Lamy, Clemence Roye and Ambroise Clément in 1870 and 1871, 3e série, 6e année, vol. XX, XXI, XXIII); cf. G. Pirou, *Les doctrines économiques en France depuis 1870* (Paris, 1925), book II; Gustave Le Bon, *Psychologie du socialisme* (Paris, 1898), 280ff.

[4] Yves Guyot, *La police* (Paris, 1884).

In the national self-examination following the Franco-Prussian War, the defeat was not blamed on French economic inferiority; on the contrary, German military superiority was sometimes explained as being the result of Germany's feudal society not yet corrupted by the new quest for material possessions.[1] Neither did there seem to exist any reason for alarm over the state of French economy during the two decades immediately following the war, when France surprised the world by a speedy payment of the war indemnity and rapid economic recovery.

This general complacency was yet hardly disturbed by a notorious pamphlet, *Au pays de la Revanche*, published in 1886 under the pseudonym of Dr. Rommel. This very one-sided but brilliant booklet mercilessly exposing the weaknesses of French economic, social and political life was at the time believed to have been written by a German; actually the author was a Frenchman, Alfred Pernessin, as should have been obvious from his perfect command of the French language and his intimate acquaintance with his subject.[2] He had a cosmopolitan background, having been born of an English mother and a Swiss father and having spent many years in Germany and England as a representative of the Crédit Lyonnais. In his many years abroad he had been in an excellent position to make comparisons between French and foreign habits in the field of business and politics and had, for reasons that are not altogether clear, developed an almost pathological aversion to all the French nation stood for. It was, however, this very antipathy that made him into one of the sharpest analysts of the weaknesses of modern France.

As may be expected, the work did not meet with a warm reception, but even its critics[3] had to admit that the author had put the finger on many of the nation's evils: the timidity and unenterprising spirit of the average French businessman, the hypertrophy of the state which was looked upon as the mama of all Frenchmen, the excessive love of decorations and distinctions among the bourgeoisie, the absence of any desire to settle in the colonies, where bureaucrats were almost the only French residents, the tumultuous scenes in the French parliament and the abusive speeches of the deputies, the lack of

[1] Cf. Renan's remarks, *supra*, 130; Blanc de St. Bonnet, *La légitimité*, 33ff., 649f.
[2] See letter of A. Raynaud revealing Rommel's true identity in *l'Éclair*, June 10, 1898, p. 1.
[3] Cf. Jean Boillot, *Le pays de la revanche et le pays des milliards, Réponse au Dr. Rommel* (Paris, 1886); Georges Montorgueil, "Opinions. L'utile enemie," *l'Éclair*, June 5, 1898, 1; Jules Lemaître, *Opinions à répandre* (4th ed., Paris, 1901), 72–81.

any local autonomy, the decline in the birth rate, the obscene language found in much of the press and the literature, the political strife and its detrimental effect on foreign and economic policies, the immense pride of the French people, still convinced to be the most powerful, courageous, and intelligent nation in the world. On the other hand, the author lacking any perspective and sense of balance, made the gross error of ignoring all evidence that contradicted his thesis and of giving the impression that no other European nations suffered from any serious evils. His conclusion was: "La France a lâché pied sur toute la ligne, tout craque en elle, tout s'affaisse, et maintenant nous pouvons en parler sans crainte et sans colère, mais avec cette pitié respectueuse qu'on doit à une grande nation qui décline.... La France n'est évidemment plus jeune; elle n'a plus le courage de pousser la charrue, de travailler au loin, de faire des enfants. ... Pourquoi tant hésiter à parler de décadence!"[1] The author perfectly illustrated the mentality that had been castigated by Fustel de Coulanges: the national tendency to self-calumniation and the idealization of the virtues of Germany and the wisdom of England.

One of Pernessin's criticisms that was most readily conceded by his contemporaries was the backwardness of agriculture. Suffering from a variety of evils such as archaic methods of cultivation, catastrophic epidemics among certain crops, and excessive division of the soil, it was in an almost continuous state of crisis after 1873. In many districts there also existed a serious shortage of labor, since the depopulation of the countryside continued to proceed at a rapid rate. It was widely realized that French peasants were no longer in a competitive position with the more efficiently producing farmers in other parts of the world, who at this time began to flood the French market with grain, wine, sugar, and other products.[2]

A still greater shock to French confidence in the soundness of their economy came in the late 1890's when a large number of books and articles called attention to the new industrial and commercial colossus that had made its appearance on the other side of the Rhine.[3] Many Frenchmen suddenly discovered that Germany, which had thus far been considered an economically almost underdeveloped country,

---

[1] Au pays de la revanche (Genève, 1886), 5–6.

[2] Cf. Marcel Braibant, L'agriculture français, son tragique déclin, son avenir (Paris, 1936); E. Guillaumin, Panorama de l'évolution paysanne, 1870–1935 (Paris, 1935), Duveau, Histoire du peuple français, 334ff.

[3] Cf. Digeon, op. cit., 476–488; see also C. Mourre, D'où vient le décadence économique de la France (Paris, 1900) and Georges Aubert, À quoi tient l'infériorité du commerce français (Paris, 1900).

was rapidly surpassing France in all branches of industry and commerce. They painfully realized that the alleged German virtues of discipline, efficiency, industriousness, and organization, which had been the secret of German military successes in the past, had been equally helpful in the development of a strong, modern economy. The impressive display of German industrial products at the Paris World Exhibition of 1900 was regarded as another debacle of Sedan.[1] It became manifest that there existed a new "German danger" – the title of a work written on this subject by the poet Marcel Schwob. But, as Gustave Le Bon and others pointed out, it was not only the German danger that the relatively stagnant French economy had to face: there also existed a British danger and an American danger, even a Russian danger and a Chinese danger.[2] Yet the circumstance that France was falling behind other leading nations in its industrial and commercial development did not rank as a major factor in the pessimism of the period. On the whole, the economic situation of the country continued to inspire optimism. France shared, though less than some other countries, in the economic progress of the times; French agriculture survived the worst crisis at the price of a high protective tariff and the financial resources of the nation remained the envy of the world.[3]

VII

It was the religious and moral state of the nation rather than the backwardness of French economy that greatly disturbed many French men of letters at the end of the century. The first thirty years of the Third Republic were, as is known, disastrous to the Catholic Church in France. The religious revival of the early 1870's was followed by the establishment of a government that surpassed all regimes since the Revolution in its hostile attitude toward Catholicism. Civil marriage and divorce were introduced, the Church was deprived of its influence on education, monastic orders were suppressed and persecuted; finally, Church and State were separated. In no other field did the young Republic display more determination than in fighting clericalism. The people who had once built cathedrals and had led Europe in the Crusades seemed to have turned their backs on the faith of their

---

[1] Luethy, *France Against Herself*, 77.
[2] Le Bon, *Psychologie du socialisme*, 28off.
[3] Cf. E. Théry, *Les progrès économiques de la France* (Paris, 1909).

fathers. This time, not only the urban population but also the rural masses fell away from the Church. "Nous assistons à une volte-face étrange," stated Renan in 1875, "le catholicisme, si longtemps soutenu par le paysan, a perdu son appui."[1] Many observers came to the conclusion that the French were the least religious nation in the world. "La France," wrote the philosopher Alfred Fouillée, "offre l'example presque unique d'un peuple qui, en somme et en masse, est libre-penseur."[2]

The reaction to this secularization process, of course, varied considerably. The loss of Catholic influence in French society was welcomed as a major victory over ignorance and superstition by the numerous Frenchmen subscribing to a secular, revolutionary ideology. Many of them were confident that they had once and for all extinguished the heavenly lights and that a purely secular morality would take the place of the otherwordly ethics preached by the Church.[3]

But not all freethinkers shared this confidence. An idealistic philosopher like Charles Renouvier, though strongly opposed to any political influence of the Catholic Church, felt that the decline of the old beliefs had left a metaphysical vacuum. He compared the moral situation of his age with that of Greek civilization at the time of its decadence and held that the world was suffering from a lack of faith in transcendental truth.[4] Ernest Renan had similar misgivings about the waning of religious faith: "Faire le bien pour que Dieu, s'il existe, soit content de nous, paraîtra à plusieurs une formule un peu vide. Nous vivons de l'ombre d'une ombre. De quoi vivra-t-on après nous?"[5] In the last decade of the nineteenth century the conviction that science and naturalism had led mankind into an impasse gained ground among French intellectuals. The philosophy of determinism was blamed for having deprived morality of its foundations and for having promoted an attitude of pessimism and materialism. Even many agnostics came to look upon the religious and moral crisis as the most alarming development of their times.[6]

---

[1] Chastenet, *Histoire de la Troisième République*, II, 15.

[2] Alfred Fouillée, *Idée moderne du droit en Allemagne, en Angleterre et en France* (Paris, 1878), 103; cf. A. Faguet, *L'anticléricalisme* (Paris, 1905), 9; Lucien Arréat, *Le sentiment religieux en France* (Paris, 1903); W. C. Brownell, *French Traits* (New York, 1888), 73.

[3] Adrien Dansette, *Histoire religieuse de la France contemporaine* (Paris, 1948–52), II, 643; Curtius, *Civilization of France*, 173ff.

[4] Renouvier, *Philosophie analytique de l'histoire*, IV, 742, 743.

[5] Renan, *Dialogues et Fragments philosophiques* (1876) in *Œuvres complètes*, I, 557.

[6] Cf. Édouard Rod, *Les idées morales du temps présent* (Paris, 1891); Paul Desjardins, *Le devoir présent* (Paris, 1892); Maurice Pujo, *La crise morale* (Paris, 1898); J. Benrubi, *Les sources et courants de la philosophie contemporaine en France* (2 vols., Paris, 1933), II, 954–963.

Other authors deplored the decline of the Catholic Church because they considered this institution essential to the support of the social order or indissolubly connected with the greatness of France. Hippolyte Taine, noting that the great mass of the French people was in the process of returning to paganism feared that this development would weaken the nation even more than the Church.[1] The seemingly dangerous political and social implications of the decline of religious convictions led many members of the bourgeoisie to revise their formerly hostile attitude toward the Church and its doctrines. The pro-Catholic views of such writers as Bourget, Brunetière, Barrès, and Maurras largely stemmed from the feeling that a strengthening of social discipline and national unity was dependent on a Catholic Renaissance. Maurras, for one, never made a secret of the fact that his admiration of the Church as an authoritarian institution did not imply any sympathy with the Church doctrine or with the (according to him) revolutionary teachings of Christ.[2]

True Catholics who realized the extent of dechristianization were naturally even more alarmed, although their faith preserved them from total despair.[3] But many French Catholics did not recognize the seriousness of the situation. Whereas recent French Catholic historians have acknowledged that at the end of the nineteenth century the Church was in a state of decline and that a large part of the French nation no longer believed in the Christian doctrine,[4] this state of affairs was not admitted by numerous Catholic leaders of the time. In 1880 Emile Keller, a prominent Catholic layman, proclaimed that in France, the first Catholic nation, the Church was younger and more vital than ever before and, in 1889, Mgr. Freppel still referred to France as "un pays foncièrement catholique."[5] Pointing to the popularity of the cult of Saint Anthony of Padua and the new shrines at Lourdes and Salette, many Catholics attributed the ordeal of the Church and the decadence of France to sinister machinations by small groups such as Freemasons, Protestants, and Jews, who represented the diabolical forces in a fundamentally still profoundly Catholic society. Many members of the clergy continued to believe

---

[1] Taine, *Les origines de la France contemporaine*, vol. XI (*Régime moderne*) (Paris, 1921), 188.

[2] Cf. *supra*, 142–143, 150.

[3] Hanotaux, *Contemporary France*, II, 684–686; Benrubi, *op. cit.*, II, 953; H. Platz, *Geistige Kämpfe im modernen Frankreich* (München, 1922), 219, 287; "Aperçu sur la situation de la religion et du clergé en France," *La réforme sóciale*, XXIX (1895), 357–387.

[4] Gabriel Le Bras, *Introduction à l'histoire de la pratique religieuse en France* (2 vols., Paris, 1942–45); F. Boulard, *Essor ou déclin du clergé français* (Paris, 1950); Dansette, *op. cit.*, II, 13ff.

[5] Dansette, *op. cit.*, II, 49–51.

that France as the eldest daughter of the Church was God's chosen
people and that by some miraculous turn of events the Church and
France would be restored to their former glorious positions.[1] With most
Catholics alternating between lamentations over the satanic Republican regime and assertions of the strong Catholic inclinations of the
French people, it is to be expected that their interpretations of the
moral and religious crisis of their times were on the whole not distinguished by a sense of realism.

Yet a minority of Catholic writers with progressive sympathies
showed a real understanding for the problems of the period. "Modernists" of one kind or another, they favored a more positive attitude
toward the popular demand for political and social equality and urged
a less uncompromising stand against the new scientific and philosophical ideas. Deeply alarmed by the decline of traditional faith and
morality, they put the blame for this deplorable situation largely
on the Church itself since it had lacked understanding for the legitimate
aspirations of the people and had become intellectually stagnant.
Unlike other Catholics, they did not identify themselves with the
forces of reaction and felt that other, predominantly non-Catholic,
nations had been more successful than France in working out a
satisfactory relationship between the Church and modern society.
At the end of the nineteenth century, many of these progressive
Catholics looked to America for inspiration, feeling that the great
freedom that the Church enjoyed in this democracy indicated the
solution of the Catholic problem in France. When in 1899 this so
called "Americanism" was condemned by the papacy, one of the
leading sponsors of the movement, the Comte Guillaume de Chabrol,
bitterly remarked: "A strong current of individual initiative in religious
matters would have been the only way of raising up the Latin races
and of giving them a decisive part in the Church; manifestly, that is
not God's plan."[2]

An outspoken and intelligent representative of this group of Catholic modernists, Paul Bureau, a professor at the Institut catholique,
wrote one of the most judicious and best informed studies on the
social and moral crisis of modern France, *La crise morale des temps
nouveaux* (1907). Influenced by the Catholic sociologist Le Play as
well as by the anti-Catholic school of Emile Durkheim, he favored

---

[1] Dansette, *op. cit.*, I, 454; II, 37–38; Epting, *Das französische Sendungsbewusstsein*, 172.
[2] Thomas T. McAvoy, *The Great Crisis in American Catholic History, 1895–1900* (Chicago,
1957), 288–289; cf. Frédéric Boudin, *L'Américanisme* (Paris, 1899); Dansette, *op. cit.*, II, 449.

a reconciliation between Catholicism and science, between what he called "les enfants de la tradition" and "les enfants de l'esprit nouveau." Unlike most Catholics he urged the upper classes to imitate the English aristocracy in their concern with the plight of the proletariat and felt strong sympathies for the latter. Bureau saw in socialism a modern religious movement and criticized the clergy for their lack of imagination in dealing with the problems of industrialized society. On the other hand, he fully shared the Catholic view of the declining birth rate, the prevalent alcoholism, and the disintegration of the family, and felt that it was up to religion not to science, to provide spiritual and moral leadership in the modern world. But he considered it an encouraging sign that many freethinkers themselves recognized the need for some form of religion and was confident that the crisis could be overcome. Even after his widely read book was placed on the Index, Bureau continued his attempt to narrow the gap between Roman Catholicism and modern civilization.[1] His point of view was shared by many other Catholic intellectuals, but their influence remained limited and their optimistic predictions were not vindicated by later events. Like Bureau, many "modernists" were forced by the Church to cease propagating their radical views, whereas others refusing to comply were excommunicated.[2]

Another group of French Catholics alarmed by the iniquities of their times but, unlike the modernists, opposed to any compromise with modern civilization continued in the old Christian tradition of prophesying disaster and the end of the world.[3] The Church did not always look with favor upon such eschatological speculations, but at least one great pope of the period seems to have shared the apocalyptic view of history. In his encyclical "All things in Christ" (1903) Pius X deplored "that at the present time society is suffering more than in the past from a terrible and radical malady, which while developing every day and gnawing into its very being, is dragging it to destruction." "There is good reason to fear," he added, "that this great perversity may be the foretaste and perhaps the beginning of the evils reserved for the last days, and that the 'son of perdition,' of whom the Apostle speaks, may already be in the world."[1]

---

[1] Cf. Benrubi. op. cit., II, 1018; see review articles by Georges Sorel in the *Mouvement socialiste*, XXII (1907), 13ff., and by Hubert-Valleroux in *La réforme sociale*, LV (1908), 292–298.

[2] Anon., *Ce qu'on a fait de l'Église; étude d'histoire religieuse avec une humble supplique à sa sainteté le pape Pie X* (Paris, 1912); Léon Chaine, *Les catholiques français et leurs difficultés actuelles* (Paris, 1903).

[3] Vulliaud, *op. cit.*, 193ff.

The most eminent French Catholic forecasting the Day of Reckoning was the novelist Léon Bloy.[2] A severe critic of his time, he did not spare the clergy in his denunciations. As early as Franco-Prussian War, at the age of twenty-four, he believed himself to be witnessing the beginning of the great catastrophe that had been predicted by many Catholic authors.[3] This feeling of living in a period of disaster never left him during the remaining forty-seven years of his life. "Nous sommes au prologue d'un drame inouï," he wrote in 1906, "tel qu'on n'en a pas vu depuis plusieurs siècles . . ."[4] Although his despondency was tempered by his expectation of the coming of the Kingdom of Heaven, it is his pessimism which seems central to this personality. "Nous périssons par impuissance, par imprévoyance, par obstination et par aveuglement," he declared as a young man, "Ah! disons tout en un mot, nous périssons parce que nous avons trop de raison, et il n'y a plus que la folie qui soit encore capable de nous sauver. J'entends la folie divine de la croix."[5]

Léon Bloy's apocalyptic views, like those of many nineteenth-century French Catholics, consisted of a blend of religious and nationalistic aspirations. Although Bloy was convinced that the French nation of his time was more corrupt than any people had ever been, he still considered the French superior to any other nation. Just like the Jews, the French were God's chosen people. Their very perdition meant that God was closer to them and had selected them for the ultimate salvation of the world. He assured his readers that other nations were so inferior to the French that they should consider themselves honored if allowed to eat the bread of their dogs. He warned that if France died, the world would be deprived of its soul and would die also.[6] As in the case of many other censors of modern France, it was only an intense nationalism that kept Léon Bloy from despairing of his country's future.

---

[1] Pius X, *All Things in Christ. Encyclicals and Selected Documents*, ed. Vincent A. Yzermans (Westminster, Md., 1954), 5.

[2] Cf. Jean Steinmann, *Léon Bloy* (Paris, 1956); Wilhelm Dillinger, *Das Frankreichbild im Werke Léon Bloys, 1846–1917* (Düsseldorf, 1937); Léon Bloy, *Choix de texte*, ed. Albert Béguin (Paris, 1946); Pierre-Henri Simon, *L'esprit et l'histoire. Essai sur la conscience historique dans la littérature du XXe siècle* (Paris, 1954), 85–87.

[3] Bloy, *Choix de texte*, 238.

[4] Jacques Chastenet, *Une époque pathétique: la France de M. Fallières* (Paris, 1949), 9.

[5] *Choix de texte*, 239.

[6] Bloy, *Jeanne d'Arc et l'Allemagne* (Paris, 1915), 14, 24; cf. Dillinger, *op. cit.*, 8, 38, 52–55; Albert Béguin, *Léon Bloy, l'impatient* (Fribourg, 1944), ch. IV.

VIII

From our present-day vantage point the views of many French intellectuals of the end of the nineteenth century about the state of their country appear unduly pessimistic. The Third Republic, present-day historians feel, displayed its weakness not before but after the First World War.[1] Especially its first thirty years now strike us as a pre-eminently constructive period. The new democratic regime, whatever its shortcomings, was more stable than any other form of government that France had known since 1789. It acquired for France a huge colonial empire and greatly strengthened France's international position by concluding treaties with Russia and Great Britain. Around 1900 France was, moreover, one of the richest countries in the world, playing a leading role in international finance. In addition, France enjoyed great prestige as the center of almost all new artistic and literary movements. A later generation is inclined to look back to the *fin-de-siècle* period as the "belle époque" and to be impressed more by its greatness than by its degeneracy.

The contrast between contemporary and present-day evaluation of the period is, however, more apparent than real. The prevalence and intensity of *fin-de-siècle* despondency can easily be exaggerated. Pessimism was clearly a countercurrent in an age that became increasingly satisfied with itself. In contrast to the many intellectuals who were convinced of the "decadence" of the present, facing this situation with an attitude of fatalistic resignation, perverse delight, or hopeful aspirations for a regeneration in the near future, the majority of the French educated public readily accepted a more complacent view of the existing situation. The pessimists themselves fulminating against the self-satisfaction of their contemporaries and their naive belief in progress admitted that optimism was all but universal.

Many observers of the French scene of this time were struck by the cheerful outlook of the majority of the French people. One of the best informed American commentators on French affairs, the critic William C. Brownell, noticed in 1888, at height of the Decadent

---

[1] Cf. David Thomson, *Democracy in France. The Third and Fourth Republics* (3d ed., London, 1958), 112–115. 168. 171–173; Rudolf Albertini, "Die Dritte Republik: Ihre Leistungen und ihr Versagen," *Geschichte in Wissenschaft und Unterricht*, VI (1955), 492–504; Donald C. McKay, "The Third Republic in Retrospect," *Virginia Quarterly Review*, XXXIII (1957), 46–60; Joseph Chappey, *Histoire générale de la civilisation d'Occident de 1870 à 1950* (Paris, 1950), I, 125, 192–193, 216.

movement in French literature, "the vivacious and confident way
of looking forward to the future, which the French, and perhaps the
French alone, share with ourselves."[1] Frenchmen often expressed
themselves in a similar vein. Pessimism, according to an "illustrious
chemist" quoted by the philosopher Elme-Marie Caro, was the natural
philosophy of a beer-drinking people. "Il n'y a pas de danger," he
added, "qu'elle s'acclimate jamais dans les pays de la vigne, ni surtout
en France; le vin de Bordeaux éclairit les idées et le vin de Bourgogne
chasse les cauchemars."[2] The historian Gabriel Hanotaux counted
vivacious optimism and an invincible national self-confidence among
the French national characteristics.[3]

The French people were fortified in their cheerful and confident
outlook by the new scientific discoveries and technological inventions
of the period. Readers of Jules Verne, they believed that there was
little to which man could not attain. The somewhat naive notion
that science would solve most of man's problem was one of the
dominating ideas of the period, accepted even by many writers who
were otherwise highly critical of modern civilization. The belief
in the saving power of science was probably the only illusion to which a
pessimist like Hippolyte Taine tenaciously clung until the very end
of his life.[4] An author like Emile Zola who portrayed such a somber
picture of French society and for this reason is sometimes considered
a leading figure in the Decadent movement of literature,[5] was actually
inspired by a strong faith in the progressive march of mankind under
the guiding light of science and truth.

In France, as in other European countries, the belief in progress
was for the first time becoming a popular creed. "Progrès" became a
favorite name for newspapers and cafés. The general public ignored
the serious criticism to which numerous philosophers and social
scientists of the period subjected the belief in science and the progressive development of history. Even a conservative historian like
Alfred Rambaud concluded his *Histoire de la civilisation française* (1887)
by asserting that "notre civilisation se distingue de plus en plus par ces
caractères: progrès scientifique, progrès démocratique, progrès de la
solidarité internationale, progrès des sentiments d'humanité ... Avec

---

[1] Brownell, *French Traits*, 315.
[2] Elme-Marie Caro, *Le pessimisme au XIXe siècle: Léopardi, Schopenhauer, Hartmann* (Paris, 1878), 286.
[3] Hanotaux, *Histoire de la France contemporaine*, II, 494.
[4] Taine to Havet, 1878 in *Correspondance*, IV, 46; cf. Chastenet, *Histoire de la Troisième République*, II, 36ff.
[5] Cf. Petriconi, *Reich des Untergangs* and Carter, *The Idea of Decadence*, 71–79.

le progrès matériel, avec le progrès intellectuel, marche du même pas le progrès moral."[1]

It was not only the development of modern civilization in general, but also that of France specifically which filled most Frenchmen with pride and confidence. They felt that the new republican regime constituted an important step forward in the direction of greater political and social equality. They fully accepted the republican credo that France was again leading the world in democratic organization and that the Republic was restoring the greatness of the country. This republican idealism, which was more than empty rhetoric dispensed in speeches on national holidays, owed much to the inspiring leadership of Gambetta, who had assured his followers: "Oui! la République, c'est désormais sous son égide que nous voulons vivre ... ce gouvernement qui implique véritablement ... le règne de la vérité, de la liberté, de la solidarité humaine. C'est sous cette forme de gouvernement qu'il faut désormais travailler tous ensemble avec un désintéressement que rien ne pourra troubler ... à la régénération de la patrie, au relèvement de la France. Et ... travailler au relèvement de la France, c'est travailler à l'avancement du genre humain, c'est travailler à la civilisation générale de l'Europe."[2]

Many Frenchmen professed their faith in the development of their country by coming to its defense against its numerous denigrators. Several historians upholding the revolutionary principles exposed the fallacies of the interpretation of the French Revolution as given by Hippolyte Taine and other conservative writers.[3] Other scholars took issue with the thesis that modern biology and anthropology had undermined the belief in political and social equality, and concluded that modern science and the principles of democracy were perfectly compatible.[4] The historian Gabriel Hanotaux asserted that it was a common mistake made by moralists of all times to exaggerate the defects of their age, illustrating his point by quoting from a sixteenth-century author, Etienne Pasquier, complaining that France had reached the state of old age.[5]

A similar mood of confidence in the strength of the country also predominated in the answers which men of letters gave to the question

---

[1] A. N. Rambaud, *Histoire de la civilisation française* (2 vols., 2d ed. Paris, 1887), II, 635–636.
[2] Léon Gambetta, *Discours et plaidoyers politiques*, III, 160.
[3] Cf. Curtius, *Civilization of France*, 81–82.
[4] C. Bouglé, *La démocratie devant la science* (Paris, 1904); Georges Guy-Grand, *Le procès de la démocratie* (Paris, 1911); D. Parodi, *Traditionalisme et démocratie* (Paris, 1909).
[5] Hanotaux, "La France est-elle en décadence?" *L'énergie française* (Paris, 1902), 339.

put to them by the newspaper *Figaro* in 1898, and again by the periodical *L'Européen* in 1904, whether France was in a state of decadence.[1] The sociologist Gabriel Tarde replied that France was suffering not from any basic inferiority but merely from bad luck. He rejected all current views that Catholicism, a rigid educational system, or blood mixture had enfeebled the French nation. Admitting that in mechanized warfare and modern industry the French were handicapped in competing with less "individualistic" nations, he predicted that the French inventive genius would in the long run restore the nation to the leading role to which it was entitled.[2] Another notable answer was given by Max Nordau, who, in spite of the bitter attack he had launched on modern French literature and French society a few years earlier, declared: "Morally and intellectually France stands in the forefront among civilized nations. Its science, its literature, and its arts are superior to most and inferior to none. France occupies now a position to which others will come later ... The Frenchman who is not proud of his nation must be a highly peculiar and ungrateful individual."[3] Other foreign authors paid a similar tribute to the persisting genius of France, with Bernard Shaw remarking that the only symptom of decadence that he could observe was that such a stupid question had been raised.[4]

Although indignantly rejecting the conservative denigration of modern France, progressive intellectuals were not utterly blind to the shortcomings of their country. Some of them like Charles Renouvier, Emile Zola, Alfred Fouillée, Charles Gide, and Emile Durkheim were seriously concerned about such social problems as depopulation, rising criminality and alcoholism, and the increasing suicide rate.[5] But it was not felt that these were signs of French inferiority, since other countries were suffering from at least equally serious problems. The public at large, moreover, largely ignored these questions; its

---

[1] *Figaro*, Sept. and Oct., 1898, answers by Francisque Sarcey, Georges Ohnet, Jules Clarétie, Juliette Adam, Albert Vandal, Paul Hervieu, Hector Malot, Maurice Maeterlinck, Marcel Prévost; *Européen*, IV (March 26, April 2 and 9, 1904), answers by Georg Brandes, Wilhelm Wundt, Björnstjerne Björnson, Max Nordau, H. G. Wells, Edmund Gosse, G. B. Shaw.

[2] *Figaro*, Oct. 11, 1898, p. 4; cf. Gabriel Tarde, *Sur la prétendue décadence des peuples latins* (Bordeaux, 1901).

[3] As transl. in Jean C. Bracq, *France Under the Republic* (new ed., Paris, 1916), 227.

[4] See also J. Novicow, *L'expansion de la nationalité française; coup d'œil sur l'avenir* (Paris, 1903).

[5] Cf. Fernand Giraudeau, *Les vices du jour et les vertus d'autrefois* (Paris, 1891); Alfred Fouillée, *La France au point de vue moral* (Paris, 1900); idem, *La démocratie politique et sociale en France* (Paris, 1910); Pierre de Coubertin, *L'évolution française sous la IIIe République* (Paris, 1896); cf. also *supra*, 158, 174.

only serious criticism of modern France was the corruption and instability of political life. But politics did not yet affect the nation as profoundly as after the First World War. "La France," said a political commentator of the period, Robert de Jouvenel, "est une terre heureuse, où le sol est généreux, où l'artisan est ingénieux, où la fortune est morcelée. La politique y est le goût des individus; elle n'y est pas la condition de leur vie."[1] After the defeat of 1870 France's position in the world might be lower than it had been in the past, but most Frenchmen felt that since that year France had not continued on the downward road but, on the contrary, had displayed spectacular vigor and recuperative power, perhaps with the only exception in the field of practical politics and biological vitality. For the majority of the French people, France was still "le plus beau royaume sous le ciel."

Apart from a few men of letters and a small segment of the laboring classes, the French were still fervent nationalists, probably even more so than ever before in their history. As such they were inclined to believe in the greatness of their nation rather than in its decadence. Republicans often outdid the traditionalists in praising the uniqueness and the superiority of French civilization, which they often identified with the cause of mankind. "France et Humanité," wrote the historian Ernest Lavisse, "ne sont deux mots qui s'opposent l'un à l'autre; ils sont conjoints et inséparables. Notre patrie est la plus juste, la plus libre, la plus humaine des patries!"[2] Republican nationalism, though more generous and liberal in nature than that of the conservatives, was hardly less insistent on a strong army allowing France to play a leading role in European politics.

It is true that in the 1890's Gambettan patriotism and the idea of revenge began to lose its former popularity,[3] but in most instances, this did not mean a loss of confidence in the future. On the contrary, new ideologies offering a better world to come began to capture the mind of idealistic Frenchmen. Pacifism, internationalism, anarchism, and syndicalism found numerous devotees among the population. The disgust with political corruption and social injustice did not lead all young French intellectuals to seek refuge in the ivory tower and

---

[1] Robert de Jouvenel, *La République des camarades* (1914) (ed. Paris, 1934), 4; cf. Onésime Reclus, *Le plus beau royaume sous le ciel* (3d ed. Paris, 1913).

[2] Pierre Nora, "Ernest Lavisse; son rôle dans la formation du sentiment national,' *Revue historique*, CCXXVIII (1962), 104; cf. Joachim Kühn, ed., *Der Nationalismus im Leben der dritten Republik* (Berlin, 1920); Carlton J. H. Hayes, *France, a Nation of Patriots* (New York, 1930).

[3] Cf. André Siegfried, *France: a Study in Nationality* (New Haven, 1930), 49–50.

to view the course of events with indifference or cynicism. At the time of the Dreyfus affair even most men of letters had broken radically with the gloomy, condescending outlook on contemporary society that had prevailed among them in the early 1890's. It was above all socialism that could count on the enthusiastic support of an influential segment of the younger generation and that with its promise of the end of exploitation and oppression inspired them with a new faith in the course of history. The socialist creed, it is true, implied the inequity and corruption of the existing, capitalistic system, but numerous French socialists refused to follow Karl Marx in his chiliastic theory that conditions had to grow worse before the world would be ready for the socialist utopia. They detected the beginnings of a truly socialistic regime in the present democratic order and believed in gradual reform rather than in catastrophic revolutions as a way to further progress.[1]

The followers of these idealistic movements were not disturbed by the "decadence" of France. They were willing to admit that existing French society was rapidly disintegrating, but this meant, according to them, that the new order of social justice and freedom for all was close at hand. The seemingly impressive following which the various progressive movements found among the French people – as clearly demonstrated by the defeat of militarism and clericalism at the time of the Dreyfus affair – convinced many Frenchmen that their country was again marching ahead of the rest of humanity on the road toward progress. As a Francophile German of this time, Hermann Fernau, remarked, what was declining in France was imperialism, authoritarianism, the police state, and bourgeois conventions, but this very "decadence" was an indication that the French democracy was pioneering in destroying all antiquated institutions and in establishing the superior social order of the future.[2] From about 1890 to 1905, when the threat of war seemed less imminent than before or after, the French people, including many intellectuals, suffered from complacency and naive illusions about the future rather than from excessive pessimism.

---

[1] Georges Weill, *Histoire du mouvement social en France, 1852–1924* (3d ed., Paris, 1924), 246–247.
[2] Hermann Fernau, *Die französische Demokratie; sozialpolitische Studien aus Frankreichs Kulturwerkstatt* (München, 1914), ch. XI.

CHAPTER VII

"FRANCE HERSELF AGAIN"
1905–1914

Nous sommes en train de nous apercevoir que notre prétendue décadence n'était qu'un mot.

ETIENNE REY, 1912[1]

Il ne s'agit pas d'une Renaissance. Il y en a dix, il y en vingt. Tout renaît.

ROMAIN ROLLAND in 1912[2]

I

During the ten years preceding the outbreak of the First World War the pessimistic mood of the *fin-de-siècle* period gradually disappeared. The concept of French decadence gave way to the notion that France was undergoing a regeneration or a renaissance. The small, but vocal segment of French society among whom national self-degradation had been the dominant temper regained their confidence in the nation. They began to propagate the view that after a long crisis in which the French people had been exposed to foreign, subversive influences France was finding her way back to the sound principles that had been the foundation of her greatness in the past. At the time that France became involved in the First World War, many intellectuals were convinced that "France was herself again."[3]

This change of mood was closely related to the revival of nationalism following the Tangiers crisis of 1905. This event, as Charles Péguy was one of the first to recognize,[4] marked the beginning of a new period for France and for Europe. Initially, it is true, the heightened international tension added to the national gloom. The immediate reaction to what seemed to many Frenchmen a capitulation to German

---

[1] Etienne Rey, *La renaissance de l'orgueil français* (Paris, 1912), 198.

[2] Romain Rolland, "Chronique parisienne," *Bibliothèque universelle et Revue suisse*, LXVIII (1912), 398.

[3] This phrase was used by Ernest Dimnet as the title of his book describing the French "Renaissance"; see *infra*, 202–203.

[4] Péguy, *Notre patrie* (1905) in *Œuvres en prose, 1898–1908* (ed. Bibl. de la Pléiade, Paris, 1959), 851; cf. Romain Rolland, *Péguy* (Paris, 1944), I, 103–115, 318–319.

imperialism was one of increasing alarm.[1] Some publicists made renewed attempts to awaken public opinion to the danger of the situation. Thus Emile Flourens, a former minister of foreign affairs, published his *La France conquise* (1906), in which he portrayed the devastating effects of the antipatriotic spirit of the country. In 1910, an even more somber picture of French impotence was given in *La France qui meurt* by Alcide Ebray, a friend of Delcassé, the foreign minister who had resigned under German pressure. By this time, however, there were already signs that the nationalistic spirit was reviving. Many politicians and men of letters renounced their previous antimilitaristic and antipatriotic convictions. Some Radicals like Clemenceau began to give serious thought to preparing the nation for another possible war against Germany. As early as 1905, Jules Renard, until this time a professed pacifist, noted in his diary that war might be preferable to further humiliating concessions to Germany.[2] But the nationalist revival did not gain real ground until after the second serious crisis in Franco-German relations, the Agadir incident of 1911. In 1912 and 1913 the rebirth of French nationalism became the topic of the day.[3] Military and patriotic themes suddenly became fashionable in novels, plays, and songs. Foreign observers also commented upon the new nationalistic and bellicose mentality of the French people.

The scope of this nationalist revival should not be exaggerated. It affected the bourgeoisie more than the lower classes, the city of Paris more than the provinces, young people more than the older generation, and, above all, men of letters and politicians more than the people at large. In the elections for the Chamber of Deputies in these years (1906, 1910, 1914) the candidates opposed to nationalism and militarism did not lose favor with the electorate, but, on the contrary, received more votes than ever before. Yet this new wave of nationalism although never a strong popular movement, became an influential factor in French politics in the last years of peace.[4] It was largely responsible for the election of a moderate "nationalist" like Poincaré to the presidency in 1913 and it was an even more important factor in the

[1] Maurice Paléologue, "La démission de M. Delcassé en 1905," *Revue des Deux Mondes* June 15, 1931.

[2] Jules Renard, *Journal* (Paris, 1935), 665 (entry for June 24, 1905).

[3] The subject is excellently treated in Eugen Weber, *The Nationalist Revival in France, 1905–1914* (Berkeley, 1959); see also Fernand Baldensperger, *L'avant-guerre dans la littérature française 1900–1914* (Paris, 1919), ch. II; Clouard, *Histoire de la littérature française*, II, 7–9.

[4] Cf. Carroll, *French Public Opinion*, 257–258; François Goguel, *La politique des partis sous la IIIe République* (Paris, 1946), 141.

enactment of the law extending military service from two to three years, a law which even the Left majority elected in 1914 was reluctant to repeal. It undoubtedly affected the image that many intellectuals formed of their country in these years and greatly strengthened the morale of those writers who in the past had been profoundly concerned about the lack of a strong patriotic and nationalistic spirit among the French people.

The nationalistic revival was the major but not the only change in French society that was greeted as an encouraging sign by the Frenchmen who had formerly despaired of their country. A closely related trend that was widely interpreted as a return to national sanity was the increased prestige that conservative ideas enjoyed among the younger generation who accepted Maurice Barrès and Charles Maurras as their spiritual mentors, whereas writers who were known for their devotion to progressive causes, like Emile Zola and Anatole France, suffered a corresponding decline in popularity. This turn to the Right was partly a result of the war threat, which called for a strong executive as had been traditionally favored by conservative parties, but it had also its source in the widespread fear of a social revolution and in the disgust with the anticlerical policies of leftist ministries.[1]

An apparent revival of religion was still another phenomenon of the time that was widely regarded as an indication that France was herself again. At the eve of the First World War, as even many anticlericals admitted, the tide seemed to be turning in favor of the Church.[2] A surprisingly large number of prominent intellectuals were converted to Roman Catholicism. Many others sympathized with idealistic or mystical theories that were at variance with the militant atheism of an earlier generation. An even more significant symptom of what was hopefully referred to as a Catholic Renaissance was that around 1910 the percentage of professing Catholics among university students was much higher than it had been ten years earlier.[3] Many of these were enthusiastic supporters of the Sillon movement which, under the

---

[1] Cf. Eugen Weber, "Un demi-siècle de glissement à droite," *International Review of Social History*, V (1960), 165–201; idem, *The Nationalist Revival in France*, 40–41.

[2] Cf. Agathon (pseud. of Henri Massis and Alfred de Tarde), *Les jeunes gens d'aujourd'hui* (Paris, 1912), ch. IV; Victor Giraud, *Les maîtres de l'heure* (Paris, 1914), II, 340–342; Georges P. L. Fonsegrive, *De Taine à Péguy; l'évolution des idées dans la France contemporaine* (Paris, 1917); Jean Prévost, *Histoire de France depuis la guerre* (Paris, 1932), 64–78; Baldensperger, *op. cit.*, 64–78.

[3] Chastenet, *La France de M. Fallières*, 218.

inspiring leadership of Marc Sangnier, aimed at a social and religious regeneration of France.

An additional change contributing to the conviction that France was returning to its traditional ideals took place in the field of literature. The vogue of French classicism started by the École Romane in 1891 gained considerable ground in the first decade of the nineteenth century.[1] The excessive individualism of the Decadents and the Symbolists was abandoned in favor of more conventional ideas in form as well as subject matter. By 1910 the decadent movement in literature definitely belonged to the past. The emphasis on neurosis and abulia, the delight in perversion and artificiality were rejected by the rising generation who became known for their realistic attitude toward life, their interest in action and sport,[2] and their antipathy to excessive speculation and self-analysis.

II

This new state of mind is revealed in a large number of contemporary publications: novels, essays, pamphlets. The most important documents testifying to the change in temper are a number of opinion polls conducted by newspapers and periodicals among young intellectuals and students. The most representative and influential of these inquiries was *Les jeunes gens d'aujourd'hui*, published in 1913 by Agathon, a pseudonym covering Henri Massis and Alfred de Tarde. Discussing the new mood under five headings (love of action, patriotic faith, moral earnestness, Catholic Renaissance, and political realism), this work presented impressive evidence for a change of mentality among a group that could be expected to provide many future leaders of the country. Although the authors were interested in influencing public opinion as well as in portraying it faithfully, and their conclusions as to the elevated moral and religious temper of young people were exaggerated, most of the testimonies given by their informants can be accepted as an accurate reflection of the opinion held by the group in question. Even many writers who were not in sympathy with the new mood (Romain Rolland, Roger Martin du Gard) agreed with most of the conclusions of the report.

Like other commentators on the state of public opinion, Tarde and

---

[1] André Billy, *L'époque contemporaine (1905–1930)* (Paris, 1956), 25–32.
[2] Cf. Georges Rozet, *La défense et illustration de la race française* (Paris, 1911); Agathon, *op. cit.*, ch. II.

Massis contrasted the confidence that the new generation had in themselves and in their nation with the mood of self-degradation that had prevailed among their elders. Young people seemed to be no longer plagued by continual doubt but had a positive, pragmatic attitude toward life and religion. They tended to be realists who were distrustful of all abstract ideologies and who resolutely accepted their responsibilities including the duty to defend their country on the battlefield. Tarde and Massis felt that a noticeable change of mentality had occurred even among the older generation, and they quoted from a letter written by an Englishwoman in which she complained that "the friends whom she had known as pacifists, antimilitarists, antinationalists, admirers of Goethe, Nietzsche, and Wagner . . . had changed considerably, still paying lip service to the old words of progress and peace, but betraying a hardly repressed desire for war by each of their words, each inflection of their voice, each look."[1]

Conservatives and moderates, Catholics and even some anticlericals agreed in welcoming the revival of the patriotic spirit, but they varied considerably in their interpretation of the so-called national renaissance, and of the alleged decadence that had preceded it. The ultraconservatives of the Action française felt greatly encouraged by the new nationalistic spirit and the increasing discredit of Leftist ideology. Their movement, though remaining small, exerted an influence far out of proportion to the number of its adherents and was increasingly appreciated as a beneficial force in national politics even by many who did not favor the restoration of the monarchy.[2] Partly as a result of the incessant press campaign of the Action française, the French parliament passed the law extending military service. Their noisy demonstrations against professors of the Sorbonne who were accused of making insulting remarks about such national saints as Joan of Arc or of poisoning the French youth with their German ideas also left their mark on public opinion. The increasing influence exerted by the new royalist movement was attested by a socialist writer complaining that the French form of government had become that of the Action française without the king.[3]

It is understandable that in these circumstances the royalist leaders felt that the worst crisis of the country had been overcome. The threat of war had seemingly shown more clearly than before that

[1] Agathon, op. cit., 40–41.
[2] Samuel M. Osgood, *French Royalism Under the Third and Fourth Republics* (The Hague, 1960), 94; Rémond, *La droite en France*, 184.
[3] Buthman, *The Rise of Integral Nationalism*, 311, Charles Maurras, *Kiel et Tanger*, 231.

France needed an authoritarian form of government. The publication of a socialist pamphlet, entitled *Faites un Roi, sinon faites la paix*, in which the preservation of peace was seen as a prerequisite for the survival of the republican form of government, was interpreted by the royalists as a sign that even their opponents had lost confidence in their principles.[1] On the other hand, Maurras and his followers felt that the situation remained critical as long as the democratic form of government had not been overthrown. They had little but contempt for the new religious and moral aspirations of their contemporaries. In 1914, according to the leader of the Action française, "the beast of democracy" was not dead but had been seriously wounded.[2]

The increasingly nationalistic and even bellicose mood of the French people also strengthened the morale of many French officers who at the time of the Dreyfus affair and the years immediately following it had often expressed themselves highly pessimistically on the outcome of a possible armed conflict. As late as 1906 a former French officer, Emile Driant, had published a work under the significant title *Vers un nouveau Sedan*.[3] After 1910, however, many of them became convinced that in a war against Germany, which they held to be imminent, the traditional ingenuity and élan of the French soldier would prove of greater military value than any numerical superiority on the part of the Germans.[4] As these alleged qualities of the French would be of greater help in the attack than in the defense, leading French officers, known as "the Young Turks," advocated an offensive strategy.[5] Some of them considered the outbreak of war not only inevitable but even desirable, since war would enhance the position of the army and also regenerate a nation corrupted by its intellectuals and politicians.

This point of view was most eloquently expressed in the works of Ernest Psichari, one of Ernest Renan's grandsons, who out of disgust with modern civilization decided to become a professional officer and soon afterwards completed his break with his family background by a conversion to Roman Catholicism. In his army career he dis-

---

[1] Marcel Sembat, *Faites un Roi, sinon faites la paix* (Paris, 1913); cf. Carroll, *op. cit.*, 257.

[2] Maurras, *La Contre-révolution spontanée*, 156–157; cf. Jacques Bainville, *La Troisième République* (Paris, 1935); Maurras, *Quand les Français ne s'aimaient pas. Chronique d'une Renaissance, 1895–1905* (Paris, 1916).

[3] Girardet, *La société militaire dans la France contemporaine.*

[4] John C. Cairns, "International Politics and the Military Mind. The Case of the French Republic, 1911–1914," *Journal of Modern History*, XXV (1953), 282–284; Girardet, *op. cit.*, 249ff.; John Bowditch, "The Concept of élan vital: a Rationalization of Weakness," *Modern France*, ed. Edward M. Earle, 32–43.

[5] M. Salm, "Der Angriffsgedanke in der französischen Militärliteratur seit 1871," *Der Nationalismus im Leben der dritten Republik*, ed. Joachim Kühn, ch. IX.

covered the simple virtues of military life and regained the confidence
in himself and his country's traditions. In his various novels he glorified
war as the most divine of all human activities and as a prerequisite
for the renewal of France.[1] "Nous allons certainement à de grandes
victoires," he wrote his mother on August 20, 1914, a few days before
his death on the battlefield, "Je me repens moins que jamais d'avoir
désiré la guerre qui était nécessaire à l'honneur et la grandeur de la
France."[2]

A republican version of the new nationalistic mood that more
faithfully reflected French public opinion of the times was presented
by the popular playwright Etienne Rey. In his *La renaissance de l'orgueil
français* (1912) he staunchly defended the record of the Third Republic against its numerous detractors. Denying that the Church had
any part in the national revival, he proclaimed that the pride of France
was the pride in the Republic. He explained how under the impact
of the *année terrible* the confidence that the French had traditionally
placed in their civilization and their military qualities had been shaken.
Most people, he felt, accustomed as they were to associate greatness
with military successes, had failed to notice the great work accomplished by the Third Republic: the economic recovery, the acquisition of
a colonial empire, and the many social and legal improvements. It
had become fashionable to denigrate the French people and to predict
that France had no future.

The idealism displayed by French youth at the time of the Dreyfus
affair was, according to Rey, the first indication that France was recovering from self-degradation, scepticism, and cynicism. The provocative actions by Germany had completed the process of national
awakening. Undisturbed by the decline of the birth rate and convinced
that French economy was more prosperous than ever, Etienne Rey
claimed that his confidence in France was shared by many of his
contemporaries. "Nous sommes en train," he wrote, "de nous apercevoir que notre prétendue décadence n'était qu'un mot."[3] "Les
jeunes gens ne connaissent plus, comme leurs aînés, l'effroi de l'existence, l'amertume des désespoirs intellectuels, la tristesse pitoyable des
désirs qui s'épuisent d'eux-mêmes. C'est cet optimisme puissant de
la jeunesse qui a le plus contribué à rendre la France la croyance en
elle-même qu'elle avait perdue."[4] Although cherishing peace, young

[1] Cf. Digeon, *op. cit.*, 514–519.
[2] Ernest Psichari, *Lettres du Centurion* (Paris, 1947), 317–318.
[3] Rey, *La renaissance de l'orgueil français* (Paris, 1912), 198.
[4] *Ibid.*, 179–180.

Frenchmen, according to the author, no longer looked upon war as a disaster to be shunned at all costs. A calm, self-assured pride had supposedly superseded the bellicose spirit that had once been characteristic of the French people.

III

Most writers who continued to believe in pacifism and internationalism were understandably disturbed by the new manifestations of chauvinism and militarism, but even some leftist idealists became more hopeful than they had been in the past. They discounted the new nationalism as a temporary vogue and were more impressed by the noble aspirations that seemed to animate a large part of the younger generation. They recognized as one of their masters the novelist Romain Rolland whose work was inspired by the hope of regenerating a world that was suffering from lack of idealism.

According to Rolland, the decline of formal religion had left a void in the human heart that could not be filled by the traditional ideologies of the Left. Pessimism, cynism, moral and social disintegration had ensued, especially in French society, which, despite its intellectual brilliancy, was morally and religiously sterile.[1] Rolland wanted to stir the fire of idealism that, according to him, was slumbering under the ashes, and for that purpose he proposed a new humanistic religion based on the worship of exemplary human beings. "La vieille Europe," he wrote in his introduction to his biography of Beethoven (1903), "s'engourdit dans une atmosphère pesante et viciée. Un matérialisme sans grandeur pèse sur la pensée ... Le monde étouffe. Rouvrons les fenêtres. Faisons rentrer l'air libre. Respirons le souffle des héros."[2]

Unlike most other critics of nineteenth-century materialism and scientism, Romain Rolland was very critical of nationalism and Catholicism. An avowed cosmopolitan, he was alarmed by the warlike spirit of French youth as revealed in Agathon's inquiry.[3] Yet in spite of his anxiety about the growing international tension, he firmly believed that a great idealistic revival was taking place and that his age compared favorably with the most glorious periods of the

[1] Romain Rolland, *Mémoires et fragments du Journal* (Paris, 1956), 197–201; "Introduction" of *Jean-Christophe* (éd. déf., Paris, 1954), p. xv; Digeon, *op. cit.*, 519–520.
[2] Rolland, *Péguy*, I, 19, 35–36; René Lalou, *Histoire de la littérature contemporaine* (2 vols., Paris, 1941), I, 301.
[3] Rolland, *La nouvelle journée* in *Jean-Christophe*, 1159ff.

past. "Il ne s'agit pas d'*une* Renaissance," he declared in 1912, "il y en a dix, il y en a vingt; tout renaît."[1]

Romain Rolland's idealism strongly appealed to numerous Frenchmen whose humanitarian feelings were not fully satisfied by the secular dogmas of the leftist parties. One of the most glowing tributes to the idealism of the author of *Jean-Christophe* was paid by Gaston Riou who, in his *Aux écoutes de la France qui vient* (1913), proclaimed his faith in the future of France. Rejecting the authoritarian principles of the French Right and of most French Catholics, this liberal Protestant urged his countrymen to return to the generous principles that had animated French nationalists in the early part of the nineteenth century. Riou took a strong stand against the idea of decadence, which, according to him, had been universally accepted at the end of the nineteenth century and still retained some of its former prestige among his contemporaries. "Comment se peut-il," he asked, "qu'une doctrine aussi puérile exerce, ici et là, sur des esprits d'ailleurs distingués une sorte de dictature?"[2] He sought the explanation in the disillusionment that had followed every French revolution. "La France, en 1789," he believed, "fut possédée par le génie de l'impossible." Instead of the expected utopia, it created "une nouvelle féodalité, la plus formidable qui ait jamais été, l'aristocratie d'industrie et de finance."[3] The Revolution of 1848 and the establishment of the Third Republic were followed by new waves of disappointment, and finally "les meilleurs Français, ceux qui avaient été l'âme même de la France, décidaient d'être stérile."[4] They became emigrants in their own country, still cherishing their old ideals but knowing that these could not by realized. In their isolation, Riou held, they rationalized their discontent in a system, the theory of decadence, and carried this theory even to the practice of complete indifference toward national welfare.

But this negativistic attitude, Riou firmly believed, was no longer characteristic of the new France that was in the making. The first sign of revival had been the idealistic reaction against scientism at the end of the nineteenth century, when an attempt had been made to reconcile the two camps into which France had been divided. This new spirit, after having been temporarily arrested in its growth by the passions unleashed by the Dreyfus case, had become increasingly strong in the

---

[1] Rolland, "Chronique parisienne," *Bibliothèque universelle et Revue suisse*, LXVIII (1912), 396, 398.
[2] Riou, *Aux écoutes de la France qui vient* (7th ed., Paris, 1915), 246.
[3] *Ibid.*, 249.
[4] *Ibid.*, 250–251.

early twentieth century when many young Frenchmen had followed in the footsteps of idealistic writers like Romain Rolland and Charles Péguy.

Henri Bergson, even more than Romain Rolland, was instrumental in liberating many intellectuals from what they called the chains of scientism or the nightmare of determinism. Numerous Frenchmen agreed with William James that Bergson had killed "the beast intellectualism . . . absolutely dead."[1] By his introduction of the concept of *élan vital* and his emphasis on intuition as the ultimate key to the understanding of life, Bergson was a powerful influence in reassuring intellectuals, bewildered by the loss of religious convictions, that modern science had not undermined all spiritual values. The tremendous popularity of his ideas in the years preceding the First World War convinced many Frenchmen that an idealistic revival was under way. In 1912, Henri Bergson himself declared that he was impressed by the numerous manifestations of what seemed to amount to a "French moral Renaissance."[2]

Bergson's influence, unlike that of Romain Rolland, was not limited to intellectuals with democratic or socialist views. It is understandable that Bergson's criticism of scientism and determinism was welcomed by many Roman Catholics and interpreted by them as a sign of a religious revival. "C'est l'étude de sa philosophie," confessed Joseph Lotte, a Catholic professor at the Sorbonne, "étude que j'ai commencée dans le plus épais matérialisme, qui m'a ouvert le chemin de la délivrance. Jusqu'en 1902 j'eus l'esprit bouclé par Taine et Renan: c'étaient les dieux de ma jeunesse."[3] According to another Catholic writer, Georges Fonsegrive, the popularity of Bergson and other idealistic philosophers was an indication that a great idealistic revival had taken place since the days when Taine's and Renan's "materialistic scientism" had dominated French cultural life.[4] In support of this thesis the author pointed to the increasingly significant contributions made by Catholics in the fields of philosophy, science, and scholarship and to conversions of prominent men of letters like Péguy and Claudel.

A similar optimism was displayed by the abbé Ernest Dimnet in

---

[1] William James to F. C. S. Schiller, June 13, 1907, *The Letters of William James*, ed. Henry James (2 vols., London, 1920), II, 291; cf. *ibid.*, 290 (letter to Henry Bergson): "You have inflicted an irrecoverable deathwound upon intellectualism,"

[2] Agathon, *op. cit.*, 285.

[3] *Ibid.*, 33.

[4] Fonsegrive, *De Taine à Péguy*, 87.

his essay *France Herself Again*, written for an English-speaking public
in the last weeks preceding the outbreak of war. Dimnet was a liberal
Catholic, who had been a Dreyfusard and whose "modernism" was
distrusted by the hierarchy.[1] He had no sympathy with the antidemocratic and paganistic philosophy of the Action française. But by
1914 he had renounced most of his earlier progressivism, and his
interpretation of the development of modern France closely resembled
that of the reactionaries. He blamed France's misfortunes on the
"baneful philosophy and the lawless literature" which had originated
in the Second Empire and had found its fullest expression in the works
of a naturalist novelist like Zola and a "decadent" poet like Mallarmé.[2]
He held this nihilistic mentality responsible for the defeat of 1870
and for the persisting weakness of France after the war, when the spirit
of materialism and scientism had been elevated to the rank of government policy. From 1876 to 1905 France had rapidly declined under
a political system which had had no other consistent principle than
that of anticlericalism. The height of decadence, according to Dimnet,
had been reached under the ministry of Combes when France had
been in a state of complete anarchy. It is against this gloomy background that the author portrayed the miraculous revival of the nation
that had taken place since the Tangiers crisis, "a flash of lightning, after
which the clouds lifted."[3] The regeneration had been prepared by
some writers of the older generation, like Brunetière, Bourget, Barrès
and Bergson, who were now accepted as spiritual guides by the younger
generation, whereas an author like Anatole France who still clung to
the old Leftist ideology was nothing more than "a fossil."[4] Like other
authors of his time, Dimnet dwelt upon the revival of patriotism, the
new respect for the army, the decline of anticlericalism and the return
to traditional standards in literature. The author's conclusion was
that what France needed was not "a conversion of the mind and the
soul, which was an indisputed fact," but "a different system of government worthy of the new spirit."[5]

Bergsonism found two of its most gifted and fervent adepts in Georges
Sorel and Charles Peguy. Both writers were former Dreyfusards who
broke with the party they had once supported and turned into its

[1] See the second part of Dimmet's autobiography, *My New World* (New York, 1937),
65-76.
[2] Dimnet, *France Herself Again* (London, 1914), 298ff., 381.
[3] *Ibid.*, 151.
[4] *Ibid.*, 213.
[5] *Ibid.*, 325.

fiercest critics. Their bitter denunciations of modern France indicate that the new idealism did not fully succeed in dispelling the anxieties of the *fin de siècle*. But, unlike the Decadents and the Symbolists, Sorel and Péguy did not accept the degeneracy of their society in a spirit of resignation. They fought a continuous battle against the materialistic mentality of their times and never fully lost their confidence in the future.

The pessimism of these two authors is another variant of the common disillusionment following high expectations of revolutionary change. Georges Sorel's case was that of a moralistic, formerly Marxian socialist, disgusted with the parliamentary tactics and reformist tendencies of French socialist leaders, whom he accused of betraying the interests of the working classes and adopting the ideology of a decadent bourgeoisie. One of the bourgeois ideas that he fought relentlessly was the belief in progress. This was, according to him, an illusion, a bourgeois invention, which had an enervating effect on the fighting spirit of the proletariat and which was, therefore, detrimental to any real advancement of civilization dependent on revolutionary action by the laborers. Actually, he held, France had been in a state of decline since 1850 when the bourgeoisie had taken over and the heroic idealism of the West had given way to a materialistic, epicurean way of life devoid of all dignity and greatness.[1]

Sorel's deep interest in the problem of cultural decline was not merely the outcome of his disillusionment in French socialism. It was already evident in his earliest work, *Le procès de Socrate* (1889), written before his conversion to an unorthodox Marxism. In his preoccupation with decadence, like in many of his other attitudes, Sorel greatly resembled the German philosopher Nietzsche. Exactly as Nietzsche, but without yet knowing his work, he described Socrates as the first rationalist and decadent, responsible for perverting the heroic Greek civilization of his time. This theme was further developed in Sorel's later studies on Greek and Roman history in which he attributed the decline of the ancient world to the same evils that, according to him, were bringing on the decadence of France: excessive individualism, an exorbitant influence of intellectuals in politics, and a rationalistic outlook on life.[2]

[1] Georges Sorel, *Les illusions du Progrès* (1908) (new ed., Paris, 1910, with chapter "Grandeur et décadence"); Michael Freund, *Georges Sorel, der revolutionäre Konservatismus* (Frankfurt a.M., 1932), 188–189.
[2] James H. Meisel, *The Genesis of Georges Sorel* (Ann Arbor, 1951), 13; Jean Wanner, *Georges Sorel et la décadence* (Lausanne, 1943); Georges Sorel, *La ruine du monde antique* (Paris,

Sorel, in spite of his devastating criticism of modern civilization, its materialism, "decadent" bourgeoisie, parliamentary institutions and democracy, believed in the possibility of a regeneration. Greatly influenced by Giambattista Vico's cyclical theory of historical change, he held that movements toward decadence and movements toward greatness are alternating and that, whereas the former are always natural, the latter require a persistent effort.[1] Like Nietzsche, he looked forward to the birth of a new culture resuming the heroic tradition of the past. It is well-known that Sorel, in striving for a cultural renewal, expected much from the revolutionary syndicalists, but that he became disappointed with this movement as he did with the Action française, which he also supported for a short time. Like Proudhon, whom he greatly admired and somewhat resembled, this moralist ended his life despairing of his country, if not of the entire Western civilization.[2]

Georges Sorel was not the only writer of his time looking upon intellectuals as perverters of the public mind. They had already come in for much abuse at the time of the Dreyfus affair when the term "intellectuals" had originated, first being used by conservative newspapers in a pejorative sense to designate the large number of scientists and scholars who had taken Dreyfus' side.[3] "Race ignoble que ces universitaires," wrote a Catholic journalist, Ernest Renauld, in 1900, ". . . qui passent leur vie à enseigner l'erreur, à corrompre les âmes . . . Je ne connais pas de fléau comparable à celui-là . . . Ils sont la cause première du mal, les véritables ennemis de l'ordre social." [4] A number of young intellectuals joined this campaign against intellectuals during the next ten years. One of Sorel's most gifted disciples, Edouard Berth, wrote various suggestive essays attempting to demonstrate that all societies in which intellectuals had held leading positions – the Byzantine Empire, eighteenth-century France, the Second Empire, and the Third Republic – had been in a state of political and cultural decline.[5] Other young writers (Henri Massis, Alfred de Tarde, Réne Benjamin, and Pierre Lasserre) concentrated

1902); *idem, Réflexions sur la violence* (Paris, 1908), ch. "La décadence bourgeoise;" *idem,* articles on the decadence of ancient civilization in *Mouvement socialiste,* 1906, 1907, and 1908.
[1] Freund, *op. cit.,* 30–31.
[2] *Ibid.,* 241; Meisel, *op. cit.,* 216, 248–249.
[3] Cf. V. Brombert, "Toward a Portrait of the French Intellectual," *Partisan Review,* XXVII (1960), 480–502.
[4] Ernest Renauld, *La conquête protestante, nouvelle eassai d'histoire contemporaine* (Paris, 1899), quoted in Soltau, *French Political Thought,* 354–355.
[5] Edouard Berth, *Les méfaits des intellectuels* (Paris, 1914); see also his *La fin d'une culture* (Paris, 1927).

their attacks on professors of the Sorbonne, who were accused of lacking insight in the greatness of French traditions, of propagating radical and socialist ideas, and of introducing pedestrian and pedantic methods of German scholarship, instead of offering a liberal education based on a study of the great books of the past.[1] Among the French intellectuals most commonly charged with these various sins were the literary historian Gustave Lanson, the influential librarian of the École Normale, Lucien Herr, and the distinguished historians Charles Seignobos, Charles-Victor Langlois, and Ernest Lavisse. The censors of French university professors harbored a special grudge against the sociologist Émile Durkheim whose positivist doctrine of morality, in the words of one Catholic critic, constituted "le plus grave péril national que notre pays ait connu depuis longtemps."[2]

Charles Péguy, the most talented of these young anti-intellectualists, wholeheartedly joined this crusade against what he called "le parti intellectuel." Péguy's views of contemporary society had much in common with those expressed by Georges Sorel. He also developed from a Dreyfusard with socialist convictions into a bitter critic of the political and intellectual leaders of the Left. Like Sorel, he glorified the heroic way of life and denounced the modern world and its bourgeois ideology (he dated the beginning of the degeneration from 1881, and not like Sorel, to 1850, the difference being explainable by the fact that Péguy was twenty-four years younger).[3] Both writers were pre-eminently moralists sharing Proudhon's almost puritan condemnation of comfort and pleasure.

Péguy was the more personally committed of the two authors. Republican idealism had meant more to him than to Sorel, and his disillusionment was correspondingly greater. With the enthusiasm and generosity of youth he had rushed to the defense of Dreyfus. Republican idealism remained sacred to him for the rest of his life, but few people will be prepared to accept his incongruous definition of the Republic: "un certain système de gouvernement ancien régime fondé sur l'honneur."[4] Unlike Sorel and other Dreyfusards, he never repented of the role he had played, but he was even more shocked

---

[1] Pierre Lasserre, *La doctrine officielle de l'Université* (Paris, 1912); René Benjamin, *La farce de la Sorbonne* (Paris, 1911); Agathon, *Esprit de la nouvelle Sorbonne* (Paris, 1911); cf. Hubert Bourgin, *De Jaurès à Léon Blum; l'École normale et la politique* (Paris, 1938).

[2] C. Bouglé, *Bilan de la sociologie française contemporaine* (Paris, 1938), 168; cf. Georges Friedmann, *La crise du progrès* (Paris, 1936).

[3] Péguy, *Notre jeunesse* (1910) in *Œuvres en Prose, 1909–1914* (ed. Bibl. de la Pléiade, Paris, 1957), 518–523.

[4] Daniel Halévy, *Péguy et les Cahiers de la quinzaine* (Paris, 1947), 200.

by what he called the sordid exploitation of the Dreyfus case by unscrupulous politicians. The degeneration of republican idealism into a despicable republican practice, according to Péguy, perfectly illustrated how decadence ensued from the replacement of a *mystique* by a *politique*. Losing all sense of proportion and noticing everywhere greed, corruption, selfishness, frivolity, and cowardice, he accused the republican leaders of betraying their country and of compromising with international finance. He was especially harsh on the once admired Jaurès, who now in his eyes was a dishonest German agent.[1]

In the *Cahiers de la quinzaine*, the distinguished periodical that he edited for fourteen years, Péguy continually vented his nostalgia for old France and his disgust with the modern world. "Le monde moderne avilit," he wrote in 1907, "Il avilit la cité, il avilit l'homme. Il avilit l'amour, il avilit la femme. Il avilit la race, il avilit l'enfant. Il avilit la nation, il avilit la famille. Il avilit même . . . ce qu'il y a peut-être de plus difficile à avilir au monde, parce que c'est quelque chose qui a en soi, comme dans sa texture, une sorte particulière dignité, comme une incapacité singulière d'être avili; il avilit la mort."[2] And three years later: "En quelques années la société moderne . . . est tombée à un état de décomposition tel, à une dissolution telle que je crois, que je suis assuré que jamais l'histoire n'avait rien vu de semblable. . . . Cette grande décomposition historique, ce grand précédent que nous nommons littérairement la pourriture de la décadence romaine, la dissolution de l'empire romain . . . n'était rien en comparaison de la dissolution et de la déchéance de cette société, de la présente société moderne."[3] Péguy held that the great power that had perverted the modern world was that of money. "L'ancien régime au moins n'avait pas commis cet abus d'être uniquement, inexpiablement le règne, le régime de l'argent. Des puissances spirituelles existaient encore, balançaient encore la puissance de l'argent." [4]

Péguy differed fundamentally from Sorel by his return to traditional values at the end of his life. After his disillusionment with republican humanism he embraced Catholicism and nationalism as the only spiritual forces capable of saving his soul and that of his country. More eloquently than any other writer has he sung the glory of France, renewing the belief that the French are a chosen people:

[1] Péguy, "A nos amis, à nos abonnés," *Œuvres en prose*, 1909–1914, 7ff.
[2] Péguy, "De la situation faite au parti intellectuel dans le monde moderne devant les accidents de la gloire temporelle," (1907), *Œuvres en Prose, 1898–1908*, 1158.
[3] "A nos amis, à nos abonnés," *op. cit.*, 37.
[4] "Clio: Dialogue de l'histoire et de l'âme," (1912), *Œuvres en Prose, 1909–1914*, 179.

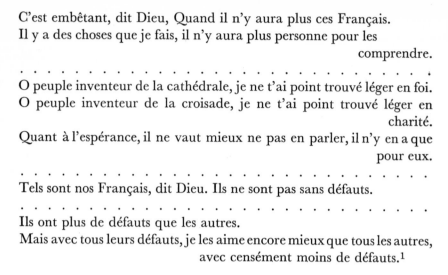

C'est embêtant, dit Dieu, Quand il n'y aura plus ces Français.
Il y a des choses que je fais, il n'y aura plus personne pour les
comprendre.

. . . .

O peuple inventeur de la cathédrale, je ne t'ai point trouvé léger en foi.
O peuple inventeur de la croisade, je ne t'ai point trouvé léger en
charité.
Quant à l'espérance, il ne vaut mieux ne pas en parler, il n'y en a que
pour eux.

. . . .

Tels sont nos Français, dit Dieu. Ils ne sont pas sans défauts.

. . . .

Ils ont plus de défauts que les autres.
Mais avec tous leurs défauts, je les aime encore mieux que tous les autres,
avec censément moins de défauts.[1]

The France which Péguy glorified was the France of the past, but
this France, he felt, was not dead. Paris was to him "capitale temporelle du monde, capitale intellectuelle . . . et capitale spirituelle,
encore, toujours, quand même."[2] He was greatly encouraged by the
nationalist revival that began to take shape during the last years of
his life.[3] A new France was in the making, a France for which he
bravely gave his life in the beginning of the First World War.

Because of his uncompromising, sincere personality and his poetic
genius, Péguy was admired as a spiritual leader by many of his contemporaries. A friend of Romain Rolland, a disciple of Bergson, an ardent
republican in spite of nationalist and Catholic views, he more than any
other writer of his time represented the new France facing the German
menace. "Dans vingt ans," wrote Georges Sorel in 1910, "le nom de
Péguy sera inséparable de la renaissance du patriotisme en France."[4]
His reputation as one of the most sincere idealists of his generation has
continued to grow after his heroic death. Many later Frenchmen have
acknowledged the debt they owed to Péguy for showing them the
way back to the real soul of France. On the other hand, it is difficult

---

[1] "Les mystères des Saints-Innocents," (1912), *Œuvres poétiques complètes* (ed. Bibl. de la
Pléiade, Paris, 1954), 379–380; cf. J. J. Tharaud's statement: "Jamais je n'ai vu personne
plus ingénument persuadé que la France était le premier pays du monde . . . ." (Digeon,
op. cit., 508).

[2] "De la situation faite au parti intellectuel," *Œuvres en prose, 1898–1908*, 1167.

[3] *L'argent* (1913) in *Œuvres en prose, 1909–1914*, 1224.

[4] Weber, *The Nationalist Revival in France*, 190.

to take Péguy seriously as a thinker. After his acquaintance with Bergson's works, Péguy was no longer plagued by any sense of inferiority in the field of rational analysis. Making a virtue of necessity, he openly flaunted all rules of consistency in his speculations on the destiny of France. His conversion to a nationalistic form of Catholicism was little more than a desperate attempt to escape the conclusion that the France of his dreams was irretrievably lost.

IV

The regained national confidence professed by so many Frenchmen on the eve of the First World War was not the result of any radical improvements in the political, social, or economic structure of the country. The parliamentary system of France had not been reformed and displayed many of the same weaknesses as in the past. The position of France in an increasingly heavily armed Europe remained as precarious as ever. The birth rate continued to decline and France persisted to lag behind most other powers in industry and commerce. Neither were there any signs that the Catholic Church was regaining its hold on the mass of the population. The limited gains that the Church was making among the bourgeoisie and intellectuals did not compensate for the severe losses which it continued to suffer among the industrial workers and the peasantry. Social unrest remained another serious problem. Conflicts between labor and capital were more frequent than before and numerous strikes suppressed by the army gave rise to a new militant antimilitarism among the laboring classes. In the last election before the outbreak of the war, in June, 1914, the leftist coalition committed to a reduction of the term of the military service won a clear majority in the Chamber of Deputies.

Neither was the change in literary attitudes as radical as many contemporaries believed. Some of the most prominent writers like Anatole France and Roger Martin du Gard remained completely foreign to the new mood of mysticism and nationalism.[1] Furthermore, the ivory tower continued to appeal to some of the most gifted authors of the period. Thus Paul Valéry, André Gide, and Julien Benda remained virtually unaffected by the vogue for action and political realism. It is especially the *œuvre* of Marcel Proust that serves to remind

[1] Roger Martin du Gard gave a very critical analysis of the new mentality in his *Jean Barois* (Paris, 1913); Anatole France's works of this period, *L'île des pingouins* (1908) and *La vie de Jeanne d'Arc* (1908) were also written in a spirit opposed to both nationalism and clericalism.

us that the individualism and estheticism of the Decadents and the Symbolists had not yet been fully superseded. His *A la recherche du temps perdu*, as far as its concentrated on the portrayal of the degeneration of the French aristocracy, may be even regarded as the supreme artistic expression of the *fin-de-siècle* mentality. Finally, in the last years before the outbreak of the war, the so-called classical revival was losing its sway. In the cafés and studios of Montmartre and Montparnasse audacious young men were professing such new creeds as Cubism, Fauvism and Futurism, which surpassed the Decadent and Symbolist movements in their emphasis on individual expression and rejection of classical rules.[1]

Many of the writers expressing their renewed confidence in France realized that the old, so-called "subversive" attitudes had not yet lost their strength. The abbé Dimnet, while asserting that France was "herself again," confessed that he was still uncertain whether this convalescence would result in a complete recovery or in a relapse.[2] Neither did the more realistic-minded conservatives abandon their misgivings about the strong popular agitation for a larger share in national prosperity.[3] In no instance did the new mood of national optimism imply the acceptance of the Leftist belief in the inevitable march of mankind toward greater happiness and enlightenment. Actually, insofar as the younger generation again received inspiration from the greatness of the past, it accepted a basically pessimistic view of the course of history. This point is clearly brought out by a leading exponent of the new nationalism, Ernest Psichari, in his novel *L'appel des armes* (1913): "Par une sorte de transmutation des valeurs, c'était le père qui signifiait le présent et le fils qui signifiait le passé, et c'était le fils qui recourait à l'histoire et c'était le père qui en appelait à l'avenir. Ainsi l'ordre ordinaire des facteurs se trouvait-il renversé."[4]

As has been noted before, the so-called "national renaissance" affected only a small part of the population. This does not mean that the great majority of the French people lacked confidence in their nation. On the contrary, of a cheerful disposition and hardly aware of the increasingly serious international situation, they did not yet see any reason for abandoning their former belief in progress and their

---

[1] Cf. Roger Shattuck, *The Banquet Years* (New York, 1958).
[2] Dimnet, *France Herself Again*, 335.
[3] Cf. André Chéradame, *La crise francaise, causes, solutions* (Paris, 1912); Jules d'Auriac, *La grande nation. La France devant l'Europe* (Paris, 1910); Guy-Grand, *Le conflict des idées*, 7; Marius-Ary Le Blond, *La France devant l'Europe* (Paris, 1913).
[4] Digeon, *op. cit.*, 517.

often overly optimistic, complacent estimate of the strength of France. Outbreak of war was held to be improbable in the enlightened twentieth century and the trend toward greater political and social equality seemed irreversible. It is true that many convinced democrats or socialists were often highly critical of existing institutions; they lamented the parliamentary corruption and inefficiency, or were concerned about social evils like the decline of the birth rate. It is also true that a number of intellectuals with progressive views became somewhat alarmed by the rising tide of nationalism and irrationalism.[1] It became evident to them that their views had lost much of the popularity which they had enjoyed around 1900. Anticlericalism was out of fashion, monarchism had become respectable, and the republic seemed once again in danger. Some old-time rationalists bitterly complained about the new wave of mysticism which had taken hold of the French mind.[2] Yet in spite of these criticisms of old standing or of recent origin, few if any French Leftists despaired of their country. On the eve of World War I, when the idea of decadence was losing its hold on French conservatives and French nationalists, it did not find any increased favor with French democrats and internationalists. France still seemed to them the standard bearer of the ideals of freedom and equality. When the First World War broke out, there existed no doubt in their minds that France was fighting for the preservation of a social and political order which was far superior to that of France's opponents.

The outbreak of World War I thus found the French nation more united behind its government than ever before in its history.[3] The French Right and the French Left, who had been fighting one another so bitterly, joined hands in defense of the fatherland. The Left willingly accepted the discipline of the army which they had disrespected in the past, while the Right fully supported the Republican regime which once had been the object of their virulent attacks. France, Renan had noted in 1854, resembled Rebecca, in whose womb two children had been struggling, each of which threatened to smother the other. But by 1914 the view that there were two Frances incapable of agreeing on any common course of action no longer corresponded to reality.

---

[1] Cf. Jean Gaumont, "Où va le nouveau socialisme?" *Revue socialiste*, LV (1912, 74–85; H. R. Weinstein, *Jean Jaurès* (New York, 1936), 173; Jean Neybour," Lettre aux jeunes," *Revue socialiste*, LVI (1912), 117–124.

[2] Cf. *supra*, 170-171; see also Jules Sageret, *La vague mystique* (Paris, 1919).

[3] Cf. Julien Benda, *Esquisse d'une histoire des Français dans leur volonté d'être une nation* (Paris, 1932).

A "sacred union," for a short while at least, had been achieved. The attitude of the French Right is in many ways the more surprising. In no other conflict between Republican France and countries representing a different system of government have Frenchmen opposed to democracy shown the same loyalty to their nation. If the war had broken out in the years of the heated controversies about the Dreyfus case, France might not have been equally fortunate in receiving the full support of many of its prominent citizens. By 1914, however, conservatives had become convinced that the "corrupt" and "decadent" France of the past was dying and that the purifying influence of the war would complete the process which had been under way during the pre-war period.[1] Like the Left, the Right now rejected the idea of decadence as a pernicious legend maliciously propagated by their political enemies.

---

[1] After the outbreak of the War Mgr. Baudrillart declared: "I think these events very fortunate. I have awaited them for forty years. France is remaking herself, and in my opinion this could not be achieved without the purifying war." (Weber, *op. cit.*, 144); cf. Victor Giraud, *Le miracle français* (Paris, 1915); *idem, Les maîtres de l'heure*, II, 60, 342ff.

CHAPTER VIII

THE FOREIGN PERSPECTIVE

> Unsere ganze europäische Kultur bewegt sich seit langem
> schon mit einer Tortur der Spannung, die von Jahrzehnt zu
> Jahrzehnt wächst, auf eine Katastrophe los.
>
> NIETZSCHE [1]
>
> As always France is far ahead on the down grade.
>
> HENRY ADAMS in 1910[2]

I

There were three major developments in French history of the nineteenth century that made a deep impression on the public mind and
inclined many Frenchmen to a mood of gloom. The first of these was
the French Revolution and similar subsequent attempts to establish a
regime allowing for a greater degree of equality and freedom. The
continual revolutionary agitation, often leading to violent and vin-
dictive measures against the classes and institutions resisting change,
alarmed those Frenchmen who, out of self-interest or idealism, favored
an aristocratic or authoritarian form of government. But despondency
was not found only among opponents of revolutionary principles;
many who believed in the ideals of the Revolution were also over-
mastered by despair when revolutionary idealism degenerated into a
reign of terror or was followed by the restoration of old institutions.
Moreover, numerous Frenchmen of all shades of political opinion
deplored that the revolutions divided the French people into opposing
camps and thus weakened the strength of the nation.

The second epoch-making event of the nineteenth century having a
depressing effect on many Frenchmen was the coming of the Industrial
Revolution. This radical, though gradual and therefore not immediately noticeable, transformation of French economy aroused a variety
of apprehensions such as forebodings of an age of vulgarity and mechanization, horror at the miserable living conditions of the working

---

[1] Friedrich Nietzsche, *Wille zur Macht*, Vorrede, Werke (19 vols., Leipzig 1899–1913),
XV, 137.

[2] Henry Adams, *Letters, 1892–1918* (New York, 1938), II, 552.

classes, and fear of bloody revolts by this new industrial proletariat. Closely related to, and often indistinguishable from the protests against certain aspects of the Industrial Revolution, were the time-honored complaints about the enervating effects of excessive wealth. Furthermore, the new industrial order, in conjunction with the impatient quest for political and social justice, was often held responsible for fostering atheism, individualism, materialism, and secularism, and thus destroying the organic, religiously oriented community of the past.

The third development of the nineteenth century that disconcerted many Frenchmen was the declining power of their country. It is understandable that diplomatic and military defeats, sometimes accompanied by foreign occupation, loss of territory, or decline of prestige, created a mood of self-examination in which the national misfortunes were attributed to an inferiority in form of government, economic production, military ardor, morality, educational system, or biological vitality. Under these circumstances the notion of national degeneration and cultural decadence gained wide acceptance. It is true that many of the authors indulging in such somber speculations were already pessimistic prior to the crisis in their nation's existence and merely used the critical situation as an occasion for venting their objections against established institutions or prevailing ideas. Yet the ordeals of France often served as a catalyst bringing about the expression of views that otherwise would have remained unexpressed or at least not have been put in such sharp and bitter terms.

France was, of course, not the only country of the nineteenth century in which the trends of the age aroused fear and anxiety. The growing demand for political equality as well as the rise of industrialism fostered despondency in many countries of the world. Similarly, in a number of states facing a decline of power comparable to that of France, failing national strength was instrumental in creating a sense of crisis and decadence.

A comparison between the apprehensions current in nineteenth-century France and some of the fears expressed in other countries (mainly Germany, England, Russia, Spain, and the United States) will be helpful in determining the significance of the French sense of decadence. The purpose of the following excursion into comparative history is not to deal, in any systematic manner, with the idea of decadence outside France, but to place French historical pessimism in a wider perspective so that its distinctive as well as its representative

features will become more evident. At the same time we hope to show
that pessimists in other countries were often of the opinion that France ✓
was the center of contemporary degeneracy, indicating, in other
words, that the decadence of France was a theme that was taken
seriously not only by French publicists but also by many foreign
writers concerned about the trends of their age.

II

It is well known that the French Revolution made a profound and
lasting impression outside France. In England, Germany, Italy,
Spain, and even in autocratic Russia and Turkey, the educated
public followed the gigantic struggle in France with passionate interest.[1]
There were few contemporary writers of any note whose works do not
bear the mark of the revolutionary events, and later generations continued to regard the Revolution as a living force of crucial significance
to their own times. Soon after the fall of Napoleon and the restoration
of the old monarchies, it was recognized that the revolutionary era
had not yet come to a close. Thus Henri de Saint-Simon wrote as
early as 1815: "The period we experience is not so much the end of
the French Revolution as the beginning of a European revolution."[2]
During the subsequent decades the outbreak of revolutionary uprisings
in many countries made it manifest to numerous European intellectuals
that the popular quest for freedom and equality had not yet lost its
strength. "The Revolution, which has so often been said to have
liquidated itself," wrote Leopold Ranke after the July Revolution of
1830, "seems never to want to come to its end. It reveals itself in ever
new, and often opposite forms."[3] This point of view became even
more common after the revolutions of 1848, when such diverse minds
as the Russian poet Tyutchev, the Spanish statesman Donoso Cortés,
and the Swiss historian Jacob Burckhardt warned their contemporaries
against underestimating the strength of the popular longing for radical

---

[1] Cf. *supra*, 43; B. Lewis, "The Impact of the French Revolution on Turkey," Journal of
World History, I (1953), 105–125; E. J. Hobsbawm, *The Age of Revolutions, 1789–1848*,
54–55.

[2] Kesting, *Geschichtsphilosophie und Weltbürgerkrieg*, 33.

[3] Leopold von Ranke, "Zur Geschichte Deutschlands und Frankreichs im 19. Jahrhundert," (1832), as quoted in Heinz-Otto Sieburg, *Deutschland und Frankreich in der Geschichtsschreibung des neunzehnten Jahrhunderts*, vol. I (Wiesbaden, 1954), 241.

innovation.[1] At this time it became a familiar saying than since 1789 mankind had been living in a state of permanent revolution.[2]

In most European countries the Revolution aroused hope and admiration as well as despair and hatred. At the outset, as is known, the general response to the overthrow of the absolute monarchy in France was one of wild enthusiasm. The fall of the Bastille was widely greeted as the happiest tiding in many centuries. "What a spectacle it is!," exclaimed a distinguished Swiss historian, Johannes Müller, "Blessed be its influence on nations and rulers. . . . July 14 is the best day since the fall of the Roman Empire."[3] Almost all leading German authors, such as Kant, Fichte, Hegel, Herder, Novalis, and the brothers Schlegel, were for a while convinced that a regeneration of the world was at hand. A similar exaltation prevailed among English writers:

> Bliss was it in that day to be alive
> But to be young was very heaven.[4]

But when the Revolution entered its phase of terror and French armies began to invade neighboring countries, these exalted feelings faded away. As early as 1790 Edmund Burke had opened the assault with his influential *Reflections on the Revolution in France*. Calling the Revolution "a strange chaos of levity and ferocity," he criticized its excessive confidence in abstract political schemes and its disregard of "natural law," tradition, and experience. Like later opponents of the revolutionary spirit he was inclined to idealize the past. "The age of chivalry," he complained, "is gone. That of sophisters, economists, and calculators, has succeeded it; and the glory of Europe is extinguished for ever."[5] Within a few years many early admirers of the Revolution were converted to Burke's point of view. Friedrich Gentz, Novalis, Hölderlin, Eichendorff, Kleist in Germany; Wordsworth, Coleridge in England voiced their hatred and disgust of regicide and atheist France.[6] By 1793, according to Johannes Müller, France

---

[1] F. I. Tioutchev, "Mémoire présenté à l'empereur Nicolas," *Revue des Deux Mondes*, June 15, 1849, 1053ff.; Juan Donoso Cortés, *Der Abfall vom Abendland* (Wien, 1948); Hans. J. Schoeps, *Was ist der Mensch?* (Göttingen, 1960), 87.

[2] Cf. Maurice Joly, *Dialogue aux enfers entre Machiavel et Montesquieu ou La politique de Machiavel au XIXe siècle* (Bruxelles, 1865); *supra*, 92.

[3] Gooch, *Germany and the French Revolution*, 46–47; cf. the enthusiastic terms in which the *Morning Post* of July 21, 1789 described the fall of the Bastille (Hobsbawm, *The Age of the Revolutions*, 53).

[4] Wordsworth as quoted in British Broadcasting Corporation, *Ideas and Beliefs of the Victorians* (London, 1949), 41.

[5] Edmund Burke, *Reflections on the Revolution in France* (2d ed., London, 1790), 113.

[6] Gooch, *Germany and the French Revolution*, *passim*.

had become the nightmare of Europe.[1] In Russia the intelligentsia expressed itself in a similar vein. In 1795 the historian Nikolai Karamzin lamented that he no longer recognized his civilized age and wondered whether mankind would again be forced to labor its way upward from barbarism, moving through the same cycles in eternal repetition.[2]

Such feelings of despair and fear remained strong among the European educated classes during the first half of the nineteenth century. At this time many conservatives were as much obsessed by the specter of the Revolution as medieval believers had been by the devil. To them the Revolution represented not a historical phenomenon, but a mythical force manifesting itself in the least expected places. They were often under the impression of witnessing the last act in a supernatural drama in which Satan was allowed a temporary triumph over the Holy Spirit. Not only uneducated peasants, but also some gifted European writers (Jung-Stilling in Germany, Willem Bilderdijk and Israel da Costa in the Netherlands, besides Lamennais and Ernest Hello in France) believed that the reign of Antichrist had begun, or at least was imminent, and that the world was approaching its end.[3]

Historically more pertinent was the fear that the revolutionary spirit was dissolving the cohesion of the body politic. This criticism was adumbrated by Edmund Burke who warned that the ideas of liberty and equality would reduce the commonwealth to "the dust and powder of individuality."[4] In the early nineteenth century this point of view was further developed by various German conservatives (Heinrich Leo, Franz von Baader, J. M. von Radowitz), arguing that the Revolution had promoted an excessive concern with selfish interests, a mentality that they designated by such various neologisms as "anarchism," "atomism," "nihilism," and "individualism."[5] All traditional values of European civilization seemed to them to be threatened by the forces unleashed by the "Great Revolution." "Since that period," complained a Russian reactionary, Konstantine Leontyev in 1884, "European thought bows down to the human being merely because he is a man . . . It no longer reveres any rare and high develop-

---

[1] *Ibid.*, 52.
[2] B. P. Hepner, *Bakounine et le panslavisme révolutionnaire* (Paris, 1950).
[3] Cf. *supra*, 42; Jan Romein, *De lage landen bij de zee* (Utrecht, 1934), 546–548, 552–553.
[4] Edmund Burke, *op. cit.*, 142–143.
[5] Ernst Benz, *Westlicher und östlicher Nihilismus in christlicher Sicht* (Stuttgart, 1949); Alexander Rüstow, *Ortsbestimmung der Gegenwart* (3 vols., Erlenbach, 1950–57), II, 114, 604; J. Goudsblom, *Nihilisme en cultuur* (Amsterdam, 1963), 3–6. Many Catholics regarded the Protestant Reformation as the first serious manifestation of these disintegrating principles; cf. *supra*, 16.

ment of human personality, but only the personality of anyone and everyone."[1]

Unlike French traditionalists, many conservatives of other European countries hated the Revolution not merely because it had destroyed the old social order, but also because it had led to French interference in the affairs of their nation. And they feared that a renewed outbreak of revolutionary sentiment would usher in another era of French domination and oppression. Hatred of the Revolution and Francophobia went therefore hand in hand. In the nineteenth century little was left of the great prestige that French civilization had once enjoyed among the European upper classes. Among English writers the flickleness, the frivolity, and the fury of French politics were proverbial. "Fickle in everything," wrote the Tory historian Archibald Alison, "the French have been faithful in one thing only – the love of change."[2] In Germany anti-French sentiments ran even higher. "I hate the French," remarked the Prussian reformer Freiherr vom Stein at the end of his life, "as cordially as a Christian may hate any one. I wish that they would all go to the devil."[3] The conservative historian Heinrich Leo (1799–1878) called France a nation of monkeys and Paris the permanent abode of Satan.[4] Russian Slavophiles were equally uncomplimentary in their opinions on modern France. They proclaimed the rottenness of entire Western Europe but often made exceptions for England and directed their severest strictures against France, the Western nation *par excellence*. France, in the words of Ivan Aksakov (1823–1886), was "the miserable land called to warn by her fate the rest of mankind, a country flying herself between popery and atheism, between superstition and unbelief, between slavery and revolt." "Her history," he wrote, "enables us to see what can happen to a 'kingdom of intelligence,' eternally carried away by the latest human theories and armed with the crippling weapons of administrative power. A kingdom of anarchy, in which parties fight for power and nothing but power, inflicting monstrous tyrannies in the name of the most liberal and democratic slogans of the world, and thus holding down a mute and morally stunned people."[5]

[1] Konstantine Leontyev, *The Average European as the Ideal and Instrument of Universal Corruption*, as quoted in Richard Hare, *Pioneers of Russian Social Thought* (London, 1951), 277.

[2] Archibald Alison, *History of Europe during the French Revolution* (1833–1842).

[3] Gooch, *op. cit.*, 583; cf. F. Gunther Eyck, "English and French Influence on German Liberalism Before 1848," *Journal of the History of Ideas*, XVII (1957), 313–341.

[4] Edgar Quinet, *France et Allemagne* (Oxford, 1908), 109–125; Hans J. Schoeps, *Das Andere Preussen* (Stuttgart, 1952), 186–187.

[5] N. V. Riasanovsky, *Russia and the West in the Teaching of the Slavophiles* (Cambridge,

Many of these foes of revolutionary France were convinced that the disease of their times was irremediable. Such was the case of Metternich, the leading statesman in the fight against the forces of the Revolution, who felt that Old Europe was going to die with him.[1] This gloomy view was even more explicitly stated by one of the rare Austrian diplomats who continued to work in Metternich's spirit, the Graf Anton von Prokesch-Osten.[2] A close friend of the Comte de Gobineau, whose pessimistic views he might have influenced, this Austrian representative to the Frankfort Diet was firmly convinced that Europe's fate was sealed and that of all nations France had always been most instrumental in promoting the corruptions of modern civilization.

The same fatalistic pessimism pervaded the scholarly philosophy of history expounded by a Protestant conservative, Karl Friedrich Vollgraff (1792–1863).[3] This obscure precursor of Oswald Spengler (whom he indirectly influenced by way of Ernst von Lasaulx, Jacob Burckhardt, and Friedrich Nietzsche) declared that all of Europe, including Germany, was suffering from the incurable malady of individualism. Like other conservatives of his times, he looked upon the French Revolution as a demoniacal movement precipitating the collapse of civilization and asserted that France had proceeded farther on the road to perdition than any other country.

Bleak visions of mankind's future were also entertained by some of the most distinguished scholars of the early nineteenth century. After hearing the news of the Revolution of 1830, the great German historian Barthold Niebuhr lamented: "Unless God gives miraculous aid, we are faced by imminent destruction akin to that which befell the

---

Mass., 1952), 105–110; Richard Hare, *Pioneers of Russian Social Thought*, 162; V .V. Zenkovskii, *Russian Thinkers and Europe* (Ann Arbor, 1953), 86ff., 194; this last author quotes the following denunciation of France from Lermontov's poem "The Last Abode":

> I wish to say to this great people:
> You are pitiful and small!
> Pitiful, because Faith, Glory, Genius,
> All that is great and sacred on the earth,
> You trampled into dust
> With the stupid mockery of childish doubts.
> You made a toy of hypocrisy and of glory,
> An executioner's axe out of liberty.
> With that axe you chopped away
> All the sacred beliefs of your fathers.

[1] Hans J. Schoeps, *Vorläufer Spenglers. Studien zum Geschichtspessimismus im 19. Jahrhundert* (Leiden, 1955), 81; cf. Henry Kissinger, "The Conservative Dilemma. Reflections on the Political Thought of Metternich," *American Political Science Association Review*, Dec., 1954.
[2] Maurice Lange, *Le Comte Arthur de Gobineau. Étude biographique et critique* (Strasbourg, 1924), 116ff.
[3] See Schoeps, *Vorläufer Spenglers*, 3–30.

Roman Empire towards the middle of the third century of the Christian era, when prosperity, freedom, culture, and science came to an end."[1] Similar doubts as to whether European civilization still had any future were voiced by Niebuhr's English admirer, the classicist Thomas Arnold. "All in the moral and physical world," he wrote in 1831, "appears so exactly to announce the coming of the 'great day of the Lord', *i.e.* a period of great visitation to terminate the existing state of things, whether to terminate the whole existence of the human race, neither man nor angel knows."[2] Many other eminent English authors were obsessed by the fear of a catastrophic revolution. The usual topic of discussion between Thomas Carlyle and Robert Southey was "the steady approach of democracy with revolution (probably an explosive) and a finis incomputable to man."[3] In 1848, when revolutions were in progress all over Europe and the Chartists were parading through the London streets, Thackeray declared that society was "in the last stage of corruption" and predicted: "There is an awful time coming for us all."[4]

The same revolutionary events of the year 1848 stirred the Spanish diplomat Donoso Cortés to develop his apocalyptic views on the course of European history.[5] In the tradition of the theocratic philosophy of Maistre and Bonald he prophesied that the decline of Christianity and the old social order would lead to unheard-of catastrophes. Convinced that the tension between the increasingly impudent rich and the increasingly discontented poor would reach the breaking point, he foretold the outbreak of a revolution of such unprecedented horror that its savagery would be forever remembered by later generations.

In the first half of the nineteenth century the opponents of the Revolution tended to be ambivalent in their evaluations of French power. On the one hand, their view that France was "the sickest of all nations," (Metternich),[6] and therefore closest to its downfall, implied the belief in French decadence. On the other hand, their fear of France testified to a high regard of the potential strength of the nation. But around the middle of the century one began to realize that

---

[1] Karl Jaspers, *Man in the Modern Age* (London, 1951), 17; cf. Franz Altheim, *Roman und Dekadenz* (Tübingen, 1951), 7.

[2] Gordon R. Taylor, *The Angel-Makers. A Study in the Psychological Origin of Historical Change, 1750–1850* (London, 1958), 269.

[3] Walter E. Houghton, *The Victorian Frame of Mind* (New Haven, 1957), 54–58.

[4] Humphrey House, "The Mood of Doubt," *Ideas and Beliefs of the Victorians*, 73.

[5] Donoso Cortés, *Abfall vom Abendland*, 44, 67; Kesting, *op. cit.*, 86–88;

[6] Metternich, *Mémoires, documents, et écrits divers*, vol. IV (Paris, 1881), 421.

revolutionary France was no longer a serious threat to other European countries. Thus, in 1850, Donoso Cortés contemptuously referred to France as the main debating club of Europe.[1] One of his most remarkable predictions was that the great revolution of the future would break out not in western Europe, but in St. Petersburg, and that a socialized and militarized Slavic race united under Russian leadership would serve as God's instrument to punish Europe for its flouting of divine commands.

Such forebodings of an impending upheaval in Russia did not yet haunt many Russian conservatives of the early nineteenth century who still liked to think of their country as the only rock of refuge in a revolutionary world. Even at this early time, however, some of them were afraid that Holy Russia would also fall victim to the satanical forces of the century. The poet Lermontov (1814–1841), for one, foresaw that:

> The day will come, for Russia, that day.
> When the Tsar's diadem will fall, and they,
> Rabble who loved him once, will love no more,
> And many will subsist on death and gore.[2]

Such fears of an imminent catastrophe increased in intensity among Russian traditionalists in the second half of the century.[3] In western Europe, on the contrary, the fear of revolution began to abate after 1848. The rising tide of democracy, it is true, continued to fill many men of letters and politicians with dark apprehensions, but it was realized that revolutionary apocalypticism had lost some of its former strength, notably in France, where aggressive Jacobinism seemed declining. Some foreign observers even came to the conclusion that France was fundamentally a conservative country that might serve as a bulwark against the dynamic forces perverting western civilization.[4] More commonly, the former fear of France gave way to a feeling of contempt

---

[1] Donoso Cortés, op. cit., 76.

[2] As translated in N. Berdyaev, The Origins of Russian Communism (London, 1948), 92.

[3] Cf. Konstantine Leontyev's foreboding: "Russian society . . . is rushing . . . more swiftly than any other society along the deadly path of universal confusion, . . . and from the womb of our state . . . we shall give birth to Antichrist," (N. Berdyaev, The Russian Idea, 205).

[4] Cf. Bodley, France, 614; "In France conservatism is the creed of the vast majority of the inhabitants;" Sisley Huddleston, France and the French (New York, 1925): "They are perhaps the most conservative nation in the world;" see also Georges Bourdon, The German Enigma, Being an Inquiry Among Germans as to what They Think, What They Want, What They Can Do (Paris, 1914); Alfred Fouillée, La démocratie politique et sociale en France (Paris, 1910), 110–112.

and indifference for the nation that was supposedly receiving its just punishment for having indulged in revolutionary chimeras.

In nineteenth-century France, as will be remembered, even many partisans of revolutionary change, frustrated by the repeated failures of their dreams, began to doubt whether history was working on their side. The same was true of many radicals in other European countries. In the period of reaction following Napoleon's downfall, the few intellectuals who remained steadfast in their loyalty to revolutionary principles tended to lose their former confidence in the future.[1] Such disillusionment with the course of history was likewise strong in a number of European countries after the revolutions of 1848. In Germany, many young liberals who had witnessed the shattering of their hopes embraced the pessimistic philosophy of Schopenhauer. One of the most radical minds of his time, Bruno Bauer, became convinced that revolutionary agitation and modern individualism had strengthened, not weakened the power of the government. Despairing of France, he urged the Germans to ally themselves with the still uncorrupted Russians and together to overwhelm the decadent West.[2]

Such a complete recantation of revolutionary hopes, it is true, remained exceptional. Actually during the second half of the nineteenth century, more than ever before, a utopian, almost apocalyptic belief in revolution gained acceptance among intellectuals sympathizing with the lot of the laboring classes. But these late nineteenth-century advocates of revolution, although highly optimistic as to the future, no longer placed much confidence in the revolutionary instincts of the French people. The repeated failures of the revolutionary uprisings in France had the effect of destroying the admiration which revolutionaries of other countries had once entertained for the French people. Thus the Italian nationalist Mazzini lost his faith in France when in the 1830's the French failed to come to the aid of the revolutionary movement in his country. "The incapacity of France to advance," he concluded "appears to be an historial necessity."[3]

---

[1] Thus William Hazlitt declared that all hopes which mankind had cherished for a radical improvement of the world "rose and set with the French Revolution. That light seems to hare been extinguished for ever;" Martin R. Adams, *Studies in the Literary Background of English Radicalism* (Lancaster, Pa., 1947), 11–12.

[2] Karl Löwith, *Von Hegel zu Nietzsche* (Wien, 1949), 120ff.; Hans Kohn, *Pan-slavism; its History and Ideology* (Notre Dame, 1953), 285; Schoeps, *Vorläufer Spenglers*, 90–93.

[3] Hans Kohn, *Prophets and Peoples* (New York, 1946), 81, 83, 89, 186.

The Russian socialist Alexander Herzen was even more disenchanted by the lack of idealism and strength displayed by the French at the time of the Revolution of 1848. Partly agreeing with Donoso Cortés and the Russian Slavophiles, he was led to the conclusion that France and Western Europe were on "the edge of an abyss, on the eve of an unavoidable, fatal cataclysm." The vulgar bourgeois mentality, he felt, had enervated the entire French people, including the working classes. "I am the first who pales and quails in the face of the approaching dark night. Farewell to the dying world, farewell to Europe."[1]

Of all French revolutionary failures, the Commune of 1871 had the most decisive effect in destroying the former admiration for French revolutionary *élan*. The nation that had given Europe the vision of human progress, complained the Russian populist Mikhailovsky in 1871, had become like England a country of "liberalism and stock exchange," ruled by the jungle laws of survival of the fittest."[2] As foreseen by Karl Marx, the outcome of the Franco-Prussian War strengthened the position of Marxism, the German brand of socialism, at the expense of French doctrines, which had hitherto held the leading position in international socialist thought.[3] At the end of the nineteenth century, many revolutionists no longer looked to France for inspiration but regarded Germany as the nation that was most likely to lead mankind in its struggle for emancipation from the yoke of capitalistic exploitation. Others felt, as did Karl Marx at the end of his life, that Russia now formed "the vanguard of the revolutionary movement."[4] All of them were in agreement with many conservatives that the French had lost their dynamic *élan* and become a "decadent" nation of cautious bourgeois, conservatively minded peasants, and individualistic artists, that was unlikely to disturb the existing social order. Such was, for example, the view of Lenin, who, in 1915, replied to fellow Bolsheviks fearing that a German victory would mean the destruction of French democracy: "Let them destroy it. France is nothing but a backward republic of usurers and rentiers fattening on

[1] Alexander Herzen, *From the Other Shore* (New York, 1956), 31ff., 155; Zenkovskii, *op. cit.*, 72; cf. Martin Malia, *Alexander Herzen and the Birth of Russian Socialism, 1812–1855* (Cambridge, Mass., 1961), 364ff.
[2] James H. Billington, *Mikhailovsky and Russian Populism* (Oxford, 1958), 75–78.
[3] Marx to Engels, July 20, 1870, Karl Marx-Friedrich Engels, *Historisch-Kritische Gesamtausgabe*, Dritte Abt., Bd. IV (Berlin, 1931), 339–340.
[4] Karl Marx in his preface to the Russian edition of the *Communist Manifesto* in 1882, Karl Marx and Friedrich Engels, *The Russian Menace to Europe* (Glencoe, Ill., 1952), 228; cf. Leopold Labedz. ed., *Revisionism* (New York, 1962), 66–67.

their gold. If Germany, who has outstripped her industrially, defeats her, there will be no harm in that."[1]

<h2 style="text-align:center">III</h2>

In the course of the nineteenth century it gradually dawned on many European intellectuals that the most important force under-mining the traditional social order was not the impatient quest for political freedom and equality but the rapid process of industrial-ization. To an even greater extent than the political emancipation of the masses, the amazing development of technology and science was widely hailed as inaugurating a new, superior phase in the history of mankind. Like the political upheavals of the century, however, the Industrial Revolution with its manifold effects aroused fear and alarm as well as complacency and hope.

Whereas most European men of letters who were opposed to the political ascendancy of the masses pointed to France as the source of all revolutionary contamination, the early foes of industrial capitalism tended to regard England as the main center of modern corruption. In agrarian Russia, for example, many intellectuals, considering their own country fortunate for being spared an uprooted proletariat which was plunging western European nations into social anarchy, declared that England above all was threatened by this process.[2] In the first half of the nineteenth century a similar view was taken by numerous Germans, Americans, and Frenchmen predicting that urbanization and industrialization were leading England either to its downfall or to a frightful revolution.[3] England appeared to many as a selfish "nation of shopkeepers," as another Carthage, which, because of its exclusive preoccupation with material gain, would in the long run be subjected by more idealistic and heroic races.

Anglophobia was especially strong among German men of letters, looking with contempt upon the allegedly utilitarian, hypocritical, and materialistic bent of the English mind. The English were, accord-ing to Heinrich Heine, "the most odious race that God in his wrath had ever created." "I might settle in England." the German poet remarked, "if it were not for two things which I cannot stand: coal smoke and

<hr>

[1] David Shub, *Lenin* (New York, 1951), 136.
[2] Donald M. Wallace, *Russia on the Eve of War and Revolution* (New York, 1961), 266.
[3] Cf. *supra*, 67; George Fitzhugh, *Cannibals All! or Slaves Without Masters* (Richmond, 1857), 79ff., 191.

Englishmen."[1] Like the French Left, many Germans with radical social and political views criticized the English for their ruthless exploitation of the industrial proletariat and of the native populations in their colonial empire. German conservatives were more likely to praise England for its respect for tradition and social order, but many of them changed their opinions when they discovered that old aristocratic England was being taken over by commercialism. In the late 1820's the historian Niebuhr, who had once called England the pride and envy of humanity, began to berate the English for their "unscrupulous practice of usury" and their "exclusive idolatry of gain." "England's rapidly accelerating decline," he lamented, "is a mournful phenomenon; it is a mortal disease for which there is no remedy."[2]

One aspect of the Industrial Revolution which many German writers of the early nineteenth century regarded with special horror was the replacement of the creative impulse by mechanized labor. In the cyclical theory of history which Goethe developed in his later years, a leveling down process of mechanization was held characteristic of the fifth phase, which he considered to be the state of his own period and which would be followed by a sixth and last one, that of chaotic disintegration.[3] "Mankind will become cleverer," he predicted, "and more perspicacious, but not better nor happier, nor more energetic. I foresee the day when God will no longer take delight in his creatures and will once again have to annihilate the world and make a fresh start."[4] Hegel was likewise struck by the pernicious effects of the use of machines on the industrial worker: the deadening of his creative instinct, his dependence upon commercial cycles, and the loss of individual freedom.[5]

Mid-nineteenth-century German socialists, enlarging upon these complaints about the breakdown of social cohesion, the division of labor, and the monotonous work on the assembly line, portrayed the modern worker as reduced to an appendage to the machine and as enslaved to capital. Applying Hegelian terminology, Karl Marx

[1] As quoted by Hermann Kantorowicz, *The Spirit of British Policy and the Myth of the Encirclement of Germany* (New York, 1932), 42 and Matthew Arnold, *Essays in Criticism* (London, 1916), I, 164.

[2] Barthold G. Niebuhr, *Life and Letters* (New York, 1852), 507, 508; G. P. Gooch, *History and Historians in the Nineteenth Century* (Boston, 1862), 17; cf. Kantorowicz, *op. cit.*, 462–466. 512–513; Schoeps, *Vorläufer Spenglers*, 21.

[3] F. Martini, "Dekadenzdichtung," *Reallexikon der deutschen Literatur*, vol I (Berlin, 1958), 225; cf. Friedrich Klemm, *Technik. Eine Geschichte ihrer Probleme* (München, 1954), 304–306.

[4] As quoted by Jaspers, *Man in the Modern Age*, 17.

[5] Kesting, *Geschichtsphilosophie und Weltbürgerkrieg*.

characterized the industrial proletarian as a "man alienated from himself," that is a person completely unable to develop his individuality. It is this deplorable situation to which Marx referred in 1856 when he complained that in the nineteenth century "there are symptoms of disintegration surpassing even the terrors of the late Roman Empire . . . Mankind becomes master of nature, but man the slave of man . . . The result of all our inventions and progress seems to be that material powers become invested with spiritual life, whereas human life deteriorates into material force."[1]

The most poignant description of the absence of any social harmony in early nineteenth-century England was given by Marx's friend Friedrich Engels, who, in his classic account of the conditions of the English working classes in 1844, reported the brutal indifference with which the inhabitants of England's capital ignored their neighbors and selfishly concentrated upon their private affairs: "We know well enough that this isolation of the individual – this narrow-minded egotism – is everywhere the fundamental principle of modern society. But nowhere is this selfish egotism so blatantly evident as in the frantic bustle of the great city. The disintegration of society into individuals, each guided by his private principles and each pursuing his own aims has been pushed to its furthest limits in London. Here indeed human society has been split into its component atoms."[2]

In England itself the Industrial Revolution was widely regarded as a plague rather than a blessing. In the long run Englishmen came to look with pride and complacency on the spectacular progress of their nation in the field of technology and industrial production. But disssenting voices were numerous and perhaps even predominant during the first half of the century when the general mood was rather one of insecurity and crisis.

It was especially the wretched condition of the new industrial proletariat – the so-called "condition-of-England question" – that explains the atmosphere of gloom among the English literate classes. Even such an enthusiastic champion of industrialization as David Ricardo felt that a mere subsistence wage was all that the working classes could hope for, and held to Malthus's morose theory that the population was forever increasing at a more rapid rate than the production of food. But what the liberal economists calmly accepted as a

---

[1] *Die Revolution von 1848 und das Proletariat* as quoted in Karl Löwith, *Meaning in History*, 36; cf. Löwith, *Vom Hegel zu Nietzsche*, 295ff.; Sidney Hook, *From Hegel to Marx* (New York, 1936), 250; Rüstow, *op. cit.*, III, 112ff.

[2] Friedrich Engels, *Die Lage der arbeitenden Classen in England* (Stuttgart, 1892), 24.

deplorable, but inevitable outcome of an iron law of supply and demand, filled less placid minds with indignation and fear. Many of the workers themselves occasionally smashed the new machinery which they regarded as the cause of their distress. The rising popular agitation in its turn alarmed the property owning classes haunted by the specter of a violent social upheaval.

Many English writers, loathing the new industrial order, idealized the rural society of the past. The English, complained Coleridge, "had purchased a few brilliant inventions at the loss of all communion with life and the spirit of nature."[1] Even a radical advocate of political reform like William Cobbett portrayed the England of pre-Reformation days in glowing colors, contrasting the social harmony of medieval England with the materialistic individualism of contemporary society. Renewing the glorification of medieval culture at the expense of a mediocre present that had been inaugurated by eighteenth century writers, Cobbett found numerous disciples among later men of letters.[2] They wished, as one of them, Augustus Pugin, declared in 1836, "to pluck from the age the mark of superior attainments so falsely assumed and . . . to direct the attention of all back to the real merit of the past and better days."[3]

Similar opinions on the degeneracy of modern England were professed by a number of Tories, known as the Young England party, who dreamed of restoring a paternalistic society in which a responsible aristocracy would rule over a once again prosperous and religious peasantry. One of the spokesmen of this group, Disraeli, described contemporary English society in almost exactly the same terms as Friedrich Engels: "There is no community in England," he wrote in his novel *Sybil* (1845), "there is aggregation. . . In great cities men are brought together by the desire of gain. They are not in the state of cooperation, but of isolation . . ."[4] Similar strictures of English society were made in many other publications of the time. As Macaulay sarcastically noted in 1848: "It is now the fashion to place the golden age of England in times when noblemen were destitute of comforts the want of which would be intolerable to a modern footman . . ."[5]

The greatest of all mid-nineteenth-century Englishmen criticizing

[1] Basil Willey, *Ideas and Beliefs of the Victorians*, 4.
[2] Raymond Williams, *Culture and Society, 1780–1950* (Anchor Books, New York, 1960), 20–21.
[3] M. R. Grennan, *William Morris, Medievalist and Revolutionary* (New York, 1945), 12.
[4] As quoted by Williams, *Culture and Society*, 105–106.
[5] T. B. Macaulay, *History of England Since the Accession of James II* (1848), at end of third chapter.

the materialism of their time, Thomas Carlyle, came closer to being a true prophet of doom than any of his English contemporaries. Profoundly influenced by the German Romantics, he shared their misgivings about modern society, "where each, isolated, regardless of his neighbour, turned against his neighbour, clutches whatever he can get and cries 'Mine'."[1] This merciless critic of his age introduced the terms "industrialism" and "Mechanical Age" to designate what he regarded as the most distinctive features of his century. He felt that mechanization had "struck its root down into man's most intimate, primary sources of conviction," and feared that this new force would have a pernicious effect on man's sense of morality and freedom.[2] "Whoever looks abroad upon the world, comparing the Past with the Present," Carlyle maintained, "may find that the practical condition of man in these days in one of the saddest, burdened with miseries which are in a considerable degree peculiar." In his crusade against the complacency of his contemporaries he went so far as to declare that "the condition of England is justly regarded as one of the most ominous, and withal one of the strangest, ever seen in the world. England is full of wealth . . . yet England is dying of inanition."[3]

With the spread of the Industrial Revolution in the second half of the nineteenth century England began to lose its reputation of being the major center of capitalistic exploitation, and instead the United States became the principal target of all intellectuals disgusted with the vulgar aspects of modern industry. Like Baudelaire and Renan, some prominent English writers (Thomas Carlyle, John Ruskin, and Matthew Arnold) pointed to the mediocrity of American civilization as a terrifying example of a society in which an almost universal preoccupation with material gain prevented the creation of great art and literature.[4] A similar anti-Americanism characterized the writings of many Germans bewailing the corrupting influence of mechanization and urbanization. Contrasting materialistic "civilization" with creative spiritual "culture," German scholars portrayed the United States as the prototype of a country in which the former was highly developed and the latter almost completely absent.[5]

[1] Houghton, *Victorian Frame of Mind*, 77.

[2] Williams, *op. cit.*, 77ff., 84–85.

[3] Carlyle. *Past and Present* (1843), p. 1; John W. Dodds, *The Age of Paradox, a Biography of England, 1841–1851* (New York, 1952), 317.

[4] Halvdan Koht, *The American Spirit in Europa; a Survey of Transatlantic Influences* (Philadelphia, 1949), 181–182.

[5] Cf. Ferdinand, Tönnies, *Gemeinschaft und Gesellschaft* (1887); Norbert Elias, *Über den*

With Germany itself becoming one of the world's industrial giants, German intellectuals steeped in the idealistic and Romantic traditions of German culture complained that their nation was being Americanized.[1]

Intellectuals of many other European countries expressed themselves with equal scorn about the civilization of the American Republic. The Norwegian novelist Knut Hamsun never grew tired of denouncing the sterility of the business civilization of the new world.[2] America, wrote the Slavophile Ivan Aksakov, "brought nothing except machines and goods, except mechanical inventions, except material improvements. Art, science, philosophy, are not the lot of North America, they are not within its province."[3] A distinguished Italian historian obsessed by the decadence of modern civilization, Guglielmo Ferrero, who investigated the causes of the decline of the Roman Empire to find a clue to the understanding of his own time, also made a study of the United States for this purpose.[4] In his *Between two Worlds* (1910), he expressed the fear that traditional European civilization with its concern for idealism and quality would be taken over by the American cult of materialism and quantity. The situation seemed to him in a sense even graver than it had been in the Roman Empire where the acquisition of wealth and the pursuit of power had at least never enjoyed the respect of moralists and of public opinion.

It should be added that in the United States itself the rapid growth of an industrialized, urbanized society often fostered a pessimistic evaluation of the present and a sense of nostalgia for the supposedly glorious era of the Young Republic in which agriculture had still been the predominant branch of economy.[5] A mere listing of a few of the major manifestations of this strain of pessimism will have to suffice to suggest its significance in nineteenth-century American society. The reader is reminded of the serious objections that so many American authors of New England and the South raised against the

Prozess der Zivilisation (Basel, 1939), I, 1–64; Fritz Stern, *The Politics of Cultural Despair* (Berkeley, 1961), 196–197.

[1] Otto Basler, "Amerikanismus. Geschichte des Schlagwortes," *Deutsche Rundschau*, CXLIV (1930), 142–146; Julius Langbehn, *Rembrandt als Erzieher* (1890); cf. Georg Steinhausen, "Verfallsstimmung im kaiserlichen Deutschland," *Preussische Jahrbücher*, CXCIV (1923), 153–185; H. Delbrück, "Die gute alte Zeit," *Erinnerungen, Aufsätze und Reden* (3d ed., Berlin, 1905), 179–212.

[2] Koht, *op. cit.*, 182–183.

[3] Riasanovsky, *op. cit.*

[4] I. Silone, "Ferrero and the Decline of Civilization," *Partisan Review*, IX (1942), 379–383.

[5] Cf. A. P. Dudden, "Nostalgia and the American," *Journal of the History of Ideas*, XXII (1961), 515–530; Richard Hofstadter, *The Age of Reform* (New York, 1960), 23–26.

supposedly increasing vulgarity of their age, of the persisting vigor of pre-millenialism among American Protestants, and of the merciless criticism to which numerous publicists, of whom Henry George was only the most influential, exposed the practices of the industrial capitalism in the Gilded Age.[1] This trend of American anticapitalism and anti-industrialism, greatly tempering the historical optimism for which nineteenth century American is, not altogether justly, noted, reached perhaps its climax at the end of the century, when the program of the Populist party proclaimed that the nation was brought "to the verge of moral, political, and material ruin" and when the pre-millenial expectation of a Doomsday became the tenet of one of the most original and vital American revival cults, the Witnesses of Jehovah.[2]

Late nineteenth-century American finally produced an eminent prophet of doom in the person of Brooks Adams, a scion of an illustrious Boston family, whose pessimism equalled or even surpassed that of many Continental censors of their time.[3] His widely translated *Law of Civilization and Decay* (1895) was one of the most somber and best documented nineteenth-century philosophies of history, anticipating many ideas of Spengler's more famous *Decline of the West*. In an economic, almost Marxian interpretation of European history since the end of the Roman Empire Brooks Adams attempted to show how energy was accumulated by the military and priestly classes and then was dissipated by the moneyed classes. After the Middle Ages, which he called "the greatest of martial and imaginary periods," Western civilization had supposedly started its decline. Brooks Adams regarded the England of his time as the epitome of decay and documented his thesis of the downfall of Europe largely with evidence from the history of this country.[4] His gloomy view of the present is well illustrated by the concluding sentence: "The architecture, the sculpture, and

[1] Elmer T. Clark, *The Small Sects in America* (Nashville, 1937); Ira V. Brown, "Watchers for the Second Coming. The Millenarian Tradition in America," *Mississippi Valley Historical Review*, XXXIX (1952), 441–458; Albert A. Ekirch, *The Idea of Progress in America, 1815–1860* (New York, 1951), esp. ch. VI and pp. 264–265; Morton and Lucia White, *The Intellectual Versus the City: From Thomas Jefferson to Frank Lloyd Wright* (Cambridge, Mass., 1962); Perry Miller, "The End of the World," *Errand into Wilderness* (Cambridge, Mass., 1956), 236–237; Roger B. Salomon, *Twain and the Image of History* (New Haven, 1961).

[2] Hofstadter, *op. cit.*, 66–67, 75, 141; Charles Taze Russell, *The Battle of Armageddon* (Brooklyn, 1912); Marley Cole, *Jehovah's Witnesses. The New World Society* (New York, 1955), ch. IV; C. Norman Kraus, "*Dispensationalism in America. Its Rise and Development*" (Richmond, Va., 1958).

[3] Cf. Arthur F. Beringause, *Brooks Adams, a Biography* (New York, 1955).

[4] See also the chapter "The Decay of England," in Brooks Adams, *America's Economic Supremacy* (new ed., New York, 1947).

the coinage of London, at the close of the nineteenth century, when
compared with those of Paris of Saint Lewis, recall the Rome of
Caracalla as contrasted with the Athens of Pericles, save that we lack
the stream of barbarian blood which made the Middle Ages."

It is, of course, by no means suggested that such pessimistic responses
were representative of public opinion. In England as well as in the
United States the spectacular advances in technology and industrial
production were generally viewed with pride and confidence. This was
also true of a large part of the educated classes in nineteenth-century
France. Many Frenchmen were more concerned about the slow rate
at which industrialization proceeded in their country than about
the evils of modern capitalism. Most French economists, as we have
seen, were greatly impressed by the new economic power of Great
Britain and urged their fellow countrymen to adopt the English virtues
of efficiency, self-reliance, and industriousness. The French public
suffered from an even more painful sense of inferiority when, at the
end of the nineteenth century, it suddenly realized that Germany
had surpassed France in most branches of commerce and industry.
This situation was considered all the more serious since the consoling view that economic prosperity leads to weakening of military ardor could hardly be entertained in the case of Wilhelmian
Germany.

It was, then, not the French, but the English, the Americans, and,
at the end of the nineteenth century, the Germans, who were widely
considered to have a special genius for the operations of capitalistic
enterprise. And many moralists pointed to these nations, and not
to France, as the frightful examples of the corrupting effects of un-
bridled industrialism. This does not mean, however, that there were
not some other forms of immorality that were regarded as more
typical of French society than of any industrially more highly developed nation. These were the vices characteristic of a frivolous, leisured
aristocracy rather than of enterprising, ruthless captains of industry:
frantic search for pleasure and entertainment, lack of social responsibility, breakdown of family relations, loose sexual morals. Such were
the corruptions for which Babylon, Alexandria, Sybaris, Rome, and
Byzantium had once been notorious, and nineteenth-century Paris
was widely regarded as the modern heir of these ancient "dens of
iniquity." The myth of Paris as the *cloaca maxima* of the world was
readily accepted by many foreigners, who tended to equate the man-
ners of France with those of its capital and to conclude that the entire

country was decadent.[1] The looseness of French morals was, for example, an ever recurrent theme in nineteenth-century German commentaries on France.[2] In German geographical handbooks the view that the French were utterly corrupt was gradually replacing the older cliché of French lightheartedness. The historian Heinrich Treitschke compiled perhaps the most elaborate catalog ever made of French vices.[3] Otto von Bismarck was also firmly convinced of French immorality. "We are also sinners," he wrote to his wife, while watching the siege of Paris in the winter of 1870–1871, "but not in such a Babylonian way and we do not defy God." [4]

Equally unfavorable opinions on France, partly stemming from the reading of French novels by Balzac, George Sand, Paul de Kock, and Zola, were common among the educated classes in other countries. Some anti-French views expressed by Americans might serve us to illustrate this world-wide Francophobia. "French literature has done much to corrupt American women," declared an American suffragette, Julia Ward Howe in 1871, "Unhappy France has corrupted the world. She is now swept from the face of the world."[5] In 1910, an American well acquainted with France as well as his own country, Archibald C. Coolidge, stated that it was not an uncommon belief in the United States that France was morally and politically decadent. "This impression," he added, "is based upon doubt as to the stability of the government, on the fact that the population is stationary, and still more on the impression of moral corruption which French literature has spread abroad."[6] Even a sophisticated intellectual like Henry Adams, who had devoted a life-long study to the history and literature of France, looked with contempt on contemporary France. "In all Paris – literature, theater, art, people, cuisine," he wrote in 1892, "I have not yet discovered one healthy new thing." [7]

[1] Cf. Roger Caillois, *Le mythe et l'homme* (Paris, 1938); Maxime Du Camp, "Le Parisien," *Revue de Paris*, XI (1874), 349–380; Carter, *The Idea of Decadence*, 15.

[2] Cf. E. Money, "La critique allemande et la littérature française contemporaine," *Revue de Paris*, XI (1874), 466–490; Carl Starck, *Die psychische Degeneration des französischen Volkes* (Stuttgart, 1871); Gabriel Hanotaux, *Histoire de la fondation de la troisième République* (Paris, 1925–26), IV, 288.

[3] See Irmgard Ludwig, *Treitschke und Frankreich*, Beiheft 32, *Historische Zeitschrift* (München, 1934).

[4] Bismarck, *Die gesammelte Werke*, vol. XIV (Berlin, 1933), 804; cf. Digeon, *La crise allemande*, 235–236.

[5] Elizabeth B. White, *American Opinion on France from Lafayette to Poincaré* (New York, 1927), 240; cf. Maria Longworth Storer, "Decadence in France," *North American Review*, CXCI (1910), 168–184.

[6] Archibald C. Coolidge, *The United States as World Power* (New York, 1910), 193–194.

[7] Henry Adams, *Letters, 1858–1891* (New York, 1930), 534–535; cf. Max I. Baym , *The*

IV

As has been noted, the sense of decadence in nineteenth-century France was fostered not only by internal political and economic upheavals but also by military defeats and other unfavorable develop- ments in the nation's relations with its rivals. It is, of course, by no means in France alone, or solely in the nineteenth century that misfortunes of this nature have been instrumental in promoting a sense of doom and anxiety. The disasters of the Jews such as the Baby- lonian captivity and the Hellenistic domination created an atmosphere propitious to apocalyptic speculations about the imminent destruction of the world; the German invasions of the Roman Empire convinced many Christians that no radical improvement in this world was to be expected and that its end was close at hand; similarly, the calamities befalling Italy in the years following 1494 and Spain in the first half of the seventeenth century were influential in destroying Renaissance opti- mism. In more recent years, the defeat of Germany in the First World War and the "Fall" of France in 1940 had a similar effect of strengthening the sense of decadence among the intellectuals of the vanquished nation.

This does not mean that defeats on the battlefield or other reverses in a state's foreign relations necessarily create a widespread mood of pessimism. Such misfortunes might leave most people indifferent and might even be welcomed by opponents of a government, which can be held responsible for the failures. This was, for example, partly the case with the Napoleonic defeats in 1814 and 1815, which, as we have seen, came as a relief to many Frenchmen. The bewilderment was more intense and widespread after the Franco-Prussian War, but even at that time some Frenchmen felt that the downfall of the Second Empire had not been bought too dearly. The intensity of pessimism provoked by disasters of such nature is in direct relation not only to the extent of suffer- ing and humiliation but also to the popularity of the government in power.

In the nineteenth century many nations did not experience any serious crisis suggestive of their decline in power or of their inferiority to other nations of the world. Some of these, in contradistinction to France, actually increased their relative strength. Of these fortunate countries, the United States had most reason to feel that history was working on its side. The spectacular growth of the young republic – in territory, population, agricultural as well as industrial production –

French Education of Henry Adams (New York, 1951), 164–165, 180; see also Christof Wegelin, *The Image of Europe in Henry James* (Dallas, 1958).

fostered not only a firm belief in progress but also an equally firm belief in the future of America. Whatever despondency there existed concerning the state of the nation did not owe its origin to any threat from abroad. Even such a hardened pessimist as Brooks Adams liked to believe that the twentieth century would be the age of America. Protected by the oceans against any involvement in major military conflicts, the American nation could afford to ignore any foreign danger. A few intellectuals with racial prejudices like Henry Adams might be alarmed by the rise of the colored races, notably the Chinese and the Japanese, but this so-called "Yellow Danger" did not by any means ruffle the equanimity of the American nation.[1]

The Russian faith in the future of their country almost equalled the optimism of the Americans. They also liked to think of themselves as a young people not yet contaminated by the corruptions of the old world. Although highly critical of existing institutions, most members of the intelligentsia, regardless of whether they were Westerners or Slavophiles, had a very high opinion of the potentialities of the Russian nation and were confident that it would have a more glorious future than any other European country. Official, tsarist Russia might be a "lie;" it was at least not as decadent as the "rotten West."

Unlike the United States, Russia suffered a number of serious diplomatic and military defeats in the course of the nineteenth century, but these reverses did not create a serious sense of alarm among Russian intellectuals. Many of them were actually pleased by the outcome of the Crimean War or Russo-Japanese War since the defeats impelled the government to make concessions to their demands. A greater sense of national frustration was experienced by numerous Russians after the victorious and fairly popular war against Turkey (1877–78) when the other great powers forced Russia to accept the humiliating conditions of the Congress of Berlin. The reaction was notably strong among the Panslavists, who had pressed for the war and now blamed Germany for the disappointing results. Hatred and fear of Germany increased in strength in the decades preceding the First World War. But such feelings remained confined to small groups of Russian nationalists and government officials. The same is true of the "Yellow Danger," which alarmed a few Russian intellectuals, but did not

---

[1] Cf. Richard Hofstadter, *Social Darwinism in American Thought, 1860–1915* (Philadelphia, 1944), 163–165; Beringause, *op. cit.*, 127; Heinz Gollwitzer, *Die Gelbe Gefahr. Geschichte eines Schlagworts* (Göttingen, 1962), 68–93.

cause much more concern in Russia than it did in the United States.[1] The profound sense of crisis experienced by the Russian intelligentsia of the nineteenth century had its origin in dissatisfaction with the domestic political situation or the painful awareness of Russian cultural inferiority, not in any concern about a threat from abroad.[2]

In the nineteenth century, while many Americans and Russians were dreaming of national greatness in the future, Great Britain could proudly point to her glory in the present. In this period no Continental nation threatened the security of England, amply protected as it was by its insular position and its powerful navy. The workshop of the world, the mother of parliaments, the mistress of the oceans, and the ruler over the largest colonial empire, Victorian England looked with a mixture of condescension and pity on the less fortunate nations of the world. In the few military conflicts in which it became involved it always emerged victorious. Occasional fears of French and Russian aggressive designs hardly disturbed the English sense of security. In the century known as that of "Pax Britannica," Great Britain seemed to have equalled or even surpassed the power of the Roman Empire. According to a representative spokesman of Victorian England, Macaulay, the English were "the greatest and most highly civilized people" the world had ever seen.[3] "I look around me," wrote another mid-nineteenth-century liberal, John Roebuck, "and ask what is the state of England? . . . I ask you whether the world over, or in past history, there is anything like it? Nothing. I pray that our unrivalled happiness may last."[4] A few disgruntled authors like Thomas Carlyle and Matthew Arnold might bewail the waxing materialism, but this did not mean that they shared the views of Continental or American Anglophobes who predicted the downfall of the English nation.

It was not until the end of the century that some English intellectuals became painfully aware of the inferiority of their nation to Germany in the fields of education, technical ingenuity, and administrative efficiency, and that British statesmen began to see the necessity of abandoning the policy of "splendid isolation."[5] Yet even the new

---

[1] Cf. Thomas G. Masaryk, *The Spirit of Russia* (new ed. New York, 1955), II, 276–279; Gollwitzer, *op. cit.*, 94–120.

[2] Malia, *Alexander Herzen*, 294, 303.

[3] T. B. Macaulay, "Sir James Mackintosh," (1835), *Critical and Historical Essays* (London, 1854), II, 77.

[4] Houghton, *op. cit.*, 47.

[5] Cf. J. A. Cramb, *Germany and England* (New York, 1914), 42–45; Dorpalen, *Heinrich von Treitschke*, 266–267.

German threat did not succeed in undermining the English ingrained sense of superiority or in creating a serious mood of national crisis.

In the course of the nineteenth century Germany became the greatest military power in the world as well as the leading industrial nation on the Continent, surpassing even England in the output of certain important industrial products. Yet this development came rather late in the century and prior to unification, the position of the German nation in the world was frequently described in very gloomy terms. Despondency about the abject state of Germany had been all but universal in the period of Napoleonic domination. At this time many German intellectuals like Fichte and Görres preached a national regeneration for their fallen country, but such hopes were not fulfilled by the post-Napoleonic settlement which left Germany weak and divided under its numerous unenlightened princelets. German intellectuals therefore continued to bemoan the utter degeneration of their country, contrasting its present weakness with the greatness of Germany in the age of the Hohenstaufen and complaining about the particularism and political immaturity of the German nation.[1]

In the first half of the nineteenth century it was still widely feared that France once again would take advantage of German weakness. For this reason some German intellectuals like Bruno Bauer advocated an alliance with Russia against the "decadent" West. Other Germans, however, were more afraid of the Russian colossus with its great reservoir of barbarian vitality and favored cooperation with the West to ward off this threat to European civilization.[2] It was true that many Germans asserted their belief in the superiority of their nation and its future greatness, but such visions, as in other cases of national messianism, served largely as compensation for an all too intolerable present.

Any misgivings about the position of Germany in the world all but disappeared after the successful unification under Prussian leadership. At the end of the nineteenth century German self-esteem soared to the point of megalomania. Although many intellectuals of Wilhelmian Germany bitterly complained about the rising tide of materialism, they generally held that western Europe and the United States suffered even more from this evil, and seldom or never questioned the superior military and economic strength of Imperial Germany. Many German

---

[1] Cf. Schoeps, *Vorläufer Spenglers*, 21; Niebuhr, *Life and Letters*, letter of Dec. 19, 1830; Gooch, *History and Historians in the Nineteenth Century*, 64–66, 115.

[2] Cf. Kurt Marko, "Amerika und Russland in der rationalen Prophezeiung nach 1848," *Jahrbücher für Geschichte Osteuropas*, n.s., VIII (1960), 171–194; Schoeps, *Vorläufer*, 92–93.

nationalists, not yet satisfied with their country's position in the world, indicted their government for its timorous foreign policy. Their daring goal was well expressed by one of Germany's leading military publicists of the time, Bernhardi: "For us there are two alternatives and no third, world dominion or ruin."[1]

To many influential intellectuals "Deutschland, Deutschland über alles" meant that no nation was a match for Imperial Germany. Russian power was no longer taken as seriously as it had been in the first half of the nineteenth century. Many German men of letters, it is true, expressed their admiration for the idealism and vitality of the Russian people, but this appreciation of the potentialities of a so-called young nation uncontaminated by the corruptions of Western civilization, did not imply any fear of the Russian colossus. Defeated in the Crimean War as well as in a war against Japan, this country stood revealed as a giant with feet of clay, far inferior to the new German Empire in the efficiency of its military machine and industrial apparatus. In their disdain of their Eastern neighbor's strength, some Germans even proposed the incorporation of parts of Russia into the German Empire.[2] England still loomed as a powerful country that was able to obstruct Germany's dream of supremacy. But many Germans recognized the greatness and splendor of the British Empire with envy rather than with admiration. And they often denied that British strength in the world was based on sound foundations, claiming that it was the product of accident or of unscrupulous exploitation of the weak and the gullible, and therefore unable to stand up in a future world conflict.[3]

After German unification, France, even more than Russia, was discounted as a weak and declining power. It was no longer feared as a bellicose, strongly disciplined country, but seen as a decadent nation weakened by pacifism, internal devisions, and slow population growth. Such derogatory views of the French were professed not only by inveterate Francophobes like the historian Treitschke but also by many intellectuals impressed by the brilliance of French culture. The French, according to a literary critic nurtured on French thought, Alfred Kerr, were suffering from an incurable weakness: "A people whose

---

[1] Cramb, *op. cit.*, 39; cf. Ludwig Dehio, "Gedanken über die deutsche Sendung, 1900–1918," *Historische Zeitschrift*, CLXXIV (1952), 479ff.; Dorpalen, *op. cit.*, 210.

[2] Roland G. Usher, *Pan-Germanism* (Boston, 1913), 48, 58–59; Aira Kemiläinen, *Auffassungen über die Sendung des deutschen Volkes um die Wende des 18. und 19. Jahrhunderts* (Helsinki, 1956), 280–281; Hans Kohn, *The Mind of Germany* (New York, 1960), 272.

[3] Kantorowicz, *The Spirit of British Policy*, 507; Usher, *op. cit.*, 34–35, 37.

men do not want to be soldiers and whose women refuse to have
children, is a people benumbed in their vitality; it is fated to be
dominated by a younger and fresher race . . ."[1]

In contrast to the states that became more powerful in the nineteenth
century than they had been before, a number of countries lost much
of the commanding position that they had previously held in world
affairs, and among these declining or so-called "old" nations, some
were faced with a much more spectacular loss in status then France.

The two most outstanding examples of countries which in the course
of the nineteenth century were reduced to a fraction of the great power
and prestige which they had once possessed in the world were China
and the Ottoman Empire. In China the idea of decadence was almost
as old as the empire itself.[2] Yet prior to the nineteenth century Chinese
writers complaining about the degeneracy of the present were hardly
concerned about the inferiority of China to other nations of the world.
Subscribing to the same cyclical theories of history as were found in
many other early civilizations of the world, they were more preoccupied with the corruption of moral and religious principles than
with any decline in national power. As late as the end of the eighteenth century Chinese literati lamenting the decline of Confucian
wisdom and piety were fully convinced of Chinese superiority over
the "white barbarians."[3] But in the nineteenth century Chinese
self-confidence was rudely tested by Western economic penetration as
well as by numerous military or diplomatic defeats. On numerous
occasions the end of the Empire seemed in sight. Some Chinese men of
letters attributed the downfall of the Empire to the corrupting influence
of the West and the disregard for ancient Confucian principles. In
sharp contrast to this point of view other writers impressed by European
technology and civilization blamed the misfortunes of their country
on excessive xenophobia.[4]

Similarly contradictory views prevailed among Turkish intellectuals
alarmed by the rapid disintegration of the Ottoman Empire. Here

---

[1] Bourdon, *The German Enigma*, 163–173; cf. *ibid.*, 92; Fouillée, *La démocratie politique et
sociale en France*, 110–112; Joséphin Péladan, *L'Allemagne devant l'humanité et le devoir des
civilisés* (Paris, 1916).

[2] See *supra*, 2.

[3] John. K. Fairbank, "Tributary Trade and China's Relations with the West," *Far
Eastern Quarterly*, I (1942), 129ff.

[4] Cf. Mary C. Wright, *The Last Stand of Chinese Conservatism. The T'ung-Chih Restoration,
1862–1874* (Stanford, 1957), 11; William T. DeBary and others, *Sources of Chinese Tradition*
(New York, 1960), 707–711, 713–716, 717–721, 722ff., 744–745.

the "Islamists" were of the opinion that the Ottoman decline was caused by the discredit into which traditional faith and law had fallen, whereas the so-called "Westerners" held the Turkisch opposition to modern civilization responsible for the weakness of the Empire.[1] The concern about the decline of the Ottoman Empire did not originate in the nineteenth century. As early as the sixteenth and seventeenth centuries a number of Turkish statesmen and political commentators had noticed with alarm that their country was falling behind the infidel in military efficiency and economic prosperity.[2] But it was not until the ninetheenth century that in Turkey, as in China, the problem of the shrinking power of the empire came to dominate almost all political discussion.

It falls beyond the scope of this study to examine in any detail how the unmistakable decline of these two Oriental powers stirred public opinion, but it is obvious that the situation which these countries faced was much more serious than that of France. Even if France lost its position of preponderance in the course of the nineteenth century, it still remained one of the great powers and actually participated in the economic exploitation and political partitioning of both China and Turkey.

In the same way France fared much better in the nineteenth century than did Austria. Multi-national and aristocratic Austria led a highly precarious existence in a world of rising nationalistic and democratic aspirations which could count on the support or sympathy of some foreign powers. Diplomats sometimes referred to Austria as the second "sick man" of Europe which was likely to follow the fate of the Ottoman Empire.[3] After two military defeats resulting in loss of territory and political influence, even the rulers of Austria lacked confidence in the continued existence of the empire. The crown prince, Archduke Rudolf, realized that he lived in a "tottering, decaying age." "The Monarchy stands there," he wrote, "a mighty ruin, which may last today and tomorrow, but which will finally disappear altogether . . . now the end has come."[4] In 1901 the Emperor, Francis Joseph, made

[1] Cf. Bernard Lewis, *The Emergence of Modern Turkey* (London, 1961), 126, 130–31. 199–200, 228–231.
[2] Cf. W. F. A. Behrnauer, "Kogabeg's Abhandlungen über den Verfall des osmanischen Staatsgebäudes seit Suleiman dem Grossen," *Zeitschrift der deutschen morgenländischen Gesellschaft*, XV (1861); Mehmed Pasha, *Ottoman Statecraft*, ed. Walter L. Wright (Princeton, 1935); see also Lewis, *op. cit.*, 21.
[3] Oscar Jászi, *The Dissolution of the Hapsburg Monarchy* (Chicago, 1929), 6–13; J. M. K. Vyvyan, "The Approach of the War of 1914," *New Cambridge Modern History*, XII (Cambridge, 1960), 340.
[4] Henry Schnitzler, "Gay Vienna – Myth and Reality," *Journal of the History of Ideas*, XV (1954), 115.

a special testamentary provision in case his rule should come to an end. Although it is still a matter of controversy as to whether the dissolution of the Danube Monarchy was inevitable, no one will deny that in the course of the nineteenth century its future became increasingly problematic.

Some perspicacious Austrians were fully aware of the critical situation. As early as 1830, after the July Revolution, the author Grillparzer declared his misgivings: "The whole world will be strengthened by the unexpected change, only Austria will go to pieces by it." In 1866 he confessed: "I am glad that I shall not see the end."[1] Yet the ordeals of Austria did not engender a widespread sense of crisis. The threatening dissolution of Austria-Hungary was welcomed rather than feared by many members of the national minorities lacking any sense of loyalty to the existing regime. As Grillparzer admitted: "There are no patriots without a fatherland, and we no longer have one."

On the surface, at least, Austrians showed little concern about the dangerous situation of their country. No other city in the world had such a reputation for gaiety as eternally waltzing Vienna. Yet this frenzy of frivolous living often served as an escape from a despressing reality. Joseph II had already noted: "When Vienna gets gay, the situation is truly grave." "In Berlin," the Viennese man of letters Karl Kraus is supposed to have said, "things are serious, but not hopeless; in Vienna, they are hopeless, but not serious."[2] It is perhaps no mere coincidence that Austria-Hungary produced a modern psychologist like Sigmund Freud pioneering in the study of suppressed feelings and of the "discontent with civilization."[3]

In contrast to the attitude of indifference or artificial gaiety with which most Austrians responded to the critical situation of their country, many Spaniards were seriously disturbed about the downfall of their once powerful nation. Spain, as one of its gifted writers, Pio Baroja put it, was a gloomy nation incapable of frivolity or joviality.[4] In no other European country, not excluding France, have intellectuals been so much obsessed with the decline of their country's position in

---

[1] Franz Grillparzer, *Briefe und Tagebücher* (Stuttgart, n.d.), II, 87; Schnitzler, *loc. cit.*, 114.

[2] Schnitzler, *loc. cit.*, 100.

[3] The threatening disintegration of the Dual Monarchy might also be seen reflected in the utter sense of despair and alienation that was expressed by writers like Kafka, Georg Trakl, and Rilke. Neither is it likely that Adolf Hitler would have become so completely uprooted from traditional loyalties if his early years had not been spent in the artificial atmosphere of Viennese society.

[4] Sáinz y Rodríguez, *La evolución de las ideas sobre la decadencia española*, 87–88.

the world.[1] As mentioned before, the Spanish preoccupation with national decadence originated as early as the seventeenth century. In the nineteenth century the problem continued to be discussed with the same sense of urgency. In this period the misfortunes of Spain had not yet come to an end. First, Spain was plagued by almost continuous civil strife and political instability. There were two Spains, even more than two Frances, irreconcilably opposed to one another. In 1836 Mariano José de Larra bitterly lamented the mortal duel between the two halves of his nation: "Here lies the Inquisition, it died of old age." "Here rests freedom of thought, it died in infancy." "Here lies military discipline." "Here lies Spanish credit," "Here lies half Spain, it died at the hands of the other half."[2] Economically, moreover, Spain fell even further behind the more enterprising nations of northern Europe than before. Finally, national self-confidence was undermined by the loss of the colonial empire. The concern about national inferiority reached its climax after the humiliating defeat in the war of 1898 against the United States.[3] At this time many of Spain's most prominent writers took up the pen to examine the reasons for the national disaster and to suggest remedies for Spain's regeneration.

In Spain as in other countries facing national decline, traditionalists and progressives presented almost completely contradictory explanations of their nation's misfortunes. Intellectuals with conservative or reactionary sympathies like Donoso Cortés and Menéndez y Pelayo blamed foreign, notably French, influences for the corruption of the Spanish soul.[4] They felt that Spanish greatness had come to an end when the people had become infected with the ideas of modern civilization such as atheism, rationalism, liberalism, and democracy. Declaring that the decadence of Spain had not started until the middle or the end of the eighteenth century, they sang the glory of religious, monarchical, and feudal Spain and defended the Golden Age of the seventeenth century, including the Inquisition and the absolute monarchy, against the denigration of Hispanophobes. They felt that

---

[1] A list of the most important publications dealing with the theme of Spanish decadence is to be found in Sáinz y Rodríguez, op. cit.; see also Rafael Altamira y Crevea, Psicología del pueblo español.

[2] Larra, "Día de difuntos de 1836. Fígaro en el cementerio," Artículos políticos y sociales (Madrid, 1927), 261; cf. Fidelino de Sousa Figueiredo, Las dos Españas.

[3] Cf. Udo Rusker, Nietzsche in der Hispania (Bern, 1962), 16.

[4] Cf. Guillermo de Torre, Menéndez Pelayo y los dos Españas (Buenos Aires, 1943); Menéndez Pidal, Spaniards in Their History, 237, 240; Carl Schmitt, Donoso Cortés in gesamteuropäischer Interpretation (Köln, 1950).

the old ideals of "Hispanidad" were still valid and should serve the Spanish people as a guiding force in its present hour of weakness and confusion.[1] Many traditionalists were actually proud of their nation for being maladjusted to the modern age of secularism and technology. Spain, said Miguel de Unamuno, was a "victim of the modern world." "I feel," wrote this great admirer of Don Quixote, "that my soul is medieval and that the soul of my country is medieval. I feel that it has passed perforce through the Renaissance, the Reformation, the Revolution, learning from them, but never letting its soul be touched; and Spanish Quixotism is but the despairing struggle of the Middle Ages against the Renaissance."[2] Like many other conservatives Unamuno hoped that Spain would remain true to its own genius and withstand the pressures of "Europeanization."

Most Spanish intellectuals, on the other hand, were highly critical of the national past. They denounced the intolerance, corruption, royal absolutism, and economic backwardness of the Old Regime, and deplored the lack of social responsibility and the suspicion of foreign ideas that had been displayed by the ruling classes. They complained that since the reign of the Catholic Kings the government had become estranged from the people as well as from the intellectual elite.[3] Some writers went even further in denying any real greatness to Spain's past. "Spain," declared Azorín, "has never, even in her most brilliant century, the sixteenth, had a moment of genuine vitality." Her glory was, according to him, merely "a flash of lightning."[4] The philosopher Ortega y Gasset reached a similar conclusion. Spain, he felt, had never been a well-organized, integrated nation. Even in the Middle Ages, Spain had been inferior to France and her short-lived preponderance in European affairs had been little more than an accident.[5] Whatever their views on the Spanish past, all these progressive intellectuals felt than Spain's weakness was the result of the country's isolation from the main currents of European culture. One of the leading critics of Spanish tradition, Joaquín Costa, there-

---

[1] Cf. Ramiro de Maetzu, *Defensa de la Hispanidad* (Madrid, 1934); Ignacio Olagüe, *La decadencia española* (4 vols., Madrid, 1950–51).

[2] Miguel de Unamuno, *The Tragic Sense of Life* (1912) as quoted in Menéndez Pidal, *op. cit.*, 13.

[3] Cf. Angel Ganivet, *Idearium español* (Granada, 1897); Ricardo Macías Picavea, *El Problema nacional* (Madrid, 1899).

[4] Azorín, "La decadencia de España," *Clásicos y modernos* (Madrid, 1919).

[5] José Ortega y Gasset, *Invertebrate Spain* (New York, 1927); cf. Gabriel Maura y Gamazo, *Algunos testimonios literarios e históricos contra la falsa tesis de la decadencia nacional* (Madrid, 1920).

fore proposed to lock up the sepulchre of El Cid with a treble lock and Europeanize Spain.[1]

The similarity between France's position and that of the "old" declining nations became a favorite theme of many French alarmists in the late nineteenth century. Some of them warned that France was following the same downward course as Spain and surmised an inability of the so-called Latin races in general to hold their own in the modern world. Other observers proclaimed France a "sick man," suffering from similar diseases as the Ottoman Empire or Austria. It is true that France, in contrast to these countries, remained one of the great powers. Yet considering the position of political preponderance that France had held at the beginning of the century, its downfall was perhaps as spectacular as that of Spain or the Ottoman Empire. Accustomed to consider France "la grande nation," many Frenchmen were bewildered by the various military or diplomatic setbacks which their country suffered in the course of the century. Of all other nations, perhaps only the Chinese were less prepared for the debacles befalling them in the nineteenth century.

As we have seen, it was especially the defeat of France in the war of 1870 that induced many Frenchmen to make gloomy estimates of their country's historical destiny. At this time numerous foreigners were even more outspoken in proclaiming the definitive end of the period of French political and cultural supremacy. "The German, not the Gaelic race are now to be protagonist in that immense world-drama," wrote Thomas Carlyle in 1870, "and from them I expect better issues. Worse we cannot well have. France with a dead-lift effort, now of eighty-one years, has accomplished under this head, for herself and for the world, Nothing, or even less, . . ."[2] Such comments on the Franco-Prussian War were also common in the United States. "The Latin races." wrote the *New York Times* on August 16, 1870, "have done their part – and not always an inglorious one – in the world's history. Now more earnest and moral and free races must guide the helm of progress."[3] After the Commune, Southern papers, who, up to this time, had generally been pro-French, expressed themselves

---

[1] Joaquín Costa, *Reconstitución y europeización de España* (Madrid, 1900).
[2] Thomas Carlyle, "Latter Stage of the Franco-German War, 1870–71," *Works* (Centenary ed., London, 1930), XXX, 57.
[3] Henry Blumenthal, *A Reappraisal of Franco-American Relations, 1830–1871* (Chapel Hill, 1959), 190; John G. Gazley, *American Opinion on German Unification (1848–71)* (New York, 1926), 347–349.

in a similar vein: "The malady which has fastened upon the Latin races," commented the *Richmond Despatch*, "seems to be incurable . . . France alone upheld the glory of the Latin name . . . The organization, the practical common sense, the wealth, the culture, the progressive spirit of England, Germany, and Russia are bound to extend their ideas over France, Spain, and Italy. There is a common element of weakness in all Latin races. They do not seem adapted to modern times."[1] Such somber prognoses of French civilization were, of course, most widely accepted in victorious Germany. Even many German Francophiles referred to France as an exhausted nation that was rapidly approaching senility.[2]

As France recovered from the wounds of defeat, such unduly pessimistic views of the country's role in the world were gradually abandoned. Yet France did not fully regain its former reputation of great world power. At least during the forty years preceding the outbreak of the First World War, France was more often considered to be in a middle position between the young, rising and the old, declining nations of the world.[3]

V

One important manifestation of nineteenth-century pessimism of European-wide significance still deserves our attention: the state of mind known as Romantic discontent or *maladie du siècle*. This melancholy mood afflicted many sensitive minds who were disgusted with the political and economic developments of the age and can therefore be partially explained as an especially intense reaction against the Industrial and French Revolutions. Yet Romantic discontent constituted not so much a moralistic or political protest against the rise of the masses and modern industrialism as a kind of metaphysical anxiety about the alleged nihilism and atomism of modern civilization, and it

[1] White, *American Opinion on France*, 209–210.

[2] See *supra*, 237-238.

[3] It is relevant to note in this connection that in the course of the nineteenth century the writers in the declining nations who favored "Europeanization" began to look less to France and more to England and Germany as the countries to be imitated. At the end of the century German philosophy and scholarship and English political and economic institutions represented to them the wave of the future; cf. Hans Juretschke, *Das Frankreichbild des modernen Spanien* (n.p., 1937); Rukser, *op. cit.*; DeBary, *Sources of Chinese Tradition*, 782. But it was frequently by way of French publications that such unfavorable views of modern France gained currency; Edouard Demolins' *Why Are the Anglo-Saxons Superior?* (1899) was, for example, favorite reading among progressive circles in Spain and Turkey; cf. Colajanni, *Latins et Anglo-Saxons*, 346–347; B. Lewis, *op. cit.*, 199–200.

assumed a great variety of forms besides disgust with the political and economic developments of the age.

The vogue of Romantic discontent originated neither in the nine-teenth century nor in France. It first became a common attitude among German men of letters belonging to the so-called *Sturm und Drang* movement which reached its greatest strength in the 1770's at a time when European society had not yet felt the impact of the Industrial or the French Revolution. These "pre-Romantics" were depressed by the spirit of complacency and conformity which prevailed among the ruling classes and against the latter's firm belief in reason and progress. The new sensibility found its first expression in the works of some of Germany's greatest authors, above all in Goethe's *Sorrows of Young Werther* (1774). Devoted disciples of Rousseau, they went even further than the French writer in praising the virtues of primitive societies at the expense of their own times and in denouncing the prevalent immorality and artificiality.[1] They were firmly convinced of the inferiority of contemporary civilization to the creative periods of the past, notably ancient Greece. Schiller declared that the individual Athenian was infinitely superior to his counterpart in modern Euro-pe.[2] Even more virulent diatribes against modern civilization, especial-ly that of France, are found in the early writings of Herder, the most original theorist of this early reaction against the Age of Reason.[3]

In order to overcome the spiritual emptiness which the Age of Reason was alleged to have promoted, these German men of letters introduced a cult of art and originality. But they soon made the painful discovery that by advocating subjectivity and worshipping "genius," by rejecting all social restraints and cultivating solitude, they had become even more estranged from the society of their age.[4]

The German Romantics of the 1790's and 1800's fully shared this profound disgust with the spirit of the times. "Oh how deeply I despise this generation," lamented Schleiermacher, "which plumes itself more shamelessly than any previous one ever did, which can scarcely endure the belief in a still better future."[5] The philosopher

---

[1] Runge, *Primitivism and Related Ideas in Sturm und Drang Literature*, esp. ch. VI; F. Martini, *loc. cit.*, 224.

[2] Shklar, *After Utopia*, 69.

[3] R. Stadelmann, *Der historische Sinn bei Herder* (Halle, Saale, 1928); Walter Schubart, *Russia and Western Man* (New York, 1950), 28; Shklar, *op. cit.*, 69–72.

[4] Cf. Rüstow, *op. cit.*, III, 114, 209ff., 604; Arnold Hauser, *The Social History of Art* (Vintage Books ed., 4 vols., New York, 1957–58), II, 114, 118ff.; III, 69–70; Arthur O. Lovejoy, *The Great Chain of Being* (Cambridge, Mass., 1957), 307, 312–313.

[5] Shklar, *op. cit.*, 69.

Fichte expressed himself in even more derogatory terms about the degeneracy of contemporary society.[1] In other writers like Kleist and Hölderlin the despair of the present took such an intense form that they were driven to insanity or suicide.[2] Hegel, one of the few intellectuals with idealistic aspirations who became reconciled with the reality of his age, characterized the mental disease afflicting many of his contemporaries as "the unhappy consciousness."[3]

The German Romantics bewailing the degeneracy of their age had at the outset many illusions about the future. At their first meeting, in 1791, Novalis and Friedrich Schlegel were in immediate agreement that the golden age was in the offing.[4] At this time nearly all German writers firmly believed in a coming regeneration. They were deeply stirred by the outbreak of the French Revolution, which they hailed as the beginning of a new era in the history of mankind. Yet, as has been mentioned, their enthusiasm soon waned and was replaced by hatred. Whatever utopianism survived this disillusionment became largely concentrated on the future of Germany alone.[5] Most German intellectuals now became vehemently anti-French and interpreted the Revolution as the logical outcome of the detestable philosophy of the Age of Reason. In large numbers they turned to reactionary ideologies or Catholicism for solace and placed the golden age in the past instead of in the future. Even more than before, many authors idealized the Middle Ages as the last great "organic" age of European civilization and as the most glorious period in German history.[6] A mood of anguish, resignation, irony, or escape into a world of fantasy took the place of the hopeful aspirations the Romantics had once cherished.[7] This increasing *Weltschmerz* among German men of letters found perhaps its supreme expression in the philosophical system of Arthur Schopenhauer who regarded any attempt at meliorating an irremediably corrupt world as the height of futility.

Romantic discontent was a common attitude among men of letters

---

[1] Cf. Löwith, *Meaning in History*, 208–209; Josef Pieper, *The End of Time* (London, 1954), 107–108.

[2] Rehm, *Der Untergang Roms*, 2–3; Karl Jaspers, *The Future of Mankind* (Chicago, 1961), 327.

[3] Shklar, *op. cit.*, 15, 22.

[4] Julius Petersen, "Das Goldene Zeitalter bei den Romantikern," *Die Ernte. Abhandlungen zur Literaturwissenschaft*, Franz Muncker Festschrift (Halle, 1926), 117–175.

[5] Cf. Oskar Köhler, *Eichendorff und seine Freunde. Ideen um die deutsche Nation* (Freiburg im Breisgau, 1937).

[6] Cf. G. Salomon, *Das Mittelalter als Ideal der Romantik* (München, 1922); Gooch, *History and Historians*, ch. V, VII.

[7] Martini, *loc. cit.*, 225.

in many other countries in the first half of the nineteenth century. This despondency in itself was not due to German influence, but rather constituted an independent reaction to a breakdown of old social and religious values similar to that which was the source of mental anxiety among German writers. But German Romantic thought did influence foreign authors in the specific theories that is offered to explain and overcome the ideological crisis. The ideas of Goethe, Schiller, Herder, the brothers Schlegel, and Schelling among others deeply impressed prominent writers in other countries: Coleridge and Carlyle in England, Quinet and Michelet in France, Channing and Emerson in America, Kierkegaard in Denmark. It was above all the Russian intelligentsia who were greatly indebted to German Romanticism for their highly developed sense of estrangement from the society of their times.[1] In all these instances German Romantic thought contributed to the formulation of a critical attitude toward the "individualistic," rationalistic trends of modern society and a greater appreciation of the organic, religious periods of the past.

It must be evident that German rather than French writers played the leading role in spreading the vogue of Romantic despair in nineteenth-century thought. It is only in its display of scepticism and abulia (foreshadowing the attitudes of the *fin de siècle*) that French Romantic discontent showed some original features. French influence, on the other hand, was preponderant in the so-called "neo-Romantic" movement of the Decadents and the Symbolists at the end of the nineteenth century. At this time, after a brief interlude in which Romantic gloom had lost much of its intensity and objective analysis and realistic portrayal had been held in high esteem, lamentations over contemporary degeneracy regained their bitterness.

The sensibility of French "neo-Romantics" initiating a European-wide, modernistic movement against many features of contemporary civilization had much in common with Romantic discontent, but differed from it in some essential aspects. Being at the same time fascinated and repelled by the corruptions of the modern world, the writers of the *fin de siècle* carried an ambivalent attitude toward perversion and decay to extremes. On the one hand, they outdid the Romantics in proclaiming the decadence and vulgarity of their times, but, on the other hand, they were less depressed and tormented by a situation which they generally accepted with a certain complaisance. As "modernists" most of them were too profoundly affected by

---

[1] Cf. Martin Malia, *Alexander Herzen*, 42–43, 126–127; Hepner, *Bakounine*.

scepticism and relativism to be nostalgic for the great art or the strong faith of a bygone age. Insofar as they were still intrigued by the past, many writers showed a preference for societies in a state of corruption and decay such as the Byzantine Empire or the waning Middle Ages. Most "neo-Romantics" were, moreover, hyperindividualists who responded to the evils of their times, not by fighting them, but by loosening all bounds between themselves and society. No longer inspired by Prometheus' proud rebellion or Icarus' daring flight, they were satisfied with a passive role in the world and suffered relatively little from the bitter disillusionments that await ambitious dreams. Despising the masses, they withdrew into their ivory towers, preaching the elitist creeds of esthetic individualism and art for art's sake and taking a delight in mystifying and shocking the detested public. It is as literary reformers rather than as social critics or philosophers of history that the so called Decadents and Symbolists left an impact on their times. By opposing conventional forms of expression and tapping new sources of poetic imagination, they inaugurated the modernist movement in literature.

This new literary sensibility found its earliest and most original expression in the works of French writers like Baudelaire, Huysmans, Verlaine, and Mallarmé. These pioneers in the cult of decadence and estheticism were highly influential in the formation of similar trends in the literatures of England, Italy, Spain, Germany and Russia at the end of the nineteenth century.[1]

As a result of this vogue of "Decadence," French literature, which had lost much of its leading position in many European countries since the French Revolution, regained some of its former prestige. Everywhere young authors proclaimed their debt to France in their emancipation from conventional taste and bourgeois complacency. English men of letters reacting against the clichés about French immorality and levity that were current in English society began to sing the praise of French culture:

> Strictest judge of her own worth, gentlest of man's mind,
> First to face the Truth and last to leave old Truths behind –
> France, beloved of every soul that loves or serves its kind.[2]

[1] Cf. A. J. Farmer. *Le mouvement esthétique et "décadent" en Angleterre, 1873–1900* (Paris, 1931); Holbrook Jackson, *The Eighteen-Ninetees* (London, 1927), 57ff.; F. Flora, "Il decadentismo," *Questioni e correnti di storia letteraria*, ed. U. Bosco (Milano, 1949), 761–810; G. Díaz–Plaja, *Modernismo frente a Novento y Ocho* (Madrid, 1951), 12–16; Enid L. Duthié, *L'influence du symbolisme français dans le renouveau poétique de l'Allemagne* (Paris, 1933); Georgette Donchin, *The influence of French Symbolism on Russian Poetry* (The Hague, 1958).

[2] Rudyard Kipling, *France* (1913).

One of the leading Austrian writers enthusiastically supporting literary modernism Hermann Bahr, exclaimed: "Paris, Paris. I have to write this word a million times to express my feelings; there I woke up a happy man, there the artist was born . . . If I ever count for anything I will owe it to Paris."[1] A fellow Viennese man of letters, Stefan Zweig, summed up his account of his happy years in Paris of this time under the title "Paris, the City of Eternal Youth."[2] Even a few Americans belatedly discovered the stimulating atmosphere of French civilization. Randolph Bourne anticipated the feelings of many later American expatriates by declaring in 1913 that French civilization was incomparably superior to the English and that Paris came as a "spiritual relief" after London.[3]

As has been pointed out, the literary sense of decadence had very little in common with either a tragic sense of life or with a clearly elaborated, pessimistic view of history. Only in a few instances did French Decadents suffer from excessive gloom or did they make any serious attempt to diagnose the maladies of their times. French literature fascinated foreign men of letters not because it added greatly to the understanding of the decline of Western civilization or because it expressed a sentiment of metaphysical anxiety with unprecedented intensity. France was rather admired because it was the cradle of all artistic and literary innovations. Insofar as foreign influences played a role in the formation of pessimistic views, German philosophers like Schopenhauer, Eduard von Hartmann, and Nietzsche, and Russian novelists like Tolstoy and Dostoevsky were more instrumental than any French writers.[4]

In western European countries (England, Spain, Italy as well as France) Decadence was primarily an esthetic posturing, significant in opening new avenues of literary expression rather than in expressing a deeply felt mood of anxiety. In Russia and Germany, on the other hand, many of the Decadents were seriously preoccupied with the cultural and social decay of modern civilization. In both countries numerous men of letters embraced the creed of literary modernism and estheticism partly under French influence, but many of them went much further than French writers in their obsession with deca-

[1] René Lote, *Les relations franco-allemandes* (Paris, 1921), 150.
[2] Stefan Zweig, *The World of Yesterday* (New York, 1943), 126ff.
[3] Philip Rahv, ed., *Discovery of Europe. The Story of American Experience in the Old World* (Boston, 1947), 415ff.
[4] Cf. Emile Legouis and Louis Cazamian, *A History of English Literature* (London, 1948), 1252–1253; Ralph H. Goodale, "Schopenhauer and Pessimism in Nineteenth-Century English Literature," *Publications Modern Language Association*, XLVII (1932), 240–261·

dence. In Russia the Decadents inherited much of the metaphysical anxiety and apocalyptic spirit which had characterized the outlook of many Russian intellectuals during the nineteenth century. One of the leading spokesmen of the "New idealism," Dimitri Meresh-kovsky, felt that Decadence was the natural end of Russian literature. He declared in 1894 that the new generation was confronting its task with fear and trembling. "There are no more barriers! We are lonely and free . . . The horror of this feeling is unheard-of. Never before did man feel in his heart such a wish to believe, nor was so aware of his inability to do so."[1] The new movement gathered considerable strength in spite of strong opposition on the part of older members of the in-telligentsia. Besides poets and novelists, many gifted Russian thinkers indulged in bleak visions of man's historical destiny. Thus the distin-guished philosopher Vladimir Solovyev, who influenced many Russian Decadents, wrote his gloomy *Story about Antichrist* (1899) in which he envisioned a near future in which all of Europe including Russia would fall under Asiatic domination and Antichrist would establish his dominion over most of the civilized world.[2] The pessimism of many Russian intellectuals deepened after the failure of the Revolution of 1905. "Decadence," declared the Russian philosopher Nikolai Berdyaev in 1907, "is now the only literature and art in Russia."[3]

A sense of despair and doom was even more widespread among German writers outraged by the drab materialism of the Wilhelmian Empire. "In no society as much as in Germany," wrote one of the devotees of the modernistic creed, Arthur Moeller van den Bruck, "did the eminent, the original, the truly individualistic men become outsiders or were isolated against their wills."[4] Here as elsewhere Decadent and other modernistic trends in literature were greatly inspired by French writers: Zola influenced many Germans naturalists; Baudelaire, Verlaine and Mallarmé were admired by some of modern Germany's most gifted poets (Stefan George, Rilke); the most famous of all German novels dealing with the theme of decadence, Thomas Mann's *Buddenbrooks* (1900), was conceived under the impression of a

---

[1] Donchin, *op. cit.*, 120; Renato Poggioli, *Poets of Russia*, 1890–1930 (Cambridge, Mass., 1960), 82–83.

[2] Donchin, *op. cit.*, 18.

[3] Cf. Masaryk, *op. cit.*, II, 274–281; similarly apocalyptic views were expounded by Vasilii Rozanov, Konstantine Leontyev, V. F. Ehrn, and Alexander Blok; see Zenkovskii, *Russian Thinkers and Europe*; Nikolai Berdyaev, *The Russian Idea* (New York, 1948), 128–129, 195, 197, 200, 204–205, 243; John M. Cohen, *Poetry of This Age, 1908–1958* (London, 1960), Ch. V.

[4] Stern, *The Politics of Cultural Despair.*

French novel, *Renée Mauperin*, by the brothers de Goncourt.[1] But many of these German authors experimenting with new forms of literary expression took the theme of decadence much more seriously than any French writer. It is well known that Thomas Mann was obsessed by decadence as perhaps no other great author of the twentieth century. Rilke's poignant description of the atomization of life in a modern metropolis and of the sense of isolation suffered by the alienated individual had no equivalent in French literature. Similarly, Kafka was unsurpassed in expressing the absurdity and anguish of existence in the modern, disenchanted world;[2] and it was finally, apart from Russia, only in Germany that the forebodings of the approaching catastrophe of the First World War inspired some young, Expressionist writers to write lyrical poems envisioning imminent doom.[3]

Most Decadents, Symbolists, and other literary modernists, whether they were truly obsessed by the social and ideological crises of their age or were only sceptics posing as Decadents, regarded the prevalent vogue of rationalistic positivism as one of the most depressing features of modern civilization. Self-confessed neo-Romantics, they renewed and intensified the irrationalistic and idealistic pessimism of the Romantic movement. But they were on the whole too exclusively interested in art and literature and too ambivalent in their attitude toward the modern world to produce any coherent philosophy of history. At the same time, however, a more substantial assault on the premises of nineteenth-century rationalism was launched by numerous philosophers and social scientists. Some of Europe's foremost intellectuals, lacking any sympathy with the esthetic individualism of the Decadents and more gifted than their literary *confrères* in analyzing the weaknesses of the rationalistic and deterministic positions, were the leading figures in what became known as "the idealistic reaction against science."

It falls beyond the scope of this study to analyze the various views of history expounded by these new "idealistic" scholars and philosophers. But it should be pointed out that in Germany again, more than in any other country, the idealistic reaction against science found a warm reception among prominent thinkers and produced a variety

---

[1] Cf. Lote, *op. cit.*, 144–147; Petriconi, *Reich des Untergangs*, 151ff.; *supra*, 248, note 1.

[2] Schoeps, *Was ist der Mensch*, 11–140; Hanna Hafkesbrink, *Unknown Germany* (New Haven 1948), ch. I.

[3] Cf. Walter H. Sokel, *The Writer in Extremis. Expressionism in Twentieth-Century German Literature* (Stanford, 1959); Kurt Mautz, *Mythologie und Gesellschaft im Expressionismus. Die Dichtung Georg Heyms* (Frankfurt, 1961), 224ff.; Martini, "Expressionismus," *Reallexikon der deutschen Literatur*, I, 430–431; Petriconi, *op. cit.*, 96–125.

of highly gloomy prognoses of modern civilization.[1] The renewed interest in the metaphysical systems of Hegel and Kant represented only the mildest manifestation of the rising discontent with positivism and scientism. Many influential intellectuals such as Ludwig Klages, Graf Keyserling, and Max Scheler went much farther in breaking with nineteenth-century intellectualism and openly sneered at reason in the name of art, life, or religion. Vitalism, activism, pragmatism, and other forms of irrationalism began to dominate much of German philosophical and historical thought by the close of the century. Even such a distinguished philosopher as Wilhelm Dilthey came at the end of his life to the conclusion that reason had failed in solving the crisis of his time and that the decline of religious convictions would lead to horrible catastrophes.[2]

The strength and originality of the sense of decadence and crisis among German intellectuals of the period might be briefly illustrated by the views of some of the most influential irrationalists. One of the most sensational denunciations of contemporary materialism was Julius Langbehn's best seller, *Rembrandt als Erzieher* (1890). Measuring his age by the romantic ideal of art as allegedly personified by Rembrandt, the author declared that the spiritual life of Germany was in a state of decay and that science and intellectualism were mainly responsible for this condition. Deploring the excessive specialization and pedantry of German scholarship, he preached a new Reformation restoring art and spontaneity to their legitimate roles. Langbehn's confused onslaught on the methods of natural science made a tremendous impression. His work became favorite reading among young Germans and contributed to the primitivism of the German youth movement in the years preceding the outbreak of the First World War.[3]

The German writer most widely known for his somber views on the course of modern civilization, Oswald Spengler, did not publish his famous *Decline of the West* until after the outbreak of the First World War, but the title of this work as well as its general conception had been determined as early as 1912.[4] Spengler was not, as he claimed, the

---

[1] Cf. Stern, *op. cit.*, Georg Lukács, *Die Zerstörung der Vernunft* (Berlin, 1954); Alfred Kämpf, *Die Revolte der Instinkte* (Berlin, 1948).

[2] Clara Misch, ed., *Der junge Dilthey* (Leipzig, 1933), 5; Georg Steinhausen, *Deutsche Geistes- und Kulturgeschichte von 1870 bis zur Gegenwart* (Halle, Saale, 1931), 44–45, 403.

[3] Cf. Stern, *The Politics of Cultural Despair*; this study also deals authoritatively with the ideas of two other leading pessimists of Wilhelmian Germany: Arthur Moeller van den Bruck and Paul Lagarde.

[4] *Untergang des Abendlandes* (München, 1918–22), I, p. x.

first intellectual of his time openly repudiating contemporary optimism; in his disparagement of the urbanized, rationalized civilization of the West and in his great expectations of the East he had been preceded by many prominent German and Russian writers. But he surpassed any of his forerunners in documenting his thesis by elaborate and often suggestive comparisons between the development of modern civilization and that of civilizations in the past.

Some of the central ideas in Spengler's philosophy of history – his cyclical view of history and his acceptance of cultural decline with a kind of fatalistic fervor – were anticipated by Friedrich Nietzsche, the philosopher who surpassed most European critics of modern civilization by the profundity of his analysis and the sincerity of his despair. Of the numerous German intellectuals who were preoccupied by the cultural crisis of their age he was perhaps the most original, the most influential as well as one of the gloomiest. According to his own testimony nothing had obsessed him as much as the problem of decadence.[1] With great subtlety and intuitive insight he diagnosed the maladies of his time and came to the conclusion that all traditional values had lost their validity. He therefore felt that Europe was heading for an age of nihilism and unheard-of catastrophes.[2] He carried his criticism of his age further than any of his contemporaries. By tracing the decadence of modern Europe back to Platonism and Christianity, he decounced not only the degeneration of the ideals that had inspired most of Western culture, but even these ideals themselves.

The views of such a complex and paradoxical thinker as Nietzsche are hard to summarize. In preaching a new gospel of heroic morality he remained within the Jewish-Christian tradition of looking forward to a regeneration of the world. Conceding that he was a "decadent" and a "nihilist," he also claimed to be exactly their opposites.[3] Unlike most German irrationalists, he was often highly critical of the cultural traditions of his own country and gratefully acknowledged his debt to French writers. His view of the approaching nihilism, for example, owed much to the theorist of French decadence, Paul Bourget, and the forceful style of his aphorisms and his often keen insight into the foibles of contemporary society were in the best tradition of French psychological analysis. On the other hand, his views of decadence were presented with an historical perspective and philo-

---

[1] *Fall Wagner*, Vorwort, *Werke*, ed. Karl Schlechta (3 vols., München, 1954–56), II, 903; cf. G. Burckhardt, *Weltanschauungskrisis* (Leipzig, 1925), I, 24ff., 29ff., 161ff., 173ff.

[2] Cf. Schoeps, *Was ist der Mensch?*, 98ff.

[3] *Ecce, homo*, *Werke*, ed. Karl Schlechta, II, 1072; Goudsblom, *op. cit.*, 20ff.

sophical depth that were outside the reach of any French writer. Although Nietzsche greatly admired contemporary French culture, he looked upon it as the last intellectual flowering of an exhausted nation and, in his historical outlook, he owed much more to German authors like Hölderlin and Kleist, Schopenhauer and Burckhardt.[1] In his heroic pessimism and his virulent irrationalism he was the heir of all the anxieties and hopes of German Romanticism. In Nietzsche's philosophy Romantic discontent with the modern world found its most disciplined and most lucid expression.

VI

From our comparative analysis of historical pessimism in a number of selected countries, it is apparent that all the principal apprehensions entering into the sense of decadence in nineteenth-century France had their counterparts elsewhere. Some of the component elements were stronger in other countries than France: the sense of national decline in Spain; Romantic despair in Germany; disgust with industrialism in early nineteenth-century England. Outside France, however, most intellectuals were almost exclusively preoccupied either with the alleged evils of modern civilization or with a decline in national power. It was only in France, holding a middle position between the declining, so-called backward nations like China, Spain, and the Ottoman Empire, and the rising, so-called progressive nations like Germany, Great Britain, and the United States that both these varieties existed in considerable strength at the same time. In other words, the sense of decadence in France was original in having its source in two developments that elsewhere did not present themselves simultaneously in the same degree of gravity: a decline in national power and the perplexing problems resulting from the advent of a democratic and economically highly developed society.

It is obvious that the declining position of France fostered a general mood of despondency. Thus the single most important shock to national self-confidence, the humiliating defeat of 1870, led Taine and Renan to formulate their pessimistic theories on the course of French history and deprived many members of the younger literary generation of any illusions as to the future. Many other international

---

[1] Cf. W. D. Williams, *Nietzsche and the French. A Study of the Influence of Nietzsche's French Reading on his Thought* (Oxford, 1952); Charles Andler, *Les précurseurs de Nietzsche* (Paris, 1920).

crises resulting in what was widely regarded as an abandonment of legitimate French interests had a similar, depressive effect on the French mind. Thus in 1830, 1840, 1848, 1866, 1887, 1898, 1905, and 1912, many Frenchmen accused their government of pursuing a policy of appeasement and indulged in somber statements as to the downfall of France and its inferiority to foreign powers.

This awareness of national inferiority, however, was only one of the factors accounting for the French sense of decadence in the nineteenth century. Most French pessimists were less concerned about the diminished position of their country in the world than about the revolutionary transformation of modern civilization. Unlike Spain, Austria, China and the Ottoman Empire, France was a modern advanced country which was confronted by the critical problems of a democratic, industrialized, urbanized, and secularized society. Decline of the birth rate, high divorce and suicide rates, industrial strikes, rural exodus, atheism and scepticism were among the many perplexing issues of the modern age which presented themselves in France with a much greater sense of urgency than in the still predominantly agrarian societies of the so-called backward nations of the world.

Insofar as the sense of decadence in nineteenth century France constituted a pessimistic response to the breakdown of the old political and social order, it had much in common with the fears that were expressed by many men of letters in other "advanced" countries like Great Britain, Germany, and the United States. Although in some respects, notably in the slow pace of industrialization after 1870, France might have appeared less "modern" than Great Britain, the United States, or Germany, in many other trends of modern civilization, such as extension of the suffrage, political centralization, growth of secularism, and decline of the birth rate, France was in advance of almost any other nation in the world. In nineteenth century, France was generally considered a very "progressive" country. "In all social phenomena," declared the American prophet of doom, Brooks Adams, in 1895, "France is a quarter of a century ahead of all other countries."[1]

It is understandable that the country in which so many aspects of modern civilization made their first appearance was also among the first in producing men of letters questioning the blessings of modern civilization. At an earlier time than almost anywhere else many Frenchmen became alarmed by the decline of faith in transcendental

[1] Brooks Adams, *The Law of Civilization and Decay* (Vintage ed. New York, 1955), 283.

values. Romantic despair or other forms of metaphysical anxiety
seriously plagued French intellectuals, who, by exposing and analyzing the spiritual emptiness of the modern world, made an important
contribution to the cultural pessimism of the nineteenth century.
It was perhaps only in Germany and in Russia that discontent with
modern secularism was more intense and widespread. Likewise,
industrial capitalism found some of its fiercest and earliest critics
among French writers. Of all socialist theorists, Fourier was perhaps
the most outspoken in proclaiming the utter decadence of modern
"civilization." The vulgarity and materialism of a mechanized,
"Americanized" world were bitterly deplored by such prominent
French writers as Baudelaire and Renan. Similar apprehensions were,
of course, voiced by publicists in many other countries affected by the
Industrial Revolution. Indeed, at the end of the nineteenth century,
the rise of a new plutocracy and the evils of urbanization and mechanization were more widely and vehemently denounced in Germany
and the United States than in France. In Victorian England, above all,
the new social abuses such as the horrifying living and working conditions of the industrial proletariat, pauperization, widespread unemployment, industrial strikes, were the subject of a solicitude and an
alarm that surpassed any concern on the part of the French about
similar problems in their country.

In France the literate classes were more preoccupied by the political
than by the economic crises of the century. Even more than the declining power of the nation, it was the new revolutionary quest for
political equality which had taken hold of the French people that
aroused their alarm. It is understandable that the French Revolution
left the most profound and lasting mark in the country in which it had
broken out. Dividing the French nation in their political loyalties, it
inaugurated a long period of political instability during which the
Revolution continued to be regarded as the most decisive turning
point, for better or for worse, in the history of France as well as in
that of the modern world in general. In no other country was political
and historical thought so much preoccupied with the seemingly
irresistible trend toward democracy. This does not mean that the
revolutionary and democratic spirit was not intensely detested by
many intellectuals in England, Russia, and Germany, but conservatives
in these countries regarded the quest for equality as a disease afflicting
France rather than their own nation and were therefore less inclined
to despair of the future than were French opponents of the Revolution.

Throughout the nineteenth century, from Joseph de Maistre to Charles Maurras, the revolutionary principles remained the main target of French conservatives. Numerous French scholars such as Tocqueville, Le Play, Renan, Taine, and Gustave Le Bon, pioneered in the study of democratic and revolutionary movements and were instrumental in strengthening the intellectuals of other countries in their abhorrence of political equalitarianism. It is by their acute psychological and sociological analysis of the French Revolution and similar manifestations of political utopianism that French historical pessimists displayed their greatest originality and exerted their most lasting influence.

CONCLUSION

Unqualified historical optimism was a rare phenomenon among nineteenth-century French men of letters. Although in the course of the century a blind belief in progress gained increased currency among the population at large, such a cheerful interpretation of the course of history met with a critical acceptance on the part of many philosophers, social scientists, and other intellectuals. It was especially in the second half of the century that a self-professed intellectual "elite" – often motivated by the desire to distinguish themselves from the complacent and utopianist "populace" – denounced the confidence with which their contemporaries viewed the trends of the times. Even many Frenchmen who fundamentally believed in the forward march of humanity were plagued by the feeling that existing society was in a state of decadence, crisis, or anarchy. Their misgivings about the state of modern civilization amounted to more than a transient mood of gloom. Many of them were firmly convinced that religion, morality, social refinement, art, and literature were losing their former vigor or brilliancy. Even if they did not anticipate the destruction of all higher forms of civilization, they no longer subscribed to the naive utopianism that had been entertained by Condorcet at the end of the eighteenth century and that had still found so many adepts among French intellectuals of the first half of the nineteenth century.

The nineteenth-century Frenchmen dissenting from their more optimistic contemporaries often vehemently disagreed among themselves. Their mutual differences pertained not only – as has been pointed out in this study – to the definition they gave of contemporary decadence, but also to the meaning or the function they assigned this retrogression of civilization in the overall course of history. Some of them still believed in the old Christian view that the increasing corruption was a manifest sign that the world was approaching its end.

Such an apocalyptic view was still accepted as a meaningful explanation of the terrors of history by numerous rural clerics as well
as by a few distinguished writers like Lamennais (in his early period),
Ernest Hello, and Léon Bloy. But with the increasing secularization of
nineteenth-century society, such eschatological speculations lost favor
with the population, and this trend was seemingly even more pronounced in France than in countries like Germany, Russia, and the United
States where numerous Protestant or Greek Orthodox sects continued
to predict the coming of Antichrist and the Day of Doom.

Most French critics of their time, holding to the secular and more
realistic interpretation of history that had been gaining ground since
the end of the seventeenth century, did not share the anxieties and
delusions that had haunted man in ancient times. Their historical
pessimism was seldom summed up in such fundamental philosophical
and religious principles as had been the case in antiquity or during the
period in which Christianity had dominated man's outlook on the
world. The view that time has essentially a corrupting influence and
that decadence is a law of nature or a part of a providential design,
was no longer accepted. Although often idealizing the past, nineteenth-
century intellectuals were seldom radical primitivists believing in
the existence of a golden age in the beginning of history. If nostalgic
for the past, they dwelled upon the excellence of relatively civilized
societies placed in a not too distant era: the Old Regime, the Middle
Ages, Periclean Greece, or of periods even less far removed in time
such as that of the Great Revolution and Napoleon, and the reign
of Louis-Philippe.

Nor did the French pessimist of the nineteenth century live in the
fearful or hopeful expectation of an imminent destruction of the world
by water or by fire. The belief once so strong in the decrease of man's
life span, the diminishing fertility of the soil, and other forms of the
decay of nature definitively belonged to the past. Although popu-
larizers of newly gained scientific knowledge might still indulge in
predictions of changes in man's physical environment that would
ultimately destroy all civilized life on our planet, such events were
placed in a too distant future to induce any serious, immediate anxiety.
It was not the vision of a sudden end of the world, but that of its
gradual vulgarization, mechanization, and disenchantment that
haunted numerous nineteenth-century men of letters.

Yet some French intellectuals holding these secular views of history
surpassed even the Christians in the gloom with which they looked

upon the course of history. Although not believing in the imminent, total destruction of the cosmos, they no longer entertained the view, so consoling to the Christians, that the end of the world would coincide with the coming of the Kingdom of Heaven. Assuming that the approaching *Götterdämmerung* constituted the final act in the human drama, they arrived at the depressing conclusion that man's destiny in this world was devoid of any ultimate purpose.

It is true that the gloomy visions of such Frenchmen generally pertained to certain fields of human endeavor or certain limited geographical areas rather than to civilization as a whole. Many, for example, taking a dim view of the future of literature and religion in a increasingly mechanized and rationalized world, granted that such losses might be accompanied by spectacular progress in the fields of science and technology. Similarly, those writers who asserted that the downfall of France was inevitable did not think that the same fate was in store for the Germanic and Slavic nations of Europe; even if all of Europe was seen as doomed to decline, it was often believed that the torch of civilization would pass to the Western hemisphere or perhaps to the colored races of the world. But the prospect of such positive developments was, of course, of little consolation to persons, who rightly or wrongly, felt that the brilliancy of literature, the purety of their religion. or the vigor of their nation was indispensable to the continued existence of civilization in the world. Thus many Frenchmen who identified the cause of their country with that of humanity tended to believe that the whole world would be debased if France ceased to exist as a strong, independent nation.

Few French critics of contemporary society, however, subscribed to such unqualified pessimism. Some of them instead endorsed the cyclical theory of history that had been so popular in ancient civilizations and that had experienced a revival with the Renaissance. Such views were, for example, encountered in the works of Gustave Le Bon, Georges Sorel, and various Social Darwinists and writers alarmed at the decline of the birth rate. In ominous reference to the future of France, they declared that societies, like individuals, have their periods of growth, maturity, and fall.

Not many of these writers were wholly consistent in their pessimistic views of the future of existing society. None of them formulated a systematic philosophy of history elaborating upon the analogies between the downward trend of modern civilization and that of past societies. It is symptomatic of the lack of interest in the theory of eternal return that the pessimistic implications of Vico's philosophy were hardly noticed by his numerous French admirers and that no French scholar made any important contribution to the study of the historical problem of Rome's decline and fall.

The rejection of any form of fatalism was indeed one of marked features of French thought in the nineteenth century, which suffered little from the infatuation with fate (*Schicksal*) that was so common among German intellectuals of the period. Almost all prominent French thinkers who severely criticized the current belief in necessary, indefinite progress were equally adamant in their opposition to its contrary, the belief in inevitable decadence. The French vindication of the freedom of the will cut across the boundaries dividing radicals and conservatives, liberals and socialists. The optimistic belief in man's ability to shape his own destiny tempered the pessimism of such diverse thinkers as the Catholic Ballanche, the democrat Quinet, the socialist Proudhon, the conservative liberal Tocqueville, and the idealistic philosophers Renouvier and Bergson.

Nineteenth-century literature, it is true, abounded in ominous – though generally false – comparisons between declining Rome and state of contemporary society. Without the example of "decadent" Rome the literary movement of Decadence would have been deprived of its most important theme. And many Decadents, as is known, liked to identify themselves with Rome at the time of its decline and accepted the ancient view that the moral dissolution of their age was irremediable. But in spite of their obsession with decadence, French litterateurs of the nineteenth century did not advance any plausible theories explaining why the modern world was going to follow the same course as Imperial Rome. Nor did the Decadents face the corruption of their times with an ancient, philosophical sense of resignation. These modernistic men of letters lacked the belief in absolute values without which a consistent belief in either decadence or progress is impossible. It was rather the new creed that all ages are entitled to their own form of morality and their own form of artistic expression, all equally valid or equally invalid, that constituted the basic presupposition of the Decadent and other modernistic movements in literature.

The lack of confidence in regeneration that characterized the historical outlook of the Decadents was not shared by most other Frenchmen concerned about the state of modern civilization. However critical of contemporary corruption, they did not face this situation with despair but continued to hope for a turn for the better. With varying degrees of conviction they looked forward to a renewal or renaissance in the near future. Thus a strong faith in the mission of France and the restoration of the nation to its former vigor and influence in the world tempered the otherwise so gloomy view that most French conservatives and Catholics took of the trends of their times. Renewing the old Jewish messianism, many of these foes of democracy and atheism lived in the constant expectation of a miracle that would save their country.

Most French leftists despondent about the present expected still more than a regeneration; they anticipated a future that would be far superior to any society that had existed in the past. Although suffering from an acute sense of crisis and deploring the fate that had destined them to be born in such an anguishing period of history, they still believed that history was moving consistently, if not necessarily rectilinearly, toward greater happiness and perfection. In their spiral theory of progress they secularized the Judeo-Christian doctrine that the course of history has an ultimate purpose. Some of these new prophets, preaching that utopia would not come into being until after contemporary society had further deteriorated and had found a catastrophic end, presented a secular version of the old apocalyptic view of history.

The exponents of these secular philosophies of history were not so much pessimists as disillusioned optimists who still clung to a belief in progress even if they admitted that the forward march of humanity was often interrupted by fairly protracted periods of retro-gression. They defined decadence, however, no longer as a deviation from old standards of simplicity and virtue, but as the persistence of antiquated institutions and ideas in a time of rapid change, and in this way broke radically with almost all notions of decadence that had been current until the end of the eighteenth century.

In conclusion we may advance a few remarks on the degree of accuracy with which nineteenth-century pessimists analyzed their society and predicted the trends of future.

Many of their views of modern civilization impress us as unduly pessimistic. Some authors were obviously blinded by political passion, or perhaps purposely overdrew the vices of their time in order to alarm their fellow citizens. Many of their gloomy prognoses were, moreover, based upon highly questionable premises such as that the existence of the temporal power of the papacy, racial purity, absolute monarchy, and a leisured, privileged aristocracy were essential to a sound political and social order.

In other respects, the nineteenth-century critics of their time strike us as overly optimistic. It goes without saying that insofar as they still suffered from the common illusion that the future would be substantially better than the present, reality has often fallen short of their expectations. But even in their worst fears the pessimists of the past century did not foresee some of the greatest horrors of our own age. Thus all of them greatly underestimated the frightful power that modern science was to place at the disposal of man. Although at the end of the nineteenth century the increasing destructiveness of modern warfare began to arouse widespread concern, the actual outbreak of the First World War and the extent of devastation and misery it caused came as a great shock to all pacifists. Certainly, few if any nineteenth-century intellectuals suffered the present-day anxiety that our entire civilization, including its highly developed technology and science, might be destroyed overnight. Nor did any of them predict some of the abominable features of modern totalitarianism like mass genocide and concentration camps.

Yet in some of their analyses of the trends of the times nineteenth-century French authors showed a remarkable insight into the development of modern society and expressed fears and anxieties that have become more widely shared in our own time. Many of them, for example, clearly perceived the dangers inherent in an increasingly standardized, centralized, and industrialized society. Similarly their prediction that France would lose its leading position in world affairs to other more enterprising or "younger" nations has largely been vindicated by the events of the twentieth century. Finally many French writers should be given credit for focussing public attention on some of the serious problems caused by the decline of old religious certainties and the breakdown of the old social order. They were the first to raise some questions that are central to many present-day discussions in sociology, psychology, and philosophy: the atomization or "anomie" of society; the alienation of man, the general acceptance of nihilism or relativism. The nineteenth-century pessimists have not been altogether false prophets.

INDEX